ADOLESCENCE

THE TRANSITIONAL YEARS

ADOLESCENCE

THE TRANSITIONAL YEARS

J. ROY HOPKINS

St. Mary's College of Maryland

ACADEMIC PRESS

A Subsidiary of Harcourt Brace Jovanovich
New York London
Paris San Diego San Francisco São Paulo
Sydney Tokyo Toronto

This book was designed by Edward A. Butler
Cover painting by R.B. Backhaus

Academic Press, Inc.
111 Fifth Avenue
New York, New York 10003

United Kingdom edition published by
Academic Press, Inc. (London) Ltd.
24/28 Oval Road, London NW1

ISBN: 0-12-355580-9

Library of Congress Catalog Card
Number: 82-70971

To my mother . . . to the memory of my father. . . .

PREFACE

Developmental Psychology is the study of changes in psychological phenomena over the life span, although in practice most developmental psychologists study a narrow age range. Adolescence has received attention as a special developmental epoch because of important changes that occur during this period—changes such as the physical transformations of puberty, the reorientation of social interests away from parents and toward the peer group, and the increased pressures for heterosexual experimentation. Psychological studies of adolescence focus attention on the contribution of these changes to the individual's development between the two great developmental epochs of childhood and adulthood. Hence, adolescence can be viewed as a period of psychological transition from one status to another.

I wrote this book assuming three major educational goals for a course in adolescent psychology. The first goal is to familiarize students with important issues in adolescent psychology, so that they might understand the importance of the issues and know the empirical data that bear on them. The second goal is to give students an appreciation of the range of methods that have been used effectively to gain information about adolescent development. The third goal is to offer some practical implications of the theoretical and empirical material students will encounter in the field of adolescent psychology.

The ideal textbook, I believe, should go beyond simply reporting what others have done; it should also attempt to organize and integrate the work of others so that an overall picture emerges. In this textbook, I have attempted to organize as well as to report in order to achieve both balance and synthesis.

FEATURES OF THE TEXTBOOK

Throughout the text, case studies and examples are used to make the reading more enjoyable and to show that the subject matter is about real people. There really *are* adolescents out there in the real world, and scientific studies ought not to be reported as if these adolescents are lifeless laboratory subjects.

Adolescence is placed in the context of the human life span. The book takes the position that adolescence is a distinct period of human development—a transitional period between the two developmental epochs of childhood and adulthood. For each of the topics covered, some discussion of developmental history is included, so that the reader will know what has gone before and what is likely to come next.

The material covered in the text is firmly grounded in the discipline of psychology; but many other disciplines have important things to say about adolescence. The physical changes at puberty require a discussion of human biology, and especially of endocrinology. A discussion of juvenile delinquency would be incomplete without emphasizing the important contributions of sociology. Throughout the text, adolescent development is placed in anthropological perspective in an attempt to avoid a narrow, ethnocentric view. Literary accounts of the adolescent transition are also discussed as prototypes of the experiences of real human beings.

THEMES OF HUMAN DEVELOPMENT

Themes of change and continuity recur in discussions of human psychological growth. While this textbook portrays adolescence as a period of transition between childhood and adulthood, it does so with full recognition that the transitions of adolescence occur within a context of continuity of subjective human experience.

On December 4, 1977, I attended the famous carol service at New College, Oxford. New College has a boys' choir, composed of prepubescent boys selected for their pure voices. They sing in the carol service along with a group of mellow-voiced undergraduates. As I listened to the carols, it occurred to me that childhood and adulthood were represented in the choir, but adolescence was missing. My mind wandered to thoughts of the transition between these two periods of life: The intricate emotional, physical, and behavioral changes that occur in the life cycle during the years between childhood and adulthood. This book is about that transition.

ACKNOWLEDGMENTS

I had the good fortune to spend the academic year 1977–1978 on sabbatical in Oxford, England, a city of striking contrasts. The crush of scurrying people and grinding double-decker buses along High and Cornmarket streets is reminiscent of any busy city. But a few steps away from these thoroughfares are more than a score of secluded courtyards and cloisters. The serenity of the setting gives one a sense of continuity with many generations of scholars. It was in Oxford that I began writing this book.

I am indebted to Lincoln College at Oxford for graciously providing me with accommodations in Bear Lane; and to Patrick Rabbitt, who, as Acting Chairman of the Department of Psychology, arranged for me to use the considerable resources of the Oxford University library system.

I also wish to thank the Vassar College Faculty Research Committee for providing a small grant to aid in the preparation of an early version of the manuscript; and St. Mary's College of Maryland, for providing student assistants. I especially appreciate the indulgence and support of John D. Underwood, Chairman of the Division of Human Development at St. Mary's College.

Several of my students have contributed material to this manuscript, whether they know it or not. Notable among them are Gregg Bachman, Michael Grunberg, Ellen Jackson, Linda Lucas, and Michael Sharp.

Many of my colleagues have graciously read various portions of the manuscript. I wish to thank them for their helpful comments: Susan E. Beers, John Bridge, Keven Bridge, Anne Constantinople, Letitia Anne Peplau, and Henrietta T. Smith. Another colleague, Laraine Glidden, was a special resource for discussing ideas as I struggled with the manuscript.

I owe a special debt of thanks to the reviewers who provided thoughtful criticisms of the manuscript:

Arnold R. Bruhn
George Washington University

Judith Gallatin
Helppie & Gallatin, Inc.

Philip Graham
Institute of Child Health, London

Martin Herbert
University of Leicester, England

Robert Hogan
Johns Hopkins University

Raymond Montemayor
University of Utah

Nora Newcombe
Temple University

Toni E. Santmire
University of Nebraska—Lincoln

Douglas B. Sawin
University of Texas

Karen Maitlandt Schilling
Miami University

Dee Shepherd-Look
California State University

Glenn W. Thompson
Allegheny College

Douglas K. Uselding
University of South Dakota

I hope that they recognize some of their suggestions in the final product.

I have used the resources of several libraries in preparing this textbook, and I would like to publicly thank their staffs: Bodleian Library, Oxford; Graduate Library, University of California at Los Angeles; The Library of Congress; Lincoln College Library, Oxford; McKeldin Library, University of Maryland at College Park; Radcliffe Science Library, Oxford; Rhodes House Library, Oxford; St. Mary's College of Maryland Library; Thompson Library, Vassar College; and Wilson Library, University of North Carolina at Chapel Hill.

I appreciate the assistance of students who helped me to gather library material in the preparation of the manuscript, notably Phoebe Carson, Cindy Rhodes, and Loretta Womer. I also appreciate the assistance of Kathy Bush-Schlemann, Mildred Fitzpatrick, Karen Garner, Cathy Loftis, Elaine Ormond, Sarah Ball Teslik, and Susan Wolfe, who helped with typing. Kennan Teslik contributed several hyphens.

Finally, I am indebted to three very fine editors in the College Department at Academic Press—Joan Goldstein, James D. Anker, and Heidi Udell—and to my excellent Project Editor, Richard Christopher.

J. Roy Hopkins
St. Mary's City, Maryland
August 1982

CONTENTS

OUTLINE

THE NATURE OF ADOLESCENCE
The Onset of Adolescence
The End of Adolescence
Adolescence as Western Invention

THEMES OF ADOLESCENCE
Searching for an Identity
Establishing Autonomy
Decision-Making about Life Goals

APPROACHES TO THE STUDY OF ADOLESCENCE
Literary Accounts
Case Studies
Observational Studies
Interview and Questionnaire Studies
Hypothesis-Testing Studies

AGE EFFECTS AND COHORT EFFECTS
Cross-sectional Research
Longitudinal Research

SUMMARY

1.

ISSUES IN THE STUDY OF ADOLESCENCE

Frankie Addams is 12 years old and she is not a "member" of anything. Her father has told her that she is too big to sleep in the same bed with him and has banished her to the sleeping porch. She is no longer interested in childish things; she has given away her doll. She is experiencing a time of transition.

It was a summer of fear, for Frankie, and there was one fear that could be figured in arithmetic with paper and pencil at the table. This August she was twelve and five-sixths years old. She was five feet five and three-quarter inches tall, and she wore a number seven shoe. In the past year she had grown four inches, or at least that was what she judged. If she reached her height on her eighteenth birthday, she had five and one-sixth growing years ahead of her. Therefore, according to mathematics and unless she could somehow stop herself, she would grow to be over nine feet tall.

Even though her arithmetic is faulty, Frankie has expressed a fundamental concern of adolescence. It can be a fearsome time, and the emotion and pathos are often captured better by the poet than by the academic. Frankie Addams is the creation of Carson McCullers in her novel *The Member of the Wedding*.

Frankie is afraid. She is not sure who she is, and her separateness, her nonmembership, frightens and mystifies her.

Listen. What I've been trying to say is this. Doesn't it strike you as strange that I am I, and you are you? And we can look at each other, and touch each other, and stay together year in and year out in the same room. Yet always I am I, and you are you. And I can't ever be anything else but me, and you can't ever be anything else but you. Have you ever thought of that? And does it seem to you strange?

In her 13th summer, the adolescent in Frankie seized upon the idea of getting away from her childhood, from all it represented. In her mind she became F. Jasmine Addams, Esq., "member of the wedding." It was her brother's wedding, and F. Jasmine decided she would accompany the couple on their honeymoon, and travel to adventure.

Boyoman! Manoboy! When we leave Winter Hill we're going to more places that you ever thought about or ever knew existed. Alaska, China, Iceland, South America. And talking of things happening. Things will happen so fast we won't hardly have time to realize them.

The adolescent's nonmembership in either the child or adult world often leads to overwhelming humiliations. For Frankie, such an event occurred at the wedding, when her brother mistook her for a child. "Frankie the lankie the alaga fankie, the tee-legged toe-legged bow-legged Frankie." Her desperate pleas to join the wedding party were rebuffed, and she was relegated, kicking and screaming, back to childhood. She was not a member of the wedding after all. Frankie learned, during that summer, what it feels like to be in transition, to be a nonmember. Her transition continued as Frances Addams the teenager, who joined her adolescent peer group, represented by Mary Littlejohn. "They read poets like Tennyson together; and Mary was going to be a great painter and Frances a great poet—or else the foremost authority on radar."

Frankie Addams is, of course, a fictitious young girl. The anxieties and hopes that she expresses are, however, typical of those of real adolescents, male and female. They are not less real for their expression through the medium of fiction. Frankie's story illustrates some of the themes of the transition from childhood to adulthood. This book is designed to survey the contributions of psychology to understanding that transition, and it is the purpose of this chapter of provide an overview to the study of adolescence.

THE NATURE OF ADOLESCENCE

A stark definition of adolescence states that it is the period between childhood and adulthood. It is a period when much personal growth takes place; and it is this growth—physical, psychological, and social—that gives the period its special place within the field of developmental psychology.

Historically, adolescence as we know it is a recent phenomenon. According to Philippe Aries, in his social history of the family, adolescence as a developmental period was merged with childhood until the 18th century (Aries, 1962). Even then, there was not much interest in adolescence as a separate developmental epoch worthy of attention. The "era of the adolescent," as Joseph Kett (1977) described our current preoccupation with youth, began in the first two decades of the 20th century. Expectations for adolescents were redefined at about that time.

The key contribution of the 1900–1920 period was not the discovery of adolescence, for in one form or another a recognition of changes at puberty, even drastic changes, had been present long before 1900. Rather, it was the invention of the adolescent, the youth whose social definition—and indeed, whose whole being—was determined by a biological process of maturation. (Kett, 1977, p. 243)

With the "invention" of the adolescent came an understanding of the nature of the developmental period—when it began and when it ended. A general definition describes adolescence as a transitional period between childhood and adulthood. As such, its onset coincides with the end of childhood, and its endpoint coincides with the beginning of adulthood.

The Onset of Adolescence

Adolescence begins when childhood ends; that point is generally considered to be reached at puberty. Two observations about the onset of adolescence, as marked by puberty, are noteworthy. First, the average age of sexual maturation differs for males and females. The best index of sexual maturation for girls is first menstruation, or menarche. For boys, the equivalent is difficult to pinpoint, although growth of testes and penis are logical indexes of maturation. Girls have their growth spurt, on the average, at age 12, and boys 2 years later at age 14 (Tanner, 1972). In about the 6th grade, girls embark on a growth curve leading to gigantic proportions—or so they, like Frankie Addams, often think. At the same time, boys show no inclination to grow an inch. It is an awkward social situation. Self-consciousness is a byword of adolescence, and intense introspection a common pastime. The cracking voice of male adolescents, breast development for female adolescents, acne, and other commonplace events accentuate the often painful self-consciousness.

Second, there has been a trend, over the last 100 years or so, for sexual maturation to arrive at earlier ages. The years of childhood are simply fewer now than in previous generations, because puberty arrives sooner.

**The End of
Adolescence**

Although the beginning of adolescence is physically defined, there is a more uncertain endpoint. Adolescence ends with "adulthood," whose arrival is vague and variable. Adulthood may be defined in sociological terms as a status distinction, involving the assumption of adult roles. Occupational roles, especially those enabling an individual to become self-supporting, and the role of spouse are such adult roles. Put in more pedestrian terms, getting married and getting a job help to confer adult status. It is not quite that simple, of course. There is a psychological *feeling* of adolescence—of not quite being prepared for the world, of dependency. The 16-year-old who quits high school to take a job and to get married may not yet be a psychological adult, despite sexual maturity and economic self-sufficiency.

Patterns of education and marriage have helped to postpone the end of adolescence for many people. A larger proportion of late adolescents have graduated from high school now than in previous decades. Figure 1-1 shows that the percentage of young people who graduated from high school has increased dramatically over the decades of the 20th century, from just over 6 percent in 1900 to about 75 percent in the decade of the 1980s. In addition, a larger proportion of high-school graduates are attending college now than in previous years. In 1960, about one-fourth of high-school graduates went to college; by 1980, that number had increased to about

**FIGURE 1-1
Percentage of high-school graduates by age 18 in the United States in the 20th century.**

(From U.S. Bureau of the Census, *Historical Abstract of the United States, Colonial Times to 1970; Statistical Abstract of the United States, 1980.*)

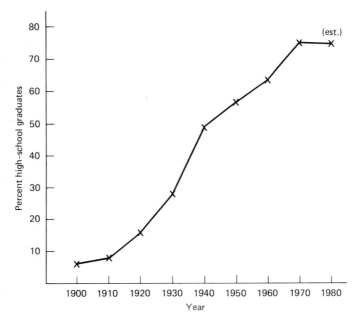

one-third. Between 1960 and 1980, actual college enrollment of persons 18–24 years old increased from 2.2 million to 7 million students (U.S. Bureau of the Census).

Age of marriage is sometimes used as one indicator of adult status. Although age of first marriage declined throughout most of the 20th century, there has been a reverse trend since about 1950. Between 1970 and 1980, median age of first marriage rose from 23.2 to 24.6 for men, and from 20.8 to 22.1 for women. Even elimination of marriage from life plans is now a more acceptable possibility. The percentage of young persons in the population who have never married has been increasing over the last few decades. In 1980, half the women and two-thirds of the men aged 20–24 had not married (U.S. Bureau of the Census).

The Current Scene: A Lengthy Adolescence When the observations about the beginning and the end of adolescence are put together, the conclusion is inescapable that adolescence is now a longer developmental epoch than it was in earlier generations. As Aries put it, "it encroached upon childhood in one direction, maturity in the other" (Aries, 1962, p. 30).

The growth at both ends of the period of adolescence implies that greater numbers of people are facing the problems of nonmem-

"Punk," a youth movement that has swept London, with reverberations among young people in the United States, exemplifies the wide variety of forms that youth subcultures may take. Here, Wendy and the Plasmatics serve as models for the uniforms and attitudes of this particular movement: outrageous dress, orange-and-purple-dyed hair, and music with lyrics that stress nihilism and anger.

(Photo by Thierry Orban/ Sygma)

bership in the child and adult worlds. On a psychological level, the anxiety and uncertainty accompanying lack of commitment have been prolonged over the last few generations. Young people are experiencing an extended period free of adult commitments. They have more time set aside for experimentation and seeking: with career plans, with sexual behavior, with fads and fashions. For some adolescents, however, freedom is accompanied by a sense of purposelessness and alienation from the adult world.

On a societal level, the growth of the period of adolescence implies a greater emphasis on youth, resulting in what has been called a "cult of youth" in North America and Europe. Advertisers celebrate the attractions of youth and identify them with their products. Young people's musical tastes dominate the airwaves. The behavior of young people often seems uniform, at least within subcultural groups. Style of dress has taken on properties of uniformity: blue jeans, sneakers, and pullover shirts with silk-screened slogans or logos—Black Sabbath, Budweiser, Southern Comfort. An explanation for uniformity of dress may rest in the tendency of young people to identify with and to imitate each other—a tendency that is not lost on business-minded manufacturers.

The term "youth culture" implies more uniformity to the adolescent experience than actually exists. Styles of passing from

Despite apparent similarities, the styles chosen by young people making the transition from adolescence to adulthood differ markedly in terms of both behavior and psychological motivation. Religious movements, such as the Hare Krishna, have a particular appeal for young people who long for membership and identity within a highly-structured framework.

(Photo by Esais Baitel from Rapho/Photo Researchers, Inc.)

childhood to adulthood are as varied as any other psychological phenomenon, perhaps more than most. Some adolescents are swept along in youth movements, such as Punks in London or Yippies in Chicago. Some become crusaders for a religious cause, as the "Moonies," followers of Korean evangelist Sun Myung Moon. Some adolescents are paragons of middle-class, middle-American virtue. Still others are violent rule-breakers—juvenile delinquents. Despite surface similarities in tastes and in dress, behavioral and psychological styles of passage into adulthood differ markedly. The psychologist, noticing these differences, wonders if there are predisposing events in childhood that can predict the style of adolescence. The psychologist is not simply exercising idle curiosity, for a predictable relationship could help to eliminate some of the misery associated with psychological and social problems in adolescence.

Adolescence as Western Invention

The stage of the life cycle that we know as "adolescence" in the Western world may not be recognized as a separate stage elsewhere. Many observers believe that adolescence is a by-product of industrialized economies (e.g., Kett, 1977), especially because industrial societies require longer preparation before assuming adult roles. In this sense, adolescence can be viewed as the "invention" of Western industrialized societies.

Adolescence in Nontechnological Societies It is a commonplace observation that different cultural groups have different norms that regulate their behavior. Among the Yąnomamö of South America, one of the most conspicuous status distinctions is that between men and women. Yąnomamö society does not value girls as highly as boys. The differential value results in greater indulgence of boys, and greater hardship for girls, which is represented clearly in adolescence.

By the time a girl is ten years old or so, she has become an economic asset to the mother and spends a great deal of time working. Little boys, by contrast, spend hours playing among themselves and are able to prolong their childhood into their late teens if they so wish. By that time a girl has married, and may have a child or two. (Chagnon, 1968, p. 85)

When Yąnomamö girls first menstruate, they are thought unclean. Isolated in their houses and hidden behind screens, they must not touch food or wear their usual clothes. They may not even scratch themselves directly, but must use a stick. Often, a girl is promised long before puberty to a future husband, a man who may even raise her for part of her childhood and therefore train her in her subservient role. Boys, in contrast, have a leisurely childhood period and experience no sharp demarcation point prior to entering adulthood. They have achieved adult status when people no longer refer to them with their personal name (Chagnon, 1968).

An alternative view of adolescence was represented by the BaBira villagers of central Africa (Turnbull, 1961). It was the custom to *initiate* male BaBira adolescents, when they were between 8 and 12 years old. During the course of the initiation, their heads were shaved; their entire bodies were smeared with white clay; they were circumcised; and they were subjected to a host of taboos, including eating or touching certain foods, eating with their initiated relatives, or getting wet. During the 2 or 3 months after the ceremony, they were "toughened up" through a series of mild tortures, such as daily switchings under the arms until the skin was raw and bleeding.

It would be a mistake to denigrate these rituals as the carryings-on of primitive peoples. Rather, they serve the function of marking the transition from childhood to adulthood. The toughening of BaBira adolescents prepares them to endure the rigors of adulthood. The Yąnomamö menstrual ritual provides a school into the ways of adults. Circumcision of BaBira males and the acknowledgement of Yąnomamö menstration both underscore genital maturation. Following the ceremonies, these adolescents are eligible to

An Australian aboriginal boy being painted before a circumcision ceremony. This ceremony is a public rite of passage that takes place when the boys approach puberty. The body paintings, animal symbols in red, yellow, black, and white, represent the clan to which the boy will belong during life and that will take care of his spirit after death.

(Monkmeyer Press Photo Service)

enter the status of adulthood. Their period of transition—of non-membership—is brief.

Adolescence in Technological Societies A long period of preparation and training is needed to prepare young people for the exigencies of life in the complex adult world of a technological society. The training is best accomplished during a period free from adult commitments. A long period of preparation for full adult status following puberty creates a separate stage in the life cycle, which we call *adolescence*.

Three major societal changes that came about around the turn of the century facilitated the creation of the separate stage of adolescence (Bakan, 1972). The first was the institution of compulsory education until the age of 16. Compulsory education, in addition to extending the period of external authority over the individual, provided training in skills useful for work in a complex industrial economic system. Second, laws prohibiting child labor prolonged the period of economic dependence on parents, and kept young, untrained workers out of the labor market. They also eliminated some of the harsh treatment of adolescents and children in industrial "sweat shops." Third, passage of special legal procedures for juveniles, beginning with the Illinois Juvenile Court Act of 1899, gave legal recognition to the concept of limited personal responsibility on the part of juveniles by virtue of their not having attained adult status.

In adolescence, individuals have some flexibility of choice—of an occupation to prepare for, of a set of characteristics that we have come to call *identity*. Freedom of choice during adolescence creates, for many, a sense of uncertainty and floundering. The identity search can be a painful quest. "Who am I?" has become a cliché-question for adolescents in technological societies, and the underlying psychological turmoil that arises when the question has no apparent answer is painfully real. In less highly developed societies, identity is less flexible and more highly ritualized. A quest is unnecessary, even irrelevant. Ritual may even extend to special relationships, with prearranged marriages and predetermined friendships.

In the best of circumstances, a long adolescence provides an opportunity for experimentation with various roles and identity anchors. Adolescents may set their minds on being poets one day and authorities on radar the next. For many young people, this indecision about the direction for adult life continues well into the college years, or even beyond. One of my students, a senior at Vassar, wrote the following to me while I was away on sabbatical:

The continuing angst of Super Senior casting about upon the sea of doubts has taken a new turn. Immediate plans call for a year off, away from full-time academics. I've no urge to travel, but I do want to stretch a bit. Seeing as I must deal with definites in my life (I cannot stand for uncertainty), I've been actively searching for an alternative for next year.

He presents two possible alternatives, opts for the second one, seemingly as he puts it into words, then goes on to say:

My decision rests easy within my psyche. I firmly believe I've been going in this direction all along and I feel good that I've taken on a quasi-concrete direction.

But he recognizes the self-convincing properties of this statement, adding:

Tune in next week for the trials and vacillations of . . .

Not all young people are fortunate enough to do their seeking within the relative safety of a college environment. The lengthy adolescence imposed by technological society is itself the context within which adolescent miseries such as delinquency occur. Many types of behavior classified as "delinquent," for example, are status offenses, acts that are applicable only to minors. Associating with immoral persons, truancy, and incorrigibility are not adult crimes. They lead to a classification as PINS—the legalese acronym for "persons in need of supervision." While cynics might argue that many adults who are in the highest reaches of government and business are "persons in need of supervision," it is not a legal classification that can be applied to them.

Despite its length and complexity, adolescence in technological society is not usually a psychologically debilitating experience. Research indicates that most adolescents do not feel they are in the midst of a stormy decade. Rather, they are going about the business of the adolescent transition with a minimum of psychological stress (Offer & Offer, 1975).

THEMES OF ADOLESCENCE

There are some common issues and tasks that all adolescents confront to one degree or another in Western society—and indeed in most societies in the world. Not all adolescents confront these issues in the same way, of course; there is great variability in style of passing from childhood to adulthood, even within one culture. Indeed, there is even great variability in reaching physical puberty. As Marshall and Tanner (1970) pointed out, "Between the ages of 13 and 15, normal boys may be found in any stage of genital development from infantile to adult." Longer adolescence in technological societies means that the issues are "stretched out." Occupational decision-making, for example, is usually a much more lengthy and uncertain process in Massachusetts as compared to Samoa.

In this section, we consider briefly some major unifying themes of adolescence, themes that are encountered throughout our subsequent discussions of research and theory on adolescence.

Searching for an Identity

In *Alice in Wonderland*, Alice wonders aloud: "Who am I? Ah, that's the great puzzle!" And indeed it *is* a great puzzle for most young people. Erik H. Erikson, a follower of Freud who wrote extensively about identity-seeking in adolescence, defined identity in terms of self-perception, upon which one bases one's behavior. *Identity* is a perception of oneself as having continuity and sameness, despite changes in physical appearance and life situation. The organization of one's experience is based on the sense of continuity as a person with a past, a present, and a future—continuity within a context of growth.

One's identity as a member of a larger social group also contributes to the sense of self. Many sociologists and psychologists have discussed the problem of youthful alienation from society, involving feelings of powerlessness, normlessness, and lack of identification with the goals of those in charge of the System. Although "alienated youth" has become something of a cliché, the questioning of society that occurs with cognitive growth in adolescence may lead to a sense of alienation. Rapid change within a technological society may create a state of uncertainty and confusion in young people, what sociologists call normlessness. Without clear norms as guides, and with a corresponding lack of heroes to emulate, young people have few guidelines for identity formation. Many young people respond to this situation by seeking their own norms within faddist and cultist youth movements.

Many of the young people who flocked to Haight-Ashbury during the late 1960s–early 1970s were *seekers*, people who had rejected even their own families in their search for an idea or a philosophy to give meaning to their lives. As such, they were vulnerable to a persuasive argument. Gurus of many sorts sought converts within this vulnerable mass of young people.

More recently, the rock music subculture has spawned a youth-culture group known as punk rock. Alienation from the mainstream is a key to punk rock, which rejects the musical conventions of other rock and blues styles. Punk rock as a youth movement also rejects other social conventions, with a nihilism reminiscent of Dadaism, an intellectual and artistic movement of the early 20th century. On stage, punk-rock musicians are given to using obsceni-

A teenager at the Mud Club in New York City. Alienation from the social mainstream is one key to understanding the "punk" phenomenon. Distinctive styles of dress represent rejection of the larger society's social conventions.

(Photo by Kleinberg/Sygma)

ties, vomiting during performances, and other nonconventional activities. Off stage, punk rockers react against almost any imaginable social convention: Violence for its own sake, wearing safety pins through the nose, and dying their unevenly cropped hair orange are nihilist signatures of the movement. I encountered representatives of punk rock in late 1977 in a wine shop in the Battersea section of London. Three teenaged girls came into the shop dressed in black from head to foot. Chains and safety pins clanged and jangled on their clothes. They had orange-dyed spots in their uneven hair, and on their faces were drawn various emblems in black, including swastikas on their cheeks.

Hippies and punk rockers are quite distinct youth groups. On a deeper level, however, they may represent similar psychological characteristics. Experimentation with alternative lifestyles, with fads and cults, may represent a norm of alienation among young people who have embarked on a collective search for identity.

Identity may be best achieved when there is a period of youthful experimentation with alternatives. Erik Erikson praised the value of youthful role experimentation in his description of the *psychosocial moratorium*, a normal period of indecision experienced by many adolescents who feel relatively free from the necessity of making adult commitments. The psychosocial moratorium is a phenomenon that may be peculiar to Western culture.

The various tasks of adolescence are highly related. Searching for an identity is perhaps the most global task, for it certainly includes occupational choice, autonomy from parents, and patterns of sexual behavior. Developing a system of values—synonyms are *moral orientation* and *ideology*—bears a strong relationship to identity. In Erikson's terms, ideology is the "guardian of identity."

Establishing Autonomy

Establishing autonomy from parents is a major issue for most adolescents. Autonomy means more than physical distance from parents. Youngsters in boarding school, or college freshmen away from home for the first time, are not always psychologically autonomous. At the same time, autonomy does not mean loss of love for parents. Strong family ties often remain throughout the life cycle; for earlier generations, this was the basis for care of elderly persons. My own maternal grandfather died in 1977 at the age of 102. "Pa" was a patriarch for his large family, and his children and grandchildren and great grandchildren were saddened at his death. My mother had long ago established psychological autonomy from her father, but she had not lost her deep affection for him.

Autonomy, then, is a concomitant of adult status, when an individual is no longer psychologically dependent on parents. A developmental analysis of social behavior places great emphasis on the adolescent period in establishing autonomy from parents.

During the adolescent years, awareness of members of the opposite sex as social objects increases and heterosexual relationships complement same-sex friendships. Although most adolescents remain tied to their parents in a psychological and affectional sense, the peer group reaches its peak of influence on the individual during adolescence. It is during this period that adolescents begin the process of breaking the ties of psychological dependence on their parents, a process that will continue into adulthood.

Some evidence, which we consider in greater detail in later chapters, indicates that males and females differ in the degree to which they establish autonomy from parents. Komarovsky (1946), for example, argued that females are subject to more parental control during the adolescent period, and as a result they develop a greater psychological dependence on parents. The risks for freedom from control are greater for women. At first glance, it would seem that parental control for this reason has been outdated by birth-control technology. Patterns of contraception among adolescent girls, especially during their first sexual experience, indicate that this may not be the case. Kantner and Zelnik (1972) studied a national group of adolescents, aged 15–19, and found that fewer than half the 1,300 sexually active teenagers had used any form of contraception on their most recent sexual experience. Although 75 percent of them used contraception at some time or other, fewer than 20 percent consistently practiced contraception.

Autonomy from parents co-occurs with a firm sense of one's self as a separate person. Sometimes this necessary development is stymied within the family. Esterson (1970) presented a case history of a young woman whose sense of autonomy was curtailed by a family that secretly investigated her boyfriends, surreptitiously listened in on her telephone calls, and restricted her movements outside the home. Esterson (1970) summarized the case with the following:

They watched her every move so closely that she felt she had no privacy at all, and when she objected, if they did not deny what they were doing, they reproached her for being ungrateful for the concern. She thus became muddled over whether or not it was right to go out with boys, or even to have any private life in the first place. (p. 18)

Decision-Making About Life Goals

"In the last five minutes I have decided to be a waitress, a teacher, a wife, a psychologist, a secretary, and a good-for-nothing." So wrote a former student requesting a letter of recommendation for graduate school in late 1977. I felt confident that her letter did not reflect a character trait of ambivalence, but rather was the typical tentativeness that accompanies vocational decision-making. For most young people, in college at least, there is a need to keep one's options open as long as possible. Dismal job forecasts account for some of this tentativeness. At the 1978 convention of the Modern Language Association, teaching jobs were advertised for fewer than half the year's crop of young Ph.D.s in English. Other disciplines are comparably "closed." High-school and college students are understandably reluctant to spend years training for a profession that will have no place for them.

Vocational decision-making may be viewed in a larger framework of movement through "the System." Those whose paths diverge while moving through the System have different forces operating in job decisions. The System includes compulsory education until 16 in the United States. This age is a decision node: One can opt for continuing education or leaving school. Participation in the labor force is lower among young people who drop out of school than among nondropouts. What drives a person to drop out of school given this gloomy statistic? Despite the rhetoric of freedom of choice in a democracy, choice is rarely entirely free. Larger social pressures, which may be called *sorting mechanisms*, lead to decisions about life orientation. Social class, race, health, physical attractiveness, and academic skill are examples of sorting mechanisms that help to determine a decision outside of the realm of free choice. In 1972, only 14 percent of white students dropped out of high school, compared to 21 percent of Hispanic students. After dropping out of school, the sorting mechanisms continue to operate. The same reasons that lead one to leave school make one less employable: Poor academic skill, poor health, and trouble with authorities may be cited as contributing sorting mechanisms.

The decision faced by high-school students on whether to go to college is also determined to some extent by factors other than free choice. For example, the decision to go to college is related to family income, and hence social class. Median family income of noncollege high-school graduates is lower than that of graduates who go on to college (Young, 1973). Motivation to seek a place in college may be lower simply because adolescents know the strain it would place on their family's financial situation. Psychological access to college is clearly related to social sorting mechanisms. Another strong factor in the college decision is the advice and encouragement a student gets from teachers and guidance counselors. "Advice" often goes beyond counsel: It may involve being placed in a nonacademic track, a decision over which the individual has little or no control.

Deciding on a job or profession is a similar phenomenon. First, one is limited by background in the categories one can choose.

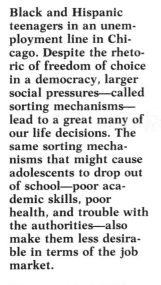

Black and Hispanic teenagers in an unemployment line in Chicago. Despite the rhetoric of freedom of choice in a democracy, larger social pressures—called sorting mechanisms—lead to a great many of our life decisions. The same sorting mechanisms that might cause adolescents to drop out of school—poor academic skills, poor health, and trouble with the authorities—also make them less desirable in terms of the job market.

(Photo copyright © 1974 by Guy Gillette/Photo Researchers, Inc.)

It would be useless, even ridiculous, for a high-school dropout to apply for a job as a physicist. Even among dropouts, jobs and background factors, such as race, are related. In 1981, one-fourth of the young adult black male dropouts were unemployed, as well as nearly one-third of young black women. These unemployment rates are double those of whites of comparable age and educational background ("Work Force," *Washington Post*, October 18, 1981).

Adolescents frequently face questions about their future work role: "What are you going to be when you finish school?" The very form of the question implies that occupation determines a person's identity. In fact, work role is probably the single most important factor in self-identity, and the factor most directly involved in the young person's identity crisis. It is also one of the most difficult commitments a young person must make. "In general it is the inability to settle on an occupational identity which most disturbs young people" (Erikson, 1968, p. 132).

APPROACHES TO THE STUDY OF ADOLESCENCE

In the following chapters on the psychology of adolescence, we encounter a wide range of research approaches. Such approaches include case studies, hypothesis-testing studies, observational studies, and cross-cultural studies. Some researchers in adolescence have used longitudinal methods of data collection, while others have used the cross-sectional method. Before commencing a detailed discussion of *topics* in adolescence, we review *methodological approaches* to the study of adolescence. This review treats several approaches to the study of one topic within the spectrum of research in adolescence—the topic of sexual behavior. The purpose of this review is to introduce the variety of methods in adolescent research, rather than to summarize the work on adolescent sexuality. A more detailed discussion of that topic can be found in Chapter 8.

Literary Accounts

This chapter opened with a description of adolescence from the point of view of Frankie Addams, the fictional creation of Carson McCullers. Literary accounts of adolescence can often highlight the themes and issues of adolescence more forcefully than academic discussions of the same topic.

Consider Herman Raucher's description of a male adolescent's sexual awakening in his novel, *Summer of '42*. In one part of the novel, a couple of 15-year-old boys, Oscy and Hermie, decided to try to lose their virginity on the beach with Miriam and Aggie. Before the big event, Oscy made copies of a step-by-step reference list of 12 acts leading up to intercourse. Oscy gave his friend a copy, but Hermie was dubious.

Hermie looked at his list. Point Six, no matter how Oscy spelled it, was fore-play. "Foreplay," said Hermie, as though the whole thing were as well known as the Declaration of Independence.

"Right," said Oscy. "That word keeps cropping up."

Hermie was feisty. "I still don't know what I'm supposed to do. What do I say—'Hi, lady, how about a little foreplay?' "

"I keep telling you, you don't have to say a word."

"Yeah? Well, Point Two definitely states that we're supposed to converse."

"Swell, Hermie. Very good. And very observant. But that's Point Two. When you get to Point Six, you'll notice that there's no more talking. Just moaning and sighing. You moan and sigh."

"She'll think I'm sick."

"She'll be moaning and sighing, too."

(Raucher, 1971, pp. 163, 165)

Literary accounts of the adolescent experience provide readers with useful collateral material. In the medium of fiction, a kernel of truth can be exaggerated, using literary license, to highlight a specific experience without having to adhere to strict, objective facts.

Case Studies

Oscy and Hermie are fictional characters, even though the description of their inexperience strikes a familiar chord. Case studies involve real people; the descriptions are as accurate as possible, given the vicissitudes of memory and of self-protective defenses.

A series of valuable case studies of adolescent experiences was provided by Goethals and Klos (1976), who asked undergraduates to write of their own lives as accurately as they could, in the context of a course on interpersonal relationships. In one case study, Sandy described her relationship to Bob. They met for the first time in 9th grade and continued to have a relationship into their college years. By the time they were in college, Sandy and Bob were identified as a couple, but they had not yet experienced a sexually intimate relationship.

Sometimes being with him was hell too. Kissing him still excited me, but it wasn't enough. I wanted him to caress and pet me, though I didn't even consider making love to him. Making love was "going all the way" and something that happened to other people.... Still it was hard longing for each other, wanting contact and physical closeness, when I couldn't conceive of "going all the way" and he couldn't conceive of anything else.

But as the relationship progressed, Sandy began to view intercourse as more of a possibility, especially after an important conversation with her mother. Her mother began the conversation.

"I . . . well . . . I don't know if I'm behind the times with this but . . . well, when you feel, at least if you do, or if you have. . . . When you and Bob come to making love," a glance at me, and finding me looking rather blank (a result of shock) *"having intercourse, I want you to come to us so that Dr. Frankel can fix you up with a diaphragm or something."*

"But really . . . I . . . we hadn't even considered it!"

"Still, when you do, I want you to tell us, because we want you to be adequately protected." (Goethals & Klos, 1976, p. 298)

Soon after this conversation, Sandy and Bob began making love, and as Sandy described it, "It was kind of like lighting a volcano."

We pirated Bob's parents' bed while they were gone and spent whole nights making love—Bob said that somehow having me there next to him put sleep pretty far down on his list of priorities, and I was so enthralled by the sinking, soaring, piercing joy of loving him I didn't regret the sleep. (Goethals & Klos, 1976, p. 301)

The case study can be a valuable tool for evaluating theoretical insights by measuring the fit between theory and real-life events. Case studies are particularly useful for providing compelling illustrations of developmental events derived from theory and research. Case studies as illustrations are best complemented by more objective research methods, such as observational studies and hypothesis-testing research, because the experiences of one individual may not be typical of very many adolescents. Focusing on only a few individuals introduces a very real danger of distortion.

Observational Studies

Observational studies attempt to locate behavior within its natural context. In studies of adult social behavior, observational studies are often conducted by researchers who represent themselves as participants in the activity under study. This type of research is called *participant observation*. An example of participant-observation research in the field of adolescent psychology is a study of social interaction in a public high school by a young man posing as a high-school senior, unknown to his fellow students or to the administration of the school (Owen, 1981). This participant-observer described the current sexual ethic in high school this way:

Ever since the 1960s adults have imagined that teenagers everywhere are coupling and uncoupling with relative abandon. Teenagers are certainly freer about sex than they were twenty years ago, but changing societal attitudes have made the most difference for kids who probably would have had reasonably active sex lives anyway. The rich get richer. The new teenage state brought into being by the "sexual revolution" is by no means a democracy. People who didn't have much luck at sex as teenagers in 1960 wouldn't necessarily be having any more luck now. In fact, the sexual revolution makes life harder, not easier, for the rank and file. A boy whose bowels unhinge at the thought of kissing a girl will not be overjoyed by the news that he is now allowed (or expected) to take her to bed. The poor get poorer. (Owen, 1981, p. 173)

Field Studies Participant observation is impractical in most studies of adolescent psychology because investigators would be easily spotted as interlopers. However, it is sometimes possible to observe the behavior of adolescents first hand in the field in which it occurs. This form of observation is sometimes referred to as a *field study*. A good example of a field study of adolescent behavior is August Hollingshead's observational study of adolescents. In the 1940s, Hollingshead and his wife moved to a midwestern town, called "Elmtown," and became actively involved with the life of the community in order to study the behavior of the town's adolescents.

Hollingshead made informal contacts with high-school students by walking his dog around the school grounds. The school officials, of course, were aware of Hollingshead's research project. After getting to know some of the students, Hollingshead began to go to places where they loafed, ate, or played games. His observations were complemented by informal interviews with many high-school students. Over the course of several months, Hollingshead was able to describe adolescent behavior and development in a number of areas, including sexual behavior. Here is his description of the casual sexuality of one group of Elmtown's adolescents:

Automobile trips to neighboring towns in search of a pick-up occur almost every night, but week ends are preferred. On these expeditions two or three boys go to taverns, restaurants, and hangouts similar to the ones they patronize in Elmtown in search of girls they hope to take on a petting party with the admitted purpose of seducing them. Particular cliques go to the same places on every trip. They may drive to two or three different ones on the same night if the "hunting" is not good. When they find girls who will go with them, the party starts out to have a good time. On these occasions, a few beers, or some more potent drink, are in order, perhaps a show, followed by a ride, some more drinks, and then the party gets down to the serious business of the evening. Generally, the boy follows the accepted aggressive male role, but every now and then the girl may be the aggressor. The evening is counted a complete success when the participants make sex contacts, but here it is each couple for itself. (Hollingshead, 1949, pp. 421–422)

Hollingshead's observational study, published under the title *Elmtown's Youth*, is one of the classic studies of adolescent social structure and social interaction; later in the textbook some of the results of Hollingshead's research are described in more detail.

Cross-cultural Studies Cross-cultural studies of adolescence, which are a special type of observational study, involve first-hand observation in other cultural settings. Cross-cultural studies can provide very valuable comparative information on styles of making the transition from childhood to adulthood. These studies help to combat some of the natural ethnocentrism to which we are prone.

Ethnocentrism is the view that what happens in one's own cultural group is right, good, natural, and normal. Cross-cultural studies show us that different cultural practices can occur naturally and normally within the context of a different social structure and social climate. Many people have traditionally held the view, for example, that adolescence is a "stormy decade," a lengthy period of inevitable psychological turmoil. Studies of adolescence from a cross-cultural perspective have shown that adolescence is not inevitably either lengthy or stormy. For example, Margaret Mead's cross-cultural studies of young women indicated that the "storm and stress" hypothesis did not apply to Samoan adolescents.

Adolescence becomes not the most difficult, most stressful period of life, but perhaps the pleasantest time the Samoan girl will ever know. . . . By common consent the nights belong to the youth for dancing, courting and love making. So the young girl has freedom but slight responsibility, assurance that she will marry but no pressure to marry quickly. (Mead, 1958, p. 344)

More recent studies of large numbers of adolescents in our own society have confirmed Margaret Mead's cross-cultural observation that adolescence need not be a stormy decade, even in a highly technological society (Offer & Offer, 1975).

Interview and Questionnaire Studies

The most commonly done studies of adolescence are those in which interviews or questionnaires are used. These studies are relatively straightforward and simple to conduct. With questionnaires, a large number of adolescents can be studied in a relatively short period of time. These methods are particularly prevalent in institutional settings, such as high schools and colleges. Among the disadvantages of this method is the fact that the behavior under study is being reported *about*, rather than being directly performed.

Adolescent sexuality has been studied primarily through questionnaires and interviews. Young people are asked a series of standard questions about their sexual attitudes and behaviors. In Chapter 8, we review studies of adolescent sexuality in some detail.

For our present purposes, the questionnaire method is of primary importance, rather than the results yielded by the method. Table 1-1 presents a version of a questionnaire which was used in a large-scale survey of adolescent sexual behavior (Sorensen, 1972). A separate version was used with girls and with boys; an excerpt from the girls' questionnaire is presented in Table 1-1.

TABLE 1-1
Excerpt from Questionnaire on Adolescent Sexual Behavior (Girls' Version)

Have your ever had sexual intercourse with a boy?

☐ Yes   ☐ No → | If your answer is "no," please skip to the next *blue* page. |

Thinking back to *the very first time* that you had sex with a boy, how old were you then?   Age: _____

Where was it that you had sex with a boy for the very first time?

☐ In my home   ☐ In the boy's home
☐ In a friend's home   ☐ In a hotel or motel
☐ In an automobile   ☐ Outdoors
☐ At school   ☐ Somewhere else

This first time that you had sex with a boy, did either you or the boy make use of any birth control method, or do anything else to cut down on the risk of your becoming pregnant?

☐ Yes   ☐ No

If you had it to do all over again, do you wish that you had waited until you were older before having sex with a boy for the first time, are you glad you did it when you did, or do you wish that you had done it when you were younger?

☐ I wish I had waited until I was older before having sex with a boy for the first time
☐ I'm glad I did it when I did
☐ I wish I had done it when I was younger

Who was the very first boy with whom you ever had sexual intercourse?

☐ A boy I had met only a little while before the time that we first had sex together
☐ A boy I was going steady with, and planned to marry
☐ A boy I knew slightly, and was more or less friendly with
☐ Someone who raped me
☐ A boy I was going steady with, but had no definite plans to marry
☐ A boy I knew well and I liked a lot, even though we weren't going together
☐ My husband, after we were married

How old was this boy when you first had sex together?   Age: _____

Source: Sorensen, 1972.

This questionnaire contains questions which are directed at the objective facts, such as "Have you ever had sexual intercourse with a boy?" It also contains questions that relate the feelings and reactions of the adolescent, such as "Do you wish you had waited until you were older before having sex with a boy?"

The questionnaire method has the virtue of being amenable to anonymity. Anonymity of participants' responses is important, especially in so sensitive an area as sexual behavior. Assuring adolescents of anonymity may encourage them to be more truthful in their responses; in addition, anonymous responses allow researchers to study important topics without invading the privacy of participants.

Hypothesis-Testing Studies

A hypothesis about how variables are related is tested when researchers observe the effect of one variable on another under controlled conditions. The most rigorous form of hypothesis testing occurs in laboratory studies, but these are rare in the study of adolescence, and almost nonexistent within the realm of adolescent sexual behavior.

However, some hypothesis-testing studies are available in the area of adolescent sexuality. Consider the following hypothesis: "Unmarried male college students are more aroused by erotic films than are female college students." This hypothesis was tested in a study at Purdue University, in which psychology students were the participants. In small same-sex groups, students viewed erotic films that portrayed couples engaging in explicit sexual behaviors. Participants were asked to rate their level of sexual arousal after viewing the films. Men and women in this study reported about the same level of sexual arousal. In other words, the hypothesis that men are more aroused by erotic films than women was not confirmed (Fisher & Byrne, 1978).

Of course, one might object that self-reported level of sexual arousal is not a valid measure, or that students in abnormal psychology courses are not representative of students as a whole or of young people in the population. One must view data in the context within which they were obtained in order to interpret them realistically. In the above study of responses to erotic films, a major problem for interpretation is the fact that participants were not randomly selected to take part in the study.

Nevertheless, it is possible to construct a research strategy to test a hypothesis about sexual behavior, and to employ the scientific practice of random selection of research participants. Consider a study on the phenomenon of volunteer bias in studies of sexual behavior (Bauman, 1973). Many of the questionnaire studies that were discussed earlier have been criticized because most of the participants who fill out questionnaires on their sexual practices have volunteered to do so. Criticisms of these studies have implied that volunteers may be more likely to claim sexual experience than nonvolunteers. One might be more likely to volunteer to take part in a study of sexual behavior if one has something to report; Bauman tested this hypothesis.

Bauman randomly selected the names of 1,000 men and 1,000 women from the Registrar's files at a southeastern university. These 2,000 students were contacted by mail, and asked to volunteer their time to fill out a sex questionnaire. Only 150 men and 196 women took the trouble to come in to Bauman's office to fill out the questionnaire. These students constitute the volunteer group.

From the same Registrar's files, Bauman randomly selected the names of 100 men and 100 women, but this time he contacted them in their dormitories, so that it was almost impossible for them to refuse to participate. These students constitute the nonvolunteer group. Figure 1-2 shows the percentages of male and female students in the volunteer and nonvolunteer groups who reported that they had experienced sexual intercourse. The differences between the volunteer and nonvolunteer groups are not statistically signifi-

FIGURE 1-2
Hypothesis-testing study of volunteer bias in reporting of sexual experience. Although differences between volunteers and nonvolunteers are not statistically significant, nonvolunteers are more likely to report being nonvirgins than volunteers.

(From Bauman, 1973.)

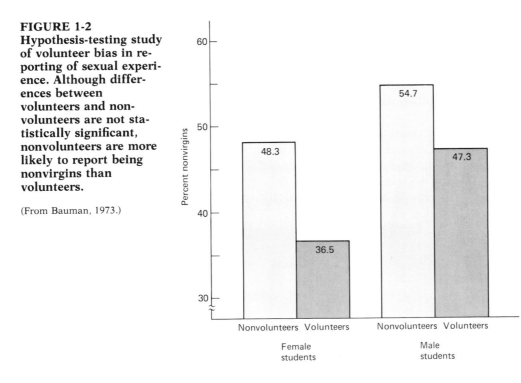

cant, but as one can see, the nonvolunteers, if anything, are more sexually experienced, contrary to the original hypothesis. The data from this study therefore failed to support the hypothesis.

AGE EFFECTS AND COHORT EFFECTS

Developmental research is usually designed to demonstrate *age effects,* which is to say differences in psychological phenomena due to differences in age or level of maturity. For example, there is a very strong age effect for the physical changes accompanying puberty. Younger adolescents are less physically mature than older adolescents. Predictions can be made about level of physical maturity on the basis of age alone in adolescence.

Many phenomena of interest to the student of adolescence are also subject to *cohort effects,* differences between people due to year of birth, rather than age. Teenagers who reached adolescence in earlier generations—that is, members of earlier birth cohorts—had somewhat different experiences in their transitions from childhood to adulthood than do teenagers today. Members of the birth cohort of the 1920s, for example, who reached adolescence in the 1940s, grew up without television, and reached puberty during the Second World War. These major differences between an earlier birth cohort and the current one might logically be assumed to exert some influence on the psychological experience of adolescence.

There are two major strategies for research on developmental change, which help to estimate age and cohort effects separately. One strategy, cross-sectional research, selects people of different ages for comparative study. Differences between age groups are assumed to be due to a combination of age and cohort differences. In the other strategy, longitudinal research, a group of people is selected for repeated study at different points in their life cycles. Since participants in longitudinal research are all from the same birth cohort, differences from one age to another are assumed to be primarily a reflection of age effects. Let us examine these two research strategies in more detail, with illustrations from research projects on adolescent sexuality.

Cross-sectional Research

Cross-sectional research essentially takes a "slice," or cross-section, of the population at a given time. In practice, cross-sectional research is usually highly restricted in terms of age groups and geographic localities studied.

A study of adolescent sexual behavior in one Wisconsin community serves as an example of a cross-sectional study (DeLamater & MacCorquodale, 1979). Two groups of young people were interviewed for a study of sexual behavior between February and July of

1973. One group consisted of male and female undergraduates from the University of Wisconsin at Madison. The other group consisted of young people between the ages of 18 and 23 who resided in Madison but did not attend the university. A total of 1,376 young people were interviewed for the study. A large majority of the participants were from Wisconsin, and nearly all were white. As the researchers pointed out, "the sample characteristics are to be expected for a middle-sized midwestern city" (DeLamater & MacCorquodale, 1979, p. 54).

Table 1-2 presents the incidences for each group of participants, separated by gender, for eight categories of sexual experience, from necking to oral–genital contact. Three points can be made from these data. First, the data indicate that almost all of the respondents have had experience with less advanced forms of sexual activity, such as necking and French kissing. Second, the data show that there is very little difference between the student and nonstudent respondents in their reported levels of sexual experience. And third, there are few noteworthy differences between males and females in their reported experience. One exception that should be mentioned is the difference between college men and women in incidence of intercourse; 75 percent of the men reported experiencing intercourse, compared to 60 percent of women.

Data from one isolated study are difficult to interpret. They provide a cross-section of two groups of young people between the ages of 18 and 23 in one midwestern community, at one historical time—from February to July of 1973. We can reasonably expect that

TABLE 1-2 **Incidence of Sexual Experience in Eight Categories of Behavior In a Cross-sectional Study**	**MALE**		**FEMALE**	
	STUDENT	NONSTUDENT	STUDENT	NONSTUDENT
Necking	97%	98%	99%	99%
French kissing	93	95	95	95
Breast fondling	92	92	93	93
Male fondling of female genitals	86	87	82	86
Female fondling of male genitals	82	84	78	81
Intercourse	75	79	60	72
Male oral contact with female genitals	60	68	59	67
Female oral contact with male genitals	61	70	54	63

Source: DeLamater & MacCorquodale, 1979.

there is an age effect operating; if these same individuals had been interviewed at younger ages, it is surely true that lower incidences of sexual behavior would have been reported. However, there is probably also a cohort effect operating. The relatively high incidence of experience at the level of intercourse in all four groups may be in part a function of the liberalization in sexual standards that occurred in the United States in the late 1960s and early 1970s. With cross-sectional data, however, such a cohort effect cannot be assessed directly.

Longitudinal Research

Longitudinal studies, in which the same individuals are repeatedly tested, have the advantage of allowing very precise estimates of age changes within a given cohort. These studies, however, provide no information on cohort differences; they might, therefore, be limited in applicability to a narrow range of birth cohorts.

Shirley and Richard Jessor's study of the transition from virginity to nonvirginity is a good example of a longitudinal study in the area of adolescent sexual behavior. The Jessors administered questionnaires annually for 4 years to the same high-school and college students in a small town in the Rocky Mountains. The percentages of students who reported that they were nonvirgins between

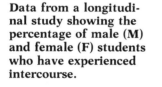

FIGURE 1-3
Data from a longitudinal study showing the percentage of male (M) and female (F) students who have experienced intercourse.

(From Jessor & Jessor, 1975.)

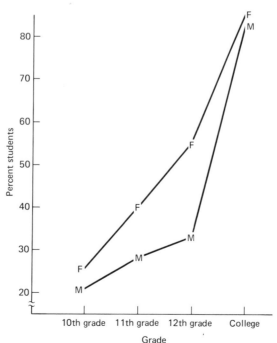

the 10th grade and college are presented in Figure 1-3. Since the same adolescents repeatedly filled out the questionnaires, these data apply to the same individuals, followed over a 4-year period. The data show that these adolescents became more sexually experienced as they grew older, as one would expect. The greatest shift in sexual experience occurred between 12th grade and college, especially for the male adolescents. Female adolescents in this study reported more sexual experience at every age than the males. This finding is interesting because it differs from results of several other surveys of adolescent sexuality, and because it violates a popular cultural stereotype. However, the trend may be a cohort effect. Recent cohorts of adolescents may, indeed, have reversed the gender difference in reports of sexual activity. Here is an instance in which comparable data from other birth cohorts, with similar longitudinal methods, would be very useful.

In the study of adolescence, as in all of psychology, it is helpful to have a variety of research approaches. Data from a variety of approaches, when their conclusions converge, inspire greater confidence in the overall results. Most of the issues which this book concerns have been approached from a number of angles and points of view. It is the task of this book to provide the reader with an understanding of the insights to be gained about adolescence from the perspective of these research approaches.

SUMMARY

1. Adolescence is the transitional period between childhood and adulthood. As Erikson pointed out, different cultures have defined this transitional period in a variety of ways.

2. Within our own culture, adolescence is a relatively new phenomenon. Until the 18th century, adolescence was merged with childhood as one, long, developmental period. Some historians believe that adolescence was "invented" in technological societies in the first two decades of the 20th century.

3. Adolescence has a physically defined onset—the beginning of puberty. Puberty is now beginning earlier than it did in previous generations, and puberty arrives earlier for girls than it does for boys.

4. There is an uncertain endpoint for adolescence—usually defined as the time when adult commitments are made. Patterns of education and marriage have lengthened the period of adolescence in our culture; more young people are extending their years of formal schooling and are postponing marriage. Both of

these events are associated with postponement of adult commitments.

5. Lengthier adolescence may be the major underlying factor in the development of "youth culture," the tendency of young people to develop a set of attitudes and behaviors distinct from the rest of the culture.

6. There are some unifying issues of the period of adolescence as it is experienced in Western societies. Adolescence is the stage of the life cycle when one confronts the psychological issue of identity—defining the nature of one's self and one's role in the world at large. Adolescents seek their identities in a cultural context. In Western society, many adolescents appear to experience a sense of alienation from the perceived norms of adult society.

7. A second theme of adolescence is the establishment of autonomy—in a psychological sense—from parents. Autonomy is one aspect of adult status, when an individual is no longer psychologically dependent on parents.

8. During adolescence, most young people make important decisions about their life goals, especially occupational goals. Many psychologists, such as Erikson, believe that occupational decision-making is the crux of the identity issue. Occupational decision-making is not entirely a matter of free choice. Sorting mechanisms, such as social class, race, and physical attractiveness come to bear on the decisions about life goals that one ultimately makes in adolescence.

9. Adolescence has been studied from a variety of points of view, and with a variety of research strategies, from literary accounts to laboratory investigations.

10. Literary accounts of adolescence often highlight important issues in human development by focusing on specific aspects of the adolescent experience without obligation to portray events exactly as they happened for any one individual.

11. Case studies involve real people; descriptions provided in case studies portray events as accurately as is possible. Case studies are valuable tools for evaluating theoretical insights with actual material from real-life experiences.

12. Observational studies attempt to locate behavior within its natural context. Field studies, which are observational studies in which researchers observe behavior in its natural habitat without any intervention, have been valuable in providing rich

sources of information about adolescent social behavior. Hollingshead's study of "Elmtown" is a good example of a field-observational study of adolescence.

13. Cross-cultural studies are another special type of observational study. Researchers observe growth and development through first-hand observation in other cultural settings. Cross-cultural studies provide useful comparative information to help researchers avoid an overly ethnocentric view of adolescent development.

14. The most common approach to the study of adolescence is the questionnaire or interview approach. This research strategy allows the researcher to collect data on a large number of adolescents in a short period of time.

15. Hypothesis-testing studies allow researchers to examine the effect that one variable has on another variable; the key to hypothesis-testing studies is experimental control of variables. Studies in which participants are randomly assigned to experimental treatment groups minimize the contamination of preexisting group differences in variable manipulation. Therefore, the interpretation of the effects of one variable on another is more straightforward when participants have been randomly assigned to groups.

16. Most research in developmental psychology is designed to uncover age effects—differences in psychological phenomena due to differences in age or level of maturity. Many psychological phenomena are also subject to cohort effects—differences between people due to year of birth, rather than age per se. Cross-sectional studies involve testing different groups of people at the same time. Because tests are conducted at the same historical time, the participants necessarily differ both in their ages and in their year of birth. Cross-sectional studies of this type cannot separate the effects of age and of cohort.

17. Longitudinal studies follow the same group of individuals through repeated testings. Because individuals from the same birth cohort are repeatedly tested, age effects can be isolated. The findings are still limited, however, because they may be applicable to only the cohort under investigation.

OUTLINE

2. PHYSICAL DEVELOPMENT AND STATUS CHANGE

Puberty, most of us would agree, brings about a great number of changes. Contours of the body become more adultlike. Interests change. Sexual desire, perhaps more frankly described as lust, is a major new interest. One's sense of "self" changes, and comes to mirror the transformations in body and behavior. Expectations for more mature behavior emerge as the body undergoes its inexorable metamorphosis.

Physical transformation of the body at puberty marks the beginning of a status transition—from childhood to adulthood. A person's sense of identity is vulnerable during a period of marked status change, and this seems particularly true during adolescence. An adolescent's task is to integrate the physical changes of puberty with the psychological transformation into adulthood. Erik Erikson (1968), who wrote eloquently about adolescence in Western society, expressed it this way:

Young people must become whole people in their own right, and this during a developmental stage characterized by a diversity of changes in physical growth, genital maturation, and social awareness . . . . The young person, in order to experience wholeness, must feel a progressive continuity between that which he has come to be during the long years of childhood and that which he promises to become in the anticipated future; between that which he conceives himself to be and that which he perceives others to see in him and to expect of him. (p. 87)

In this chapter, we examine the phenomenon known as the "secular trend," which refers to changes over time in the average age at which physical maturation occurs, and changes in average height and weight attained by members of given populations. Next, we review the changes at puberty, including the sequence of development for boys and

These trumpeters in a volunteer high-school band illustrate the great size differences that can occur between adolescents of the same age. Although the secular trend is toward earlier maturation and increased height and weight, there is a wide range of individual variation.

(Photo by George E. Jones III/ Photo Researchers, Inc.)

girls and the underlying physiological mechanisms responsible. Timing differences in maturation are also explored for their psychological ramifications.

Finally, we look at cultural variations in the mode of transition from childhood to adulthood. Many cultural groups have traditionally practiced dramatic puberty rites, often called *initiation ceremonies*, to mark this status transition. These rites are contrasted with our own protracted and unritualized status transition in adolescence.

THE SECULAR TREND

Varsity football players at the University of Texas at Austin have been measured since the turn of the century. Team members are larger now. In the decade 1961-1970, they averaged 6.6 cm (2.6 in) taller and 16 kg (35.2 lbs) heavier than in the decade 1899–1910 (Malina, 1972). Although these data are probably confounded by changes in recruiting practices, they are consistent with a trend toward increased stature among young people.

In fact, people are getting larger, and they are maturing earlier, than in previous generations. The average age for first menstruation, for example, is now just under age 13; in the mid-1800s it was over 16. The trend toward earlier maturation and toward increased stature is referred to as the "secular trend." Larger athletes at the University of Texas provide just one example of this trend at work.

Dimensions of the Secular Trend

Increase in Stature In the United States, large-scale data on stature are provided by the armed forces. Like Texas athletes, army recruits are a special population, but they reflect the average male more closely than the small Texas sample. In both cases, the data conform to the drift toward increased stature, which is part of the secular trend. Army recruits in the Vietnam era were taller and heavier than recruits in the Second World War. Similarly, soldiers in World War II were taller and heavier than inductees of the First World War (Karpinos, 1961).

The trend toward increased stature has been quite regular since the mid-1800s. For example, measurements of Iowa boys from 1961 to 1963 were compared with measurements from 1881 on boys in Wisconsin. Both groups of boys were from European ancestry. The differences in height for the two groups of boys over this 80-year time span were large and systematic, as shown in Figure 2-1. At age 14, there is a 15 cm (6 in) difference between the two groups (Roche, 1979).

Stanley Garn (1980) summarized the trends in stature increase this way:

Children are taller, adolescents are taller, and adults are taller, at a rate approximating 1 centimeter per decade, or 1 inch every twenty-five years. As a result of this secular change, we now stand over 10 centimeters (4 in) taller than our Civil War ancestors, and we are also far heavier. (p. 124)

Earlier Maturation Human beings, in addition to growing taller, are growing up earlier. The average European or American man did not reach his full height at the turn of the century until he was in his mid-20s; now, full height is reached by age 18.

A convenient index of maturation is age of first menstruation, known as menarche. This dramatic event has shown a regular trend toward earlier occurrence since the mid-1800s. Figure 2-2 shows the regular nature of the trend for girls in Europe and America. It represents a drop in age of menarche of 4 months per decade for the past 100 years, from roughly age 16½ to age 13.

The trend toward earlier maturation is illustrated in the United States by a group of girls and their mothers in a longitudinal growth study in Boston. Average age at first menstruation was 14.4

FIGURE 2-1
A comparison showing the differences in height between boys in Iowa in the 1960s and boys in Wisconsin in the 1880s.

(From Roche, 1979. Copyright © 1979 by the Society for Research in Child Development.)

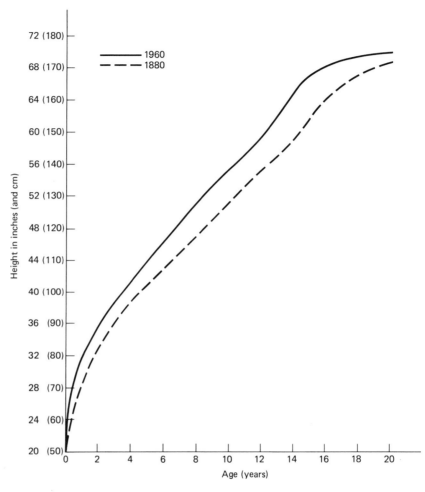

among the mothers, who were born between 1894 and 1917. For their daughters, all born in the 1930s, average age was 12.9 (Damon, Damon, Reed, & Valadian, 1969).

Origins of these women were predominantly European. A similar trend holds for other ethnic groups. The Japanese Ministry of Education has compiled physical measurements on essentially all children in school since 1900 (except during the Second World War). Records of all girls who were 6 years old in 1900 and in 1950 were examined for age of menarche. Selected age groups at distinct points in time are called cohorts; average age of menarche of the 1900-cohort was 14.5; for the 1950-cohort it was 13.6 (Kimura, 1967). Similarly, average age of menarche among samples of girls in

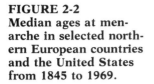

FIGURE 2-2
Median ages at menarche in selected northern European countries and the United States from 1845 to 1969.

(From Roche, 1979. Copyright © 1979 by the Society for Research in Child Development.)

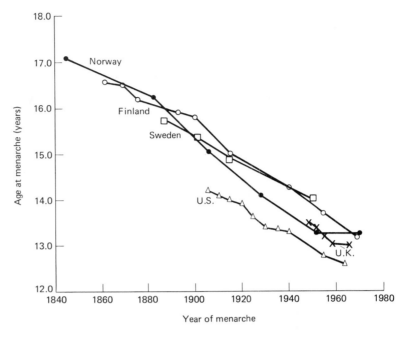

Leningrad was 14.2 in 1927–1930, and 12.9 in 1959 (Vlastovsky, 1966).

Clearly there must be limits to this trend. Extending it backwards in time, say to 1066 when William the Conqueror won the Battle of Hastings, would lead to a prediction of an average age of 39 for first menstruation among women of that era. Obviously, this cannot have been the case. A rough estimate for age of menarche in Medieval Europe is 14, culled from such sources as the 6th-century physician Aetius and from the 12th-century nun Hildegard of Bingen, the earliest German medical writer (Amundsen & Diers, 1973). The same age, 14, is estimated as the age of menarche in classical Greece. Here is one of history's first descriptions of puberty, from Aristotle's *Historia Animalium.*

For the most part males begin to produce sperm when 14 years have been completed. At the same time pubic hair begins to appear.... At the same time in females a swelling of the breasts begins and the menses begins to flow.... In the majority the menses are first noticed after the breasts have grown to the height of two fingers' breadth. (Amundsen & Diers, 1969, p. 125)

These are only estimates, of course, in comparison to the documented ages of the mid-1800s which show menarche at age 16½.

The age of 14 might more accurately reflect the beginning of visible signs of puberty than menarche, as the quote from *Historia Animalium* suggests.

Recent estimates are that menarche remained stable at about age 14 or 15 through the Medieval period, at which time age of menarche was delayed until age 16 or older. This delay in age of first menstruation appears to have been coincident with the growth of large cities during the Industrial Revolution, perhaps as a function of disease, malnutrition, and social stress that the new phenomenon of urban poverty brought about (Malina, 1979).

Factors Affecting the Secular Trend

As the social stresses of the Industrial Revolution began to subside in the mid-1800s, the secular trend (really a return) to earlier maturation began. Although no one knows for sure why the secular trend began after the Industrial Revolution, several contributing factors have been suggested. Among these are decreased family size; changes in world temperature and humidity; improvements in urban life; reduced child labor; lighter and less restrictive clothing; improved personal hygiene; improved medical care; and improved nutrition (Meredith, 1976). Some of these hypothesized factors deserve closer scrutiny.

Ecological Factors Some ecological factors, such as altitude, are known to affect the average age of onset of sexual maturation. Girls who live in higher altitudes, such as Denver, Colorado, experience menarche at later ages, perhaps because altitude slows the overall rate of growth and development (Frisch & Revelle, 1971). Altitude also affects the average height attained by adolescents. Male adolescents in Peru's coastal Tambo Valley averaged 12.9 cm (5.2 in) taller than agemates in mountainous Puno, Peru, at an altitude of over 4000 meters (13,000 ft). The low-altitude boys also weighed more by about 11 kg (24 lbs). These rather dramatic differences decrease during late adolescence, suggesting that altitude affects rate of growth more than final growth attained (Beall, Baker, Baker, & Haas, 1977). In any case, altitude obviously has had no effect on the changes in age of maturation or of stature over time, represented by the secular trend.

Although mean world temperature has increased since the mid-1800s, it is a gross summary statistic with little meaning for our present purposes. Controlled studies of the effects of temperature on mice indicate that maturation is speeded by warmer temperatures. Among humans, effects of temperature on maturation have not been demonstrated. Both Eskimo girls and Nigerian girls reach menarche at about age 14½ (Tanner, 1962). Humidity also appears to exert little influence. Girls in Assam, a hot and wet climate, reach menarche at the same age as girls in the hot and dry Burmese climate (Foll, 1961).

Environmental Factors Increased urbanization, reduced child labor, and changes in clothing style are all directly associated with technological advances following the Industrial Revolution and have been proposed as factors contributing to the secular trend. As Garn (1980) observed, "The school bus, improved home heating, the availability of snacks, and even the shift to spectator sports may all contribute to this trend" (p. 124). Apart from rural–urban differences, little research is available which bears on these factors. Even the rural–urban question is difficult to separate from effects of social class. One study, for example, showed that girls in rural Ceylon reached menarche a year-and-a-half later than urban Ceylonese girls (Wilson & Sutherland, 1950). It is not clear what aspect of a rural–urban difference may account for such a wide gap. Data on maturation among laboratory rats are interesting with regard to this point. Laboratory rats cannot strictly be described as urbanized, of course; but they are reared in a more densely populated area than free-roaming rats. Sex glands develop earlier in the lab rats than in "wild" rats (Damon, Damon, Reed, & Valadian, 1969).

Family Size Family size is associated with physical growth rate, on the average. One study, for example, showed that 8-year-old boys who were only children averaged 4 cm (1.6 in) taller than those having four or more siblings (Scott, 1961). In general, children from smaller families are larger, and mature earlier, than children from larger families (Malina, 1979). Consider the data on family size and age at menarche in the United States from 1850 to 1970, shown in Figure 2-3. There has been a regular decrease in family size over this 120-year span of time. Data on average age at menarche have been collected for much of this time span, and show a corresponding decrease. While the similarities in these two curves are interesting and suggestive, when considered in conjunction with what is known about family size and growth, the similarities cannot be said to show a direct relationship between family size and age of sexual maturation. Family size may indeed contribute to the secular trend, but the estimate is that it can account for no more than one decade's worth of increase in growth—about 2.5 cm (1 in) in height (Tanner, 1962).

FIGURE 2-3
Trends in family size and age at menarche in the United States from 1850 to 1970.

(From Roche, 1979. Copyright © 1979 by the Society for Research in Child Development, Inc.)

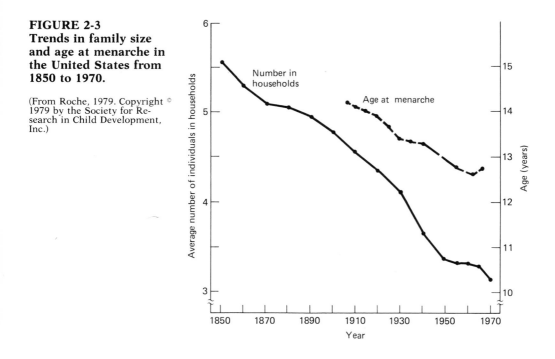

Health and Nutrition Improved personal hygiene and improved medical care are often cited as factors contributing to earlier maturation. There was a marked reduction in infant mortality during the 19th and 20th centuries as a result of medical advances, especially in Western countries. For example, after Robert Koch's discovery of the cholera bacillus in 1883, cholera was nearly eliminated in Western Europe and North America (Malina, 1979). Many other infectious diseases, such as smallpox and intestinal infections, were also drastically reduced. As a result, more children survived into adolescence, and fewer individuals experienced the drain of bodily resources caused by these diseases. Medical advances are probably the most important contributing factor to the secular trend (Malina, 1979). Nevertheless, the trend began before scientific medicine was widely available and before information on personal hygiene was widely disseminated (Cone, 1961). Medical advances, therefore, cannot completely account for the phenomenon.

Improvements in diet and nutrition, strongly related to social class, are also important factors in accounting for the secular trend. Studies that have examined age of menarche by social class have consistently shown that upper-class girls reach menarche before lower-class girls. For example, upper-class Hong Kong girls had their first menstrual periods, on the average, 9½ months before their lower-class counterparts in the early 1960s (Lee, Chang, & Chan, 1963). Similarly, middle-class girls in Baghdad reached menarche seven months before slum girls (Shakir, 1971).

The argument that the secular trend is influenced by nutrition and living conditions is bolstered by data from wartime, when shortages of food are common. Adolescent boys in the Soviet Union showed a diminished height and weight during the Second World War (Vlastovsky, 1966). Reports of delayed adolescent growth are also available from wartime Germany, France, and Belgium, and during the economic depression (1929–1933) in the United States (Tanner, 1962).

Girls in more privileged classes, who enjoy better nutrition, reach menarche 2–3 months earlier than poorer girls. Bantu girls in southern Africa have among the highest menarcheal ages. "Poor" Bantu girls, who were reported to have meat in their diets only when a cow died from accident or disease, began menstruating at age 15.4. "Not-poor" Bantu girls with a weekly ration of meat or poultry, menstruated at about age 15 (Burrell, Healy, & Tanner, 1961).

Limits to the Secular Trend   Secular trends in height and in age of physical maturation must have some limit. In fact, there is evidence that the trend has ended among the most economically favored Americans (Roche, 1979; Garn, 1980). Students who came from private schools to Harvard, for example, were somewhat taller and heavier than those coming from public schools, whose families were presumably somewhat less well-off. Furthermore, the private-school students at Harvard had reached their growth potential even in the 1930s (Bakwin & McLaughlin, 1964).

The women at Wellesley showed no sharp increases in height or weight over the decades of the 1930s to 1950s. In addition, there were no public versus private school differences. One hypothesis to account for this gender difference is that males respond more to improved conditions than females. "Females, as compared to males, are less easily thrown off their growth pathway by environmental adversities such as malnutrition or disease" (Bielicki & Charzewski, 1977, p. 265). Growth curves for girls are also less affected by the privations associated with wartime (Tanner, 1962).

Age at menarche, too, appears to have stabilized in America at an average age of about 12½–13 (Roche, 1979). It must be remembered, however, that there is considerable variability around this average age. Menstruation can begin several years earlier or later.

Effects of the Secular Trend

We have discussed at length some of the possible causes of the secular trend. There remains the task of speculating about some of the effects of this phenomenon.

One effect of the secular trend in earlier maturation is a greater span of reproductive capability. Although the average age of menarche has decreased dramatically over the last 100 years to just under age 13, the average age of menopause in American women has remained stable at about age 50. Decisions about sexual behavior have to be made earlier now than in previous generations, and must be made for a longer period of time.

Obviously, the lowered age of menarche means that decisions about sexual behavior affect the teenage years most critically. A possible indirect result of the secular trend toward earlier sexual maturation is the phenomenon of teenage pregnancy. There has been a dramatic increase in pregnancies among girls below the age of 15 in recent years (Furstenberg, 1976). There is also a relationship between age at sexual maturation and age at first marriage. Adolescents of both genders who reach sexual maturity earlier enter marriage and parenthood earlier, on the average (Kiernan, 1977; Malina, 1979). The social implications of the secular change in reproductive capacity may be far reaching: "As a result of the secular decrease in the age at menarche, there is an increasing number of mothers who are ill prepared for the task of mothering, thus creating both biological and psychological hazards to themselves and their progeny" (Garn, 1980, p. 125).

The major implications of changes brought about by the secular trend center around the need for appropriate educational intervention to prepare young people for the physical changes of puberty earlier now than in previous generations. Girls should be informed about the physical nature of menarche, starting at around age 9. Both boys and girls should be prepared for the changes in their bodies and informed about the sexual decision-making that will be necessary once reproductive capability is attained—earlier now than in previous generations (Malina, 1979).

Gap Between Physical and Social Maturity A major result of the secular trend has been an increased gap between physical maturity and social maturity. What is the relationship between physical and social maturity, and how is the adolescent's sense of self affected by the two?

One's sense of identity is anchored, in large part, in the reactions of other people. Such a view of self-identity was central to the theories of George Herbert Mead (1934), and Cooley (1909/1962) and implicit in the work of Sullivan (1953) and Erikson (1968) as well.

Naturally, the way other people behave toward you is based on many different factors. One of these factors is physical maturity.

In American society, it is generally assumed that children and adults differ in their ability to get along in the world. In comparison to adults, children are assumed to lack judgment, intellectual maturity, experience, and general knowledge. For example, we do not allow children to vote, even though they may know who the candidates are and how to operate a voting machine. We assume they need more practical experience in representative democracy, which the schools instill in them through classwork and extracurricular activities such as student government.

There is no magical formula for deciding when a person has reached a plateau of social maturity. Legal voting age in the United States is now 18, although only a few years ago it was 21. Age at which young people can marry without parental consent differs from state to state, and sometimes by gender. In Mississippi, young men may marry without parental permission at age 17, while in Alabama they must wait until they are 21. Women may marry in Mississippi at age 15, and in Alabama at 18. Adolescents are allowed to drive at age 15 in Hawaii, but must wait until they are 21 in Colorado. Drinking age shows similar variation: In New York it is 18, in Alaska 19, in Delaware 20, and in Missouri 21. Many states, such as Maryland, have recently raised the legal drinking age from 18 to 21.

Note that we do not assume that social maturity—the ability to make decisions and assume adult roles and responsibilities on one's own—is attained at the same time as physical maturity. In the United States, most adolescent boys are physically mature by about age 15 or 16, girls a year or two earlier. The period of adolescence, therefore, involves three separate but closely related transitions. First, in the physical transformation of puberty, one becomes mature sexually; full reproductive capacity is attained and the desire to engage in sexual activity intensifies. Second, adolescents gradually assume more adult rights and responsibilities, come to be treated as "grown up" by others, and therefore finally attain social maturity. A third transition concerns one's sense of identity, and follows directly from the first two. Identity is based in part on the reactions of others, and undergoes changes that parallel the physical and social transitions.

Although these three elements cannot be isolated from each other, we may consider physical changes as the cornerstone, the transition that sets the process of status change in motion. Growth of the body toward mature sexual functioning dictates new interests and desires. Further, people begin to react differently toward the adolescent who is now more adultlike in behavior and appearance.

The new treatment by others, in turn, brings about new views of the self (Petersen & Taylor, 1980). Others begin to expect adolescents to assume more and more mature social roles; indeed, the movement toward adulthood virtually demands the assumption of socially mature roles. The physical transformations of puberty, therefore, are a key element in the psychological—as well as the physical—transition from childhood to adulthood.

TRANSFORMATIONS OF PUBERTY

The Initiation of Puberty

Ultimate responsibility for brain and body characteristics rests with the chromosomes, although the mechanisms are not clearly understood at this time. However, geneticists have isolated chromosomal patterns, or karyotypes, which differ in males and females. The human brain, too, shows some degree of gender differentiation from early fetal life. For example, a part of the lower brain converts a male hormone into the female hormone estrogen. Such conversion, it is suggested, may direct the brain to become either a "male" brain or a "female" brain (Naftolin, Ryan, & Petro, 1971).

Brain Regulation of Puberty　At a critical level of maturity prior to puberty, the hypothalamus, a control center in the brain regulating such states as hunger and thirst, relays a message to the pituitary. Among other functions, the pituitary manufactures growth hormones. At about age 11, the hypothalamus signals the pituitary to release gonadotrophic hormone (GTH), which stimulates growth of the gonads (testes in boys, ovaries in girls), and adrenocorticotrophic hormone (ACTH), which stimulates growth of the adrenal cortex. This gland, near the kidneys, produces in boys and girls sex hormones characteristic of both genders.

During puberty, pituitary secretion of growth hormones increases sevenfold (Root, 1973). Interestingly, the pituitary itself shows a considerable growth spurt at puberty, a growth spurt that is greater among girls than among boys (Tanner, 1962).

Apparently, the brain puts in motion the events of puberty when the hypothalamus signals the pituitary to secrete growth hormones. We may ask why the hypothalamus, after 10 to 12 years, suddenly sends out this signal. The answer to this question is not clear-cut at this time, but there are some interesting possibilities.

An intriguing line of research suggests that body weight may trigger some of the events of puberty. When height and weight show their initial growth spurt, at about age 9½ for girls and 11½ for boys, girls weigh about 30 kg (66 lbs) and boys 36 kg (80 lbs). This represents, for both sexes, the point at which daily basal bodily heat production is 35 calories per kilogram (Frisch & Revelle, 1971b).

The body's energy balance, expressed as a production of calories per kilogram, might signal the hypothalamus that the proper growth has been attained for initiation of puberty (Frisch & Revelle, 1969).

Hormonal Regulation of Puberty In specialized endocrine glands, cholesterol is synthesized into hormones with drastically altered physiological properties. Following growth and development stimulated by GTH, the gonads convert cholesterol into highly active sex steroids. In the human body, three major endocrine glands synthesize cholesterol into sex-steroid hormones. They are the testes in males, the ovaries in females, and the adrenal cortex in both males and females (Doering, 1980). The hormones produced by these specialized glands are outlined in Figure 2-4.

All body tissues are exposed to the same amounts of circulating sex-steroid hormones, but only special tissues are receptive to their action. For example, the breasts, in both males and females, are responsive to estradiol, while the ears, intestines, and most other body tissues are not.

Puberty, from the point of view of the endocrine system, involves a change in the activity level of glands that are already functioning (Kulin, 1974). Hypothalamus, pituitary, adrenal cortex, and gonads are interrelated in a complicated fashion. Sex hormones operate as a link in a feedback mechanism because the hypothalamus modifies its action on the pituitary when the level of hormones in the bloodstream exceeds a certain threshold. This feedback mecha-

FIGURE 2-4
Major endocrine glands that convert cholesterol to sex-steroid hormones.

(Based on a discussion in Doering, 1980.)

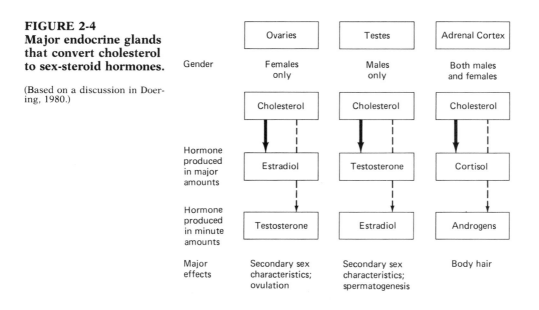

	Ovaries	Testes	Adrenal Cortex
Gender	Females only	Males only	Both males and females
	Cholesterol	Cholesterol	Cholesterol
Hormone produced in major amounts	Estradiol	Testosterone	Cortisol
Hormone produced in minute amounts	Testosterone	Estradiol	Androgens
Major effects	Secondary sex characteristics; ovulation	Secondary sex characteristics; spermatogenesis	Body hair

nism safeguards the system from going haywire and resulting in gigantic growth. The sensitivity of the hypothalamus to gonadal secretions changes following puberty.

Girls' brains appear to regulate release of gonadotrophic hormone cyclically, while boys' brains maintain a more constant level of secretion. Cyclical release of GTH maintains the periodicity characteristic of the reproductive system in women (Harris, 1964).

Typical Physical Changes at Puberty

To minimize the language of tables and statistics, we follow the physical changes of puberty in two typical, but fictitious, adolescents. (Descriptions of puberty for the typical boy and girl were extracted from the following sources: Faust, 1977; Katchadourian, 1977; Marshall & Tanner, 1970; Nicolson & Hanley, 1953; Stolz & Stolz, 1951; Tanner, 1962, 1972, and 1978.) Although there is considerable variation in average ages, the sequence of events during puberty is fairly consistent. There is no such thing as a "typical adolescent," of course. An adolescent's development through puberty may differ markedly from the following pattern and still be "normal." The following descriptions are, however, a reasonable reflection of *average* physical timetables, based on data from large numbers of males and females.

A Young Girl's Puberty: The Case of Claire

Claire celebrated her 10th birthday on New Year's Day. She could accurately be described as a preadolescent, for although she had not yet experienced any of the outward changes associated with puberty, she seemed ready to begin (Figure 2-5). Indeed, about a month after her birthday, Claire had begun to experience the event that gave puberty its name—the growth of pubic hair. For Claire, as for most girls, pubic hair began as downy, uncurled, and only slightly darkened hair, and very little appeared that first spring. By late summer, she noticed some slight changes in her breasts: They had begun to grow into small mounds, and the dark area around the nipple (called the areola) had enlarged in diameter. In the language of biological development, this is called the *breast-bud stage* of puberty. Although less visible, the walls of the uterus and vagina increase in thickness at this time.

Claire was aware that she had been growing throughout the year. Her height growth began sometime before she was 11 and steadily intensified. Around her 12th birthday, she was growing at her fastest rate—the point called *peak height velocity*. Claire did not reach her full adult height until about age 16, but this major spurt in height growth was to fall off from its peak during the next 2 years. Her breasts had also continued to grow during the year, and the areola had enlarged further.

Early in adolescence, subcutaneous fat was deposited in greater quantities, rounding the contours of Claire's body. Estradiol probably controls these fat deposits, since girls experience them to a greater extent than adolescent boys. About two-thirds of the boys in one study (Stolz & Stolz, 1951) showed noticeable fat increases in early adolescence. Boys, too, produce some estradiol, which could be responsible for their fat increase.

By the spring after her 12th birthday, Claire had noticed that her pubic hair, although still very sparse, had grown considerably darker, coarser, and more curled. And by the middle of autumn, her pubic hair resembled the adult pattern. The only difference was that the area covered was much smaller than among adults. Growth of underarm (or axillary) hair had also begun by this time.

By Claire's 13th birthday, she had noticed that the darkened areola of her breast actually formed a slight secondary mound from the contour of her breast. This secondary mound is a transitory stage in breast development and disappears later.

Menarche   When Claire was 13, approximately 3 years after the appearance of pubic hair, she had her first menstrual period. First menstruation is given the label menarche, while last menstruation is known as menopause. Menarche is an important time in a girl's life, for psychological and social reasons. An extract from Anne Frank's diary provides a rich example of the psychological importance of menarche (Figure 2-6). More than any single event at puberty, menarche signals the point of transition from childhood to adolescence. Menarche does not imply full reproductive capacity, however. Many girls are effectively sterile for a period of 12 to 18 months following menarche, at which time ovulatory cycles begin (Tanner, 1972). However, this period of sterility is not reliable and does not apply in all girls. There is no guarantee against pregnancy in unprotected intercourse.

There is a great deal of individual variation in age of menarche, even apart from cases of precocious puberty brought on by malfunctions in the central nervous system. The earliest menarche on record was at just under one year of age. At the other extreme, a few girls do not experience their first menstruation until they are in their 20s (Johnston, 1974). More normal age range for menarche, in the United States, is 10½–15½ years, while average age is just under 13 (Faust, 1977; Nicolson & Hanley, 1953).

FIGURE 2-5
Photographs of "Claire's" development from age 10 through puberty.

(From Tanner, 1962.)

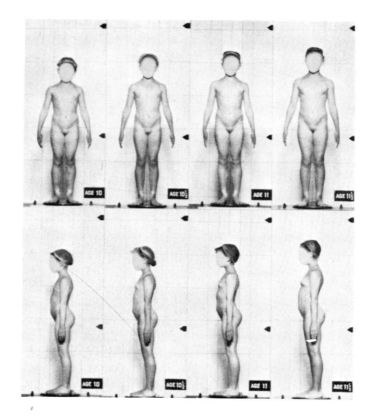

The Critical-Weight Hypothesis Frisch and Revelle presented evidence that menarche is delayed until a critical weight is reached, about 46 kg (or just over 100 lbs). Among Caucasian girls, mean weight at menarche has been roughly 46 kg for over a century. Persuasive evidence for the notion that a critical weight triggers menarche comes from data showing that early-maturing girls weigh about the same as late-maturing girls at menarche. The early and late maturers differed in mean height, however, with late maturers being taller. These findings are consistent with other work showing that malnutrition delays menarche; that twins and later-born children—who weigh less than first borns—experience menstruation later (Frisch & Revelle, 1971a); and that menstruation stops in the disorder anorexia nervosa, which involves severe weight loss (Bruch, 1978).

Support for the critical-weight hypothesis is not unanimous, however. One researcher expressed the issue this way: "Even if such an index or weight factor were shown to precede menarche, one

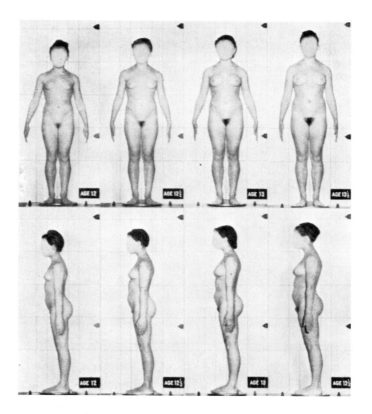

would not be justified in inferring a causal relationship between the two. As an example, development of secondary sexual characteristics begins before menarche but is not presumed to be a cause of menarche" (Faust, 1977, p. 54).

In many other cultures, especially in earlier time periods, menarche was the time for a girl's initiation into the full status of adulthood. Initiation rites marking the transition to adulthood in some other cultures are discussed later in this chapter.

Physical Maturity At age 14½, Claire had reached the adult stage in pubic hair development, with coarse, pigmented, and very curly hair in the "feminine" pattern of the inverse triangle. She had also attained almost 99 percent of her ultimate height.

By the spring following her 15th birthday, Claire's breasts had reached the mature stage. Now the areola had receded, so that only the nipple projected from the breast's general contour. The

FIGURE 2-6
Extract from the diary of Anne Frank, a young Jewish girl who came of age in the 1940s during the Nazi holocaust in Europe.

(From Anne Frank, *The Diary of a Young Girl,* 1952.)

Yesterday I read an article about blushing by Sis Heyster. This article might have been addressed to me personally. Although I don't blush very easily, the other things in it certainly all fit me. She writes roughly something like this—that a girl in the years of puberty becomes quiet within and begins to think about the wonders that are happening to her body.

I experience that, too, and that is why I get the feeling lately of being embarrassed about Margot, Mummy, and Daddy. Funnily enough, Margot, who is much more shy than I am, isn't at all embarrassed.

I think what is happening to me is so wonderful, and not only what can be seen on my body, but all that is taking place inside. I never discuss myself or any of these things with anybody; that is why I have to talk to myself about them.

Each time I have a period—and that has only been three times—I have the feeling that in spite of all the pain, unpleasantness, and nastiness, I have a sweet secret, and that is why, although it is nothing but a nuisance to me in a way, I always long for the time that I shall feel that secret within me again.

(From the diary entry of January 5, 1944. Anne Frank died in March 1945, in the concentration camp at Bergen-Belsen. Her diary, published in 1952, is entitled The Diary of a Young Girl.*)*

physical changes most clearly associated with puberty, the secondary sex characteristics, had occurred for the most part during the 4-year interval from age 11 to 15.

A Young Boy's Puberty: The Case of Mark

Boys are older than girls, on the average, when they enter puberty. But let us review the events of puberty for a typical boy, Mark, in the way that we did for Claire (Figure 2-7).

Mark celebrated his 11th birthday on New Year's Day. By the time he returned to school the following September, the first external signs of puberty had begun. These consisted of an enlargement of the testes and scrotum. The scrotum became reddened and more wrinkled, but at this point there was no accompanying enlargement of the penis. The growth spurt had barely begun and was not yet noticeable.

Testosterone Production A year later, when Mark was 12, his testes increased production of the hormone testosterone about 20 times the prepubertal amount (Kulin, 1974). Testosterone, in turn, caused growth of the penis, as well as many of the other physiological changes that differentiate between boys and girls.

Areas of the body differ in their susceptibility to the action of testosterone. For example, cartilages of the shoulder joints are induced to growth through action of this hormone (Tanner, 1972). Hormones typical of both genders (androgen and estrogen) are secreted by the adrenal cortex in both boys and girls. Although the precise nature of the adolescent growth spurt is not known, it may occur as follows: Adrenal androgens and growth hormone account for the growth spurt in girls, as well as for much of the spurt in boys. In boys, an additional growth element is provided by testosterone, which is primarily produced in the testes (although it is produced in minute amounts in the ovaries).

By September following Mark's 12th birthday, his testes and scrotum had also become quite a bit larger. Appearance of pubic hair, an eagerly anticipated event for Mark, began when he was 13. At this time, there was a sparse growth of downy hair at the base of his penis. Mark also had some acne throughout the period of puberty. The underlying skin changes that result from the action of androgen create conditions favorable to acne. Consequently, boys are somewhat more likely to be plagued with skin problems than girls.

Fat Deposits Some adolescent boys experience fat deposits in a typical female configuration, at the hips and thighs, and around the nipples. Psychological hazards accompanying such developments may be great. For example, one boy in the California Adolescent Study who experienced such "feminine" fat deposits was described as follows:

He was quite unhappy about the fat period, which peaked at about the midpoint of his puberal height growth, and was particularly sensitive concerning his breast enlargement. . . . From this boy's reaction one may hazard the guess that a delayed fat period occurring when other boys have outlived this inconvenience is particularly apt to cause emotional distress. (Stolz & Stolz, 1951, pp. 386–387)

Androgen and testosterone production among these boys, however, is at the same level as among boys not experiencing the changes. Penis and pubic hair growth are average among them (Stolz & Stolz, 1951).

First Ejaculation Near age 14, Mark's pubic hair was dark, coarse and curled. He experienced his first ejaculation of semen near his 14th birthday. It was a nocturnal emission, which Mark learned to refer to as a "wet dream." He had now reached his *peak height velocity*, the point of maximal rate of growth. He would continue to grow, but the rate would now taper off until around age 16, when

FIGURE 2-7
Photographs of "Mark's" development from age 11½ through puberty.

(From Tanner, 1962.)

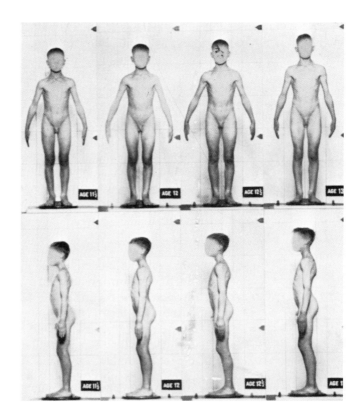

he attained 99 percent of his ultimate height. Mark, like the majority of boys, reached his full adult height by age 18.

Body Hair By the spring after Mark's fourteenth birthday, his pubic hair was very nearly adult in type—curly, pigmented, coarse. He now had some axillary, or underarm, hair and was also beginning to show a darkened fuzz around his upper lip. This gradually filled into a mustache, and finally a beard. His facial hair was not complete until after age 16. Mark's body hair continued to appear well into his 20s, on the abdomen, chest, and so on.

Body hair, of course, is one distinguishing characteristic between men and women. Growth of body hair appears to be under the influence of male hormones: Some areas of the body are susceptible to androgens, produced by the adrenal cortex in both males and females, others to testosterone, produced by the testes in males. The pubic area has the lowest threshold for sensitivity to androgen, and therefore produces pubic hair very early in the adolescent period in both boys and girls. Underarms are also highly responsive to

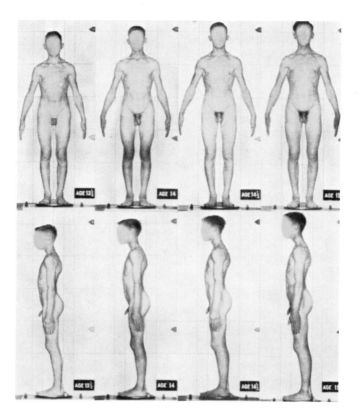

androgen. Face, chest, and abdomen, however, may respond only to testosterone. Thus, girls rarely develop hair in these places. Among boys, hair appears on face and chest relatively late in puberty because these areas have a high threshold for a response to testosterone. Differences among boys in amount of facial and body hair are probably a result of genetic differences in susceptibility of the body

Adolescent Milo talks to his mirror.

(From Berke Breathed, "Bloom County," *The Washington Post,* January 12, 1981.)

to testosterone's effects, rather than a difference in actual amounts of male hormone produced. Androgen, then, rather than estrogen, controls the growth of body hair in girls as well as boys (Tanner, 1962).

Before his 15th birthday, Mark's larynx was also enlarging. Soon his voice began to "crack" and deepen. The deepening of his voice was a gradual process, completing near the end of adolescence.

Physical Maturity By age 15, Mark's genitals were mature in size and shape. No further increase in size will take place. On the contrary, the penis may decrease slightly in size following its adolescent peak. Pubic hair had reached a fully adult distribution at about the same time that the penis was fully mature in size. Mark, along with about 80 percent of males, continued to show some pubic hair dispersal, mostly in a peak up the body midline toward the navel, into his mid-20s, however.

Gender Variation and Individual Variation

Claire and Mark illustrate that boys and girls differ on major indicators of physical maturity, such as the point of maximal rate of growth in height. In fact, studies indicate that girls mature earlier than boys in every physical comparison, except age of walking, from 21 months to 18 years (Nicolson & Hanley, 1953). One convenient measure of physical development is the average age at which adolescents reach maximal rate of height growth. This measure indicates the commonly accepted 2-year lag of boys behind girls: Mean age for boys is about 14, while for girls it is 12 (Tanner, 1978). The visible events of puberty, as exemplified by Mark and Claire, begin at around age 10 or 11 for most Western children.

The age at which pubertal changes begin is generally taken to be the beginning of adolescence. Although most of the process of physical maturation is complete 4 or 5 years from onset of puberty, the period that we refer to as adolescence may last considerably longer. Length of adolescence is determined in part by the age at which puberty begins.

THE TIMING OF PUBERTY

Considerable variation exists in the timing of puberty from one individual to another. Figure 2-8 illustrates this variation in photographs of three male adolescents, each exactly 14¾ years old, and three female adolescents, each 12¾ years old. It is reasonable to expect differences in the interests, abilities, and popularity of the adolescents illustrated by these three levels of development. Sense of

FIGURE 2-8
Individual variation in pubertal development. Each of the three boys is 14¾ years old, and each of the three girls is 12¾ years old.

(From Tanner, 1972.)

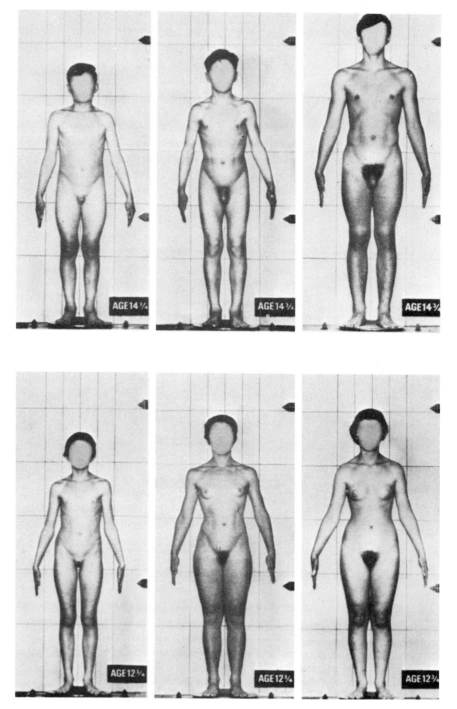

self-identity varies as a result both of one's own perceptions of self relative to others and of the actual reactions of others (Petersen & Taylor, 1980). The girl in the right-hand photograph, for example, is likely to elicit quite different reactions from the boys in her school than the first girl despite their identical ages. Similarly, her parents and teachers treat her as more mature and more likely to have adult interests.

Exact age norms for early or late maturation would be misleading because there is so much normal variation. One convenient index is the percentage of a given age group who have reached a certain level of maturity. The first 20 percent of a given cohort to reach puberty, for example, may be described as early maturers, and the last 20 percent as late maturers.

Early Maturation

Problems associated with early maturation are usually assumed to be less severe than those occasioned by late maturation. Boys who mature early are particularly likely to receive favorable reactions from others. Because competitive physical events are more central to adolescence among boys, the earlier growth spurt conveys prestige to boys who are able to outperform their peers.

Still, psychological hazards do exist for early maturers. They have a longer period of time to experience the normal traumas of adolescence, such as lack of independence and vocational indecision. They may experience a longer period of frustrated sex drive. Their anomalous appearance relative to the majority of their agemates may heighten their self-consciousness. Early-maturing girls are socially and psychologically disadvantaged in adolescence (Peskin, 1973). Girls who tower over their friends, including all of the boys in their classes, may feel acutely embarrassed. Sixth-grade girls who had reached puberty received lower prestige ratings from their schoolmates than prepubertal girls. In later grades, when their size was no longer anomalous, the most mature girls received the high prestige ratings (Faust, 1960).

Some girls may experience scholastic difficulties in conjunction with their earlier sexual maturation (Gallo & Savoia, 1978; Davies, 1977). However, there is considerable disagreement on this point; other studies indicate that early maturing girls are high achievers in school (Douglas & Ross, 1964; Garfagna, Figurelle, Matarese, & Matarese, 1972).

It has been suggested that early maturation has social advantages for boys and disadvantages for girls. The social disadvantage might, in turn, be translated into negative self-conceptions for early-maturing girls. Psychologists have used several techniques to assess self-conceptions. One straightforward method is to ask people how they feel about themselves on various dimensions, such as physical appearance. Such techniques have revealed that girls who mature early assign more negative self-ratings than late maturers. Psychologists are often skeptical of such results, however, because people might be motivated to hide their negative feelings, even from themselves. Another technique involves projective methods, such as asking for stories about ambiguous pictures. For example, an adolescent might be asked to write a story about a picture of a girl sitting alone in a library. Statements in the story, assessed for emotional and motivational content, are assumed to reflect the author's self-perceptions and mood. Early-maturing girls tend to write favorable stories, despite their *direct* negative self-ratings (Jones & Mussen, 1958). These results are puzzling until the age of the girls is considered. When they wrote the projective stories, the girls in the study were 17 years old; negative effects associated with early maturation may not last after puberty is complete.

Negative self-conceptions or not, girls who have reached menarche have a clearer sexual identification than girls of the same age who have not reached menarche (Rierdan & Koff, 1980). This finding implies that girls who have matured physically may be expected to show more heterosexual interests, reflected in such behavior as dating. The relationship between physical maturity and dating is not so clear-cut, however. In fact, there is a much closer relationship between chronological age, regardless of physical-maturation status, and dating than there is between physical maturation and dating (Dornbusch, Carlsmith, Gross, Martin, Jennings, Rosenberg, & Duke, 1981). This finding concerns only whether the girl had *ever* had a date; no information was available in the study on frequency of dating once it was initiated.

The expectation of adults in the larger culture for a match between physical maturity and social maturity is not actually reflected in the behavior of adolescent girls, at least in the area of first dates. Rather, there is a lag between physical maturity and social maturity for early-maturing girls. Dating interests are more clearly reflected in chronological age than in physical maturity.

Early-maturing girls, as one would logically expect, are taller and heavier in early adolescence when compared to late-maturing girls. However, they are ultimately *shorter* and heavier than late-maturing girls, a difference that persists into adulthood. Furthermore, "from infancy through adolescence, for boys and girls, and for whites and blacks, children of early-maturing mothers are taller and heavier than the children of late-maturing mothers" (Garn, 1980, p. 140).

Late Maturation

Early-maturing girls and late-maturing boys both appear to suffer psychologically from timing of puberty (e.g., Livson & Peskin, 1980). Researchers have painted a gloomy picture of late-maturing boys. They are said to have feelings of inferiority, depression, guilt, and parental rejection; to have little leadership potential; to have low self-images; and to be mildly rebellious. Adults rate them as less attractive, more tense, and more affected. Peers describe them as bossy, restless, and less grown-up (Mussen & Jones, 1957; Weatherley, 1964). One researcher summarized the effects of variation in boys' development with the following:

During the adolescent period late-maturing is a handicap for many boys and can rarely be found to offer special advantages. Early-maturing carries both advantages and disadvantages. In our culture it frequently gives competitive status, but sometimes it also involves handicaps in the necessity for rapid readjustments and in requiring the adolescent to meet adult expectations which are more appropriate to size and appearance than to other aspects of maturing. (Jones, 1957, pp. 127–128)

Negative feelings associated with early maturation in girls, we have seen, disappear when they enter adulthood. A group of late-maturing boys in a longitudinal growth study were compared with early-maturing age-mates in adulthood. They did not differ in objective indices of life adjustment, such as marital status, number of children, social class, or education. Size differences, too, had nearly disappeared by age 33. Although there were few personality differences, early maturers did continue to present a more consistently favorable personality profile (Jones, 1957).

Precocious and Delayed Puberty The discussion of timing of puberty has centered on early and late maturation falling within the range of normal, despite wide individual variation. Sometimes *major* timing errors occur, referred to as precocious or delayed puberty. Some children, through early release of gonadal hormones, perhaps brought about by erroneous pituitary stimulation, undergo the changes of puberty as early as age 6. They grow taller, and develop the usual secondary sex characteristics associated with their gender.

Consider a hypothetical girl, in 1st grade, who has such a developmental misfortune. She looks odd to her classmates—and to herself. Adults inevitably treat her differently, often expecting her to have interests far beyond her years. Socially, she may prefer the company of her age-mates, but they find her a peculiar companion. Adults, in turn, often view her childlike interests as inappropriate. In short, her physical and social development are grossly out of phase. Her sense of identity suffers from such a developmental asynchrony. The problem has been stated succinctly by specialists in errors of developmental timing. "As a result, precocious children tend to view themselves as freaks or misfits . . ." (Money & Clopper, 1974, p. 176).

Happily, major timing errors are relatively rare. For our purposes, they illustrate the complex interplay among physical, social, and identity development that adolescents normally experience in moving from childhood to adulthood.

STATUS CHANGE AND INITIATION

Thus far in the chapter, the focus has been on the physical phenomena of puberty. Although the psychological ramifications of physical maturation have been taken into account, little has been said about the *social transition* into adulthood that also takes place during adolescence. A social transition to adulthood, as distinct from a purely physical transition, is a relatively new phenomenon, dating perhaps as far back as the 18th century, but probably not earlier (Aries, 1960/1962).

Adulthood is no longer defined solely in terms of physical size or capacity for mature sexual functioning. Rather, economic and educational criteria are more often used to signify adulthood. Age at which indicators of adulthood are attained has been progressively postponed. For instance, 10 times the percentage of persons over 17 had completed high school in 1980 compared to 1900 (Figure 2-9).

FIGURE 2-9
Percent of persons over 17 years of age who were high school graduates during the years 1920–1980.

(From U.S. Bureau of the Census, *Statistical Abstract of the United States, 1980.*)

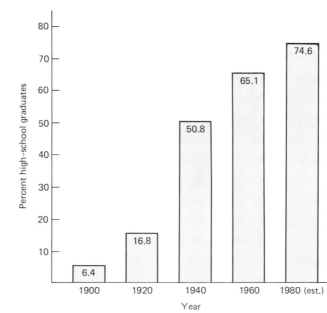

Combining these data with the secular trend to earlier maturation reveals that adolescence, in technological societies, has been greatly extended since the Industrial Revolution. The long and complex gap between physical and social maturity provides a period of ambiguous status: past-childhood but not-quite-adult. Norms guiding behavior during this period are not always clear. These factors have contributed to a view of adolescence in our society as a period of identity-seeking—a quest for a clarification of how to behave and what to become. In many nontechnological societies, dramatic ceremonies were traditionally held to confer adult status and thereby avoid the gap between physical and social maturity. At the same time, a young person's identity as an adult member of the community was clarified.

Rites of Passage

The most influential analysis of celebrations to mark transition from one status to another is the highly influential work of van Gennep (1909/1960). Rites marking status transition from childhood to adulthood are variously referred to as initiation rites, puberty rites, and rites of passage. Three major elements characterize such rites, according to van Gennep: separation, transition, and reincorporation. In adolescent initiation rites, for example, the physically maturing person is usually separated from the family and taken to an initiation hut with other candidates for adulthood. There they undergo a period combining seclusion, trials of endurance, instruction, and ritual operations. Following the transition phase, they are ceremonially reincorporated into the community as low-status adults.

Status change following rites of passage can be illustrated by examining the adolescent transition in several nontechnological societies. It should be noted that written descriptions of initiation ceremonies come primarily from classic anthropological studies, such as Cora DuBois's *The People of Alor*, published in 1944. As the technological world has spread its influence, the number of societies practicing these "primitive" rituals has correspondingly decreased.

Kaguru Initiation Rites   The Kaguru, a cultural group living in what is now Tanzania, illustrate van Gennep's phases in rites of passage. (The anthropological fieldwork on which this discussion is based [Beidelman, 1971] was conducted in 1957–1958.) The Kaguru hold initiation ceremonies around the time of puberty for both boys and girls. Candidates must "die" as children and be "reborn" as adults. Several differences are evident in the rites for boys and girls, typical of societies having status distinctions between adult men and women.

Rites for Boys Boys are initiated in groups. Their *separation* from childhood is emphasized when they are stripped and shaved over their entire bodies. Ritual abounds in the ceremony, with songs and dances symbolically underscoring the lessons. As the boys are circumcised, for example, songs emphasize themes of danger and wild animals which the male role evokes: "People! The lion is biting the cow!" A doctor cuts off the boy's foreskin with a cold knife, an operation undoubtedly anticipated with both dread and eagerness. Although painful, the resulting mark distinguishes adult men from mere uninitiated boys, and emphasizes the link between this rite and sexual maturation.

The several days of seclusion that follow circumcision constitute a period of *transition* which includes instruction in the ways of adult men. *Reincorporation* into community life as a full social person is celebrated with a feast when the initiates emerge from seclusion.

Rites for girls Initiation among Kaguru girls coincides with first menstruation and, therefore, is an individual ceremony. The label given to the ceremony, *igubi*, means "wild pig," emphasizing a girl's wild nature that can be subdued by male hunters. Genital operations are not now mandatory among Kaguru girls. At one time, however, cutting off the tip of the clitoris was typical of their initiations.

Although the girl's *separation* now lasts but a few days, in the past she was required to remain indoors many months, growing fat and pale—and hence more desirable. Her *transition* phase included instruction in household matters, and especially in sexuality: "The mouth of the wildcat is always open; let it be so, for it will never fill up" (Beidelman, 1971, p. 110). That is, women are sexually insatiable, with much "hotter" sexual natures than men. Girls are reincorporated into community life at a 2-day feast only women may attend.

Initiation ceremonies emphasize, through drama and ritual, a new identity. A period of uncertainty and seeking is unnecessary because adult status is conferred. The initiation's transitional instruction period emphasizes those roles, obligations, and cultural practices required for identification with the adult reference group.

Initiation Drama and Social Communication

Identity involves social communication—feedback from other people that helps an individual to clarify sense of self. Dramatic ceremonies with prescribed rituals provide such social communication in a highly memorable form. One function of the dramatic—and, to the Western mind, peculiar—rites may be to reinforce a new identity and status for impressionable adolescents.

Genital operations provide a good example. It is likely that several reasons exist for such cultural practices. Among the reasons are beliefs that procreation is more likely following removal of clitoris or foreskin and that physical maturity is hastened by circumcision. Performing an operation on the genitals further establishes one's identity as an adult of the appropriate gender, with all the roles and obligations of adult status. In addition, the practice renders the ceremony unforgettable to the initiate by associating it with a painful and frightening operation.

Adolescents would not be likely to forget events and instruction surrounding a genital operation carried out with little or no anaesthetic. The resulting scar is a mark of distinction associated with adult status: "Among primitive nonliterate peoples for whom a written diploma is an impossibility, an unalterable bodily mark, a pattern of scars, a mutilation of a kind which no person is likely to attempt to perform on himself, is an excellent means of classification" (Young, 1965, p. 7).

Many of the more colorful aspects of initiation ceremonies can be viewed in this light. Hazing and flogging are common practices, especially during boys' initiations. Among the Big Nambas of the New Hebrides, adolescent males are not only circumcised, they also have nettles rubbed on their backs so harshly that scars may

Initiations into organizations where "pledges" must complete ridiculous or unpleasant requirements may promote stronger identifications with the group. Here, a group of high-school students in Georgia are undergoing ritualistic hazing as part of their induction into the school's marching band.

(Photo by Will McIntyre/Photo Researchers, Inc.)

form. Further, they are kept awake almost continuously for 10 days after the genital operation, and frightened by adults who rub luminous mushrooms on their hands and mimic ghosts in the middle of the night. After 30 days of fear and discomfort, they are welcomed to adult society at a feast and dance. Such an emotional and painful experience would be hard to forget. A severe initiation ceremony may also serve to strengthen the young initiate's identification with the society. Such a result has been demonstrated in laboratory studies: Individuals who have been initiated severely tend to show a stronger liking for the group into which they were initiated (Aronson & Mills, 1959). Sorority and fraternity initiations with ridiculous and unpleasant requirements for "pledges" presumably operate on this principle. Having successfully completed the difficult initiation, members will feel a stronger sense of identification with the group.

Functions of Initiation Rites

Transition in status from childhood to adulthood, as we have emphasized, concerns physical maturity, social maturity, and self-identity. Initiation rites highlight the physical, social, and psychological aspects of status change in a relatively brief and dramatic ritual.

Emphasis on Physical Maturity Considerable variability exists in timing of puberty from individual to individual and from culture to culture, as we saw earlier in the chapter. Initiation rites do not coincide with any universal aspect of puberty, but they almost invariably occur sometime during the early-adolescent period.

Among girls, the rites are very often individually held at the time of first menstruation. Among the Maroni River Caribs in Surinam, for example, girls go into seclusion at menarche for about 8 days. Certain restrictions must be observed, such as avoiding the river. It was believed that *Oko:yumo*, the water spirit, disliked the smell of anything associated with female reproduction and might harm the menstruating girl (Kloos, 1971).

In the Dutch Indies, girls of the cultural group known as the Alor have no special menstrual ceremony, but they are tattooed about the forehead and cheeks when their breasts begin to develop. Both adolescent boys and girls have their teeth blackened and filed, and are allowed a period of sexual experimentation at the time of these ceremonies (DuBois, 1944).

Emphasis on Gender Identity Puberty rites very often involve a modification of norms surrounding sexual behavior. There may be increased sexual freedom for a short period of time, as among the Alor, or a period in which sexual behavior is completely taboo. Among other things, norms regarding sexual behavior during the rites emphasize their link to gender identity.

It is reasonable to ask why some societies find it necessary to clarify gender identity with a dramatic puberty ritual, while others do not. One suggestion is that gender identity must be clarified when childhood socialization practices conflict with requirements of the adult role.

Among a group of aborigines in the Highlands of New Guinea (Meggitt, 1964), for example, adult men and women coexist in a highly antagonistic society. Although both boys and girls are raised by their mothers, they learn the cultural opposition between genders before becoming adults. Adolescent boys, for example, are taught that any contact with menstruating women, especially sexual contact, will "sicken a man and cause persistent vomiting, turn his blood black, corrupt his vital juices so that his skin darkens and wrinkles as his flesh wastes, permanently dull his wits, and eventually lead to a slow decline and death" (Meggitt, 1964, p. 207). Not surprisingly, Highland initiation rites at menarche include seclusion from men, while rites for boys teach the magic needed for protection from women.

Societies that have exclusive mother–child sleeping arrangements, in part because fathers have separate houses, might be expected to result in feminine identification among boys. One function of male initiation ceremonies, especially those involving genital operations and tests of endurance, may be to transfer identification from females to males (Whiting, Kluckhohn, & Anthony, 1958).

A similar gender-identity conflict exists for girls in matrilocal societies—those in which married couples live near the wife's family. A girl must function as an adult in the same community that had formerly treated her as a child. Rites for girls in matrilocal societies dramatize new roles girls will play as adults. "The purpose of the rites appears to be an announcement of status change both to the initiate and to those around her, made necessary because she spends her adult life in the same setting as her childhood" (Brown, 1963, p. 841). Accordingly, the symbols of such rites for girls suggest their adult roles. In Surinam, Carib girls' hands are placed in a large bowl of ants at one point in the initiation rites. This symbolically reminds the girls to be industrious and busy, like determined ants (Kloos, 1971).

Emphasis on Social Maturity In addition to signifying capacity for adult sexual functioning and clarifying gender identity, initiation rites dramatize a change in social status. The lag between physical and social maturity experienced by Western adolescents is avoided by a specific and dramatic rite.

In most societies there is some association in people's minds between the notion of sex maturity and that of social maturity, but in those cultures in which puberty ritual is most developed, the coincidence of the two is considered quite specific, and the puberty ritual is either made the occasion of the assumption of adult roles in the political, legal and economic sense, or regarded as the first step in the gradual assumption of a series of such roles. (Richards, 1956, p. 18)

Cultural groups where subsistence is based on hunting or agriculture often depend on the labor of young people. Adolescence may, therefore, be a relatively short period in which more and more adult tasks are assumed. Such is the case among the Kwoma, a tribe in New Guinea (Whiting, 1941). Ceremonies marking adolescence for both boys and girls indicate their readiness to assume their adult duties.

Initiation rites appear to be particularly likely in societies where adults form a very close-knit group. A cohesive group demands group loyalty and identification. Initiation ceremonies announce to all concerned, both candidates and others, that adult status has been achieved and membership in adult society accepted. The ceremony may dramatize that "men are quite different from women and uninitiated boys" (Young, 1965, p. 24). Such a dramatic statement is important both for the identity of the initiate and for the solidarity of the group.

Such a psychological contribution to identity is akin to a certificate of graduation. The ceremony suggests readiness and fitness for adulthood, as Richards pointed out in her detailed description of Bemba rites: "The series of ceremonial acts of her *chisungu* [initiation] may be regarded as giving her the assurance that she is fit to assume her new role and providing an acceptable proof that she has successfully reached a new stage in life" (Richards, 1956, pp. 161–162).

Status Change in Western Culture

Initiation rites, then, serve as a societal mechanism for reinforcing the links between physical, social, and psychological adulthood. The dramatic ritual helps to accomplish the transition to adult status in a relatively brief period of time. Technological society, with its increasingly protracted adolescence, has only vestiges of initiation ceremonies. The Jewish Bar Mitzvah, for example, is held during the pubertal period at age 13. Although the ceremony technically celebrates the boy's becoming a man, nobody, including the initiate himself, really believes it.

The increasingly rare debut, in which "society" girls announce their availability for marriage, is really only pretext for a party. No one expects the debutante to marry right away, or to assume the characteristics of full-fledged adult womanhood.

No modern technological society is cohesive enough to promote identification of adolescents with the larger society through a ceremony. High-school graduation perhaps comes closest to such an initiation rite. It is a ritualized ceremony, even though it is not very dramatic, or even particularly memorable. It vaguely suggests readiness for assumption of adult economic roles, but less so all the time. But high-school graduation does not differentiate male and female roles; it does not apply to all adolescent boys or girls; and it does not lead to any notable change in identity within the culture.

In Western societies, minor events on the road to adulthood, such as graduating from high school or obtaining a driver's license, do not serve to dramatize adulthood. Rather, they are elements in the gradual acquisition of adult status, whose final arrival is very difficult to pinpoint.

SUMMARY

1. Beginning in the mid-1800s, the secular trend toward greater adult stature and earlier sexual maturation operated continuously for about 100 years. A cluster of factors probably contributed to the trend, many of them concerning living conditions associated with social class. Improved nutrition, improvements in medical care—including inoculation of infants against common diseases—and increased urbanization are possible contributing factors. Among the most favored segments of the population, the trend appears to have ended.

2. Puberty signals the beginning of the transition from childhood to the physical, social, and psychological status of adulthood. The physical transformations of puberty are under complex hormonal control directed by the brain. Hypothalamic stimulation of the pituitary initiates release of gonadotrophic (GTH) and adrenocorticotrophic (ACTH) hormones, which in turn stimulate the adrenal cortex and the gonads to increase their production of hormones that regulate the physical changes of puberty. Girls mature earlier than boys by an average of 2 years. Boys and girls are out of phase with each other in physical development and in social interests throughout junior high and early senior high school.

3. There is considerable normal variation in the ages at which young people reach puberty. Early physical maturation appears to pose special psychological hazards for girls, while late maturation is more problematical for boys. Long-term effects of differences in age of physical maturation are minimal.

4. It is convenient to think of adolescence as the period that begins with physical maturation and ends with the assumption of adult roles—often called social maturity. The secular trend indicates an earlier onset of adolescence. Furthermore, in Western society, adult roles are being postponed for large segments of the population, with increasingly lengthy educational preparation.

5. Historically, many nontechnological societies accomplish the individual's status transition with dramatic ceremonies called initiation rites or rites of passage. The overall function of these rites is one of social communication. When adolescents reach a requisite level of physical maturity, they are separated from their families or from normal social interaction. In a transition period lasting a few days or weeks, they are taught the expectations and beliefs associated with the social status of adulthood. Lessons are highlighted by events such as genital operations and tests of endurance, rituals that serve to dramatize the status transition for the entire community. Initiates are reincorporated into the group with the status of adults, eligible to take on increasing responsibilities in the community. Initiation rites also accomplish a change in identity status. Finding that they were expected to behave as adults, adolescents begin to view themselves as members of the adult reference group of the appropriate gender. Only vestiges of initiation rites exist in technological societies; the Jewish Bar Mitzvah is one example.

OUTLINE

3. IDENTITY DEVELOPMENT

"Who in the world am I? Ah, that's the great puzzle!" So Alice wonders aloud as she begins her adventures in Wonderland. Alice's reflective question is not always easy to answer. One's sense of self, or sense of identity, is difficult to put into words. You can experience this difficulty yourself by trying the "Who am I?" test, one approach to the study of self-identity. On a blank sheet of paper, write the question "Who am I?" at the top of the page. Now write 20 answers to the question.

Children are more concrete than adolescents and adults in their approach to the "Who am I?" test. Their answers reflect a lack of the complexity and confusion which shows up in the answers of many adolescents. For example, Bruce, a 9-year-old, provided concrete answers that betrayed no psychic conflicts about the issue of the self.

My name is Bruce C. I have brown eyes. I have brown hair. I have brown eyebrows. I'm nine years old. I LOVE! Sports. I have seven people in my family. I have great! eye site. I have lots! of friends. I live on 1923 Pinecrest Drive. I'm going on 10 in September. I'm a boy. I have a uncle that is almost 7 feet tall. My school is Pinecrest. My teacher is Mrs. [Vernon]. I play Hockey! I'm almost the smartest boy in the class. I LOVE! food. I love fresh air. I LOVE School. (Montemayor & Eisen, 1977, p. 317)

The answers of a typical 17-year-old girl, however, contained many more abstractions and ironies. Her answers were more personal in a psychological sense.

I am a human being. I am a girl. I am an individual. I don't know who I am. I am a Pisces. I am a moody person. I am an indecisive person. I am an ambitious person. I am a very curious person. I am not an individual. I am a loner. I am an

American (God help me). I am a Democrat. I am a liberal person. I am a radical. I am a conservative. I am a pseudoliberal. I am an atheist. I am not a classifiable person (i.e., I don't want to be). (Montemayor & Eisen, 1977, p. 318)

Adolescence is the stage of the life cycle that is most crucial in the crystallization of identity. Erik Erikson, who is sometimes called the "father of the identity crisis," declared that "not until adolescence does the individual develop the prerequisites in physiological growth, mental maturation, and social responsibility to experience and pass through the crisis of identity" (Erikson, 1968, p. 91).

We begin this chapter with a brief overview of the psychological dimensions of self-identity. The contributions of Sigmund Freud and Erik Erikson to our understanding of identity development are reviewed. Finally, research on sequential progress in the development of self-identity is examined in detail, especially as it relates to Erikson's theoretical model.

PSYCHOLOGICAL DIMENSIONS OF SELF-IDENTITY

Identity as a concept refers to a collection of traits and personal characteristics. *Traits* are habitual patterns of behavior, such as honesty/dishonesty, happiness/sadness, or intelligence/stupidity. Personal characteristics include physical attributes, such as height, color of hair and eyes, and condition of skin; and background factors, such as ethnic-group membership and religion.

Aspects of Identity

Objective Identity It may be helpful to distinguish between three aspects of identity (Miller, 1963). Objective identity refers to other people's perceptions of the individual's identity. Objective identity is not necessarily "real," but rather reflects the way that other people view an individual. I have a student, for example, whom I consider to be a very good-looking young man from New York. He is Jewish, in the sense of being a member of an ethnic group, but is not at all religious. Although he is something of a Don Juan, he likes to have one serious love affair at a time, albeit brief and tempestuous. He has a good deal of money, and likes to "court" women. He is considered by many people, including myself, to be a "joker," always laughing, always plotting something funny or cultivating a bizarre image. At the same time, he is bright and capable in classes. As far as I am concerned, this is Michael's objective identity; and when he is in my presence, I treat him accordingly. We laugh and joke a lot; and unless he is being serious about a personal problem or an academic matter, Michael invariably has a pet scheme, which he tells me about with great relish. Objective identity, then, is one aspect of each individual's identity; all of us have a set of objective identities, because each person with whom we interact has a view of us. Some consistency among these different views of us is to be expected, of course.

Subjective Identity A second aspect of identity, subjective identity, refers to the individual's perception of the way other people view him or her. It is this aspect of identity that is most closely associated with *impression management*. As an example, modern political candidates devote a great deal of attention to portraying a set of traits and characteristics that will attract votes. A truly Machiavellian candidate might be expected to attempt to figure out what the voting public wants in a candidate and then to behave in a manner consistent with that image. If the candidate believes he is thought to be aloof, he may attempt to create the impression that he is warm and open in his personal relationships. In other words, his subjective identity may include the trait aloofness but he may attempt to change that image by modifying his behavior or by selectively disclosing information about himself.

Self-Identity The final aspect of identity, the one this chapter primarily concerns, is self-identity. Self-identity is the person's own private version of the set of traits and personal characteristics that best describe her or him. Self-identity is a complex self-definition, including diverse emotional and personal information that relates to the individual's understanding of self. Self-identity is not necessarily congruent with subjective identity.

These three aspects of identity—objective identity, subjective identity, and self-identity—were captured beautifully by a 14-year-old girl who was reflecting on the question, "What is someone's self?":

Your real self is things you may show to yourself but not show to others—the way you think inside of you. Sooner or later you are going to find out that there are kinds of things that you don't feel like telling anybody else. That is more your self. And things you are sharing is your outer self. Things inside are more yourself to you. (Broughton, 1981, p. 21)

James Marcia, who has written extensively about the development of identity in adolescence, argued that the emotional and personal information contributing to an understanding of the self—

information such as drives, abilities, beliefs, and individual history—form a more or less well-developed structure of self-identity. Individuals with relatively undeveloped self-structures are more confused about themselves and less appreciative of their own individuality. Individuals with relatively better developed self-structures are more sure of themselves. The self-structure undergoes its greatest transformation during the period of adolescence (Marcia, 1980). Transformations in the self-structure during adolescence are the subject of this chapter.

FREUD'S THEORETICAL APPROACH TO ADOLESCENT IDENTITY DEVELOPMENT: THE TRANSFORMATIONS OF PUBERTY

Sigmund Freud was indisputably one of the most influential figures in the history of psychology. Freud's insights into human psychological development, although they have been refined and modified considerably since their publication in the early 1900s, have continued to provoke discussion and to shape thinking in a number of critical areas. The role of psychosexual development in the emergence of self-identity in adolescence is one such critical area.

The sexual instincts, always important in Freudian theory, are at their peak of importance during the adolescent period. Understanding that period requires a review of the earlier psychosexual stages of development.

Stages of Psychosexual Development

Human psychological development, in the Freudian view, follows a biologically predetermined course, with different zones of the body having a special time of ascendancy as the major source of

The psychoanalytic movement began with Sigmund Freud (1856–1939) and grew to become one of the most important forces operating in the 20th century. Freud's work has had a profound influence on the development of modern psychology, as well as a far-reaching impact on Western culture as a whole.

(Culver Pictures, Inc.)

sexual instincts. This notion is the key to Freud's psychosexual stages of development, which are outlined in Table 3-1.

Pregenital Sexuality   In the first year of life, the region around the infant's mouth—similar to an "erogenous zone"—is the primary source of sexual instinct. Gratification of this instinct is accomplished through the use of the mother's breast, the child's own thumb, or some other easily suckable object. Freud's assertion that such mundane childhood events as thumb-sucking and breast-feeding had sexual overtones was highly controversial in the medical community in Victorian Vienna.

Between the ages of 1 and 3, the primary erogenous zone is the anal region. Again, the child derives sexual pleasure from this region of the body, especially during elimination. The oral and anal stages of psychosexual development are together referred to as pregenital sexuality. Pregenital sexuality does not differ for boys and girls. Not until the first stage of genitality, the Oedipal period, does psychosexual development diverge for the two genders.

Genital Sexuality   Between the ages of 3 and 5, the primary source of sexual excitation originates from the genital region, defining the first stage of genital sexuality. This stage of childhood sexuality is accompanied by strong feelings of sexual attraction to the parent of the opposite sex as an object for gratification. This stage is referred

TABLE 3-1 Freud's Psychosexual Stages	STAGE	AGE	MAJOR CHARACTERISTICS
	Oral	Birth–1	Mouth region primary erogenous zone; sucking for gratification; relative primacy of id.
	Anal	1–3	Anus primary erogenous zone; elimination as form of gratification; feces as gifts; ego as aid in adaptation to external reality.
	Oedipal	3–5	*Boys:* Penis as source of sexual excitation; incestuous fantasies toward mother and rivalry with father; culminating in intense castration anxiety and sexual repression, as well as superego development.
			Girls: Clitoris as source of sexual excitation; anatomical enlightenment leads to castration complex (feeling that she has been castrated and is inferior to boys), culminating in repression of sexual instincts.
	Latency	5–puberty	Period of sexual repression during which the ego becomes significantly strengthened.
	Adult Genital	Adolescence	Development of sex-role identity and nonincestuous heterosexual object choice.

to as the Oedipal stage, named for Oedipus, the character in Greek tragedy who unwittingly killed his father and married his mother.

Psychosexual development diverges in important ways for boys and girls during the Oedipal stage. Nevertheless, there are some common themes in this stage of Freud's theory that we wish to emphasize in this exposition. Both boys and girls are sexually attracted to the parent of the opposite sex, and as a result, they experience frustration and anxiety. Frustration and anxiety intensify throughout this stage of development; finally, the child must make use of psychological defenses against these negative emotions. Both boys and girls accomplish their psychological defense through identifying with the same-sex parent, internalizing their parents' value system, and repressing (or temporarily "forgetting") their sexual impulses. Repression of sexual impulses characterizes the later-childhood years, which Freud referred to as the *stage of latency*. Psychosexual latency lasts until the physical transformations of puberty begin.

The Transformations of Puberty From the psychoanalytic perspective, a series of transformations take place during the adolescent period that lead to adult heterosexual functioning. One very important transformation is the transition from infantile sexuality to normal genital sexuality. "With the beginning of puberty changes set in which transform the infantile sexual life into its definite normal form" (Freud, 1905/1962, p. 66). An inevitable element in psychosexual development is the normal sexual perversity of childhood, such as obtaining sexual gratification through sucking. In adolescence, pregenital erogenous zones become subordinate to the genital zone as the primary source of sexual excitation. Pregenital zones do not lose all their erotic power; rather, they become less important as sources of sexual excitation. For most adults, primary gratification is obtained through use of the genital erogenous zone in heterosexual intercourse. It is in adolescence that this mode of sexuality is established.

A second transformation occurring during the adolescent period is the change from a primarily autoerotic or masturbatory sexual impulse to an external object choice. Several adolescent phases of sexuality are necessary before the final phase of heterosexual object choice is reached. In particular, early adolescence is characterized by *narcissism*, in which erotic interest is expressed toward the self, as well as toward persons very much like the self (Blos, 1962).

Breaking away from parental authority, a third transition in adolescence, is a very important step in psychosexual identity. This

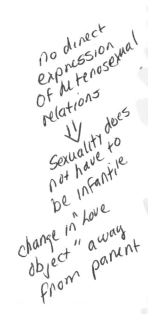

[handwritten margin notes] no direct expression of heterosexual relations ↓ Sexuality does not have to be infantile change in "love object" away from parent

transformation, involving a redefinition of the adolescent's relationship to parents, is one of the most difficult of adolescence.

Individuation   Establishment of psychological autonomy from parents, with the clear appreciation by adolescents that they have their own independent ideas, has been referred to as individuation (Blos, 1962). It is not necessary for adolescents to reject parental standards and values for them to accomplish individuation. Indeed, the value differences between adolescents and parents are not striking (e.g., Gallatin, 1980; Jennings & Niemi, 1974). Here is the description of the individuation process as one young woman, Debbie, experienced it.

Up to a certain age, I believed everything my parents said. Then, in college, I saw all these new ideas and I said, "Okay, I'm not going to believe all that stuff you told me," and I rejected everything and said to myself, "Okay, now I'm going to make a new Debbie which has nothing to do with my mother and father. I'm going to start with a clean slate and what I started to put on it were all new ideas. These ideas were opposite to what my parents believed. But slowly, what's happening is that I'm adding on a lot of the things which they've told me and I'm taking them as my own and I'm coming more together with them." (Josselson, 1980, p. 192)

Psychosexual Phases of Identity   The later childhood years of latency are a time of sexual repression. The physiological changes of puberty arouse the sexual instincts once again in their full force. Following puberty proper, there is a qualitative shift from indiscriminate sexual impulses to specific genital urges. Freud referred to these urges as the *second genital phase* of psychosexual development, and believed that the new genital urges were initially directed toward parents. He believed that the anxiety created by adolescent Oedipal wishes caused a redirection of sexual energy toward objects as much like the self as possible. A series of strong attachments to friends of the same age and gender is the result. These so-called narcissistic friendships often contain an erotic component that may be expressed in overt behavior such as mutual masturbation.

According to the psychoanalytic model of development, heterosexual identity becomes clearly patterned in late adolescence. Although they have achieved psychosexual identity, adolescents may not experience heterosexual intercourse. Still, genital urges are primarily gratified, in fact or in fantasy, through the opposite-sex.

Freud's psychoanalytic approach to adolescence, therefore, presented adolescence as the period during which psychosexual identity becomes crystallized. According to Freudian theorists, instinctual pressures are primarily responsible for the sequence of events (Adelson & Doehrman, 1980).

In recent years, the traditional view that psychosexual development in adolescence is dominated by drive pressures following puberty has been refined and modified (Josselson, 1980). Major studies have failed to find evidence that most adolescents are at the mercy of instinctual pressures in their psychological development. Adolescents appear not to be preoccupied with control of instincts (Douvan & Adelson, 1966) or repudiation of parents (Offer & Offer, 1975). Perhaps the major revisionist of the Freudian position on adolescent development is Erik Erikson.

ERIKSON'S PSYCHOSOCIAL THEORY

Stage Crises

Working within the psychoanalytic tradition, Erikson refined Freud's stage sequence and extended it throughout the life cycle. In Erikson's model, each stage has a dominant theme or task, which can result in a positive or negative outcome. Psychological tension surrounding the task builds up until it requires that an individual come to some sort of resolution. Although this tension, or crisis, may be experienced as a very unpleasant psychological state, Erikson did not view it as a debilitating catastrophe. Rather, it is "a

Erik Erikson (1902–), father of the identity crisis, extended Freud's stage sequence of psychosexual development throughout the human life cycle in an expanded stage sequence of psychosocial development.

(Photo by Olive R. Pierce/Black Star)

necessary turning point, a crucial moment, when development must move one way or another, marshalling resources of growth, recovery, and further differentiation" (Erikson, 1968, p. 16). In late adolescence, young people experience a *crisis of identity*.

Because identity is so central to psychological functioning, it is important throughout the life cycle. Identity in adolescence is shaped by resolutions of earlier crises and will evolve further in later stages. The basic elements of Erikson's eight stages of the human life cycle are shown in Table 3-2. Infancy and childhood are important because they result in identifications and identity ele-

TABLE 3-2
Erikson's Eight Stages of the Human Life Cycle

NORMATIVE CRISIS	AGE	MAJOR CHARACTERISTICS
Trust vs. Mistrust	0–1	Primary social interaction with mothering caretaker; oral concerns; trust in life-sustaining care, including feeding.
Autonomy vs. Shame and Doubt	1–2	Primary social interaction with parents; toilet training; "holding on" and "letting go" and the beginnings of autonomous will.
Initiative vs. Guilt	3–5	Primary social interaction with nuclear family; beginnings of "Oedipal" feelings; development of language and locomotion; development of conscience as governor of initiative.
Industry vs. Inferiority	6–puberty	Primary social interaction outside home among peers and teachers; school-age assessment of task ability.
Identity vs. Role Confusion	Adolescence	Primary social interaction with peers, culminating in heterosexual friendship; psychological moratorium from adult commitments; identity crisis; consolidation of resolutions of previous four stages into coherent sense of self.
Intimacy vs. Isolation	Early adulthood	Primary social interaction in intimate relationship with member of opposite sex; adult role commitments accepted, including commitment to another person.
Generativity vs. Stagnation	Middle age	Primary social concern in establishing and guiding future generation; productivity and creativity.
Integrity vs. Despair	Old age	Primary social concern is a reflective one: coming to terms with one's place in the (now nearly complete) life cycle, and with one's relationships with others; "I am what survives of me."

ments which contribute to the resolution of the adolescent crisis of identity. These early stages are preludes to the central normative crisis of identity in adolescence.

Differences Between Erikson's and Freud's Views

Erikson's framework differs in three important respects from Freud's views. First, Erikson has shifted the period of decisive personality formation from early childhood to adolescence. Freud, in a very real sense, "discovered" childhood in terms of its place of importance in later psychological functioning. Erikson respected this discovery, modified it to suit his own theoretical purposes, and incorporated it into a revised stage model of development. Thus, the first four stages in Freud's system—the oral, anal, Oedipal, and latency stages—are incorporated into Erikson's model as well. Although Erikson's first four stages have different labels, they retain their Freudian psychosexual characteristics but are subordinate to the identity concerns of adolescence.

A second difference between Erikson's and Freud's contributions to stage development concerns the emphasis on sexuality. Freud insisted that sexual instincts provided the motivating energy behind all behavior. Although Erikson respected Freud's discoveries regarding infantile sexuality, he nevertheless felt that such radical sexual determinism overstated the facts of human development. He wrote that

Knowing what we know today, it is obvious that somebody had to come sometime who would decide that it would be better for the study of human motivation to call too many rather than too few things sexual, and then to modify the hypothesis by careful inquiry. (Erikson, 1964, p. 33)

Erikson's stages of development, deemphasizing sexuality, are called *psychosocial* stages. Normative crises at each of the eight stages of the life cycle have a social aspect that is rooted in the individual's interaction with other people who constitute a social world.

The third difference concerns Freud's overemphasis on innate drives to the neglect of social factors. Identity is most closely related to what Freud called the ego. Freud believed that ego functions somehow developed as a way of accommodating to external reality, but only late in the pregenital phase of development. In Erikson's view, Freud's rendering of the ego as an after-thought did not give sufficient respect to the concept of social identity. According to Erikson, identity evolves within a social world. Without reference to an environment including other people, identity is a meaningless term.

The traditional psychoanalytic method . . . cannot quite grasp identity because it has not developed terms to conceptualize the environment. Certain habits of psychoanalytic theorizing, habits of designating the environment as "outer world" or "object world," cannot take account of the environment as a pervasive actuality. (Erikson, 1968, p. 24)

Senses of Identity in Erikson's Theory

Identity is one of those concepts in psychology that people are able to grasp intuitively but find very difficult to define. Erikson recognized this difficulty when he attempted to specify the many senses of the term he wished to admit into his definition.

So far I have tried out the term identity almost deliberately—I like to think—in many different connotations. At one time it seemed to refer to a conscious sense of individual uniquencess, at another to an unconscious striving for a continuity of experience, and at a third, as a solidarity with a group's ideals. (Erikson, 1968, p. 208; emphasis added)

These senses of identity respect the dimensions of self-structure discussed earlier, and at the same time add an element of developmental continuity. Erikson's definition of identity emphasizes the importance of an autonomous sense of self, a private version of traits and characteristics that set one apart from all others. It is also important to view one's "self" as a continuous phenomenon. One's sense of self does not undergo radical alterations with changes in group membership or with age.

The crisislike period for clarifying one's identity, the period of heightened vulnerability and sensitivity, occurs during adolescence or early adulthood. The most positive outcome of the crisis is an optimal sense of identity experienced as psychosocial well-being. Identity achievement, experienced as psychosocial well-being, is a result of an examination of alternatives available, followed by commitment to one alternative within the range of the possible. Erikson wrote that "without some such ideological commitment, however implicit in a 'way of life,' youth suffers a confusion of values" (Erikson, 1968, p. 188). Thus, two extremes of the identity-clarifying process are identified: *identity achievement*, on the one hand, and *identity confusion*, on the other.

Crisis and Commitment in Identity Status

Erikson's scheme for the development of identity is based upon astute observation and upon clinical practice. The strong intuitive appeal of his identity scheme led subsequent researchers to seek empirical support for the identity statuses he outlined. One such attempt is the work of James Marcia and his colleagues. Marcia (1966) developed a semistructured interview for use with older adolescents, particularly college students. Erikson's identity statuses are defined by psychosocial criteria, which reflect the person's own thinking about how he or she is dealing with major tasks of adolescence. Decisions about occupational goals and about religious and political ideologies are among the tasks outlined by Erikson, tasks that can be verified by observation and discussion with an average group of college students. Marcia's interviews use these tasks as content areas for eliciting information about identity status. Sample questions and answers from Marcia's interview are provided in Table 3-3. In Marcia's research, trained scorers agree on how to classify identity status between 75 and 90 percent of the time, based on presence of crisis and commitment in students' responses to interview questions.

Marcia reasoned that four identity statuses can be distinguished on the basis of an adolescent's experience of a psychological crisis and on the degree of commitment to a decision, once made. "Crisis refers to the adolescent's period of engagement in choosing among meaningful alternatives; commitment refers to the degree of personal investment the individual exhibits" (Marcia, 1966, p. 551) These four identity statuses are presented in Table 3-4, together with their criteria with respect to crisis and commitment. They are

---

TABLE 3-3
Sample Questions and Answers from Marcia's Identity-Status Interview

I. OCCUPATIONAL AREA

"How willing do you think you'd be to give up going into _____ if something better came along?"

Achievement: "Well, I might, but I doubt it. I can't see what 'something better' would be for me."

Moratorium: "I guess if I know for sure I could answer that better. It would have to be something in the general area—something related."

Foreclosure: "Not very willing. It's what I've always wanted to do. The folks are happy with it and so am I."

Confusion: "Oh sure. If something better came along, I'd change just like that."

II. RELIGIOUS AREA

"Have you ever had any doubts about your religious beliefs?"

Achievement: "Yeah, I even started wondering whether or not there was a god. I've pretty much resolved that now, though. The way it seems to me is . . ."

Moratorium: "Yes, I guess I'm going through that now. I just don't see how there can be a god and yet so much evil in the world or . . ."

Foreclosure: "No, not really, our family is pretty much in agreement on these things."

Confusion: "Oh, I don't know. I guess so. Everyone goes through some sort of stage like that. But it really doesn't bother me much. I figure one's about as good as the other!"

Source: Marcia, 1966.

TABLE 3-4
Identity Statuses and Their Criteria in Terms of Crisis and Commitment

	IDENTITY STATUS			
	PSYCHOSOCIAL MORATORIUM	IDENTITY FORECLOSURE	IDENTITY CONFUSION	IDENTITY ACHIEVEMENT
Position on Occupation and Ideology				
Crisis	In crisis	Absent	Present or absent	Present
Commitment	Present but vague	Present	Absent	Present

Source: Marcia, 1980.

called psychosocial moratorium, identity foreclosure, identity confusion (and the related negative identity), and identity achievement.

Psychosocial Moratorium   For the crisis of identity to end happily, an adolescent must be allowed a period in which adult commitments are delayed. Delay provides time to try out different roles, both in reality and fantasy, until a rational choice can be made.

Psychosocial moratorium—a period of time during which adult commitments are delayed—can take a variety of forms. Here, a group of West Point cadets walk down a street in New York in 1971 as Vietnam protesters read antiwar poetry under Vietnamese and American flags. Whether conventional or unconventional in form, the psychosocial moratorium provides the adolescent with an important period of transition between the morality learned as a child and the ethics to be developed as an adult.

(Photo copyright © 1971 by Margot Granitsas/Photo Researchers, Inc.)

Erikson called this delay a psychosocial moratorium, a period characterized by postponement of adult commitments and by "selective permissiveness on the part of society and of provocative playfulness on the part of youth" (Erikson, 1968, p. 157). Ways of experiencing a psychosocial moratorium on a large scale are often institutionalized. Among middle-class young people, going away to college is a way of experimenting with roles prior to adult commitments. Still other means of finding one's "self" include psychotherapy, drug experiences, the armed forces, the Peace Corps, and perhaps even juvenile delinquency. Whatever form the psychosocial moratorium may take, it provides the adolescent with a subjective experience during the period of transition from childhood to adulthood. "The adolescent mind is essentially a mind of the *moratorium*, a psychosocial stage between childhood and adulthood, and between the morality learned by the child, and the ethics to be developed by the adult" (Erikson, 1963, pp. 262-263).

Students classified as experiencing a psychosocial moratorium are *in* a period of crisis. Their commitments are vague, and yet they are engaged in an active struggle to clarify them, as this student was.

I don't know what I'll do. I've got a long time. It's a big place out there. I know lots of nice people. I'm going to leave school at the end of the semester and take off for 4 or 5 years. . . . Until you've extracted yourself on your own, without your culture to support you, you don't know what you've got. (Donovan, 1975, p. 48)

Identity Foreclosure When an adolescent makes commitments contributing to an adult identity, particularly occupational decisions, before having a chance to experiment freely with possible roles, the sense of identity that results has no proper foundation. Such an identity results from commitment before the experience of an identity crisis has run its course.

Consider the case of one of my college friends, whose father was a successful doctor and his mother a nurse. His parents, not surprisingly, strongly encouraged him to choose medicine as his life's work. Despite his personal misgivings, he capitulated to parental pressure, even though he wanted to pursue his musical talents. Happily, his immediate postcollege years were spent studying medicine and music in a flexible British university. Distance from his parents' interference allowed him to abandon medicine in favor of an occupational identity that more clearly expressed his own sense of self. Although his early decision can be taken as an example of identity foreclosure, he was able to experience a year of study abroad that served as a psychosocial moratorium away from the influences that had originally led to foreclosure. When I saw my friend after his independent decision, he was a happily married music student, whose proudest possession was a lovely secondhand piano.

Students who are in a state of identity foreclosure often have parents who pressure them into early decisions about careers or ideologies. One foreclosed student described his occupational plans this way.

I plan to be a clinical psychologist. Have since high school. Mother said she would have been a psychologist. She has a lot of influence on me. (Donovan, 1975, p. 45)

Identity Confusion The process of psychosocial self-definition may demand of the adolescent too many commitments all at once. Decisions about sexual behavior, about preparation for a job or career, about drug use, may converge and result in acute identity confusion. A prototypical case of identity confusion is Holden Caulfield, J.D. Salinger's wry "catcher" who, trying to figure out where he stood, rejected most of the adult world as "phony." Introspective and intelligent, Holden spoke for a whole generation of young people who were aware of their confusion but unable to do much about it. As he is being thrown out of yet another prep school, he tells his faculty advisor, "Look, sir. Don't worry about me, I mean it. I'll be all right. I'm just going through a phase right now. Everybody goes through phases and all, don't they?"

Identity confusion may be particularly acute with respect to intimacy and sexuality. Plagued by increased sexual drives, many adolescents nevertheless fear interpersonal intimacy. They fear a loss of the identity gains they have made if they engage in premature intimacy with others. Seeking their own identities, they look for partners like themselves. True intimacy, healthy in a psychosocial sense, is possible only following the resolution of the identity crisis late in adolescence, according to Erikson.

A frequent accompaniment of identity confusion is the inability to settle down to serious work. Academic work suffers, concentration lags, the individual may withdraw into a limited social world to avoid competitive situations. Identity confusion that takes this form has the danger of affecting the adolescent's sense of adequacy. In extreme forms, the result is "work paralysis." When this happens, according to Erikson, it is extremely difficult to develop an occupational identity as a prelude to adult role commitments because the adolescent experiences a self-imposed exile from the competitive situations and role experiments that lead to such commitments.

Students showing identity confusion might or might not have had an identity crisis, but in either case they are not committed to an occupation or an ideology. Rather, they appear to be uninterested in ideology and steeped in relativism. Here is one confused student's response to the interview.

I have no major, General Studies. I have enough credits in Psych. and Math. No plans. Nothing crosses my mind. . . . No tangible ideas right now. I'm waiting for the summer. In the winter I'm on a down. This summer I'm going to split. (Donovan, 1975, p. 42)

Negative Identity One logical conclusion to the dilemma of identity confusion is "a scornful and snobbish hostility toward the roles offered as proper and desirable in one's family or immediate community" (Erikson, 1968, pp. 172–173). Again, Holden Caulfield serves as a prototype, the young person who removes himself from the "phoniness" of the precommitment world of the prep school. Parents often play an unwitting role in the negative identity of their offspring by imposing ideal standards that are too strict before developmental readiness for commitment has been reached. Parents who insist that their children grow into their own professional roles—doctor or lawyer or cabinetmaker—may find that their child opts instead for the most undesirable role imaginable. Some cases of juvenile delinquency and adolescent escapism seem to follow this pattern. Negative identity appears more intelligible when viewed as an attempt to regain some mastery over the course of one's own destiny. Negative identity can be viewed as autonomy and initiative gone awry because of faulty communication between adolescent and parent during the crisis of identity.

The most severe form of negative identity culminates in suicide or in a suicide attempt. Erikson described one such case, a pretty young girl whose father was a mill worker. Her family expressed the view that they would rather see her die than become a prostitute, while suspecting her every move when it came to a natural interest in the opposite sex. In extreme circumstances complicated by this girl's assumptions that no other avenue was open to her, she hanged herself. Erikson described this circumstance as one of "those rare cases where 'to be a suicide' becomes an inescapable identity choice in itself" (Erikson, 1968, p. 170).

Identity Achievement Students classified as showing identity achievement have had an identity crisis and are committed to an occupation or ideology. These students have firmly decided on careers and on ideological positions after carefully examining alternatives available. In relationships to their parents, they appear to be fully autonomous. Among college students, relatively few people have reached the status of identity achievement (Donovan, 1975).

Reflecting about occupational choice is not new to adolescence. Young children are asked many times what they want to be when they grow up; and children give that question a lot of thought, even when they are not specifically asked it. In an interview in which 8-year-old Kurt was asked to talk about any subject he wanted to, he lapsed into the following monologue about future occupations.

When I grow up I think I'd like to be an airplane driver and hope that I don't wreck, and that I might be an . . . let's see . . . an artist maybe. And I might be a train driver, I sorta b'lieve I wanna be. I might be a policeman, or a station manager, or maybe a gunfighter, and maybe be . . . Let me see. Maybe I might be able to go travel around the world, or stop people from stealing—things like that. (Hopkins, 1968)

There is a fantastic quality to Kurt's occupational ramblings, unlike the concerns of adolescents who are facing actual decisions. Erikson cited work-role as one of the central problem areas among young people. "In general it is the inability to settle on an occupational identity which most disturbs young people" (Erikson, 1968, p. 132).

Marcia's criteria for identity achievement in the area of occupational choice were quite stringent, as described in a study conducted with a sample of college women.

With respect to the interview criteria for "commitment to an occupation," mere selection of a college major is not sufficient. In order to be judged "identity achievement," a subject has to have made a decision about an occupation after having considered and discarded alternatives. She has to have a fairly good knowledge of the day-to-day activities of a person in the occupation chosen, and she has to be taking some concrete steps beyond just course selection toward her occupational goal. (Toder & Marcia, 1973, p. 289)

It is not surprising that very few college students show occupational identity achievement using these criteria (Donovan, 1975). In fact, relatively few college students have made concrete commitments to their future occupations. About three-fourths of a sample of students in a career-orientation survey at Vassar gave specific answers to the question: "What are your ultimate career or occupational plans?" Even among those who did give specific answers, however, many showed a lack of logical relatedness, which would indicate a real commitment. For example, one 19-year-old male sophomore answered, "Anthropological research; or broadcasting; or bicycle mechanic." An 18-year-old female sophomore gave this reply. "Either teaching, law, medicine, business, or mechanics."

It appears safe to conclude that both male and female adolescents and young adults are concerned about occupational decision-making and that this concern is reflected in their own sense of "self." Commitment to an occupational category eases the psychological difficulties associated with identity development.

Achievement of identity is a prerequisite, according to Erikson, for the kind of true interpersonal sharing found in psychologically intimate relationships. "It is only when identity formation is well on its way that true intimacy—which is really a counterpointing as well as a fusing of identities—is possible" (Erikson, 1968, p. 135). Studies with college students have shown a strong relationship between identity achievement and higher levels of intimacy (Constantinople, 1969; Kacergius & Adams, 1980).

Identity and Individuation

A crucial property of identity is the sense of individual separateness and uniqueness. Theorists in the Freudian tradition, as we saw earlier, refer to the development of this sense of autonomy as individuation; and they suggest that the process is central to adolescent development. Because individuation reserves a special place for parents in the psychological development of adolescent offspring, we might expect different styles of parenting to affect the individuation process.

The Role of Parents in Individuation It is clear that parents play an important role in the identity development of their children. This role can be seen clearly in deviant cases, in which peculiar patterns of family interaction have resulted in disturbed senses of identity among adolescent children. Intensive case studies, such as the one of Sarah Danzig (Esterson, 1970), show the effects of family interaction gone awry. Sarah's family secretly investigated the boys she was interested in, monitored her telephone calls, and became alarmed by any indication that she had thoughts that were secret from them. Her parents felt that she spent too much time in bed, which was an indication either of laziness or of sickness. In a family interview, this issue was raised:

Father: *Well I don't want you to do it, Sarah, because we feel so strong. Don't make a condition of it. You must in your own mind make up your mind whether, er—you should get up early or not.*

Mother: *You must feel it's right, your own self, Sarah—not because we tell you to, but—*

Sarah: *Well yes, it'll be all right to get up.*

Mother: *You think we're right to—? [Father starts to speak.] Just a moment. No, let me get her opinion.*

Sarah: *Yes, I think so.*

Father: *That's submissive. I don't want a submissive attitude. (Esterson, 1970, pp. 73–74)*

Sarah began to exhibit bizarre behavior and thought patterns starting around age 17, and finally was admitted to a psychiatric hospital. One perspective on her illness is that it resulted from a thwarted individuation process. Sarah may have become confused about who she was because she had such a difficult time divorcing her own thoughts and feelings from those imposed on her through her family interaction. The sense of continuity in time and the sense of individual uniqueness that are so critical to identity require a reasonable latitude for the individuation process, in childhood and adolescence.

The degree to which parents control their adolescent children may influence the extent to which adolescents can achieve an independent sense of identity. Moderate control, neither too lax nor too stringent, appears to provide the best framework within which identity may develop. Identity development also proceeds more smoothly when parents agree on the control measures that they use with their children (Pable, 1965).

Adolescents' styles of individuation probably reflect their general status in psychosocial maturity. Adolescent males who scored high in psychosocial maturity were likely to have internalized their parents' expectations for them, allowing a peaceful transition toward a sense of autonomy. Those who scored low on psychosocial maturity, however, were more likely to show their independence through rebellion and testing the limits of parental rules (Josselson, Greenberger, & McConochie, 1977; Bernard, 1981).

The importance of parent–child relationships in the adolescent period is emphasized later in the book, when we discuss interpersonal interaction with parents and peers in Chapter 7.

Sex Differences in Identity Status

The interviews quoted above were conducted with male students using questions on occupation and ideology. Attempts to assess the identity statuses of college women have been based on a different set of interviews for the most part, with questions involving interpersonal issues such as attitudes toward premarital intercourse. In interviews concerned with this issue, college women at the State University of New York at Buffalo were classified into the

FIGURE 3-1
Percentage of men in each identity status by content area. (*Ach*= identity achieved; *Mora*=moratorium, *Fore*=foreclosure; *Conf*= identity confusion.) Men and women are similar in identity status for areas of occupation, religion, and politics; in the area of sex, more men are classified in the status of foreclosure.

(From Waterman & Nevid, 1977.)

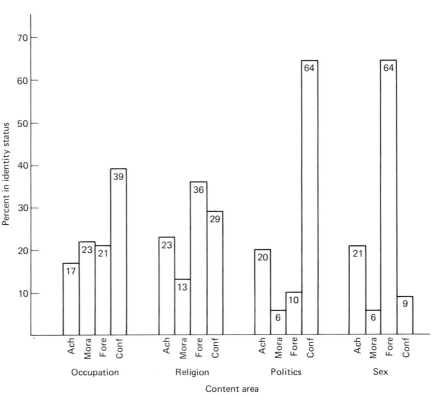

four identity statuses described by Marcia. Identity-achievement women had settled on a set of sexual standards after a period of experimentation and confusion. Moratorium students were vague about the standards that guided their behavior; and those classified as showing identity confusion lacked a position on sexual standards. Foreclosure students expressed puritanical standards, and they were determined to remain puritanical (Marcia & Friedman, 1970).

Interviews on premarital sexual standards sometimes yield a different pattern of identity statuses for women than interviews on occupation or ideology. In addition, those college women who showed identity achievement in the sex interview had a higher level of "psychological comfort" than those who showed identity achievement on the occupation and ideology interview (Marcia & Friedman, 1970). Some researchers believe that the issues on which men and women define their identities may, on the average, differ (Hodgson & Fischer, 1981; Marcia, 1980; Schenkel & Marcia, 1972). In this view, interpersonal issues, such as sexual standards, are more germane to female identity, while occupational issues are particularly important in the determination of male identity. These facets of identity might be expected to determine some of the psychological difficulties experienced by men and women. As Carol Gilligan put it, "Since masculinity is defined through separation

FIGURE 3-2
Percentage of women in each identity status by content area. (*Ach*= identity achieved; *Mora*= moratorium; *Fore*=foreclosure; *Conf*= identity confusion.) Men and women are similar in status for areas of occupation, religion, and politics; in the area of sex, more women than men are classified in the status of identity achieved.

(From Waterman & Nevid, 1977.)

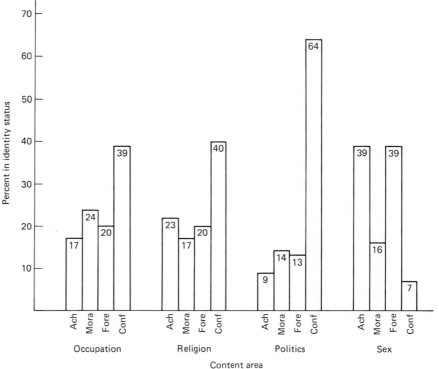

while femininity is defined through attachment, male gender identity will be threatened by intimacy while female gender identity will be threatened by individuation. Thus males will tend to have difficulty with relationships while females will tend to have problems with separation" (Gilligan, 1979, p. 434).

Other researchers, however, believe that occupation and ideology are just as important concerns for women as they are for men. At least one study has found that questions on occupation are better for prediciting the identity statuses of college women than questions on premarital sex (Hopkins, 1980).

Obviously, the best method for comparing men's and women's identity statuses is to use the same interview with both men and women in the same study. Surprisingly, none of the above studies used this method. However, in those projects that have included interviews with both men and women, few striking sex differences have been found (e.g., Podd, Marcia, & Rubin, 1970).

Another study comparing college men's and women's identity statuses found that the women's pattern of identity status was similar to that of men for all content areas *except* premarital sex. Data for the 70 men and 70 women in this study (Waterman & Nevid, 1977) are presented in Figures 3-1 and 3-2. More of the women had reached identity achievement in the area of sex, and more of the men were classified as in the status of foreclosure for this content area—implying that the men had reached a level of commitment to a sexual ideology without experiencing any exploratory crisis. Men were more likely than women to have achieved identity in the content area of politics, but they showed similar patterns for occupation and religion.

Not all identity-status research has used Marcia's interview technique. Another approach to the study of identity is to present students with statements derived from Erikson's theory that reflect successful and unsuccessful resolutions of stage crises. Students are asked to indicate how characteristic of themselves these statements are. Some research using this technique indicates that women enter college at a more mature level of identity development than men, but that men make greater and more consistent gains in identity during the college years (Constantinople, 1969). Sex differences may, therefore, reflect differences in the impact of college on identity formation as well as the importance of different content areas. Data from a more recent generation of college students indicate no clear pattern of sex differences (Whitbourne, Jilsma, & Waterman, 1982).

Role Contradictions for Women Marcia (1980) suggested that identity resolution may take longer for women, while resolution of the crisis of intimacy may take longer for men. The psychological process of clarifying the sense of identity may pose special difficulties for women because two contradictory roles are presented as models for them. On the one hand, women are expected to be glamorous and socially attractive; on the other hand, they are expected to meet the same challenges of an achievement-oriented society that men must meet. These contradicitions may pose difficulties for establishing an integrated identity for many young women, such as the college student who wrote

All through high school my family urged me to work hard because they wished me to enter a first-rate college. At the same time they were always raving about a girl schoolmate who lived next door to us. How pretty and sweet she was, how popular, and what taste in clothes! Couldn't I also pay more attention to my appearance and to social life? They were overlooking the fact that this carefree friend of mine had little time left for school work and had failed several subjects. (Komarovsky, 1946, p. 185)

College men also recognize the role strain that cultural contradition pose for women. Almost one-third of the college males randomly selected from the senior class at an Ivy League school reported experiencing insecurity on dates with bright women. As one of them put it,

I enjoy talking to more intelligent girls, but I have no desire for a deep relationship with them. I guess I still believe that the man should be more intelligent. (Komarovsky, 1973, p. 874)

Conflicting societal attitudes, reflected in the advice of parents and the treatment of dates, reinforce the potential difficulty faced by young women in establishing an occupational identity and a sex-role identity that are congruent with each other.

It is probably fair to say that sex-role identity is a difficult process for both boys and girls. Boys, for example, must shift from early identification with the mother to identification with the father. In addition, more severe sex-typing demands are made of boys, in terms of games that they may play and clothes that they may wear. These stricter demands, however, are correlated with greater social advantages that go along with the male role, as society is presently constituted. Some evidence suggests that adolescent boys and girls have internalized this set of attitudes about sex roles.

Many young women have difficulty establishing an occupational identity that is congruent with the sex-role demands placed on them by the larger society. Still, many young women, such as the fork-lift operator pictured here, are electing occupations that go beyond traditional, sex-stereotyped occupations.

(Photo by Aster and Bill Magee/ Freelance Photographer's Guild)

High-school students in the New York metropolitan area rated scales that contained traits stereotyped as either masculine or feminine. Boys rated adjectives stereotyped as masculine as more desirable than girls did adjectives stereotyped as feminine (Rudy, 1968). Even so, sex-role preference, as measured by the Femininity Scale of the California Psychological Inventory, was found to be unrelated to social acceptance among either male or female high-school students (Webb, 1963).

Research on the issue of sex differences in identity status has been made somewhat more complicated than it need have been by studies that examined identity status for only one sex or the other. Those projects that have included both men and women find many more similarities in identity status than differences. When differences in identity status are found, they appear to reflect two related phenomena: First, there are some overall differences in the issues on which men and women clarify their identities, with women showing somewhat more concern for interpersonal issues for identity clarification in adolescence than men do. Second, the developmental timetables for resolution of the crises of identity and intimacy are slightly different for men and women, with women taking longer to resolve the identity crisis, and men taking longer to resolve the intimacy crisis.

DEVELOPMENTAL VALIDITY OF IDENTITY STATUS

Erikson's discussion suggests that identity change should follow a developmental sequence. Identity confusion and psychosocial moratorium, in which no commitments have been made, should be early developmental statuses, preceding identity achievement. Identity foreclosure, characterized by commitment without crisis, is an early and immature identity status. Some support has been obtained for the developmental validity of this identity sequence (Waterman, 1982).

Among younger adolescents, identity status is related to developmental maturity. Identity achievement occurs with increasing frequency from the sophomore to senior years in high school. Furthermore, students with higher identity-status scores also show more positive self-concepts and higher scores on measures of trust and industry (LaVoie, 1976).

Marcia reinterviewed 30 of the college men who had served in his original 1967 study of identity status again in 1973. As one would expect, the moratorium status was the most unstable over time. All of those originally classified as moratorium students had changed status in the intervening 6 years. In addition, a surprising finding was that those who had achieved an identity in college were more likely to change later than those who had not.

The results of this study lead one to surmise that achieving an identity during the college years may or may not yield continued identity achievement, while not achieving an identity in college seems to mean not achieving identity in the subsequent 6 or 7 years. (Marcia, 1976, p. 152)

A sequence of identity status that goes from achievement or moratorium to the status of foreclosure seems theoretically implausible, yet it was obtained in 6 of the 30 cases in Marcia's follow-up study. The explanation may lie either in the interview procedures for assessing identity status, or in the procedures Marcia used to select the follow-up sample. Marcia contacted only those men who were still living within a 50-mile radius of Buffalo, New York, 6 years after their original participation. Those who stick close by their undergraduate institutions may be preselected for a more rigid personality style, which is reflected in their subsequent classification into the status of identity foreclosure.

Longitudinal Studies Longitudinal studies of identity status over the college years have yielded information on its developmental validity. One such study (Waterman, Geary, & Waterman, 1974) involved 53 college seniors who had been interviewed as freshmen at Rensselaer Polytechnical Institute. Among these men, there was a net increase in achievement status between freshman and senior year; this result supports the notion that identity achievement is a developmentally mature stage. A net decrease in moratorium and foreclosure statuses reinforces the point. Again, however, a downward shift in identity status does occur for some of the students, which is theoretically inconsistent. Marcia's interview may be responsible for misclassifying some students, which would confound the developmental sequence. In the study just cited, judges agreed on the identity classification of the seniors only 63 percent of the time. Thus, in more than a third of the cases, trained judges could not agree on assigning an identity status based on what students said in their interviews.

Longitudinal studies at liberal-arts colleges have shown a pattern of increase in identity status (Waterman & Goldman, 1976). Identity achievement shows its greatest developmental increase in the content area of occupational choice, at least among male college students. Percentages of students in the four identity statuses are shown by content area in Table 3-5. Identity status undergoes very little developmental change in the areas of religious and political

TABLE 3-5
Percentage of Freshmen and Seniors in Each Identity Status by Interview Content Area

STATUS AND CONTENT AREA	FRESHMAN YEAR	SENIOR YEAR
Occupational Choice:		
Achievement	9	41
Moratorium	24	4
Foreclosure	30	35
Confusion	37	20
Religious Beliefs:		
Achievement	25	32
Moratorium	12	14
Foreclosure	36	18
Confusion	27	36
Political Beliefs:		
Achievement	27	29
Moratorium	4	4
Foreclosure	16	16
Confusion	53	51

Source: Waterman & Goldman, 1976.

beliefs over the college years. Identity achievement in occupational choice, however, is shown by 41 percent of the seniors, as compared to only 9 percent of the freshmen. Measures of identity based on questionnaires rather than interviews have yielded similar results on developmental validity. For example, consistent increases in the percentages of students who showed successful resolutions of the identity crisis were found from the freshman to the senior year at the University of Rochester (Constantinople, 1969).

Cross-sectional Studies Longitudinal studies follow the same students, giving them the same or similar tasks for assessing their identity statuses. In cross-sectional studies, students in different age groups are tested at the same time. Meilman (1979) used the cross-sectional technique with five age groups of males: 12, 15, 18, 21, and 24 years old. These males showed a trend toward more mature identity statuses with age, as shown in Figure 3-3. None of the 12-year-olds were in the identity-achievement status, whereas, a majority (56 percent) of the 24-year-olds showed identity achievement. Late adolescence appears to be the age of greatest sensitivity to the identity crisis.

Predictive Efficiency of Identity Status The validity of identity status is further strengthened by its predictive efficiency. Students in the moratorium status might be expected to be more changeable in their academic plans than students in other identity statuses.

FIGURE 3-3
Percentage of males who were in the identity-achievement status at five age levels. Older males are more likely to be classified in the more mature identity-achievement status.

(From Meilman, 1979.)

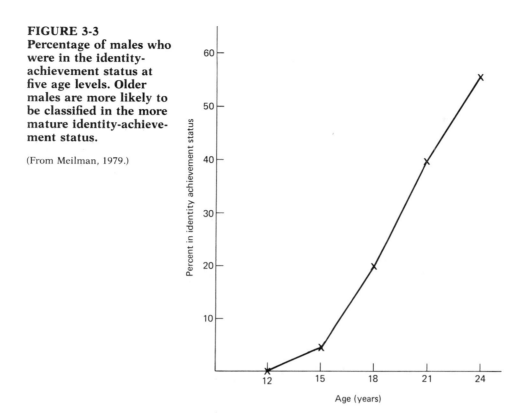

Among 92 students who were interviewed as freshmen at Rensselaer, 32 had changed their occupational plans by their sixth semester. Changed plans were indicated either by transfer to a different academic program, or by withdrawal from school. Among those freshmen classified as experiencing a psychosocial moratorium, 80 percent changed their plans; among all other identity statuses, only 30 percent changed plans (Waterman & Waterman, 1972). Logically consistent behaviors are associated with other identity statuses as well. Identity-achievement college students performed better on a concept-attainment task while under stress than did students in other identity statuses. Foreclosure students, who are susceptible to the influence of authority, were most likely to endorse authoritarian values such as obedience and respect for authority figures (Marcia, 1966).

In the studies of identity achievement discussed thus far, high-school or college students served as subjects. Research has rarely been conducted on young people out of school, and identity status may vary as a function of the characteristics or concerns of the population studied. This point is strengthened by research in Canada, which compared the identity statuses of college students and working youth of the same age, race, and social class (Munro & Adams, 1977). Percentages of young people in each identity status, determined by responses in a private interview, are shown in Figure 3-4. More of the working youth were classified in the identity-achievement category; they had achieved identity in the content areas of religion, politics, and ideology. Other studies support this conclusion (e.g., Morash, 1980). It is possible that some students avoid commitments in these areas by using college as a psycho-social moratorium. Working youth did not differ from college students on occupational identity.

Erikson's model of identity, therefore, appears to enjoy empirical support. Identity statuses characterized by crisis and commitment can be distinguished in standard interviews and can be reliably classified. The proportion of developmentally higher identity-achievement responses increases with age. Students who have been studied longitudinally tend to progress toward identity achievement in the later college years. The validity of identity development is further demonstrated by studies showing a relationship between identity status and other personality dimensions. Moratorium students appear to be more changeable in their occupational plans; identity-achievement students appear to have greater self-esteem, autonomy, trust, and industry. Research comparing men and

FIGURE 3-4
Percentages of college students and working youth in each identity status. (*Ach*=identity achieved; *Mora*=moratorium; *Fore*=foreclosure; *Conf*=identity confusion.) More working youth than college students are classified in the identity-achievement status.

(From Munro & Adams, 1977.)

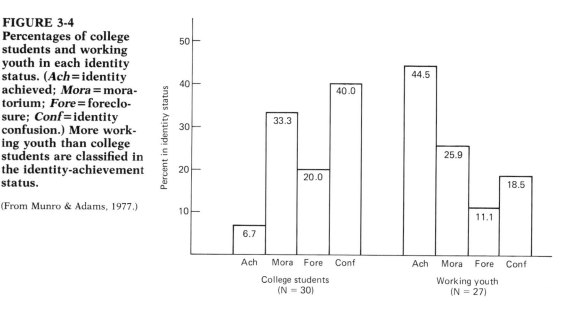

women, while not conclusive, suggest that they may differ on a few of the content areas on which identity is based. Content areas may differ systematically among other groups as well, such as young people who are working versus those who are pursuing college educations.

Methodological Difficulties

Recall that Erikson's outline of psychosocial development included a stage in which identity concerns reached a crisis point. This stage is seen as typical of the period of adolescence and youth in American society, a stage that most people experience. Since stage-conceptions of development posit qualitatively different levels of thought or behavior occuring in an invariant sequence, any overlap or stage mixture clouds the data in support of the theory. Behavior of a given person appears continuous, posing additional difficulties for classifying the person's behavior as indicative of a given stage.

Another difficulty with this area of research concerns the tasks used to measure the construct in question. No task exists that is certain to elicit crucial information relevant to identity. A person may be operating at different levels depending on the content area of the questions. Marcia's interviews for identity-status classification provide a good example of this problem. A person's identity status is usually not identical for the different content areas of occupation, religion, politics, or sexual standards. The problem of measurement validity recurs in developmental psychology because there is no sure-fire behavioral sign of complicated cognitive and emotional constructs, such as "formal operations," identity status," and "ego level."

As Loevinger (1966) pointed out, all kinds of development occur within a person simultaneously. It may be useful to separate different channels of development for purposes of exposition and discussion, but they are closely related in the natural context of the person. Thus, physical, psychosexual, intellectual, and emotional aspects of development influence each other. Attempts to measure them and chart their developmental course inevitably lead to some loss of clarity because important influences have to be ignored.

SUMMARY

1. The self-structure, or self-identity, changes most during the adolescent period. Adolescents, in comparison to children, include more abstract, and more psychological, elements in their self-structures. Self-identity is an individual's own private version

of the traits and personal characteristics that best describe him or her.

2. Freud believed that psychosexual self-identity grows out of three key transformations of puberty: First, there is a transition from infantile sexuality to normal genital sexuality. Second, there is a transformation from autoerotic sexual impulses to heterosexual impulses. Third, there is a breaking away from parental authority with its Oedipal ties, a process referred to as individuation.

3. The traditional Freudian view that identity development is dominated by drive pressures at puberty has been revised in recent years, primarily by Erikson. Although Erikson retained the psychoanalytic stages of childhood, he deemphasized the sexual instincts in the process of adolescent identity development in favor of concerns about socially determined issues such as occupational choice and premarital sexual standards.

4. Adolescence, according to Erikson, is the time for an identity crisis, a period of heightened vulnerability and sensitivity about the "self." The crisis generally concludes with commitments to occupation and ideology.

5. Researchers, most notably Marcia and his colleagues, have described four identity statuses based on Erikson's scheme. *Psychosocial moratorium* is a period in which adult commitments are delayed. Students in psychological moratorium are *in* an identity crisis, and their commitments, if any, are vague. *Identity foreclosure* results when commitments are made before the identity crisis has had a chance to run its course. *Identity confusion* results when students have had an identity crisis, but are still unable to make commitments. And finally, *identity achievement* describes those students who have had an identity crisis, and have made commitments to occupation and ideology.

6. Successful resolution of the identity crisis in late adolescence is a prerequisite for the emotional sharing of the next stage of the life cycle, involving the crisis of intimacy.

7. Individuation, the process of clarifying one's uniqueness and separateness from others, is particularly influenced by parental behavior. Moderate parental control, neither too lax nor too strict, appears to provide the best context for individuation.

8. Relatively few studies of identity development have used the same set of interviews with both male and female adolescents.

Speculation that women and men differ on the issues around which they clarify their identities has received only moderate research support. Identity development in both men and women is heavily influenced by occupational decision-making. In addition, women appear to be somewhat more concerned than men are with interpersonal issues, such as premarital sexual standards, as they bear on identity clarification.

9. Women may take longer to resolve the crisis of identity, while men take longer to resolve the crisis of intimacy.

10. Evidence supports Erikson's views on the developmental progression of identity development. Individuals show increasingly mature identity statuses throughout the adolescent years. This conclusion is supported by the few longitudinal studies available (in which the same students are interviewed about identity issues at more than one age), and by cross-sectional studies (in which interview responses of students of different age groups are compared). The greatest shift in identity status appears to occur in late adolescence, at least for those people who go to college.

11. More young people who do not attend college appear to have reached the status of identity achievement than those who are in college. College may provide an institutionalized psychosocial moratorium for delaying the process of identity development.

OUTLINE

4. SEX-ROLE CONSOLIDATION IN ADOLESCENCE

OPENING EXERCISE

At the risk of opening this chapter on a depressing note, I offer a sad story, which is in fact a riddle. Read the story, and see if you can figure out the answer to the question at the end.

The Surgeon–Patient Riddle

On a bright, sunny day in February, a boy and his father were driving on a country road. As they came to the crest of a hill, going perhaps a little faster than they should have been, they met a truck taking too much of the road. They were unable to avoid a collision; the truck and the car crashed together head-on. The father was killed instantly, and the son was very seriously injured. The truck driver, however, was unhurt and was able to summon an ambulance immediately. The boy was rushed to a nearby hospital, where he was taken to the operating room for emergency surgery. The surgeon walked into the operating room, took one look at the boy, and said: "I can't operate on this boy. He's my son!"

How can you explain the surgeon's comment? The riddle confuses many people who are accustomed to associating certain occupational categories with gender. The gender of the surgeon is never mentioned, but most people assume that the surgeon is male. The solution to the riddle is, of course, that the surgeon is the boy's mother. The riddle illustrates the extent to which we view the world along sex-typed dimensions. Perhaps we believe that traits that make a person a good surgeon—such as strength and cool-headedness in an emergency—are found more often among males than among females. Perhaps we are simply making inferences based on the real disparity in the percentage of surgeons who are men as opposed to women. In any case, each time I have used the riddle in a classroom, I have found that a majority of college students are stumped by it. Furthermore, college women do not seem to be any better at solving the riddle than men.

In this chapter we are concerned with sex roles, the behaviors associated with the biological gender distinction. Within psychology, the term "sex role" refers to sex-typed behaviors in a general sense, behaviors that are expected for males and females in a stereotypical fashion. Writings under the rubric "sex roles" also include more strictly psychological sex differences, such as personality trait differences by gender. In the course of the chapter, references to sex roles include these general connotations. Readers, however, should be aware of the origins of the term in role theory: the different prescriptions for behavior based on biological gender.

Our first task is to describe the distinction between roles and stereotypes and to examine some of the stereotypes associated with being male and female. Next, we discuss the concept of sex-role orientation—the degree to which people view themselves as masculine, feminine, or neither. The heart of this chapter is the discussion of the developmental history of sex-typed behavior; here we emphasize adolescence as a period for sex-role consolidation. To reinforce this point, we focus on research in one area of cognitive functioning—spatial ability—which shows a typical developmental history: Few sex differences prior to adolescence, with increasing differentiation through adolescence, until differences level off in early adulthood. Although we concentrate on spatial ability in this discussion, the same pattern may hold for other important areas that demonstrate sex differences because some of the major influences on sex-role consolidation exert particular influence during the developmental phase of adolescence.

ROLES AND STEREOTYPES

A role is a social category that implies a set of behaviors that distinguish it from other social categories. Within a college community, several roles may be mentioned that together form an organized social network. Students are expected to take a certain number of classes and to perform the tasks associated with those classes in order to accumulate the credits necessary to graduate. Graduation enables them to move from the college community and to take on additional roles in the larger society because some roles are restricted to individuals with educational credentials. Pediatricians, for example, must have medical degrees with specialization in the medical aspects of child development. Professors are expected to teach a prescribed number of courses and to sit on college committees that formulate educational policy or interpret the rules of the college. Administrators are charged with carrying out such day-to-day operations of the college as paying bills, scheduling class meeting times and places, and recruiting students for future sessions. Other employees of the college carry out essential support functions: preparing meals for the dining halls, typing course examinations, maintaining buildings and grounds.

Roles vary in the degree to which the behaviors are specified. *Parent* and *child* are reciprocal roles defined by a biological relationship. Wide variation in the performance of the behaviors associated with these roles is tolerated. Parents are expected to provide for the support of their dependent children and to oversee their educational, medical, and social upbringing. In satisfying these broad role requirements, parents may run the gamut from warm and supportive to aloof and neglectful. Within the broad range of expected behaviors, role performance becomes a matter of the individual's interpretation, just as a role on stage is interpreted by the actor who fills it.

A role is a social category entailing a set of expected behaviors, attitudes, and traits associated with successful performance of the role. A stereotype, on the other hand, involves a caricaturelike set of behaviors and attributes that presumably apply to members of a social category. Stereotypes may or may not be based on actual performance of the behaviors; they are abstract expectations. Like caricatures, they often distort reality out of all proportion.

The college community provides an example of the distinction between roles and stereotypes. The role of college professor includes prescribed behaviors, such as teaching a certain number of courses, serving on college committees, and advising students on their courses of study. Many popular stereotypes exist of the college professor, including traits such as absentmindedness and knee-jerk liberality. Professors are stereotypically seen as individuals who are knowledgeable and erudite in their own highly specialized fields, but who are helpless and inept when faced with the reality of the larger society. A role is a social category that prescribes certain expected behaviors; a stereotype is a caricature of expected behaviors and traits ascribed to persons who belong to a social category. Not all social categories are roles. It is not proper to say that "black," "Oriental," or "Presbyterian" are roles, but they are social categories; and they do have stereotypes associated with them.

Sex-Role Stereotypes

The distinction between roles and stereotypes is blurred when we consider sex roles. It is unclear which behaviors associated with being male or female should be considered prescribed. Must girls be nurturant in order to be considered successful performers of the female sex role? If boys are nurturant, are they violating the rules for successful performance of the male role? In other words, is nurturance one of the behaviors prescribed by the female sex role, or is it simply a caricaturelike stereotype applied to girls and women? It seems clear that behaviors generally associated with one or the other sex role are not prescribed in the same sense as behaviors associated with occupational roles. Current research on femininity and masculinity implies that behaviors and traits associated with gender are response tendencies rather than roles. As a first step toward untangling the confusion of sex roles, we examine some of the popular stereotypes associated with gender.

Stereotyped Trait Assignment Trait assignment by gender does exist. In one study in New England (Rosenkrantz, Vogel, Bee, Broverman, & Broverman, 1968), a large number of college students agreed substantially on trait assignment by gender. Among both men and women, 75 percent or more agreed on a list of items that differentiated between the genders (see Table 4-1). Furthermore, the masculine traits were evaluated as more socially desirable than the feminine traits. In self-ratings using the items on the list, these students indicated that they saw themselves along sex-typed dimensions.

A common technique for gauging sex stereotypes is to present a list of adjectives, such as "friendly," "intelligent," "kind," and so forth. Respondents are asked to indicate the degree to which the adjectives characterize males or females. Using this technique, Rudy (1968) established a set of masculine stereotypes and a set of feminine stereotypes. Ninth- and 10th-grade students of both sexes subsequently rated these traits for their desirability. They rated the sex-appropriate traits as more desirable, which indicates that sex stereotypes do influence the characteristics that one would choose to possess, at least among adolescents. Boys in this study did not rate feminine traits as any less desirable than girls did the masculine traits. That sex-appropriateness is rated more desirable is an important finding because some have argued that traits stereotyped as masculine are in general more desirable. It appears that adolescents evaluate the desirability of traits by the degree to which they match sex-appropriate stereotypes. It is possible, of course, that this tendency may reflect conformity pressures in adolescence because research with college students generally does show a more positive evaluation of "masculine" traits (e.g., Rosenkrantz et al., 1968).

Males and females from a broad age range, from age 12 to adults up to 76 years old, have been asked to rate the "ideal male"

TABLE 4-1
Sex-Role Stereotypes

MALE TRAITS

Aggressive	Feelings not easily hurt
Independent	Adventurous
Unemotional	Makes decisions easily
Hides emotions	Never cries
Objective	Acts as a leader
Easily influenced	Self-confident
Dominant	Not uncomfortable about being aggressive
Likes math and science	Ambitious
Not excitable in a minor	Able to separate feelings from ideas
crisis	Not dependent
Active	Not conceited about appearance
Competitive	Thinks men are superior to women
Logical	Talks freely about sex with men
Worldly	Knows the way of the world
Skilled in business	
Direct	

FEMALE TRAITS

Does not use harsh	Interested in own appearance
language	Neat in habits
Talkative	Quiet
Tactful	Strong need for security
Gentle	Appreciates art and literature
Aware of feelings	Expresses tender feelings
of others	
Religious	

Source: Rosenkrantz, Vogel, Bee, Broverman, & Broverman, 1968. Copyright © 1968 by the American Psychological Association. Reprinted by permission of the publisher and author.

and the "ideal female" on a number of traits. All age groups concerned subscribed to a stereotyped view of ideals. Ideal males were thought to possess traits of dominance, aggressiveness, exhibitionism, autonomy, and self-confidence; ideal females were thought to possess traits of abasement, succorance, and deference. The raters in this study were both males and females, and they agreed on the above stereotypes (Urberg & Labouvie-Vief, 1976). Although stereotypes for the ideal male and ideal female were held across the age range, the strongest stereotyping occurred among adolescents (Urberg, 1979). Other studies have confirmed that adolescence is an important stage for sex-role stereotyping (e.g, Emmerich & Shepard, 1982).

Even though the tendency to stereotype along gender lines appears stong and consistent, it has undergone some changes in the past few years. For example, submission and dependence are now

In 1981, Sandra Day O'Connor became the first woman appointed to the Supreme Court of the United States. A political cartoon about Justice O'Connor's appointment capitalized on sex-role stereotypes.

(From Don Wright, *Miami News*, July 1981.)

seen as somewhat more appropriate and impulsiveness as less appropriate for the ideal of either sex (Urberg, 1979).

The picture that emerges from research on sex-role stereotypes is one of consensus about traits that differentiate males and females. Within American society, an individual is likely to hold a set of stereotypes for sex-appropriate behavior, and is also likely to evaluate sex-appropriate traits as more desirable.

Stereotypes in Behavior

So far, we have been concerned with the stereotyped expectations people hold for men and women, in terms of what they *think* men and women are like, or what their *ideal* man or woman is like. Earlier, we described a stereotype as a caricature-like set of expectations for behavior. Now it is time to consider the behavior itself. To what extent do real males and females differ along stereotyped lines in their behavior? Since stereotypes have been viewed as trait differences, our discussion centers around some of the more common sex-stereotyped traits: nurturance and dominance, cooperation and competition.

Nurturance and Dominance Nurturance and dominance are often mentioned as traits that are characteristic of women and men, respectively. Nurturance refers to the tendency to extend emotional support to other people, or occasionally, to animals. Dominance refers to the tendency to seek and maintain leadership roles, or in general, to influence other people. Several studies have shown that men and women are expected to behave along these stereotyped lines.

One study, for example, showed adherence to these stereotypes among students of both genders, aged 7–14 (Rothbaum, 1977). Students were asked to tell stories involving themes of dominance ("an adult who takes charge of things; someone who is the leader and tells others what to do") and nurturance ("an adult who is known as being kind to others, especially to those in need"). Although the researcher was a male and may have subtly influenced the results, both boys and girls used male characters more often in their dominance stories than in their nurturance stories. Interestingly, this sex-stereotyping tendency increased through age 14, the upper limit of the age range studied.

Although some studies indicate that college students rate the male stereotypes more highly, the set of characteristics embodied in these stereotypes is not unanimously praised. "These stereotypes reflect a conception of adulthood that is itself out of balance, favoring the separateness of the individual self over its connection to others and leaning more toward an autonomous life of work than toward the interdependence of love and care" (Gilligan, 1977, p. 482).

Behavioral Nurturance   Attempts to confirm the stereotyped difference in behavioral nurturance have yielded mixed results. Many studies of nurturance have not found any striking sex differences among children (e.g., Silverman, 1967; Staub, 1971), or among adolescents (e.g., Gruder & Cook, 1971; Isen, 1970).

Sandra Bem and her colleagues have attempted to evoke real life nurturance among undergraduates at Stanford. In one study, students were given an opportunity to be nurturant toward babies (Bem, Martyna, & Watson, 1976). The babies wore sex-neutral clothing, and were "assigned" one of two names, "David," or "Lisa," regardless of their actual gender. The undergraduates were observed in their interaction with the babies, and instances of kissing, nuzzling, holding the baby to the chest, smiling, and talking to the baby were noted. Male and female undergraduates did not differ in their nurturance toward the babies, but, interestingly enough, the attributed sex of the baby was responsible for differences in nurturance. The undergraduates were significantly more nurturant to the baby when they thought it was "David" than when they thought it was "Lisa." The researchers speculated that undergraduates may, on the whole, think that female infants are too "fragile" to tolerate much nuzzling, a notion that is also highly stereotyped.

The same research group designed another study to evoke sex differences in nurturance (Bem, Martyna, & Watson, 1976). Again, undergraduate men and women from Stanford participated, this time in what they thought was a study of "disclosure." Students always participated in same-sex pairs; one student was to be a "listener," and the other a "discloser." In fact, the "discloser" was always a paid confederate of the researchers because the "random" assignment of roles was rigged. After the confederate had disclosed some personal and emotional information, the students were asked to fill out questionnaires, and while they were doing so, the "discloser" admitted feeling better because of talking to the student, who was the real subject of the experiment. It was at this point that the researchers looked for signs of nurturance. Some of the students did not acknowledge the discloser's statement; this was a very low-nurturant response. Others looked at the discloser and made reassuring remarks, even suggesting that they get together again; this was a high-nurturant response. Overall, female undergraduates were more nurturant in this situation than were male undergraduates. Sex-role orientation of the students was also a factor in their nurturance. Students of both genders who were more masculine, as measured by the Sex-Role Inventory, were less nurturant (Bem, Martyna, & Watson, 1976).

Anthropologists have observed children in other cultures for the incidence of nurturance among boys and girls. In one careful cross-cultural study, children's nurturing behavior was observed over a period of 2 years in six very different cultures: Nyansongo, Kenya; Khalapur, India; Tarong, Philippines; Taira, Okinawa; Juxtlahuaca, Mexico; and Orchard Town, U.S.A. Girls in all six cultures were more likely to offer emotional support to another person than boys were (Whiting & Pope, 1974). Sex differences in nurturing were stronger among older children than among younger in these six cultures.

Research on nurturance, while not completely conclusive, suggests that there are behavioral differences by gender. Studies that show a sex difference almost always indicate more nurturance among girls than among boys. Furthermore, there appears to be an age effect: Sex differences in which girls are more nurturant are stronger in adolescence than are sex differences in childhood.

Dominance The cross-cultural study of six cultures that was just described revealed less striking sex differences in dominance than in nurturance. Younger boys were found to be more dominant than younger girls; however, among the older children, no sex differences emerged. Nevertheless, it is clear that in our own culture, dominance is stereotypically viewed as a masculine trait (e.g., Rothbaum, 1977; Urberg & Labouvie-Vief, 1976).

One technique for studying this stereotype is to look at patterns of dominance *in women* as a function of their sex-role orientations. If the stereotype is accurate, one would expect that women who are classified as having masculine sex-role orientations would be more dominant than other women. Such a study was done by Klein and Willerman (1979). Women in this study were first divided into four sex-role orientations: feminine, masculine, androgynous, and undifferentiated. They then participated in a problem-solving discussion with two other students who were actually confederates of the researchers. One of the problems for discussion used in this study is presented verbatim in Table 4-2.

During the course of the discussions, students were surreptitiously observed, and their behavior was recorded. The contents of their speech were analyzed for forceful and assertive statements; and the actual amount of time they spent talking was recorded. The researchers did find the predicted relationship between sex-role orientation and dominance: Feminine female students were less dominant than the masculine women. Furthermore, they were less dominant when the confederates were male than when they were female (Klein & Willerman, 1979).

Cooperation and Competition Stereotypes hold that women are more cooperative and men more competitive. Research provides some support for these stereotyped differences. For example, more than 2,400 young people participated in a self-assessment study of cooperation and competition. Each of these two traits was measured by three true–false items, which are presented in Table 4-3. Self-reported cooperation and competition both declined with

TABLE 4-2 **One of the Discussion Problems Used in the Study of Sex-Role Orientation and Dominance**	Imagine that our country is under threat of imminent nuclear attack. A man approaches you and asks you to make the following independent decision: There is a fallout shelter nearby that can accommodate 4 people, but there are 12 people vying to get in. Which 4 do you choose to go into the shelter? Here is all the information we have about the 12 people. 1. A 40-year-old male violinist who is a suspected narcotics pusher. 2. A 34-year-old male architect who is thought to be a homosexual. 3. A 26-year-old lawyer. 4. The lawyer's 24-year-old wife who has just gotten out of a mental institution. 5. A 75-year-old priest. 6. A 34-year-old retired prostitute who was so successful that she's been living off her annuities for 5 years. 7. A 20-year-old black militant. 8. A 23-year-old female graduate student who speaks publicly on the virtues of chastity. 9. A 28-year-old male who will only come into the shelter if he can bring his gun with him. 10. A 12-year-old girl who has a low IQ. 11. A 30-year-old MD who is an avowed bigot. 12. A high-school student.

Source: Klein & Willerman, 1979.

TABLE 4-3 True–False Items Used to Measure Cooperation and Competition	COOPERATION **T F** I like to help other students learn. **T F** I like to learn by working together with other students. **T F** Other students like to help me learn. COMPETITION **T F** I like to get better marks than other students do. **T F** I like to do better work than my friends. **T F** My friends want to do better work than me.

Source: Ahlgren & Johnson, 1979.

grade in school, but there were systematic sex differences at each grade level. Females were more cooperative at each grade, and males were more competitive at each grade, consistent with the stereotype (Ahlgren & Johnson, 1979).

Another study of competition confirmed the decline over grade level, from 5th to 12th grade. In addition, some situational determinants appeared to influence competitive behavior. Female students in 12th grade worked faster at mechanical tasks, such as assembling a doorbell or making gold necklaces with pliers, when they were competing with male students than when they were competing with other females or working alone. Sex of competitor had no effect on the scores of male students (Krauss, 1977).

Situational aspects of competition were also demonstrated with a study of college dating couples. Women did not do as well on a verbal task when they were competing against their dates as they did when they cooperated with their dates on the same task to score higher than another couple. This tendency was especially strong among women who held traditional sex-role attitudes (Peplau, 1976).

SEX-ROLE ORIENTATION

Sex-role orientation refers to the degree to which one incorporates into one's self-identity the traits associated with gender. Some of the characteristics and labels associated with the "masculine" and "feminine" principles are listed in Table 4-4.

The traditional view of sex-role orientation holds that masculinity and femininity are opposite sides of the same dimension. An individual who is highly feminine, in this view, is by definition low in masculinity. Indeed, as Constantinople (1973) pointed out, measures of masculinity and femininity have traditionally exploited this view, taking the measurement of one to be the opposite of the other. This traditional view has recently come into serious question. Masculinity and femininity are separate personality attributes that can vary independently of one another (Bem, 1974; Spence & Helmreich, 1978).

TABLE 4-4 Various Terms for the "Masculine" and "Feminine" Principles	MASCULINE PRINCIPLE	FEMININE PRINCIPLE
	Agency	Communion
	Instrumental	Expressive
	Impersonal	Interpersonal
	Initiation	Conservation
	Internal	External
	Inner-directed	Other-directed

Because masculine and feminine attributes are actually two separate dimensions, it is possible to measure them separately. One instrument used to measure them is the Sex-Role Inventory (Bem, 1974), which contains 60 items. Each item is checked on a seven-point scale according to how strongly it applies to one's self—from "never or almost never true" to "always or almost always true." The Sex-Role Inventory contains 20 masculine items, 20 feminine items, and 20 neutral items, yielding four sex-role orientations: masculine; feminine; androgynous (both highly masculine and highly feminine); and undifferentiated (low in both dimensions).

Sample items from another instrument used to measure sex-role orientation, the Personal Attributes Questionnaire (Spence & Helmreich, 1978), are presented in Table 4-5; Table 4-6 provides

TABLE 4-5
Sample Items from a Checklist of Personal Attributes

PERSONAL ATTRIBUTES QUESTIONNAIRE

The items below consist of pairs of characteristics, with the letters **A** through **E** in between. Each pair describes contradictory characteristics—that is, one cannot be both at the same time, such as very artistic and not at all artistic. The letters form a scale between the two extremes. Individuals are asked to choose a letter that describes where thay fall on the scale. For example, if they think they have no artistic ability, they would choose **A**. If they think they are pretty good artistically, they might choose **D.** If they are only medium, they might choose **C**, and so forth. (In all, there are 24 items on the Personal Attributes Questionnaire.)

Not at all artistic	**A B C D E**	Very artistic
Not at all aggressive	**A B C D E**	Very aggressive
Not at all excitable in a major crisis	**A B C D E**	Very excitable in a major crisis
Not at all helpful to others	**A B C D E**	Very helpful to others
Not at all aware of feelings of others	**A B C D E**	Very aware of feelings of others
Not at all self-confident	**A B C D E**	Very self-confident

Source: Spence & Helmreich, 1978.

TABLE 4-6
Percentage of College Students Who Are Masculine, Feminine, Androgynous, and Undifferentiated

MALE COLLEGE STUDENTS

		Masculinity (Agency)	
		Above median	Below median
Femininity (Communion)	Above median	Androgynous 32%	Feminine 8%
	Below median	Masculine 34%	Undifferentiated 25%

FEMALE COLLEGE STUDENTS

		Masculinity (Agency)	
		Above median	Below median
Femininity (Communion)	Above median	Androgynous 27%	Feminine 32%
	Below median	Masculine 14%	Undifferentiated 28%

Source: Spence & Helmreich, 1978. Copyright © 1978 by Janet T. Spence and Robert L. Helmreich.

percentages of college students who scored in each of the four categories of sex-role orientation. Two points should be made about the pattern of results for the 715 students in this study. First, a large number of students of both sexes scored in the two extreme categories, androgynous and undifferentiated. Second, the expected relationship between gender of subject and sex-role orientation is obtained. A higher percentage of males is classified as masculine than feminine; and a higher percentage of females is classified as feminine than masculine.

Masculinity and Femininity

Several terms have been proposed for the "masculine" and "feminine" principles. Masculinity and femininity are rather like a yin and yang of personality, essential elements both present to some degree in each human being. The "masculine" principle includes such elements as individualism, selfishness, alienation, denial, mastery, and autonomy. It is a highly instrumental orientation. The "feminine" principle includes elements of community, mystery, affirmation of feeling, participation, and other-directedness. It is an interpersonal orientation (Brown & Marks, 1969).

These orientations can be illustrated using examples from a study with college students. The students were given the names of various emotions, and told to "recall an occasion in your life which matches this emotion." One male student recalled this incident from his childhood that illustrated the emotion of joy.

After saving my allowance for a year, I was allowed to buy a .22 rifle. My father carefully taught me how to use the rifle, safety care, etc. Finally, I was allowed to go hunting myself. Several days of hunting went by, with no success, but I finally shot a rabbit. I was so delighted that I ran all the way home with the game. That night I dreamed of African safaris. (Carlson, 1971, p. 272)

This example, scored as reflecting the masculine principle, contains themes of self-assertion, autonomy, and achievement. In contrast, another male college student recalled the following childhood incident to illustrate his experience of joy.

My mother was returning to Los Angeles by train. I was standing between my aunt and uncle as we stood on the platform. My uncle was holding my arm. My mother stepped from the train. I was so happy to see her I could not control myself. I broke my uncle's grasp on my arm and ran to my mother, nearly toppling her with the force of my embrace. I felt happy, accepted, and very comfortable as my mother and I held each other close. Tears were in my mother's eyes. I do not recall if I was crying or not. I was very happy. (Carlson, 1971, p. 272)

The themes running through this example are togetherness, being loved and accepted, a sense of oneness and closeness. It, of course, was scored as illustrating the feminine principle.

Masculinity and femininity are attributes that can vary within both men and women, although there are some average differences in responding. In Carslon's (1971) study, from which the above examples are quoted, 60 percent of the males' responses were coded as masculine, compared to 40 percent of the females' responses. Within gender, 10 of 14 males were primarily masculine, while only 5 of 20 females were primarily masculine in sex-role orientation.

Sex-Typed and Cross-Sex Identity Females who score high on the feminine principle and men who score high on the masculine principle are said to be exhibiting sex-typed identity. Men and women who show the reverse pattern ("feminine" men and "masculine" women) are said to have a cross-sex identity.

Young people who have a sex-typed identity prefer sex-typed tasks and feel more comfortable when they are performing sex-typed tasks than cross-sex-typed tasks. For example, a group of introductory psychology students at the University of Texas at Austin, who had been classified by their sex-role orientation, rated their preference for and comfort in a dozen common tasks, some traditionally feminine, some traditionally masculine, and some neutral.

The tasks are listed in Table 4-7. Sex-typed students preferred the sex-typed tasks; this tendency was especially strong for the males (Helmreich, Spence, & Holahan, 1979).

A similar, but somewhat more direct, technique for measuring young people's responses to sex-typed and cross-sex-typed tasks was devised by Bem and Lenney (1976). They asked two dozen college students of each gender in three sex-role orientations (sex-typed, cross-sex-typed, and androgynous) if they would be willing to be photographed doing tasks which were sex-typed, cross-sex-typed, or neutral. The tasks, 20 in each group, included the ones listed in Table 4-7. Sex-typed students reported feeling more nervous, more peculiar, less likable, and less masculine (if male) or feminine (if female) on sex-inappropriate tasks than the students who were either androgynous or cross-sex-typed. Sex-typed male students experienced the greatest sex-role conflict when confronted with cross-sex-typed tasks (Bem & Lenney, 1976).

Another study (Heilbrun, 1976) extended these findings. College students were asked to deliberately fake masculine and feminine adjective checklists, in order to appear as psychologically healthy or unhealthy as possible. Table 4-8 shows that the prototype for psychological unhealthiness among college males was low masculine and low feminine scores. Among college women, psychological unhealthiness came about through a drastic reduction in femininity, with no appreciable effect on masculinity.

Sex differences arise in actual reports of psychological health

TABLE 4-7
Common Tasks
Classified as Masculine,
Feminine, or Neutral for
Preference Ratings of
College Students
	MASCULINE TASKS
	    Oil a squeaky hinge on a metal box
	    Nail two boards together
	    Tighten a screw
	    Attach fishing tackle to a line
	FEMININE TASKS
	    Iron a cloth napkin
	    Set a table
	    Measure out a cup of flour
	    Sew a button to a piece of fabric
	NEUTRAL TASKS
	    Play with a yo-yo
	    Sharpen a pencil
	    Peel an orange
	    Put a jigsaw puzzle together

Source: Helmreich, Spence, & Holahan, 1979. Copyright © 1979 by the American Psychological Association. Reprinted by permission of the publisher and author.

TABLE 4-8
Masculinity and Femininity in Faked Scores of Psychological Health

	FAKED TO BE AS PSYCHOLOGICALLY HEALTHY AS POSSIBLE		FAKED TO BE AS PSYCHOLOGICALLY UNHEALTHY AS POSSIBLE	
	MALES	FEMALES	MALES	FEMALES
Masculinity	56.5	52.7	43.3	51.3
Femininity	46.3	46.4	32.8	19.6

Source: Heilbrun, 1976. Copyright © 1976 by the American Psychological Association. Reprinted by permission of the publisher and author.

as well. High-school students in metropolitan Toronto, aged 13–20, filled out anonymous questionnaires about aspects of life stress, such as "concerns about the way I look," and "feeling awkward in social situations." Female students were more likely to disclose negative feelings than their male counterparts. These results are interpreted as demonstrating the sex differences in role expectations.

In adolescence, societal and familial expectations of females become more diffuse and sometimes full of contradictions and inconsistencies. The net result for females is a delay in evolving a definition of the self, and with this comes a sense of uncertainty and lack of control of their lives. (Burke & Weir, 1978, p. 287)

Father Absence and Cross-Sex Identity

A family constellation in which the father is absent provides an interesting case for examination of cross-sex identity in boys. In the Freudian Oedipal scenario, the father is necessary for sex-role consolidation in both boys and girls. Social-learning theory emphasizes the father as sex-role model for boys, with much less of an effect hypothesized for girls. Cognitive-developmental theory places least emphasis on the presence of a father figure for the development of gender identity, but argues that fathers are used as models for imitation once gender identity is established.

Effects of Father Absence on Boys   Research suggests that the effects of father absence may be less a function of the father's absence as such than of reasons for that absence and the child's age when the absence occurs. One study, for example, examined 29 2nd-grade boys whose fathers were present and 29 whose fathers were absent. Three aspects of sex-role were used: sex-role orientation, or awareness of being a boy or a girl; sex-role preference, defined by positive evaluation of sex-appropriate toys; and sex-role adoption, indicated by a test of the boy's actual masculine or feminine behavior. Father absence, in this study, affected only sex-role orientation. Reasons for father absence were examined separately. Boys whose fathers were present were more likely to draw a male figure when asked to "draw a person." Time of father's absence did not affect these results (Drake, & McDougall, 1977).

Male aggression is sometimes viewed as an attempt by boys, especially adolescents, to assert their masculinity; this has been referred to as "protest masculinity" (Whiting, 1965). Aggression among adolescent boys, in the form of acts of juvenile delinquency, might reflect sex-role identity conflict stemming from an early feminine identification and a later masculine identification. Such sex-role confusion could result from early father absence followed by presence of a father figure later in childhood. Harrington (1970) tested this hypothesis among 133 adolescent boys who appeared for help at mental-health agencies in upstate New York in 1966. These boys ranged in age from 13 to 19. Harrington found that neither sex-role identity scores nor behavior ratings for masculinity were related in any systematic fashion to father absence. He concluded that father absence is not a good predictor of sex-role behavior, at least in the United States.

Tests of ego identity using Erikson's model as a guide have yielded some effects for father absence. Male college students who grew up in fatherless homes scored lower on measures of Erikson's first six identity-crisis resolutions than did students from homes with a father or a stepfather (Oshman & Manosevitz, 1976). However, these effects are only peripherally related to sex-role development.

Although the effects of father absence on sex-role development appear to be less striking than expected, such effects have been reported. Sex-typed behavior of black and white boys between the ages of 9 and 12 was rated by male recreation directors in an urban center. Boys who lost their fathers early—through desertion, divorce, death, or illegitimacy—were rated as being less aggressive than either boys who lost their fathers after age 5 or boys who had fathers present in the home. Boys with no fathers, whether separation occurred early or late in childhood, were more dependent on peers than father-present boys (Hetherington, 1966).

A relationship between intellectual performance and father absence has also been demonstrated, at least for sons. Male undergraduates at the University of Virginia whose fathers were absent for a significant period during their upbringing had lower SAT scores than men who grew up in intact families. Young men who had stepfathers present had scores which fell between the other two groups (Chapman, 1977).

Effects of Father Absence on Girls   Father absence appears to have some effect on personality development in girls, but not on cognitive performance or on sex-role development per se. Hetherington (1972), who studied adolescent girls aged 13–17 at a community recreation center, concluded "that the effects of father absence on daughters appear during adolescence and are manifested mainly as an inability to interact appropriately with males, rather than in other deviations from appropriate sex typing or in interactions with females" (p. 323). One mother, a divorcée, described her daughter this way:

That kid is going to drive me over the hill. I'm at my wits' end. She was so good until the last few years then Pow! At eleven she really turned on. She went boy crazy. When she was only twelve I came home early from a movie and found her in bed with a young hood and she's been bouncing from bed to bed ever since. She doesn't seem to care who it is, she can't keep her hands off men. It isn't just boys her own age, when I have men friends here she kisses them when they come in the door and sits on their knees all in a very playful fashion but it happens to them all. Her uncle is a sixty-year-old priest and she even made a "ha ha" type pass at him. It almost scared him to death! (Hetherington, 1972, p. 322).

Overall, the effects of father absence on sex-role development, which the theoretical models might lead us to expect, are not confirmed by research. While it does appear that father absence has an effect on childhood and adolescent cognitive and personality development, specific effects on sex-role development have not been demonstrated convincingly.

In part, the lack of a relationship between father absence and sex-role development may underscore the findings on childhood similarities in sex-role behavior between the genders. It appears that boys and girls behave more nearly alike than many people have been led to believe. It is in adolescence, when hormonal pressures combine with adult-role expectations to differentiate the sexes, that a cluster of sex-typed behaviors begins to emerge.

Androgyny

Androgyny is based on the notion that masculine and feminine qualities do not necessarily preclude one another (Constantinople, 1973; Bem, 1974; Spence & Helmreich, 1978). Individuals who score high on both masculinity and femininity are described as androgynous. Several researchers have suggested that androgynous men and women are more psychologically healthy than students in any other sex-role orientation. For example, high-school students who were androgynous in their responses to questions about sex-role orientation had higher self-esteem than students who were high on masculinity alone or who were high on femininity alone (Spence & Helmreich, 1978). The relationship between self-esteem and androgyny appears to be particularly strong for women (Schiff & Koopman, 1978).

Androgyny tends to increase with age among males. In a cross-sectional study of androgyny, males and females, aged 13–60, were given the Sex-Role Inventory. There were no striking age differences in the percentages of people classified as sex-typed, as Figure 4-1 shows; however, the percentage of males classified as androgynous increased dramatically (Hyde & Phillis, 1979). One interpretation of these data is that rigid sex-typing decreases over the life cycle for males (Fischer & Narus, 1981). Furthermore, our cultural notions of masculinity may tap a youthful set of attributes, such as "athletic" and "ambitious." About a third of students of both sexes in high school and college are androgynous (Bem, 1975; Spence & Helmreich, 1978).

Culture and Sex-Role Orientation

Margaret Mead (1949) placed the problem we have been discussing in a cross-cultural perspective.

In any human group it is possible to arrange men and women on a scale in such a way that between a most masculine group and a most feminine group

FIGURE 4-1
Age changes in sex-typed identity and androgyny. There are no striking gender differences in percentages of people classified as sex-typed; however, the percentage of males classified as androgynous increases with age, while the percentage of females classified as androgynous decreases with age.

(From Hyde & Phillis, 1979.)

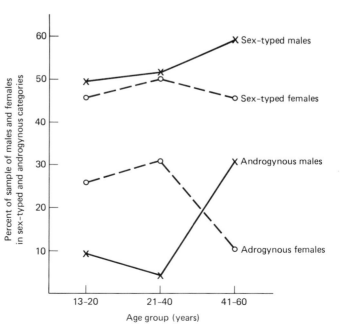

there will be others who seem to fall in the middle, to display fewer of the pronounced physical features that are more characteristic of one sex than of the others. (p. 141)

So the child, experiencing itself, is forced to reject such parts of its particular biological inheritance as conflict sharply with the sex stereotype of its culture. (p. 148)

Mead (1935) found three cultural groups that have different sex stereotypes from those found in the United States. Among the Arapesh, few sex differences were noted. Both men and women were nonaggressive and sensitive, with personality types similar to those described above as exhibiting a feminine sex-role orientation. The Mundugamor people, on the other hand, were ruthless and unpleasant, an exaggerated example of the masculine orientation. Sex differences were found among the Tchambuli people, but the stereotypes were the reverse of those we have come to expect. The women were the dominant, "masculine" types, while the men were more emotional, "feminine" types.

Major cultural differences such as those reported by Mead are instructive. Variations from our own cultural pattern place greater emphasis on the influence of socialization practices for the development of sex differences. Notice that this argument does not require that we reject the influence of biological factors, such as genetic and hormonal influences. Such factors may still exert a strong influence, but one that is overshadowed by cultural expectations.

For example, there is a great deal of support for the hypothesis that sex differences in aggression are strongly influenced by biological factors (Maccoby & Jacklin, 1974). Socialization practices with respect to aggression may still determine, to a large extent, the behavioral expression of aggressive behavior. Boys are much more aggressive among the Yąnomamö, an Indian group living in the rain forests of South America, than in our own culture. Child-rearing practices help to enhance Yąnomamö boys' aggressive behavior.

The boys alone are treated with considerable indulgence by their fathers from an early age. Thus, the distinction between male and female status develops early in the socialization process, and the boys are quick to learn their favored position with respect to girls. They are encouraged to be "fierce" and are rarely punished by their parents for inflicting blows on them or on the hapless girls in the village. (Chagnon, 1968, p. 84)

Sex differences were examined in various social groups around the world by carefully coding references to "strength of socialization from age 4 or 5 years until shortly before puberty" (Barry, Bacon, & Child, 1957, p. 327). Aspects rated on a seven-point scale included responsibility, nurturance, obedience, achievement, and self-reliance. As can be seen in Table 4-9, socialization of girls strongly fostered nurturance, while socialization of boys emphasized achievement and self-reliance. These data indicate that there is some cross-cultural consistency in the behavioral attributes that are emphasized for each sex. At the same time, cultural diversity in sex-typing does exist. For each category of behavior, several cultures emphasize no differential socialization by gender.

Within our own culture, the dominant socialization themes for girls are those directed at attributes in the "feminine" cluster; an emphasis on interpersonal relationships and physical affection characterizes this cluster. For boys, the aim of sex-role socialization is the "masculine" cluster, including achievement and competition combined with controlled affection (Block, 1973).

Socialization of affectionate behavior will serve as an example of sex-typing in our culture. Children learn about expression of affection through several sources, including observation of their parents, and in particular, through their own interactions with their parents. Fathers and mothers were observed in interactions with their children in a child-care center. Boys experienced less interaction with both parents than girls did. Affection shown in father–son dyads was particularly low (Noller, 1978).

Adolescents view themselves as having personality characteristics congruent with sex-role stereotypes. Across the age range from 12 to 19 years, girls reported themselves to be more sociable, nurturant, conscientious, and help-seeking than boys. The sex difference in reported characteristics was combined with a developmental increase for both sexes in achievement, conscientiousness, and rule-boundedness (Noller, 1978). The developmental increase strongly suggests a socialization factor.

TABLE 4-9
Cross-Cultural Incidence of Socialization Practices by Gender

	NUMBER OF SOCIETIES	PERCENT OF CULTURES WITH EVIDENCE OF SOCIALIZATION PRACTICES IN THE DIRECTION OF		
		GIRLS	BOYS	NEITHER
Nurturance	33	82%	0%	18%
Obedience	69	35	3	62
Responsibility	84	61	11	28
Achievement	31	3	87	10
Self-Reliance	82	0	85	15

Source: Barry, Bacon, & Child, 1957. Copyright © 1957 by the American Psychological Association. Reprinted by permission of the publisher and author.

Parental Influences on Sex-Role Orientation

Many agents of socialization, particularly parents, have a potential for affecting a child's sex-role development. Major theories of sex-role socialization emphasize the important part played by parents. Regardless of theoretical orientation, most researchers believe that sex-role behavior develops at least in part through observation and imitation. Children are encouraged to imitate their same-sex parents, receiving approval for doing so. Children pick up models of behavior to imitate through observation. They observe what their same-sex parents do and say, and later imitate this modelled behavior in play and fantasy.

In 1979, I observed a family in the natural setting of their home, and saw some of these socialization pressures at work. The family included a 4½-year-old boy, whose favorite television program was the then popular "Donny and Marie" show. The little boy, Jared, liked to play with dolls, and had nagged his parents into getting him a Donny-and-Marie doll set for Christmas. His parents, however, thought that dolls were inappropriate for a little boy. To discourage his interest in dolls they told him that playing with dolls was "silly" for a boy. They did not diminish his interest in dolls; but he felt the disapproval in their reaction. When he told me what he had received for Christmas, he added, "you probably think I'm silly."

This type of family interaction, over time, presumably leads to sex-typed behavior. Boys and girls form a notion of sex-role expectations, and adopt behavior in accordance with those expectations in order to avoid disapproval and to receive positive reactions from others. As children grow older, sex-role expectations are communicated in the larger society of the peer group and the school. The same mechanisms of gaining positive reactions and avoiding disapproval guide them into behavior which matches the sex-role expectations which they perceive.

Understanding of Sex-Role Orientations   Sex-role concepts and attitudes undergo regular changes in accordance with the child's cognitive growth, according to cognitive-developmental theorists. Lawrence Kohlberg (1966) summarized the approach in this way:

Our theory, then, is cognitive in that it stresses the active nature of the child's thought as he organizes his role perceptions and role learning around his basic conceptions of his body and his world. (p. 83)

Young children do not fully understand the constancy of gender until they have mastered some of the other constancies of perceptual and cognitive organization between the ages of 4 and 6. A child's understanding that a quantity of liquid remains the same when it is poured from a bowl into a glass requires the cognitive ability to untangle reversible transformations. Understanding that some states such as gender, are irreversible, is presumably linked to this cognitive accomplishment.

Kohlberg (1966) quoted a 4-year-old boy, Jimmy, who had not mastered the notion of sex-role identity.

Johnny: *I'm going to be an airplane builder when I grow up.*

Jimmy: *When I grow up, I'll be a Mommy.*

Johnny: *No, you can't be a Mommy. You have to be a Daddy.*

Jimmy: *No, I'm going to be a Mommy.*

Johnny: *No, you're not a girl, you can't be a Mommy.*

Jimmy: *Yes, I can. (p. 95)*

Jimmy's problem is a cognitive one. He must untangle the labels that are ordinarily applied to people and their relationship to arbitrariness. A person's name is arbitrary, but it does not change over time. Age is not arbitrary, yet it does change from year to year. Gender is neither arbitrary nor changeable. Until a child has mastered these relationships, he may be confused about sex-role issues and expectations. Once the child has mastered the gender classification, he or she will begin to match behavior to sex-role expectations that are perceived in the surrounding world.

Cultural Expectations for Gender Roles

The traditional view of masculinity and femininity, as we have suggested, was tied to a harsh view of sex-role expectations. Adolescent boys were expected to orient themselves toward a future work role, and an instrumental, active approach to the future. Adolescent girls were expected to aspire to the interpersonal goals of wifehood and motherhood, with less emphasis on career. Douvan and Adelson, two influential researchers in the field of adolescent psychological development, conducted a major study on these sex-role orientations in the 1950s. They described the sex-role pressures on adolescents as follows:

There is no inherent conflict for the man between work and realization of his sex role in marriage and parenthood, but there is for the woman. . . . We should point out in this connection that the boy has different problems with activity–passivity because the culture allows him virtually no choice. The boy must choose activity, no matter what the personal cost, or be suspected and disapproved by his society. Nonetheless, the approved path for the boy is at least clear and unambiguous, whereas the girl's choice or solution is always something of an individual invention, and seems never to carry complete approval. (Douvan & Adelson, 1966, pp. 34–35)

In a high-school vocational-training class, a young woman learns how to operate a lathe. The traditional view that young women should not be strongly committed to a work role outside the home has diminished in recent years, providing many young women with the opportunity to train for occupations that were formerly sex-restricted.

(Photo copyright © 1981 by S. Oristaglio/Photo Researchers, Inc.)

Douvan and Adelson may have elicited sex differences on the instrumental–interpersonal focus because of differences in the form of their interviews for use with boys versus girls. Both boys and girls were asked, "What are the things you'll have to decide or make up your mind about in the next few years?" Girls were subsequently asked about jobs only if they mentioned jobs as one of these things. Boys, on the other hand, were asked about jobs whether they mentioned them or not. In addition, only girls' forms included probe questions on marriage:

"Could you tell me a little about the kind of person you'd like to marry?"

"What kind of work would you like your husband to do?"

Perhaps the researchers would have concluded that the boy's focus was more interpersonal if he had been asked questions about future marriage plans. Indeed, Spence and Helmreich (1978) found that somewhat more males (17 percent) than females (14 percent) saw marriage as their most important goal. Spence and Helmreich distinguished between sex-role behaviors and psychological attributes of the person doing the behaving. Although the behavior of an adolescent male may match perfectly the sex-role stereotype for his gender, his personality orientation may be much more congruent with the feminine principle.

Female Sex-Role Strain   Sex-role expectations are more ambiguous for girls than they are for boys. Both boys and girls are expected to meet the demands for school achievement, and family pressures for achievement are more or less equal for sons and daughters. A cultural contradiction, as Mirra Komarovsky (1946) called it, appears when girls in late adolescence and early adulthood are expected to make achievement aspirations secondary to their goals for wifehood and motherhood. In Chapter 3, we saw that the pattern of issues on which identity is built may be different for women than it is for men. One might, therefore, expect adolescents to differ on measures of their self-concept.

Self-concept, like self-identity, is a tricky and elusive research issue because it involves a private, subjective evaluation of the adolescent experience. The technique most often used to measure self-concept is an adjective checklist, like the one presented in Table 4-9. Aspects of the person's self-view are rated using the items on the list. Psychologists assume that the pattern of ratings indicates a self-evaluation in positive or negative terms.

This technique has yielded some sex differences in self-concept by the late adolescent years. Male and female college students in their freshman and senior years, as well as graduate students, rated their "self" and "ideal" intelligence scores (Bailey & Minor, 1976). Women at each grade level showed a greater discrepancy between "self" and "ideal" ratings than men did.

Measures of self-concept begin to diverge for men and women during the college years, a phenomenon that appears to be related to other aspects of identity development. In Erikson's formulation, identity development is in part defined by a perception of the self as having continuity across time and across situations. Cultural ambiguities in sex-role demands, which are greater for women than for men, would be expected to lead to differences in self-concept as identity issues become more salient in late adolescence. For example, men should view themselves in a consistent manner in a variety of situations, while women should view themselves differently, depending on perceived role demands in a given situation. Heilbrun (1964) found some support for this view. Undergraduates at the University of Iowa (54 men and 61 women) were asked to rate themselves on an adjective checklist in eight different interpersonal situations. For example, they rated themselves when with "someone in whom sexually interested," or with "a close male friend," or with "an employer." A separate checklist determined the extent to which they matched the stereotyped views of masculinity or femininity. There was a direct relationship between masculinity and role consistency for these college men: The more masculine men saw themselves as more consistent across situations. Among women, the pattern was less straightforward. Women who rated themselves as low or high in femininity also viewed themselves as more consistent. The women who were moderate in their femininity, however, showed less role consistency.

Erikson's model of development helps to interpret these data. In late adolescence, issues of identity are important in several content areas, including sex-role conceptions. Males who have strong sex-typed identities view themselves as consistent across situations; cultural expectations are more clear-cut for them. Female college students experience more ambiguous role demands, which can lead to confusion in self-concept. This may be especially true for women whose sex-role commitment is neither masculine nor highly feminine.

The discussion of gender-role expectations indicates that age differences are important in sex-role behaviors. Adolescents appear to be more stereotyped in their views of sex-typed behaviors for men and for women than any other age groups. Furthermore, behaviors such as nurturance and competition show systematic changes with age. Cultural contradictions in sex-role expectations for women become acutely pronounced during adolescence, when girls must consolidate their sex-role identities with their occupational identities. Adolescence, therefore, appears to be a critical time in the development of sex-role behaviors. The developmental history of sex-typing demands closer scrutiny.

DEVELOPMENTAL HISTORY OF SEX DIFFERENCES IN BEHAVIOR

Girls and boys are fairly similar in their interests and behavior through most of childhood, until early adolescence. In the most comprehensive review of sex differences in behavior to date, Maccoby and Jacklin (1974) surveyed representative research in perception, intellectual performance, achievement, and social behavior across the life span. Some areas of behavior, most notably aggressive behavior, yield consistent sex differences from childhood on; boys appear to be more aggressive than girls at all ages studied. Many of the stereotyped expectations for sex differences in behavior, however, appear to be unfounded. Furthermore, in many of the areas for which there is evidence for sex differences, consistent results do not appear until adolescence. Adolescence is an important age for consolidation of sex differences, for a combination of reasons. Hormonal changes accompanying puberty may be responsible for some of the differences that emerge in adolescence. More importantly, adolescence is the age for clarification of identity, as we saw in Chapter 3. Sex-role identity is one of the central issues in the process of identity development, and contributes to emerging gender differences in behavior at adolescence.

For good or ill, adult gender roles are construed differently by most adolescents growing up in American society. Most young people assume that they will some day marry and have children. The adult male role includes the assumption that he will "head" the family, in the sense of becoming its chief economic provider. The adult female role includes the assumption, on the part of most people, that she will assume primary responsibility for child care and supervision, and that she will oversee the running of the household. Although it is difficult to classify these expectations about adult behavior as either roles or stereotypes, they are commonly held assumptions about male and female behavior. Like the sex-role stereotypes reviewed earlier, there is considerable agreement about these expectations among adolescents, who are at a point in their life cycles when they must make tentative plans about the character of their own adulthood.

The fact that adolescence is such an important time in the life cycle for the development of sex differences makes it an appealing period for study. Several questions are important as they relate to the development of such differences in adolescence. Are differences in behavior by gender related in any systematic way to hormonal secretions? Is any genetic influence apparent? To what extent are the expectations of the cultural group related to gender differences in behavior? Answers to all of these questions are incomplete at this point; however, examination of some of the major areas of research yields intriguing clues for untangling the confusion about sex differences in behavior.

The areas of psychological behavior that have been examined for sex differences are many and varied. Maccoby and Jacklin's review covered 86 major areas of research, from achievement demands to visual afterimages and illusions. It would be impossible to cover all of these areas of research in one chapter. However, we can examine some of the possible influences on sex differences in one area of research where differences are well documented. For our purposes, we have chosen an area of behavior related to intellectual functioning in which boys and girls begin to diverge in adolescence. This area of intellectual functioning concerns spatial ability.

SPATIAL ABILITY

Some sex differences in intellectual functioning, which begin to appear consistently only in adolescence, are well documented. Boys and girls from preschool to early adolescence, for example, perform at similar levels on most measures of verbal ability. Beginning around age 11, however, girls' verbal superiority is demonstrated with increasing consistency (Maccoby & Jacklin, 1974). In a similar fashion, boys and girls do not differ on spatial tasks throughout childhood. Beginning in adolescence, boys show increasing superiority on spatial tasks and on mathematical skills (Maccoby & Jacklin, 1974; McGee, 1979). In one study, male and female 8th graders were similar in their attitudes toward math; but by 11th grade, males performed significantly better than females (Sherman, 1980).

Figure 4-2 is a schematic representation of the magnitude of the differences in spatial ability from childhood through early adulthood. The differentiation of spatial ability by gender appears to emerge in early adolescence. Maccoby and Jacklin (1974) summarized the age trend in spatial and visual tasks as follows: "The male advantage emerges in early adolescence and is maintained in adulthood for both kinds of tasks" (p. 94).

Measures of Spatial Ability

Several types of tasks exist for measuring spatial ability. Two of the most commonly used tasks are the rod-and-frame test and the embedded-figures test, which are illustrated in Figure 4-3.

These tests require a subject to overcome confusing information provided by the surrounding field. In the rod-and-frame test, a luminous rod must be oriented vertically with respect to the subject and the "real" vertical, rather than with respect to a surrounding luminous frame. The embedded-figures test requires the subject to find line drawings embedded in a context of confusing and superfluous lines. Because these tests require the subject to ignore an irrelevant context, they are sometimes said to measure an element of cognitive style called *field independence*. Field-independent people are presumably able to perform the tasks well because they are not overly confused by the surrounding context, or "field."

FIGURE 4-2
Schematic representation of the magnitude of sex differences in spatial ability at various stages during the life cycle.

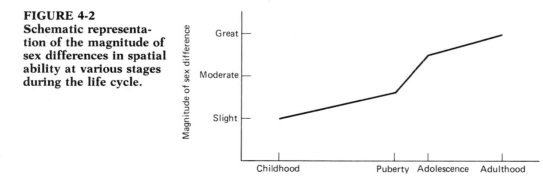

FIGURE 4-3
The rod-and-frame test and the embedded-figures test. (a) In the rod-and-frame test, the rod must be oriented to the "true" vertical, irrespective of the orientation of the surrounding frame. (b) An example of one of the embedded figures in the embedded-figures test. The "A" figure is embedded in the corresponding "B" pattern, as shown by the heavy-lined area.

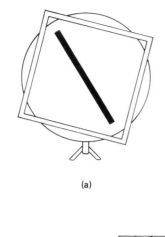

(a)

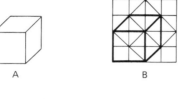

A   B

(b)

Spatial ability is also measured by other types of tasks. For example, one of the major IQ tests, the Wechsler intelligence test, contains block-design items. An individual is shown a pattern that must be reproduced using a set of cubes with differently painted surfaces.

One simple test of spatial ability also taps the individual's understanding of the physical world. This test is the water-level problem designed to show age differences in physical understanding (Piaget & Inhelder, 1948/1967). In this test, illustrated in Figure 4-4, an individual must indicate the water level in bottles turned at sev-

FIGURE 4-4
The water-level problem. Imagine that the drawings represent two bottles on a table. Draw the water line in each of the bottles to represent how it would look if half-filled with water.

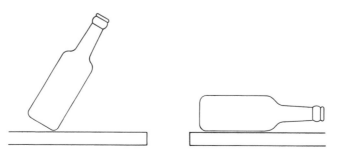

Rubik's cube, a popular puzzle, requires spatial ability for solution. Like Piaget's water-level problem, mastering Rubik's cube depends heavily on visualization.

(Ideal Toy Corporation)

eral angles. Performance on the test is easiest when the bottle is upright; it is most difficult when the bottle is at an oblique angle, as it would be if turned to the one-o'clock position.

Spatial ability, as a general category of cognitive performance, probably consists of two related abilities, visualization and orientation (McGee, 1979). Visualization involves the ability to mentally rotate objects and includes mental manipulation. The water-level problem and some common puzzles, such as Rubik's cube, depend heavily on visualization. Orientation, on the other hand, is the ability to orient with respect to one's body and to remain unconfused by irrelevant information. The rod-and-frame test and the embedded-figures test require orientation abilities for their solution. These somewhat separate abilities are collectively known as *spatial ability*.

Sex and Age Differences in Spatial Ability   Differences in performance on these tests by gender are not striking until about the time of puberty. Adolescent males, however, show consistently better performance on these items than adolescent females (Witkin, Goodenough, & Karp, 1967; Saarni, 1973; and Nash, 1975).

The trend in sex differences can be illustrated with the water-level problem. In one study, students from nursery school to college were given a version of the water-level problem. The results are illustrated in Figure 4-5, which shows that boys made somewhat fewer errors than girls even in childhood, but the differences remained slight until performance began to diverge in 6th grade. The researchers described their results this way:

Boys showed orderly improvement in performance with increasing age such that by the seventh or eighth grade they performed as well as college men. The course of development for girls, however, was much less clear and even by college age, girls as a group were doing no better than children many years younger. (Thomas & Jamison, 1975, p. 36)

Research using the other tasks show similar age trends (e.g., Liben, 1978; Witkin et al., 1967). Age differentiation of spatial performance by gender roughly coincides with puberty, when hormonal changes begin to exert their greatest influences in sexual dimorphism.

Spatial Ability and Hormonal Influences

Some research indicates a relationship between hormonal action and spatial ability. More specifically, the better performance of

FIGURE 4-5
Age and sex differences in performance on the water-level problem.

(Reprint from "On the Acquisition of Understanding that Still Water is Horizontal" from *Merrill-Palmer Quarterly*, Volume 21, No. 1, 1975 by Hoben Thomas and Wesley Jamison by permission of the Wayne State University Press. Copyright © 1975 by the Wayne State University Press.)

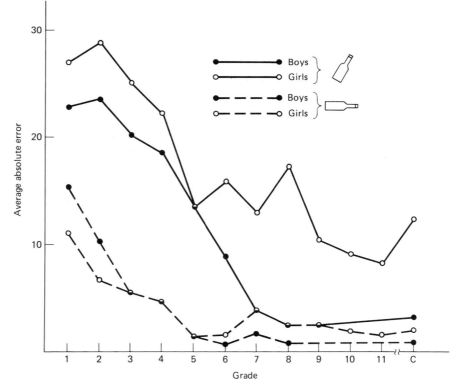

adolescent males is thought to result from differential influences of the male and female hormones. Consider, for example, the results from a longitudinal study of spatial ability in which data were also available on the development of secondary-sex characteristics, such as genital and breast development (Petersen, 1976).

Data from the files of the Fels longitudinal study (one of the famous comprehensive studies of development from childhood into adulthood) included scores on the Wechsler block-design task. Also available were nude photographs for 35 male and 40 female adolescents who took the tests at ages 13, 16, and 18. Hormonal levels were inferred from the relative development of secondary-sex characteristics rated from the nude photos. As expected, a greater sex-hormone action was found as age increased. Scores on the spatial-ability task increased over the age range for both genders, but males outperformed the females at each age (Figure 4-6).

Sex differences in spatial ability scores were significant at each age. Furthermore, by age 18, girls who were rated as having a more "masculine" body shape from their nude photographs scored higher on the spatial tasks.

The precise nature of hormone action is not clearly understood at this time. The fact that more masculine-appearing girls had higher scores on the spatial task suggests that androgen action

FIGURE 4-6
Spatial ability as compared to adolescent development for males (M) and females (F), aged 13–18.

(From Petersen, 1976.)

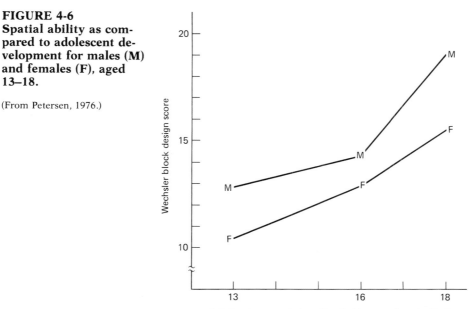

Age (in years, as an index of level of hormonal production)

might influence spatial ability. Other studies indicate that this is not the case for boys, however. High levels of androgens, which are "male" hormones, are actually associated with *lower* spatial scores in boys (e.g., Broverman, Klaiber, Kobayashi, & Vogel, 1968; Maccoby & Jacklin, 1974).

Rate of Physical Growth Rate of physical growth may itself be a determinant of behavioral sex differences. As we saw in Chapter 2, girls experience the peak growth in height about 2 years earlier than boys. In a study of both spatial and verbal abilities, patterns of physical maturation were examined in relation to sex differences in cognition (Waber, 1977). Several measures were obtained for early and late maturing boys and girls at two grade levels (5th and 8th for girls, 8th and 10th for boys). First of all, stage of sexual development was rated during physical examinations. Overall IQ measures were also obtained. Spatial abilities were measured by the Wechsler block-design task and by the embedded-figures test; verbal ability was measured with "word fluency" tests. Performance on these cognitive tasks was then examined as a function of rate of physical maturation. Late-maturing adolescents of both sexes did better on the spatial tasks than they did on the verbal tasks. Just the reverse pattern was found among early-maturing adolescents. These data suggest that patterns of cognitive ability vary systematically with rate of maturation; since girls ordinarily mature earlier than boys, their greater verbal abilities and poorer spatial abilities reflect this maturational difference (Waber, 1977).

So far this pattern of data is descriptive. Boys do better on spatial tasks and girls do better on verbal tasks. Boys mature later than girls, on the average. One interpretation of this descriptive pattern, which is consistent with the data, postulates that gonadal steroids—sex hormones produced by the ovaries and testes—differentially affect brain development depending on the point at which they are produced and released into the bloodstream. Gonadal steroids that reach the brain relatively early in adolescent development may influence the brain to develop its verbal centers more extensively than its spatial center.

Male high-school students who perform better on the "feminine" repetitive spatial tasks were found to have wider shoulders, more body hair, and more facial hair (Broverman, Broverman, Vogel, Palmer, & Klaiber, 1964). The hairier, more masculinized 16-year-olds in this study are probably earlier maturers than their less hairy, less repetitive peers. Their pattern of spatial task performance is therefore associated with earlier maturation; this is the set of events which holds for most adolescent girls.

Brain Lateralization

The left hemisphere of the brain contains the primary verbal centers in most people, and may be "primed" by early action of gonadal steroids; the right hemisphere, which is the spatial-ability center among most people, may be "primed" by later action of gonadal steroids. Sex differences in cognitive abilities, in this view, are the result of hemispheric lateralization produced through the mediation of hormonal action. Hormonal action, in turn, results in part from the maturation timetable, which itself varies systematically by sex.

Because the right hemisphere of the brain is primarily responsible for spatial processing, individuals who are differentially lateralized for right-hemisphere dominance would be expected to perform better on spatial tasks. One simple method for obtaining a crude measure of brain hemispheric lateralization is to ask people questions and record the direction of their gazes while they think of answers (Ray, Georgiou, & Ravizza, 1979). Looking to the left while thinking of answers generally indicates a cognitive style mediated by the right (or spatial) hemisphere of the brain. Looking to the right generally indicates a cognitive style mediated by the left (or verbal) hemisphere (Tucker & Suib, 1978).

Brain lateralization of students in introductory psychology classes was assessed using this method. Women who solved the water-level task were more likely to be left-lookers, which indicates a right-hemisphere lateralization. This relationship did not hold for male students, however (Ray et al., 1979).

Brain lateralization for spatial abilities is presumably independent of hemispheric dominance in the brain. The majority of both boys and girls are left-hemispheric dominant, as seen by the fact that the majority of both sexes are right-handed.

However, current research on spatial processing suggests that males have spatial abilities more differentially localized in the right hemisphere than females do, and this difference is reflected in their better performance on spatial tasks (e.g., Kimura, 1969; McGee, 1979). Since adolescence is the time when the greatest divergence in scores of males and females is obtained on spatial tasks, brain lateralization for spatial ability might also undergo shifts following puberty. Brain lateralization is one of the hypotheses currently receiving wide attention for explaining sex differences in spatial ability (McGee, 1979).

Spatial Ability and Genetic Influences

Evidence for hormonal influence on spatial ability does not rule out other influences. In fact, some evidence in favor of a genetic component to spatial ability also exists. The so-called sex-linked traits are easiest to demonstrate using data on similarity of performance by different degrees of familial relationship, such as father–daughter correlations. Recall that each human being has 23 pairs of chromosomes, the hereditary units which carry genes. Each biological parent contributes 23 chromosomes at fertilization. One pair of chromosomes contains the genetic information for gender differentiation; this chromosome pair is designated the XX pair for females and the XY pair for males.

As far as is known, the Y-chromosome carries only information relevant to maleness, such as the testis-differentiating factor. The X-chromosome, however, contains information for several traits other than femaleness, and these are designated the sex-linked traits. Among sex-linked traits are color-blindness, baldness, and hemophilia. Even though females may carry genes for the negative expression of these traits on one X-chromosome, they still have another X-chromosome carrying "positive" information to override the expression of the trait. Males, on the other hand, are likely to show full expression of any sex-linked trait because there is no overriding information contained on the Y-chromosome (Lehrke, 1972).

Genetic influences alone cannot account for the fact that sex differences in spatial ability begin to appear consistently only in adolescence. The genetic information is present at birth and might be expected to yield sex differences in childhood as well. In combination with the results of studies of hormonal influences, however, the research on sex differences in spatial ability lead to the following conclusions. Consistent sex differences in spatial ability manifest themselves in early adolescence and continue into adulthood. Sex-linked genetic influences may be important in spatial ability, in combination with hormonal factors. It appears that timing of maturation in adolescence is implicated in spatial ability; early maturation leads to relatively poorer performance on tasks with a component of field independence. Early maturation is, of course, the norm for adolescent girls in comparison to boys.

Spatial Ability and Differential Socialization

Differential socialization might account for some of the observed differences between males and females in spatial ability. Schools, parents, and other agents of socialization probably influence the interests of boys and girls on a variety of intellectual dimensions, including spatial ability. Girls, for example, might be discouraged from displaying much interest in spatial and mathematical problems and puzzles because it is not considered "feminine."

Differential socialization suggests a hypothesis about the development of spatial abilities in girls: "If sex role measures reflect past experiences, then masculine girls should have had experiences like those of most boys that facilitate performance on spatial tasks and other masculine sex-typed activities" (Signorella & Jamison, 1978, p. 690). Adolescent girls in 8th grade provide partial support for this notion. These girls were given both the embedded-figures test and the Sex-Role Inventory. Those who scored high in masculine sex-role orientation also did better on the embedded-figures test, which measures spatial ability (Signorella & Jamison, 1978).

Socialization practices that have been studied cross-culturally also provide evidence consistent with this notion. Comparisons of cultures that differ in the socialization of autonomy suggest that higher spatial ability scores are obtained by children who are given more autonomy (Berry, 1966; MacArthur, 1967). In our own culture, boys are allowed more expression of autonomy than girls are (Douvan & Adelson, 1966), and boys may indirectly reap the benefit of advanced spatial ability relative to girls.

Further evidence for a socialization contribution to the sex difference in spatial ability is derived from research on father absence. Several studies have shown that males score higher on quantitative portions of standard aptitude tests, such as the SAT, than women do (e.g., Bieri, Bradburn, & Galinsky, 1958). To the extent that this sex difference is a product of observational learning and socialization within the home, males whose fathers were absent for a significant portion of their childhoods would be expected to show lower performance on SAT quantitative tests. This pattern has in fact been demonstrated among college males at Harvard (Carlsmith, 1973) and the University of Virginia (Chapman, 1977).

BEYOND SEX ROLES

Research indicates that for many behaviors, adolescence is the critical time for consolidation of sex differences. Intellectual competencies, such as spatial and verbal ability, and personality factors, such as self-concept, follow this developmental pattern. It is important to reiterate that sex differences, when they are observed, are average differences in performance of men and women. There are large areas of overlap in the behavior of males and females despite arithmetical means that differ statistically. Furthermore, research on sex differences is not always as rigorous or as representative as we might hope. Of the 298 studies of sex differences reported in consecutive issues of one journal *(Journal of Abnormal and Social Psychology)*, 38 percent of the studies tested only male subjects, and 5 percent tested only female subjects. In the 108 studies with both male and female subjects, there were statistical tests of sex differences in only 32 of them, with significant differences obtained in just 22 studies, less than 10 percent of the total group (Carlson & Carlson, 1960).

Debates about the source of sex differences in behavior have gone on for years, sometimes taking on the character of battles. One of the reviews of psychological sex differences, in fact, was titled *The Longest War* (Tavris & Offir, 1977). It seems clear that there is no single source of sex differences; behavior is under the influence of many factors, and we have isolated a few of the important ones. Spatial ability, for example, seems clearly under the influence of genetic and hormonal factors. We can also be fairly certain from cross-cultural research that cultural expectations play a role in eliciting different patterns of behavior from males and females. All of the major theoretical orientations in psychology emphasize the important role played by parents in the socialization of sex differences. Research on the nature of parental influence leads to no clear and concise conclusion, however. Parents certainly provide models for their children—some good and some bad. It seems irrefutable that children often imitate the behavior and attitudes of their parents, for whatever reasons. And yet, when the father is missing from the family constellation, there are few consistent effects on the sex-role development of either sons or daughters.

Finally, what are we to make of the existence of sex roles, of stereotypes of masculinity and femininity? We need to move away from the notion that masculinity is the opposite of femininity. Rather, we should recognize the existence of two separate principles: the feminine-interpersonal-communion principle and the masculine-instrumental-agency principle. Both of these attributes can logically exist within the same individual, resulting in a state of psychological androgyny. Already there is evidence that individuals who are psychologically androgynous have higher levels of self-esteem and in general seem happier with themselves.

On a more global level, there is no longer a compelling economic reason to differentiate the adult roles of men and women. One should expect pronounced sex differences in behavior when a value is placed on superior strength of adult males for securing food and defending the family unit against attack (Barry, Bacon, & Child, 1957). A highly technological society does not need to make this distinction, and changes in the societal structure should eventually lead to less and less differentiation of sex roles—to a greater degree of psychological androgyny.

Adolescence is a period of particular vulnerability with respect to sex differences (Rosenkrantz et al., 1968; Signorella & Jamison, 1978). Not only are hormonal secretions at their peak for generating physical sex differences during adolescence, as we learned in Chapter 2, but it is also the time when societal pressures operate most forcefully. Sexual and sex-role identity are primary issues in adolescence, and the status changes that accompany physical maturation provide a basis for differentiating adult role requirements by gender.

SUMMARY

1. Sex roles are behaviors associated with a biological gender distinction; within psychology, "sex roles" are behaviors that are stereotypically associated with males and females.

2. Masculinity and femininity are separate personality dimensions that can vary independently. People can have both masculine and feminine traits at the same time. Individuality, selfishness, and alienation are part of the masculine principle, while community, participation, and other-directedness are part of the feminine principle.

3. Men who exhibit masculine traits and women who exhibit feminine traits are said to be *sex-typed*. The opposite pattern—"feminine" men and "masculine" women—illustrates a cross-sex identity. People differ in *sex-role orientation*, defined as the degree to which they incorporate sex-typed traits into their self-identities.

4. Despite theoretical predictions to the contrary, father absence in childhood has no striking effect on the sex-typing of boys or girls. Father absence, however, does appear to exert a negative effect on daughters' social skills with boys.

5. People who exhibit both masculine and feminine traits are described as *androgynous*. Androgynous adolescents score higher on measures of psychological adjustment than either sex-typed or cross-sex-typed adolescents.

6. Each culture has its ideal set of traits for males and females. Our culture generally values dominance and achievement for males, and emotionality and sensitivity for females. Other cultures value different sets of traits for the two genders.

7. Sex-role behavior develops in part through childhood sociali-

zation, through observation and imitation. Parents are important models for sex-role socialization.

8. Children become progressively more sophisticated in their awareness of sex-typing and cultural expectations. Young children are not fully aware of gender constancy until they have mastered other cognitive constancies, such as conservation of quantity.

9. *Roles* are social categories that call for a set of behaviors; these behaviors distinguish one role from another. *Parent* and *child* are roles, defined by a biological relationship, which require certain reciprocal behaviors.

10. *Stereotypes* involve caricatured behaviors and attributes that are applied to members of a social category. The stereotype of college professors as bumbling and absentminded is an example. Stereotypes are abstract expectations rather than required behaviors. Most trait assignment associated with gender is a blur of roles and stereotypes.

11. Nevertheless, people in our culture generally agree on trait assignment by gender. *Ideal males* are thought to be dominant, aggressive, and self-confident. *Ideal females* are thought to be succorant, nurturant, and deferent. Adolescents are particularly likely to subscribe to sex-role stereotypes.

12. Nurturance and dominance are often mentioned as sex-typed traits for females and males, respectively. Attempts to confirm these stereotypes suggest that there *are* behavioral differences by gender. For example, studies of nurturance that show a sex difference almost always indicate more nurturance among girls. This effect is strongest in adolescence. Studies of dominance yield less consistent sex differences.

13. In our culture, sex-role expectations are more ambiguous for girls than for boys. Both genders are expected to achieve in school, but girls are sometimes required to make achievement secondary to family roles. Such expectations rarely apply to boys.

14. Adolescents are more stereotyped in their views of sex roles than any other age group. Boys and girls show fairly similar interests until adolescence. Hormonal changes that accompany puberty may be responsible for some of the differences which

emerge in adolescence. For example, measures of spatial ability yield few sex differences until adolescence, when boys begin to do better than girls.

15. A combination of factors may contribute to this developmental history, including genetic, hormonal, and socialization influences prior to and during the critical adolescent years.

OUTLINE

5.

COGNITIVE DEVELOPMENT

This chapter begins with a simple test of one aspect of thinking, involving propositional logic.

THE CHECK-CHECKING PROBLEM

Emily Earnshaw is a clerk in the Westminster Bank, which has a rule that any check made out for $50 or more must be approved by the bank manager, Oliver Fawley. Mr. Fawley shows his approval by initialling the check on the reverse side. Occasionally, a teller in the bank makes a mistake, and the rule is not followed. It is Ms. Earnshaw's job to make sure the rule has been followed with the previous day's checks, so that payment can be stopped on large checks not approved by Mr. Fawley. About half the checks in Ms. Earnshaw's stack are face up, and half face down. Here are four examples.

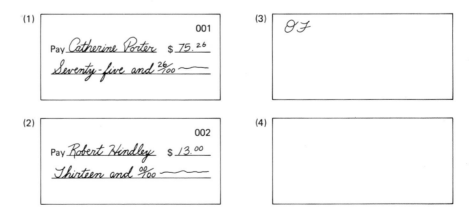

(1)
```
                              001
Pay Catherine Porter   $ 75.26
Seventy-five and 26/100 ———
```

(2)
```
                              002
Pay Robert Hindley   $ 13.00
Thirteen and 00/100 ———
```

(3) `OF`

(4)

Which of these four checks must Ms. Earnshaw turn over to see if the rule has been followed? Select all those checks, but only those checks, which Ms. Earnshaw would have to turn over to make sure the rule has been followed.

Mrs. Earnshaw's check-checking problem involves reasoning about a rule and is a modification of a task described by Wason (1968). To solve the problem, individuals need to use elements of cognitive processing similar to propositional logic. Let P equal a check made out for $50 or more, and P (or not-P) equal a check of less than $50. Let Q stand for an initialled check, Q an uninitialled one. Therefore, to follow the bank's rule, "if P then Q," two checks must be turned over: Check 1 must be turned over to see if it has Mr. Fawley's approval; it is a P-check, and "if P then Q." Check 4 must be turned over to see if it is a case of P-Q, that is, a check of more than $50 which was not approved. Checks 2 and 3 are irrelevant to the rule: Check 2 is a P-check, and the rule only concerns P-checks. Even if Mr. Fawley did approve a check of less than $50, it should not disturb Ms. Earnshaw. Likewise, Check 3 is a Q-check; it may be made out for more than $50 or less than $50, but it has been approved, and in either case would satisfy the rule, "if P then Q."

Wason (1968) found that college students, in a similar task almost always turned over Number 1, as they should have, and almost never turned over Number 2. But a majority of subjects (60–75 percent) turned over Number 3 which was irrelevant to the rule; and only a minority checked the other side of Number 4, which *was* relevant. Wason's subjects were introductory psychology and statistics students at University College, London.

Although many adolescents and adults do not solve this problem according to the rules of propositional logic, there are age differences in performance. Eighth graders in one study, for example, solved propositional-logic problems less than a fourth of the time, whereas college graduates solved the same problems more than half of the time (Roberge & Flexner, 1979). Research and theory on cognitive development indicate that adolescent thinking differs in important respects from thinking in childhood. In general, there appear to be dramatic improvements in the ability to solve tricky propositional-logic problems such as Ms. Earnshaw's check-checking problem, during the adolescent years.

In this chapter, we examine the nature of adolescent thought. We review ways in which adolescent thinking differs from thinking in other stages of the life cycle. We focus particular attention on Jean Piaget's influential discussion of adolescent thinking, which he called formal-operational thinking. Some of the characteristics of Piaget's stage theory of cognitive development are discussed, along with a review of research on formal operations.

THE NATURE OF THOUGHT IN ADOLESCENCE

In comparison to thinking found in childhood, adolescent thought involves several new characteristics. First, it is more logical, as exemplified by the check-checking problem. Second, adolescent thought includes the possibility of reasoning about hypothetical situations. Third, it is more abstract, less tied to concrete concepts. Fourth, it is more introspective; thinking about thinking itself is far more characteristic of adolescents than of children. Each of these major characteristics of adolescent thinking is examined below.

Increased Use of Logic

The major description of the use of logic in adolescence is Inhelder and Piaget's *The Growth of Logical Thinking from Childhood to Adolescence*, published in French in 1955 and translated into English in 1958. While Piaget's theory is a general theory of cognitive growth, he was most intrigued by the development of scientific thinking. The tasks designed to measure logical thinking reflect this bias. The tasks that Inhelder and Piaget used have been imported to laboratories in the United States that have investigated adolescent thinking.

Stages in the growth of logical thought can be illustrated using Inhelder and Piaget's billiard game. A special apparatus is used when questioning children, but the basic physical relationships are the same as in a standard billiard game. In Figure 5-1, aficionados of billiards will see immediately that hitting a billiard ball from point X to point O (against the buffer) will deflect it throught point X'. A hit from point Y, on the other hand, will deflect it through

FIGURE 5-1
The billiard game. A billiard ball hit from point x to 0 against the buffer will deflect through point x', angle α_I = angle α_D. Similarly, a ball hit from point y to point 0 against the buffer will deflect through point y'; angle β_I = angle β_D

(Based on a discussion in Inhelder & Piaget, 1958.)

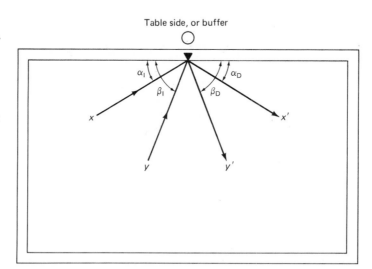

Table side, or buffer

point Y'. Pool sharks can make use of this predictable relationship even if they cannot put it into words: The angle of incidence is equal to the angle of deflection, independent of the force of the hit. In Figure 5-1, angle α I = angle α D and angle β I = angle β D.

Young children faced with the billiard game are concerned with whether the ball goes where they want it to, without considering why it happens. When asked why it happens as it does, they merely describe the result, as did Wirt (age 5 years, 5 months): "It came out here and went over there" (Inhelder and Piaget, 1958, p.6).

Older children are able to see a serial relationship in the order of the angles; that is, they have a vague idea which hit will yield a sharper angle of deflection, but they cannot go beyond the concrete facts to any implications. Vir (7 years, 7 months) gave this analysis: "To aim more to left, you have to turn to the left" (Inhelder & Piaget, 1958, p. 7). Children stick to the facts as they see them.

Adolescents begin to formulate hypotheses as they try to figure out the billiard game; when they figure it out, they view the results as a logical necessity, confident in the generality of the law. Having verified the equality-of-angle law, Def (14 years, 8 months) replied to Piaget's "objection" that the law might not be very general.

It depends on the buffer too; it has to be good and straight—and also on the plane—it has to be completely horizontal. But if the buffer were oblique, you would have to trace a perpendicular to the buffer and you would still have to take the same distance [to the line and from it] up to the target: The law would be the same . . . The law doesn't vary. (Inhelder & Piaget, 1958, p. 12)

The development of logical thinking, in Piaget's system, primarily concerned logic applied to physical phenomena. In addition to the billiard game, Inhelder and Piaget (1958) evaluated the logic of children and adolescents on a chemical-combination task, flexibility of metal rods, a pendulum task, and eleven other natural-science experiments. Many of these tasks have been used in American research on adolescent thought as well. For example, Siegler (1981) used Inhelder and Piaget's balance game. The apparatus used in this task is illustrated in Figure 5-2. Loops of different weight can

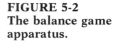

FIGURE 5-2
The balance game apparatus.

(From Seigler, 1981.)

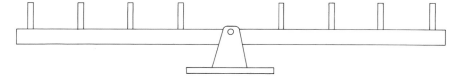

be hung on the balance's pegs, and at varying distances from the fulcrum. Thus, there are two important dimensions in this task: the weight on each side of the fulcrum, and the distance of the weights from the fulcrum. Young children typically consider only the weight on each side, and if the weights are unequal, they predict that the side with the greater weight will go down regardless of counterbalancing distances from the fulcrum. If the amounts are equal, they predict that the apparatus will be in balance. Older children behave much as younger ones do in the unequal-weight situation; but if the weights are equal, they take distance from the fulcrum into account. Adolescents, on the other hand, take both dimensions into account and begin to compute the simultaneous action of weight and distance to predict whether the arms will balance (Siegler, 1981). Several researchers have confirmed the increasing use of logical thinking in adolescence as compared to childhood (e.g., Elkind, 1962; Lovell, 1961; Moshman, 1977; Roberge & Flexner, 1979; Shantz, 1967).

Piaget viewed the difference between child and adolescent logic as a qualitative difference with major significance for cognitive development in general. "The adolescent's logic is a complex but coherent system that is relatively different from the logic of the child, and constitutes the essence of the logic of cultured adults" (Piaget, 1972).

Hypothetical Reasoning

Adolescents are more capable than children of formulating hypotheses and examining evidence for or against them. They are able to engage in this type of reasoning even when the original premises are false. For example, consider the following problem: "All three-legged snakes are purple; I am hiding a three-legged snake; guess its color." An adolescent can accept the false premises of the problem and arrive at a logical solution, where children get caught in the absurdity of the original false premise (Kagan, 1972).

Piaget and Inhelder described hypothetical reasoning this way:

By means of a differentiation of form and content the subject becomes capable of reasoning correctly about propositions he does not believe . . . He becomes capable of drawing the necessary conclusions from truths which are merely possible, which constitutes the beginning of hypothetico-deductive or formal thought. (Piaget & Inhelder, 1969, p. 132)

Research has confirmed a shift toward greater hypothesis use in adolescence. For example, students in different grades were shown cards that illustrated several dimensions, any one of which could be relevant in a discrimination-learning task. Color, shape, size, and position on the card were all potentially relevant dimensions. The dimension selected by students indicated their hypotheses about dimensional relevance. Older students were more consistent in their responses across trials, indicating more sophisticated understanding of hypothesis testing (Eimas, 1969). It should be noted, however, that a task of this type requires rather complex language, and younger students' poorer performance might result from not understanding the task, rather than their inability to generate consistent hypotheses. Instructions for this task, in part, were that "one of the colors, or letters, or sizes, or positions is always correct" (Eimas, 1969, p. 163).

The ability to generate alternatives and hypothetical solutions is related to creative thinking. Ironically, adolescents appear to be less creative in their thinking than children. One suggestion to explain this apparent discrepancy is that adolescents have a greater *potential* for creativity, but that they express the potential less frequently than children because they also become more sensitive to peer judgment during adolescence (Wolf & Larson, 1981).

Abstract Thinking

The opening problem, Ms. Earnshaw's check-checking problem, has been shown to be a difficult problem in propositional logic, but it is tied to a concrete example in the real world. Problems have also been devised which are abstract, involving manipulation of symbols rather than real objects. These abstract problems are more difficult still but are easier for adolescents than they are for children. Consider the following problem:

There is an A *if and only if there is a* B.

There is an A.

Write a conclusion that follows necessarily from this pair of premises. (Roberge & Flexner, 1979)

Performance on problems like this one improves dramatically from childhood to adolescence. The answer: There is a *B*.

Abstract thinking extends to many areas of cognitive performance in adolescence. In a study of creativity, for example, high-school students differed from 6th graders primarily in their increased use of abstract and complex solutions to creativity tasks (Milgram, Milgram, Rosenbloom, & Rabkin, 1978).

One study compared the performance of the same students on problems in both concrete and abstract thought. Abstract problems, similar to the one described above, provided symbols for students

An exercise in abstract thinking and propositional logic . . . .

(*Peanuts* by Charles Schultz © 1981 United Features Syndicate, Inc.)

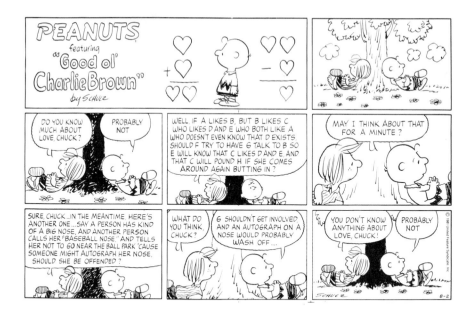

to manipulate. Concrete problems, on the other hand, were written about concrete situations. Here is one of the concrete problems, assessing mathematical combinations.

At a party there were only four bowls of food. The first contained rice, the second chicken, the third tomatoes, and the fourth mushrooms. Everybody took some food. Some people took just one kind of food, some took two kinds, some took three, and one person had some of all four kinds. Everybody at the party took a different mixture of foods. What is the maximum number of people who could have attended and what did they each have to eat? (Barratt, 1975, p. 701)

Students in this study were 12–14. As Table 5-1 shows, more of the older students performed successfully on these problems. There was a linear increase in successful performance by age on both types of problems. In addition, the concrete problems elicited dramatically superior performance from students in each age group (Barratt, 1975). The answer to the party food problem is provided in Table 5-2.

TABLE 5-1
Percentage of Students Correct on at Least One Problem of Each Type

	AGE		
	12	13	14
CONCRETE PROBLEMS	30	57	72
ABSTRACT PROBLEMS	10	21	31

Source: Barratt, 1975.

TABLE 5-2
Answer to the Party Food Problem

How many guests could there have been, maximum? __15__
What did they each have to eat?

PLATE FOR GUEST NUMBER	CONTENTS OF PLATE
1	Rice
2	Chicken
3	Tomatoes
4	Mushrooms
5	Rice and chicken
6	Rice and tomatoes
7	Rice and mushrooms
8	Chicken and tomatoes
9	Chicken and mushrooms
10	Tomatoes and mushrooms
11	Rice, chicken, and tomatoes
12	Rice, chicken, and mushrooms
13	Rice, tomatoes, and mushrooms
14	Chicken, tomatoes, and mushrooms
15	Rice, chicken, tomatoes, and mushrooms

Thinking about Thinking

Children have no difficulty thinking about *things* or *events*. The most casual observations of children's play lead to the conclusion that imagination is a key element. However, children do have difficulty thinking about *thinking* to a greater extent than adolescents do. In one study of the phenomenon of reflective thinking, as it is called, students in grades 1 through 6 were asked to use cartoon bubbles to demonstrate their ability to think about things versus thinking (Miller, Kessel, & Flavell, 1970). Consider these two situations, for example: "Think about William eating ice cream." "Think about William thinking about Mary thinking about jumping rope." Both children and adolescents are able to think about William in the first situation with no difficulty. Adolescents are much better at thinking about William in the second situation, however.

Although adolescents are better at this sort of task than children, they have not achieved the adult stage in reflective thinking. Adolescents have little difficulty thinking about the thoughts of others, but they sometimes fail to differentiate between what they are thinking about and what others are thinking about (Looft, 1972).

This characteristic of adolescent thinking is related to adolescent self-consciousness, as David Elkind has pointed out. "Accordingly, since he fails to differentiate between what others are thinking about and his own mental preoccupations, he assumes that other people are as obsessed with his behavior and appearance as he is himself" (Elkind, 1967, p. 1030). Elkind likened this form of reflectivity to a kind of egocentrism referred to as the *personal fable.* The adolescent personal fable is an exaggerated belief in one's own uniqueness and immortality. Writing diaries for posterity, confiding in one's own personal god, and believing that bad things "can't happen to me," all are aspects of the personal fable. Incidentally, one never completely overcomes the personal fable, but it tends to lessen after adolescence (Elkind, 1967).

Stages in Cognitive Development

The characteristics of adolescent thinking presented above suggest that adolescent thought is different from childhood thought in important and predictable ways. Piaget has proposed that human thinking, or cognition, proceeds through four stages, characterized by qualitatively different modes of thinking. Cognitive development, in this view, is not simply a matter of learning more facts and strategies as one grows older; rather, there are transformations in the *way* a person thinks. Before we examine Piaget's theory of cognitive development, we briefly consider the notion of *stage* in developmental psychology.

Stage is a hypothetical construct within a formal developmental theory. Freud's division of human development into five psychosexual stages, and Piaget's theory of cognitive development as a four-stage model are two examples. Formal theories satisfy four criteria to be classified as stage theories: qualitative difference, invariant sequence, logical relationship, and stage generality.

Qualitative Difference Each stage must differ from all other stages, either in form of functioning or in terms of a distinguishing characteristic. In Freudian theory, for example, the young child's earliest erotic impulses center around the mouth and result in behavior aimed at oral gratification; the second stage finds interest focused on the anal region with behavior aimed at anal gratification.

Invariant Sequence Development through stages always occurs in an invariant order. While there may be age guidelines for stage development, there is no one-to-one correspondence between age and stage. Rather, stage theories recognize rate of progression through stages as variable, with sequence or order of stage movement constant.

Logical Relationship Stages must bear some logical relationship to each other. Gesell and Ilg's (1943) stages of motor development illustrate this criterion. Crawling occurs before toddling, and tod-

Jean Piaget (1896–1981), a Swiss psychologist associated with the University of Geneva, was the major theorist in the cognitive-developmental tradition. He called his approach to mental development *genetic epistemology*—the study of an individual's growth of knowledge from the reflexive actions of infancy to the hypothetical and deductive thinking of adulthood.

(Photo copyright © 1980 by Ives de Braine/Black Star)

dling before running; the logical relationship centers on human locomotion. If Gesell had provided age norms on crawling, followed by puberty, the sequence would have been correct; but these phenomena are not logically related.

Generality within a Stage   The nature of functioning at a given stage should generalize across situation. In Erikson's theory, for example, adolescence is the stage of the identity crisis. Adolescents are concerned about their identities in several areas of their lives, such as sex-role identity, occupational identity, and political ideology. Inhelder and Piaget (1958) referred to this generality within a given stage as a "structured whole."

PIAGET'S COGNITIVE-DEVELOPMENTAL THEORY

Cognitive-developmental theory is primarily concerned with stages in modes of thinking. The major theorist in the cognitive-developmental tradition was Jean Piaget of the University of Geneva. Piaget's colleagues in Geneva, most notably Bärbel Inhelder, have also made significant contributions to Piagetian theory. Developed over the past 50 years, Piaget's theory traces the growth of mental development from reflexive actions in infancy to hypothetical and deductive thinking in adulthood. Piaget called his approach to development "genetic epistemology," the study of the individual's growth of knowledge. Knowledge entails *cognitive structures*, organizing features of the mind which determine the individual's understanding of the world.

Cognitive structures undergo progressive elaboration, in Piaget's stage model, through a process known as *equilibration*. The individual uses cognitive structures to interpret features of the environment—external reality. Environmental information, in turn, causes the structures themselves to change when the structures are inadequate for handling new information.

Piaget's Stages

Piaget's four stages of cognitive development are outlined in Table 5-3. The sensory-motor action schemes that characterize infancy are overshadowed in early childhood by internalized representations of objects and events, and by symbolic representation made possible by language. In later childhood, true operations—internalized actions that are reversible—are applied to situations in the here-and-now. Beginning at adolescence, true operations of hypothetical and deductive thought extend the concrete to the possible. Formal-operational thought is the highest stage of cognition described by Piaget.

Cognitive growth at adolescence involves a transition from concrete to formal operations. Our discussion therefore focuses on these two stages. First, we discuss a task used to assess formal-operational thought, with characteristic approaches to these tasks used by individuals operating at concrete and formal-operational levels.

Two aspects of Piaget's theory relating to adolescent cognition require close attention in our discussion. One is the mechanism of transition from concrete to formal thought; we examine in some

TABLE 5-3 **Piaget's Four Stages of** **Cognitive Development**	**Stage I**	**Sensory-Motor Stage** (*birth to age 1½*) Sensory-motor action schemes, such as sucking, grasping. Reflexes.
	Stage II	**Preoperational Stage** (*age 1½ to 6*) Internalized representations of objects and events. Symbolic representation and language.
	Stage III	**Concrete-Operational Stage** (*age 6 to puberty*) True operations applied to objects in the here-and-now.
	Stage IV	**Formal-Operational Stage** (*adolescence and adulthood*) Hypothetical and deductive thinking. Propositional logic.

detail stage movement as it applies to cognitive growth from later childhood to adolescence. A second aspect of Piaget's theory is the concept of the "structured whole." Piaget insisted that the structures of a stage of thought show general applicability from one type of problem or event to another. We need to ask two questions about the structured whole: (1) Do adolescents who have reached formal operations show consistency in their application of those operations? (2) Is formal operations a stage that most normal adolescents and adults, who are exposed to normal environmental stimulation, inevitably reach?

Concrete versus Formal Operations

Thinking in later childhood is characterized by concrete operations; children can solve some logical problems tied to concrete objects in the real world, such as conservation of quantities of liquid when poured from one container into another. Children are able to see that this action is reversible, and that the amount of liquid must inevitably remain the same.

Isolated logical skills, such as reversibility, remain isolated and fragmented until adolescence. In adolescence, a stage of formal operations emerges in which these logical capabilities are integrated into a single logical system. With the emergence of formal-operational reasoning, adolescent thinking is systematic. Hypotheses can be formulated and tested. Thinking can be abstract.

The Chemicals Problem The difference between concrete and formal operations can be best seen with one of Inhelder and Piaget's logic problems. Consider the chemicals problem presented in Figure 5-3. A student is presented with several beakers of colorless liquid: water; diluted sulphuric acid; oxygenated water; thiosulphate; and some combinations, including one of oxygenated water and diluted sulphuric acid. The interviewer uses a dropper to add potassium iodide to each glass. Because oxygenated water oxidizes potassium iodide in an acid medium, the liquid in the beaker with oxygenated water and sulphuric acid turns yellow. The student is asked to reproduce this result.

In the stage of concrete operations, children combine the agent, potassium iodide (PI), with all the other liquids singly, one at a time. They do not, however, think to try the agent with any combinations. For example, Ren (age 7) combined 4 and PI, then 2 and PI, and 1 and PI, and 3 and PI, and then remarked, "I think I did everything. I tried them all." When asked what else he could have done, he replied, "I don't know." (Inhelder & Piaget, 1958, p. 111).

FIGURE 5-3
The chemicals problem. This diagram illustrates the problem of colored and colorless chemicals. Four similar flasks contain colorless, odorless liquids: (1) diluted sulphuric acid; (2) water; (3) oxygenated water; (4) thiosulphate. The smaller flask, labeled *g*, contains potassium iodide. Two glasses are presented to the subject; one contains 1 + 3, the other contains 2. While the subject watches, the experimenter adds several drops of *g* to each of the glasses. The liquid in the glass containing 1 + 3 turns yellow. The subject is then asked to reproduce the color, using all or any of the five flasks.

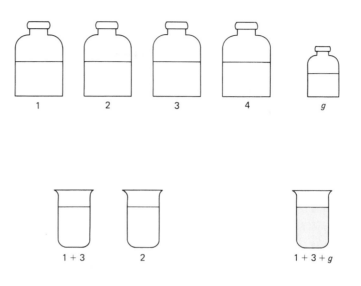

(From *The Growth of Logical Thinking from Childhood to Adolescence: An Essay on the Construction of Formal Operational Structures* by Barbel Inhelder and Jean Piaget. Translated by Anne Parsons and Stanley Milgrim. Copyright © 1958 by Basic Books, Inc. By permission of Basic Books, Inc., Publishers, New York.)

In a transitional phase between concrete and formal operations, students generally begin by combining PI with each liquid singly, and then progress by adding PI to a combination of all four liquids. Finally, they hit upon the idea of taking the liquids two at a time and then three at a time, but they are not very systematic in their approach. For example, Tur (at age 11½) first tried PI with each liquid singly, and observed, "That doesn't work. You have to mix all four." When that did not work either, Tur tried changing the order several times without success, and then tried a few unsuccessful two-by-two combinations, 1 and 4 and PI, 2 and 3 and PI, 3 and 4 and PI, 2 and 1 and PI. When none of these worked, he said, "I wonder if there isn't water in all of them!" He moved on to three-by-three combinations, and finally hit upon 1 and 3 and 2 and PI, leading to the following dialogue with the examiner:

That's it.

[*What do you have to do for the color?*]

Put in 2.

[*All three are necessary?*]

One at a time doesn't work. It seems to me that with two it doesn't work; a liquid is missing.

[*Are you sure that you have tried everything with two?*]

Not sure. (Inhelder & Piaget, 1958, p. 115)

At the formal stage, adolescents are capable to trying all of the combinations systematically. Cha (age 13), for example, began by combining PI with each liquid singly, then moved on to two-by-two combinations. When he discovered that 1 and 3 and PI worked, he said, "It turned yellow. But are there other solutions?" He proceeded to try all possible combinations systematically, so that he was able to speculate about the action of each liquid. Here is part of the interview:

[*What is there in 2 and 4?*]

In 4 certainly water. No, the opposite, in 2 certainly water since it doesn't act on the liquids; that makes things clearer.

[*And if I were to tell you that 4 is water?*]

If this liquid 4 is water, when you put it with 1 and 3 it wouldn't completely prevent the yellow from forming. It isn't water; it's something harmful. (Inhelder & Piaget, 1958, p. 117)

Cha has so systematically tested the liquids that he can dispute the interviewer's suggestion that water is in beaker 4.

Transition from Concrete to Formal Operations

One of the most perplexing problems for a stage theory of development is accounting for transitions from one stage to another. In accounting for stage progression, we must specify the characteristics of the child's thought at the two stages; then, the nature of thought during the transitional phase must be specified. If stages represent pure structured wholes—modes of thinking with complete generality—we would expect children in the concrete and formal stages to show nearly 100 percent of their thinking, as represented by their answers to several of the tasks presented earlier, at those respective stages. According to the notion of the structured whole, an adolescent who shows formal reasoning on the chemicals problem should also show formal reasoning on the billiard game and the balance problem. Very few studies have shown such pure stage performance.

For example, Keating (1975) found that fewer than two-thirds of even the most advanced seventh graders used formal thought consistently. Average 7th graders performed at that level consistently only one-fourth of the time. It therefore seems appropriate to characterize stage thinking as representing a dominant stage rather than a pure stage. In a dominant stage, students might exhibit 60 percent or so of their thinking in standardized tasks at that stage, with the remaining 40 percent of thinking distributed in the immediate lower or higher stages.

How, then, can the transition between dominant stages *A* and *B* be characterized? Two possibilities consistent with Piaget's model are suggested. First, the stage transition could be abrupt, occurring as an epiphany or "Aha!" reaction. Schematically, such an abrupt transition may be described as shown in Figure 5-4(a). The second possibility is a gradual transition characterized by a longer period of stage mixture, which may be diagrammed as shown in Figure 5-4(b).

The transition problem is not a trivial one, since it goes to the heart of a stage theory that posits qualitatively different states in an individual's thinking. It is necessary to specify the mechanism involved in getting from one state to another. Unfortunately, the experiments that address the problem entail complicated difficulties in research design. Piaget's own studies have been cross-sectional, which is to say he has tested different age groups, noted the differences in their responses, and constructed a model of development to account for the differences. Piaget's only longitudinal studies were conducted with his own three children and resulted in his model for sensory-motor development in infancy.

Longitudinal research has the advantage of testing the same children over time, so that their transitional periods may be examined closely. As Porges (1976) pointed out, however, longitudinal research is complicated by practice effects; children's transitional phases may differ from spontaneous cases because these children are confronted with similar problems at different points in time.

Experimental difficulties notwithstanding, there are data available that favor the interpretation of gradual stage transition.

FIGURE 5-4
Two alternative stage transitions for the progression from concrete to formal operations.

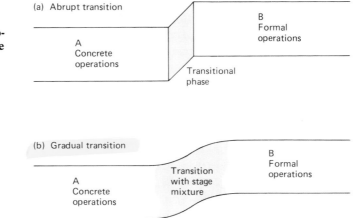

Flavell and Wohlwill (1969) proposed that stage movement be viewed as transitional between two relatively stable ways of viewing the world. Individuals coming into formal operations, according to this model, go through four phases: (1) failure on all formal-operational tasks, characteristic of children who are still in the concrete-operations stage of thinking; (2) an initial transition in which they exhibit minor formal-operational competence; (3) a phase in which formal operations are available within their competence, but performed inconsistently; and (4) a final phase of full and consistent formal-operational reasoning. Evidence from several studies is consistent with this model (e.g., Moshman, 1977; Danner & Day, 1977; Siegler, 1981). Consider once again the movement from concrete to formal operations on the chemicals problem. Children in the concrete operations stage fail the task, as Ren did. The transitional stage is marked by only partial success because individuals do not systematically apply their logical insights. Finally, at the formal operations stage, adolescents are capable of success on the task.

Training Studies

Training studies, in which attempts are made to *induce* upward stage movement through instruction, are a special case of stage transition. Training studies provide a means of studying mechanisms that are most successful at inducing stage movement, as well as a means of studying the characteristics of the transitional period itself.

In training research, students are usually given a pretest to assess their current level of cognitive functioning. They are then presented with solutions to tasks that are either at their dominant level, one stage below, one stage above, or two stages above their dominant level. Following this intervention, the children are retested on the original problem, and any stage movement in their answers is noted. A retest with a delay of a few days or weeks provides a limited longitudinal assessment of stage transition. One such study (Snyder & Feldman, 1977) used a map-drawing task, and only 5th-grade students operating at the same dominant stage were selected for instruction following the pretest. Although they had the same dominant level of cognitive functioning, they exhibited differing degrees of stage mixture in their performance on the pretest. Those students whose pretest answers are highly consistent may be characterized as "entrenched" in their dominant stage, whereas students with high-stage mixture are more transitional. Following Flavell and Wohlwill's model, one would expect upward stage movement to be greater among high-mix, transitional students than among low-mix, entrenched students. This is exactly what Snyder and Feldman's experiment showed, both for performance in an immediate posttest and in a posttest administered 5 weeks after intervention. In this experiment, both the pretest mixtures of stage responding and the greater stage advance of students showing high-stage mixture imply a gradual transition from stage to stage.

Interventions that present models at or below a subject's dominant stage should not induce stage advancement because the student is already thinking at that level. Arguments one stage above the subject's dominant level are not so advanced that they cannot be grasped, but they produce some disequilibrium because students are not yet "fluent" in higher-stage reasoning. Resolution of this disequilibrium is accomplished by stage advance. Models that are two or more stages above a subject's dominant level cannot be understood because they are so far removed from current ways of reasoning. The theory predicts little stage advance with interventions of this magnitude. Turiel (1969) found just this theoretical relationship in the realm of moral thought, which we discuss in the next chapter.

Snyder and Feldman (1977), however, found an equivalent amount of stage movement when interventions were one or two stages above the dominant stage. Nevertheless, the movement that occurred was always to one stage above the subject's dominant level; even when advance in stage was stimulated by a solution two stages higher, the advance was only one stage. This result is important for two reasons: First, it suggests that stage movement occurs in sequence, even when it occurs through training; second, it rebuts an explanation of stage advance through imitation. If subjects were imitating responses rather than showing orderly stage transition, one would expect two-stage models to provoke two-stage (rather than one-stage) responses.

Equilibration As individuals gain more experience with problems of a similar type, they discover ways of analyzing the problems that lead them to solutions. With enough experience, their whole approach to similar problems evolves so that new problems of a similar type can be solved readily. Their thinking has evolved into a new mode, qualitatively different from the old approach to problems. Piaget described this evolution as *equilibration*. Let us examine a research project on equilibration.

Fourth and 5th graders participated in this research project (Kuhn & Angelev, 1976). They were initially given a battery of tests to assess their ability to solve some of the physical-science problems that Inhelder and Piaget (1958) designed. One of these problems, called the pendulum problem, required the students to predict how fast a string with a weight attached would swing (see Figure 5-5). The amount of weight attached and the length of the string were varied in the problem.

FIGURE 5-5
The pendulum problem. This problem utilizes a simple apparatus consisting of a string, which can be shortened or lengthened, and a set of varying weights. The other variables that at first might be considered relevant are the height of the release point and the force of the push given by the subject.

(From *The Growth of Logical Thinking from Childhood to Adolescence: An Essay on the Construction of Formal Operational Structures* by Barbel Inhelder and Jean Piaget. Translated by Anne Parsons and Stanley Milgrim. Copyright © 1958 by Basic Books, Inc. By permission of Basic Books, Inc., Publishers, New York.)

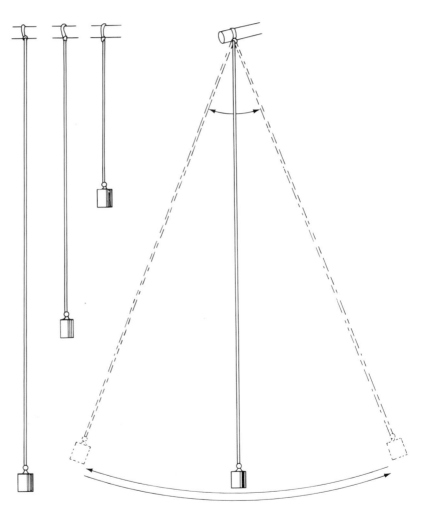

Following this assessment, the students spent the next 15 weeks solving similar problems, but with entirely new materials. One group had problem sessions once every 2 weeks, another group once a week, and a third group twice a week. They were then given posttests on the first set of problems, including the pendulum problem. Those students who had more experience in the intervening 15 weeks showed more advanced problem solving abilities on the posttests (Kuhn & Angelev, 1976). The evolution of their thinking in these problem situations was orderly, and stagelike, entirely consistent with Piaget's description of the equilibration process.

Stage transition, then, appears to be a gradual phenomenon, of the sort diagrammed in Figure 5-4(b). Piaget asserted that transition from stage to stage results from cognitive disequilibrium. He described overall stage development as a process that restores relative equilibrium (Piaget, 1950; Piaget & Inhelder, 1969; Piaget, 1970; Piaget, 1971; Piaget, 1973).

Formal Operations as a Structured Whole

Each equilibrated stage in Piaget's theory supposedly represents a structured whole. At the formal-operations stage, the structured whole implies a generality of application. Structures of propositional logic may be applied to a host of different problems, as a mode of thinking about the world. Piaget recognized the theoretical difficulties such a view of epistemology entails: "The existence of these overall structures raises a problem: Do they in fact really exist in the mind of the subject being studied, or are they merely an invention of the psychologist who studies children or adults?" (Piaget, 1971, p. 3).

Piaget's own data do not always support the notion of a structured whole. For example, the operations of class inclusion, which are characteristic of concrete-operational thought, are not generally applicable once they are attained. Children presented with an array of flowers, such as five primroses and three tulips, are asked: "Are there more primroses or more flowers?" By about age 8, children correctly apply class-inclusion operations and answer, "More flowers." At the same time, they fail a class-inclusion problem involving animals: Confronted with a picture of five squirrels and three rabbits, they reply that there are more squirrels than there are animals. This is a predictable sequence in the child's competence—class inclusion of flowers before animals. Yet a view of the stage as a structured whole implies a general application of class inclusion to different problems.

Consistency of Formal Thinking in Adolescence and Adulthood
According to Piaget, formal operations is the final stage in cognitive development, and is attained in adolescence. When it is attained, formal thinking should be relatively consistent, from situation to situation, according to the notion of the structured whole.

Inhelder and Piaget imply that most adolescents achieve formal-operational thought. Here is what they have to say:

The subjects' reactions to a wide range of experimental situations demonstrate that after a phase of development (11–12 to 13–14 years) the preadolescent comes to handle certain formal operations (implication, exclusion, etc.) successfully, but he is not able to set up an exhaustive method of proof. But the 14–15-year-old adolescent does succeed in setting up proofs. (Inhelder & Piaget, 1958, p. 347)

Inhelder and Piaget's discussion is misleading on this point; their failure to include any indication of the number of individuals in this age range who did *not* attain formal-operational thought is the major difficulty. Subsequent researchers have found that formal thought is far from universal, even among older adolescents and adults. For example, 37 percent of 11th graders in one study failed to operate at the formal-operational level on several of the physical-science tasks, such as the pendulum problem (Keating & Clark, 1980). In another study, almost one-fourth of college students failed a formal reasoning problem in probability (Murray & Armstrong, 1978).

Although Inhelder and Piaget did not provide data on how many adolescents succeed at formal-operational tasks, several investigators have used their tasks to provide this useful normative data. For example, Martorano (1977) gave 10 of the physical-science problems to 80 female students from 6th to 12th grades and found a transition to formal thinking between the 8th and 10th grades. Even so, performance indicated that formal thinking "cannot be said to represent the characteristic mode of thought for that developmental period" (Martorano, 1977, p. 671). Twelfth grade subjects, who scored highest, passed an average of only 6 of the 10 tasks at the formal level.

Another investigator (Lovell, 1961) also used a subset of 10 of the formal-operational tasks. Only 31 of his 52 older subjects, including college and noncollege adults, used formal thought. Dulit (1975) selected tasks including the chemicals problem. Using several groups of students, including older adolescents (aged 16–17) and some adults (aged 20–55), he found a minority to be fully formal-operational in their approach to the problem. He summarized, "Fully developed formal-stage thinking seems to be far from common-place or routine among normal adolescents and adults" (Dulit, 1975, p. 551).

Criticisms of Piaget's work with Inhelder on formal thought prompted him to reconsider his position on the structured whole. Formal thought, he said, is a structural system; but the 15 tasks he and Inhelder devised to measure it are not very general. These tasks are useful for measuring the subset of formal operations dealing with mathematical and physical relationships. In this revised view, Piaget still argued that all adolescents are capable of formal thought, *but in their own special area of aptitude.* This revision of the theory brings us once again to the problem of the structured whole. If formal operations entails such a general structure, it ought to be applicable to any reasonable problem that an individual encounters.

"Natural Experiments" Most adolescents do not encounter problems like the chemicals task very often in their everyday lives. Performance on problems of logic applied to more commonplace situations might yield different results. Deanna Kuhn and her associates have designed a more natural experiment to examine logical thinking.

Kuhn's "natural experiment," called the plant problem, is illustrated in Figure 5-6. Students were shown four real plants, two of which appeared healthy, and two of which appeared sickly. Adjacent to each plant were a glass of water (either large or small) and a dish of plant food (either dark or light). In addition, two of the plants, one sick and one healthy, had a bottle of leaf lotion next to them. Students were then told the following:

I've been raising some plants. I'd like to show them to you and ask what you think. Let's look at this plant first. It seems quite healthy, doesn't it? Every week I gave this plant a large glass of water, some of this dark-colored plant food, and a little of the leaf lotion in this bottle. Now I have another plant like this at home that I've just started working on. My plant at home I'm giving a small glass of water each week, some of the light-colored plant food, and I'm not giving it any of the leaf lotion. How do you think my plant at home is going to turn out?. . . How do you know? (Kuhn & Brannock, 1977, pp. 10–11)

Young children simply have no conception of the isolation of variables in this problem. When asked if the plant will be healthy, for example, one child said, "Not healthy, because leaf lotion and a small cup of water makes it grow good. My grandfather grows them. Leaf lotion and a small cup of water and if the sun shines, maybe it'll be healthy" (Kuhn & Brannock, 1977, p. 12).

FIGURES 5-6
The plant problem: a "natural experiment" in formal operations. Students are shown four plants, two healthy and two sickly. The amount of water, type of plant food, and presence of leaf lotion are the variables that must be considered in predicting growth of plants.

(From Kuhn & Brannock, 1977. Copyright © 1977 by the American Psychological Association. Adapted by permission of the publisher and authors.)

Children in concrete operations have some notion of the necessity to isolate variables, but either they do not select the important variable or they fail to exclude the unimportant ones. For example, one concrete-operational child said, "It'll be sick because you didn't use no leaf lotion." When asked if water had anything to do with it, the reply was, "No, because you always use the same amount" (Kuhn & Brannock, 1977, p. 12).

Formal-operational solutions to the plant problem are characterized by isolation of the correct variable and exclusion of irrelevant variables. College students were far more likely to use formal thinking on the plant problem than were students in elementary or junior high school, as shown in Figure 5-7. The percentage of students using formal-operational thinking increased from 15 percent in Grade 4 to 65 percent among college students (Kuhn & Brannock, 1977).

FIGURE 5-7
Percentage of students from 4th grade to college that show formal-operational reasoning on the plant problem.

(From Kuhn & Brannock, 1977. Copyright © 1977 by the American Psychological Association. Adapted by permission of the publisher and authors.)

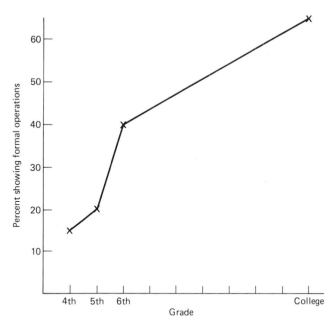

Levels of Availability of Formal Thought Although studies of adolescent and adult thinking show that formal operations are not consistently used by a majority of people interviewed, the capacity for formal thinking may nevertheless be present. Three formal-operational problems were used to test this notion (Danner & Day, 1977). Students aged 10, 13, and 17 were coached if they failed to demonstrate formal operations on the first and second problems. Figure 5-8 shows that none of the 10-year-olds showed formal thinking on the first problem without prompting, compared to about half the 13 and 17-year-olds. Thus, formal-operational thinking was spontaneously available to about half of the students 13 and over, but to none of the 10-year-olds. Among those who did not spontaneously exhibit formal thought, the coaching had a differential effect by age. Only 25 percent of the 10-year-olds showed formal thought even after two prompts. By comparison, 75 percent of the 13-year-olds and all of the 17-year-olds showed formal thought after two prompts. The older students also required fewer prompts to engage their formal reasoning (Danner & Day, 1977). Formal thinking, as described by Piaget, is apparently more readily available to older adolescents, even though they may not spontaneously demonstrate it. Studies that assess formal reasoning without prompting may underestimate the competence of adolescents and adults to reason at

FIGURE 5-8
Levels of availability of formal thought. Percentage of adolescents showing formal thought, with and without coaching.

(From Danner & Day, 1977.)

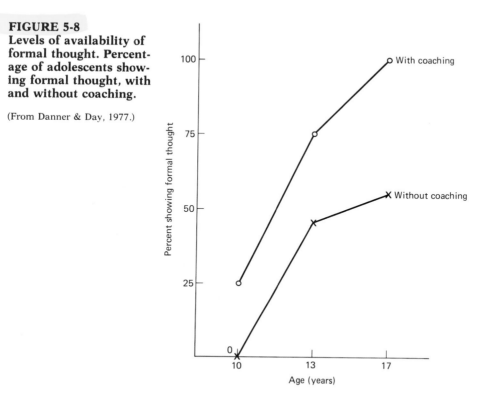

the formal-operational level. Similar differences in levels of availability of formal thinking have been demonstrated in other research (e.g., Kuhn & Angelev, 1976; Moshman, 1977; Stone & Day, 1978).

Environment and Formal Operations

Differential levels of availability of formal reasoning may be affected by environmental effects, such as culture, educational background, and physical handicap.

Piaget and his colleagues are primarily interested in the sequence of qualitative stages in human thought. Individual differences and differences among subgroups are of little interest to them for studying universal sequences of developmental stages. It is fair to say that American psychologists have been far more interested in individual differences, which are useful for diagnostic purposes and for discovering which conditions favor development.

Cognitive-developmental theory is an interactionist model between innate and environmental factors. Although developmental structures are elaborated through interaction, environmental factors can be expected to play a significant role in rate of progress through stages.

In some social environments the stages are accelerated, whereas in others they are more or less systematically retarded. This differential development shows that stages are not purely a question of the maturation of the nervous system but are dependent upon interaction with the social environment and with experience in general. (Piaget, 1971, p. 7)

Experience in school might, therefore, be expected to play a significant role in stage progression. Furthermore, if attainment of formal operations is not universal among adults, schooling might be expected to exert an influence on its ultimate attainment. A series of studies (Goodnow, 1962; Goodnow & Bethon, 1966) examined the effects of schooling, social class, and cultural background on cognitive development. Two findings are relevant to the present discussion. First, the similarities among cultural groups were more striking than the differences, implying a universal sequence in cognitive development. Second, formal-operational tasks were more affected by schooling than concrete-operational tasks. Availability of formal reasoning might therefore be expected to vary as a function of background characteristics, such as educational level.

Deaf and hearing adolescents have been compared on a "symbol-picture logic" task to assess formal operations (Furth & Youniss, 1971). Around one-half of the hearing subjects (21 of 40) showed formal-operational thought, compared to one-fourth of deaf subjects (11 of 40). These results imply that language is not necessary for formal thought, but that linguistic experience facilitates its development. In line with our conclusions, these researchers described formal operations as "a potential that requires personal interest and environmental occasions" (Furth & Youniss, 1971, p. 62). Formal reasoning may be less readily available to individuals without language. The separation of language from cognitive level is illustrated in another study (Glick, 1975). The Kpelle language, used in Liberia, expresses size comparisons of increasing order ("*A* is bigger than *B*"), but not decreasing order ("*B* is smaller than *A*"). Kpelle subjects performed equally well on nonverbal tasks measuring size comparisons in either direction. When asked to *explain* the basis of their performance, however, they could express it only for increasing-order comparisons. For *A* is larger than *B*, one subject said: "I chose the one that was big past the other." Typical explanations for *B* is smaller than *A* were, "God told me" or "My Kpelle sense told me." These studies of the relationship between cognition and language, especially the work with deaf adolescents, indicate that language facility influences the availability of formal thought.

IQ and Formal Operations

Both IQ and achievement tests are designed to measure individual differences. As we have said, cognitive-developmental theory has not been concerned with these differences. The Piagetian perspective of interaction between maturation and experience, however, does imply an important role for experience. Although IQ and Piagetian intelligence are conceptualized differently, they should bear some relationship to each other if they both contain an experiential component. Several studies have been designed to determine the extent of this relationship.

Kuhn (1976) studied students who were in transitional phases, from preoperations to concrete operations and from concrete to formal operations. Her subjects were middle-class 1st to 3rd graders and middle-class 5th to 7th graders who were given the Wechsler IQ test (WISC) and several of Piaget's tasks. Kuhn found a significant correlation between "mental age" from the WISC and Piaget scores for younger students only, and concluded that the factors responsible for performance on IQ tests are not identical to those responsible for progress through Piaget's stages. An alternative conclusion is that formal thought is more liberated from IQ than concrete thought.

Children who have very high IQs resemble older children in their mental age; thus, if mental age were responsible for movement through Piaget's cognitive stages, one would expect those students to reach formal operations earlier than their average-IQ peers. Webb (1974) tested 25 students aged 6 to 11 who had IQs above 160, which is a very high IQ, indeed. Chronologically, they would be expected to perform at the concrete-operational level. Webb used two of the formal-operational tasks (Specific Gravity and Balance). Only four students gave formal-operational answers to both problems, and an additional five students on one of the two problems. IQ, therefore, appears to facilitate Piagetian stage movement; but high IQ alone is not sufficient for eliciting formal thought.

Other researchers have also reported relationships between IQ and Piagetian stage. Schoolboys in the United States, 11 years old, were given several of Piaget's tasks. The "dull" students (IQs 64–88) scored lower on all of them than students with IQs ranging from 100–120. But when the dull 11-year olds were matched with 8-year olds for *mental* age, there was no significant difference in their performance (Goodnow & Bethon, 1966). When average and very bright 5th and 7th grade boys were given three formal-operational tasks, none of the average 5th graders showed formal operations on all three tasks, compared to nearly half of bright 5th graders. Among the 7th graders, 23 percent of the average students versus 62 percent of bright students passed all three tests at the formal level (Keating, 1975).

All of these studies suggest that very bright students are precocious on Piaget's tasks. Children and adolescents with lower than average IQs may not be "retarded" on Piaget's tasks, however. DeVries (1974) tested children aged 5–7 who had low and average IQs, and aged 6–12 who had low IQs. In addition to the IQ test, she administered an achievement test and the 15 Piaget tasks of formal operations. Her data showed that IQ was a poor predictor of Piaget-task performance.

The research on IQ and Piagetian intelligence suggests the following conclusions. Above-average IQ facilitates progress through Piaget's stages for some children and adolescents. This does not mean that everyone who has a high IQ shows precocious stage movement, however; we have seen that formal thought is not consistently used even by highly-intelligent college students. There appears to be little relationship between IQ and Piagetian intelligence among children and adolescents whose IQ scores are average or moderately low. Severely retarded individuals are difficult to test using either IQ tests or Piagetian tasks. Nevertheless, it seems safe to conclude that children and adolescents whose IQ scores indicate severe retardation would also show low scores on Piaget's tasks.

Methodological Issues   Piaget's approach to the study of cognitive development differs in important ways from the dominant experimental orientation in American psychology. The clinical method, favored by Piaget, cannot be described as an experimental method. Prior to 1920, Piaget worked in Bleuler's psychiatric clinic and in Binet's IQ-test-development program in Paris. Both clinical interviews and individual IQ-test administrations require face-to-face interaction. Piaget's probing and flexible clinical method for studying a child's approach to cognitive problems grew out of these experiences. Although he was criticized for a lack of controlled experimental verification of his hypotheses, Piaget steadfastly adhered to the clinical method. Inflexible experimental control, he argued, might miss the fundamental nature of child thought. Piaget changed his procedure from child to child; he attempted to *diagnose* the thought of the individual child. The clinical method follows the child's thought wherever it might lead; a standardized experiment follows it only as far as the preplanned experimental design allows (Flavell, 1962).

The clinical method loses experimental control; it also places a heavy reliance on verbal interaction between the subject and the interviewing experimenter. It is plausible that verbal instructions are more difficult for younger children. Furthermore, the effect of Piaget's explanations to a child is often impossible to assess, for he did not always present the instructions or questions he used in his published reports.

Because Piaget was most concerned with the development of scientific thought and an epistemological approach to child development, his studies have emphasized logic. Logical operations do not necessarily reflect the complexity of a child's cognitive status. A research methodology designed to assess logical operations may distort one's actual cognitive status. One critic put it this way: "Complexity of logical structure demands a parallel complexity in the corresponding psychological processes. But the two structures are not necessarily identical, and it is the second which is fundamental to the cognitive development of children" (Lunzer, 1960, p. 201).

This criticism appears most pertinent at the formal-operational level; Piaget describes formal thought with specific propositions of formal logic. Wohlwill criticized Piaget's description of formal-operations as indicative of his tendency "to see nothing but perfect logic and rationality in adult intelligence" (Wohlwill, 1962, p. 82). As we saw earlier, a large number of adults appear *not* to reason this way, and those who do are not consistent in their use of formal reasoning.

It bears repeating that Piaget's studies, with the exception of his observations of his own children, were cross-sectional. In other words, he did not study the stage development of the same subjects over time, but rather noted the tendency of cognitive competencies to appear in roughly similar developmental periods in different subjects. As Lunzer (1960) pointed out, the only experimental test of the structured whole of stages is to study the development of a psychological phenomenon in the same subjects.

The above issues concern Piaget's approach to data collection. His presentation of data also lacks the rigor associated with scientific reports, as well as the clarity which would make his results more comprehensible. As a friendly critic put it, Piaget shows an "indifference to clarity in style of writing" (Furth, 1970, p. 242). Surely part of the difficulty is a translation problem. His major works have been translated from French to English, but by different translators, some of whom are psychologists and some of whom are not. The terms in Piaget's theory are complex, and often have multiple meanings. For example, the translators of *The Growth of Logical Thinking from Childhood to Adolescence* noted that

In the translation "structured whole" we have had to sacrifice some of the connotations of the original in the interest of securing a meaningful and commu-

nicable equivalent. The French term is ensemble des parties, *where ensemble means both "whole" (with the implication of integration as used by Gestalt psychology) and "set" as used by mathematical set theory. For logicians the term should be translated "the set of all sub-sets." (Parsons & Milgram, 1958, p. xix)*

The reader may complain, with Lewis Carroll's Alice, that a word ought to mean what it says!

Piaget's research reports are incomplete. He seldom provides even a summary statistic, such as a mean. Indeed he does not report how many subjects were seen in a given study. A misleading picture of normative cognitive accomplishments often emerges, as in the case of adult functioning at the level of formal operations.

Despite the problems of data collection and presentation, scores of replications by other researchers have confirmed the sequential nature of cognitive stages. Although adolescents and adults may fail to show criterial formal-operational performance on the physical tasks designed by Inhelder and Piaget, most of them probably have the potential for formal thought. Most preadolescents at around age 12 begin to shift their cognitive focus from immediate reality to the world of possibilities and to the future. Rudiments of formal thinking, involving manipulation of logical propositions, begin to enter into their problem solutions. They demonstrate an ability to reason about hypothetical situations, and to reflect upon their own thoughts. For most individuals in Western society, these general cognitive accomplishments are well integrated into their functioning by the late teens, which are also the years of initial decisions on professional or occupational specialization and "life programs" that will carry over well into the years of adulthood. The transition from child to adult thought renders this period one of the most interesting and diverse in the life cycle, a period of lofty ideals and mundane realities. As Piaget put it, "This is the age of great ideals and the beginning of theories, as well as the time of simple present adaptation to reality" (Piaget & Inhelder, 1966/1969, p. 130).

SUMMARY

1. In many ways, adolescent thinking differs from the type of thinking found in childhood. Adolescents are capable of thinking in a more logical fashion, of reasoning about hypothetical situations, of thinking more abstractly, and of thinking about the process of thinking itself.

2. The differences in childhood and adolescent thinking suggest that cognitive development may proceed through stages. Stages of thinking are qualitatively different from each other; they oc-

cur in an invariant sequence; they bear a logical relationship to each other; and they apply generally to a wide range of issues.

3. Jean Piaget's cognitive-developmental theory is primarily concerned with stages in modes of thinking. According to his theory, there is a progressive elaboration of cognitive structures, which are organizing features of the mind determining the individual's understanding of the world.

4. Piaget outlined four stages of cognitive development; the *sensory-motor stage* of infancy is superceded by the *preoperational stage* of early childhood. In later childhood, true mental operations are possible, but still tied to concrete reality in the *concrete-operational stage*. The final stage of cognitive development arises in adolescence: Hypothetical and deductive thinking, which make use of propositional logic, characterize the *formal-operational stage* of cognitive development.

5. The concrete-operational thought of later childhood is not systematic. Students are haphazard in their approach to logic problems in this stage of thinking. In a transitional phase between concrete and formal operations, students gradually become more and more systematic, until finally, in the stage of formal operations, they have tested their alternative solutions thoroughly enough to be sure of the logical necessity of the answers they have arrived at.

6. Training studies, which attempt to induce movement from concrete to formal operations, have demonstrated that the growth of stages is gradual, and that this growth involves a fairly long transitional phase marked by a mixture of concrete- and formal-operational thinking.

7. Piaget described the movement from one stage to another as *equilibration*—the progressive elaboration of cognitive sophistication through experience.

8. Although adolescents appear to develop the systematic approach to logic problems that Piaget suggested, they are not entirely consistent in their use of their newly acquired potential for formal operations. Their approach to problems is not a true "structured whole," defined as thought that is entirely consistent from one problem to another. Rather, adolescents appear to have access to formal thinking only in certain specific situations, perhaps in areas where they have a special aptitude. Some "natural-experimental" situations, such as Kuhn's plant problem, appear

to be more likely to elicit formal thinking than Piaget's natural-science tasks, such as the chemicals problem.

9. By early adolescence, most people seem to have developed the potential for formal-operational thinking. Whether their approach to specific problems makes use of this potential depends on several factors, such as the type of problem, their educational experience, and their interests.

OUTLINE

6. MORAL DEVELOPMENT

One of the major themes of adolescence is value conflict and moral questioning. In this chapter we examine moral development in adolescence. Before we begin the discussion, consider the following moral dilemma concerning plagiarism.

PLAGIARISM

An elective, or nonrequired, course in college had a reputation as being very difficult. All of the students who took the course were aware of this reputation. One of the reasons that the course was so difficult was that five lengthy papers were assigned throughout the term. Consider the circumstances surrounding the following senior's case of plagiarism, and try to answer the questions posed about the dilemma.

A senior in college took this course and wrote the first four papers. When the time came to hand in the fifth paper, he had many other things to do in order to graduate. One of his friends had taken the course two years previously and still had his papers. He asked this friend for one of the papers. He rewrote some parts of it and handed it in, believing that the teacher would never remember a paper that had been written that long ago, especially since many people take the course. However, the professor recognized the paper and the name of the student who had originally written it.

1. What should the teacher do? Why?

2. Suppose the set punishment for plagiarism is explusion from school. Should the professor consider the fact that the student is a senior and is about to graduate? Why or why not?

3. Is expulsion from school a fair punishment for plagiarism? Why? If not, what is a fair punishment? Why?

4. Is the student who loaned the paper guilty in some way? Why? Should he be punished? Why? (Blatt, Colby, & Speicher, 1974)

Psychologists have used the technique of posing moral dilemmas as a major means of assessing moral judgment and charting its developmental history. They believe that answers to questions posed about a moral dilemma such as the one presented above reflect aspects of moral development that change across the life cycle.

In very general terms, moral development concerns the relationship between the individual and society, for moral issues are issues of human social conduct. In considering moral judgment, we need to examine not only people's understanding of moral situations, but also their understanding of social exchange with fellow human beings.

In this chapter, moral development from childhood to adulthood is examined in detail. Several questions guide the discussion: Are there stages in moral thinking, similar to general cognitive stages? Does moral judgment influence moral behavior? Is morality a trait, part of a person's character? Are there absolute values—such as respect for human life—that transcend situations? Does a person's background determine judgment and behavior in moral situations?

DEVELOPMENTAL HISTORY OF MORAL JUDGMENT

Piaget's Position

We begin with a brief discussion of Piaget's position on moral development. The dilemmas that Piaget (1932) presented to children concerned "naughtiness." For example, he asked which child was naughtier, one who accidentally broke 15 cups while on his way to dinner, or one who broke one cup while taking some jam from the cupboard. Piaget found that children up to age 7 or 8 based moral judgments on consequences. The child who caused more objective damage was the naughtier, regardless of intentions. Here is Piaget's interview with Schma, who was 6 years old.

[Have you understood the stories? Let's hear you tell them.]

A little child was called in to dinner. There were fifteen plates on a tray. He didn't know. He opens the door and he breaks the fifteen plates.

[That's very good. And now the second story?]

There was a child. And then this child wanted to go and get some jam. He gets on to a chair, his arm catches on to a cup, and it gets broken.

[Are those children both naughty, or is one not so naughty as the other?]

Both just as naughty.

[How would you punish them?]

The one who broke the fifteen cups: two slaps. The other one, one slap. (Piaget, 1932, p. 120)

In contrast, older children based their judgments on the subjective intentions of the children, as did 9-year-old Gros.

[What did the first one do?]

He broke fifteen cups as he was opening the door.

[And the second one?]

He broke one cup as he was taking some jam.

[Which of these two silly things was naughtiest, do you think?]

The one where he tried to take hold of a cup was because the other boy didn't see.

[Then which one would you punish most?]

The one who broke one cup.

[Why?]

He did it on purpose. If he hadn't taken the jam, it wouldn't have happened. (Piaget, 1932, p. 124)

These replies illustrate the two major aspects of moral judgment outlined by Piaget. *Heteronomous morality* lasts until the stage of concrete operations begins at around age 6. It is characterized by a view of rules as absolute and unchangeable, enforced by adult authority. Wrong-doing is judged to occur when rules are not followed; and badness of an act is judged by its consequences. *Autonomous morality* characterizes adolescent and adult judgments; rules are seen as flexible, and acts are judged by intentions.

Intentions and Consequences The transition from heteronomous to autonomous morality is a result of general cognitive growth, as well as social experiences with peers. Although much later work has confirmed a general shift from a morality of consequences to a morality of intentions, these orientations do not reflect true, unified stages. Piaget recognized this fact and was careful to point it out. "In detail, therefore, the material cannot be said to embody stages properly so called" (Piaget, 1932, p. 119). Research has subsequently documented the mixture of moral judgments on the basis of consequences and intentions, while supporting the general shift. Lickona (1976), for example, reported that younger children are able to judge by intentions, evaluating a plausible intentional lie ("I can't shovel snow from the driveway because I have a headache") as worse than an implausible exaggeration ("The snow in our driveway is way over my head").

Armsby (1971) convincingly argued that Piaget's cup-breaking stories failed to take intentions into account, inasmuch as the damage was accidental in both cases. He asked children to judge which child was naughtier, one who broke one cup on purpose, or one who broke all the family's dishes accidentally. A majority of even the 6-year-old children in this study based their judgments on intentions. In addition, Armsby's data also showed that children make fewer judgments based on intention in situations that have extreme consequences, such as breaking the new color television accidentally.

Children who are given an explanation for misbehavior that indicates mitigating circumstances also take intention into account in deciding on punishment about as often as adolescents and adults do. Students in 1st and 4th grades, as well as adults, were presented with stories in which one child harmed another. A child in one story, for example, threw a bucket of water on another child. With mitigating circumstances, such as the explanation that the doused child was playing dangerously with matches, children and adults alike judged by intentions (Darley, Klosson, & Zanna, 1978).

One study—using students in kindergarten, 2nd grade, 5th grade, and college—revealed that more of the college students focused on intentions in making moral judgments than the children did (Surber, 1977). Mature moral judgment may involve learning that consequences are less relevant than intentions. At the same time, most of us do take consequences into account; the majority of students took consequences into account to some extent in judging behavior.

Cognitive abilities of young children may not permit them to balance intentions and consequences. In answering a dilemma in which a girl accidentally breaks a jar of mustard while trying to help her tired mother finish shopping, 19 of 24 children (all younger than 6) showed that they could use intentions in making their judgments, but they were unable to consider both intentions and consequences at the same time (Gottlieb, Taylor, & Ruderman, 1977). Such an ability awaits further cognitive growth.

Inability to simultaneously consider intentions and consequences may stem from the memory demands of the dilemmas children are asked about. Most of the dilemmas first present a description of the intentions of the central character, then a description of the consequences. If children are less able than adolescents and adults to remember all this information, they might simply judge the act by the most recent—and hence the best remembered—information. In fact, there is some evidence that memory problems are in part responsible for children's judgments based on consequences (Feldman, Klosson, Parsons, Rholes, & Ruble, 1976).

Finally, children may judge acts by consequences because children themselves are often judged by a different set of standards than are adults. For example, when I broke a plate while washing dishes during my early adolescence, my mother scolded me by saying, "Don't be so careless. You broke a plate." On the other hand, when she broke a dish, there was no suggestion of responsibility at all: "Oh, that plate broke," she would say.

Kohlberg's Theory

Lawrence Kohlberg's influential work on moral judgment grew out of Piaget's cognitive-developmental approach. Like Piaget, Kohlberg uses the clinical method to assess an individual's level of moral thought. This method relies on responses to standard moral dilemmas, and on answers to follow-up probe questions, for classifying reasoning into a moral stage. Kohlberg questioned people on nine standard moral dilemmas, which address difficult issues such as commitments involved in promises, mercy killing, and the value of human life. One of Kohlberg's nine dilemmas is presented in Table 6-1; this one is called Heinz's dilemma.

Levels of Moral Judgment

Responses to Kohlberg's nine moral dilemmas fall into three levels of moral judgment, each with two stages. Levels and stages are outlined in Table 6-2. According to Kohlberg, these stages occur in an invariant sequence of forward movement. Furthermore, it is the reasoning behind a reply which is important for classifying stages, rather than the content of the answer per se.

TABLE 6-1 **Heinz's Dilemma**	In Europe, a woman was near death from a very bad disease, a special kind of cancer. There was one drug that the doctors thought might save her. It was a form of radium that a druggist in the same town had recently discovered. The drug was expensive to make, but the druggist was charging 10 times what the drug cost him to make. He paid $200 for the radium and charged $2,000 for a small dose of the drug. The sick woman's husband, Heinz, went to everyone he knew to borrow the money, but he could only get together about $1,000, which was half of what it cost. He told the druggist that his wife was dying and asked him to sell it cheaper or let him pay later. But the druggist said, "No, I discovered the drug and I'm going to make money from it." Heinz got desperate and broke into the man's store to steal the drug for his wife. Should Heinz have done that? Why, or why not?

Source: Kohlberg, 1976.

TABLE 6-2
Levels and Stages in Kohlberg's Theory of Moral Development

LEVEL I. PRECONVENTIONAL LEVEL	WHAT IS RIGHT	REASONS FOR DOING RIGHT
Stage 1. Punishment-and-Obedience Orientation	To avoid breaking rules backed by punishment, obedience for its own sake, and avoiding physical damage to persons and property.	Avoidance of punishment, and the superior power of authorities.
Stage 2. Instrumental Relativism	Following rules only when it is to someone's immediate interest; acting to meet one's own interests and needs and letting others do the same. Right is what's fair, what's an equal exchange, a deal, an agreement.	To serve one's own needs or interests in a world where you have to recognize that other people have their interests, too.

LEVEL II. CONVENTIONAL LEVEL	WHAT IS RIGHT	REASONS FOR DOING RIGHT
Stage 3. Good-Boy/Good-Girl Orientation	Living up to what is expected by people close to you or what people generally expect of people in your role as son, brother, friend, etc. "Being good" is important and means having good motives, showing concern about others. It also means keeping mutual relationships, such as trust, loyalty, respect and gratitude.	The need to be a good person in your own eyes and those of others. Your caring for others. Belief in the Golden Rule. Desire to maintain rules and authority that support stereotypical good behavior.
Stage 4. Law-and-Order Orientation	Fulfilling the actual duties to which you have agreed. Laws are to be upheld except in extreme cases where they conflict with other fixed social duties. Right is also contributing to society, the group, or institution.	To keep the institution going as a whole, to avoid the breakdown in the system "if everyone did it," or the imperative of conscience to meet one's defined obligations (easily confused with Stage 3 belief in rules and authority).

LEVEL III. POSTCONVENTIONAL, OR PRINCIPLED, LEVEL	WHAT IS RIGHT	REASONS FOR DOING RIGHT
Stage 5. Social-Contract Orientation	Being aware that people hold a variety of values and opinions, that most values and rules are relative to your group. These relative rules should usually be upheld, however in the interest of impartiality and because they are the social contract. Some nonrelative values and rights like *life* and *liberty*, however, must be upheld in any society and regardless of majority opinion.	A sense of obligation to law because of one's social contract to make and abide by laws for the welfare of all and for the protection of all people's rights. A feeling of contractual commitment, freely entered upon, to family, friendship, trust, and work obligations. Concern that laws and duties be based on rational calculation of overall utility, "the greatest good for the greatest number."
Stage 6. Universal Ethical Principles	Following self-chosen ethical principles. Particular laws or social agreements are usually valid because they rest on such principles. When laws violate these principles, one acts in accordance with the principle. Principles are universal principles of justice; the equality of human rights and respect for the dignity of human beings as individuals.	The belief as a rational person in the validity of universal moral principles, and a sense of personal commitment to them.

Source: Kohlberg, 1976.

The Preconventional Level Individuals at the preconventional level of moral judgment recognize labels of good and bad, right and wrong, but do not interpret these labels in terms of social conventions or standards. In Stage 1 of moral judgment, the "punishment and obedience orientation," the focus is on physical consequences of an act, and on unquestioning obedience to authority. This stage is very similar to Piaget's heteronomous morality. In response to Heinz's dilemma, one child at Stage 1 answered: "He shouldn't

Lawrence Kohlberg (1927–   ) is a leading American theorist on moral development whose research on moral judgment grew out of Piaget's cognitive-developmental approach. Kohlberg emphasizes role-taking ability as a component of moral development.

(Photo by McElroy/*Newsweek*)

steal the drug, it's a big crime. He didn't get permission, he used force and broke and entered. He did a lot of damage, stealing a very expensive drug and breaking up the store, too" (Kohlberg, 1969, p. 379). In this reply, physical consequences in terms of damage to the drugstore take precedence over the suffering of Heinz's wife, who is not even mentioned.

Stage 2 is called the stage of "instrumental relativism." Judgments at this stage are based on an act's instrumental value in serving the needs of an individual. Consider this reply to Heinz's dilemma: "He shouldn't steal it. The druggist isn't wrong or bad, he just wants to make a profit. That's what you're in business for, to make money" (Kohlberg, 1969, p. 379). The druggist's selfish needs are seen as central to the solution of the dilemma by this child. Again, the suffering of the wife is not alluded to at all.

Preconventional morality is exemplified by most children under age 9 or 10, some adolescents, and many adolescent and adult criminals (Kohlberg, 1976).

The Conventional Level Individuals at the conventional level make moral judgments on the basis of expectations—in the family, the social group, or the nation. Maintaining conventional expectations has a value in its own right.

Stage 3, the first of two conventional stages, is called the "good-boy or good-girl orientation." In this stage, actions in the dilemmas are judged by motive. Good motives lead to good acts, bad motives to bad ones. Conformity to stereotypes of what is good and what pleases others contributes to moral judgments. Here is a Stage 3 reply to Heinz's dilemma: "He shouldn't steal. If his wife dies, he can't be blamed. It isn't because he's heartless or that he doesn't love her enough to do everything that he legally can. The druggist is the selfish or heartless one" (Kohlberg, 1969, p. 379). Stage 3 reasoning emphasizes the need to be a good person in the eyes of others as well as oneself.

Stage 4, the "law-and-order orientation," bases moral judgments on rules, authority, and the maintenance of a social order. Thus, a person at Stage 4 answers Heinz's dilemma as follows: "It is a natural thing for Heinz to want to save his wife but it's still always wrong to steal. He still knows he's stealing and taking a valuable drug from the man who made it" (Kohlberg, 1969, p. 379).

At the conventional level, moral judgments show a loyalty to conformity, as well as identification with persons or groups who maintain the social order. Conventional morality is the level shown by most adolescents and adults in American society, and indeed, in most societies (Kohlberg, 1976).

The Postconventional Level Postconventional moral judgments transcend the authority of persons or conformity to groups; values and principles have their own validity. Individuals at this level understand and accept society's rules, but they view the rules in terms of the principles that underlie them. Rules have no validity for their own sake, however.

Stage 5, the "social-contract orientation," bases moral judgments on individual rights and on standards that have been critically examined and agreed upon as guidelines for behavior for all members of society. The relativism of human values places emphasis on procedural rules, but possibilities for changing the rules are recognized. Here is the reasoning of a person at Stage 5 in response to Heinz's dilemma: "You can't completely blame someone for stealing but extreme circumstances don't really justify taking the law in your own hands. You can't have everyone stealing whenever they get desperate. The end may be good but the ends don't justify the means" (Kohlberg, 1969, p. 380).

The final stage in Kohlberg's postulated sequence is Stage 6, the stage of "universal ethical principles." Judgments of rightness at Stage 6 are based on self-chosen but absolute principles of justice and reciprocity, logical comprehensiveness, universality, and consistency. True moral principles permit no exceptions. Here is a Stage 6 reply to Heinz's dilemma: "Heinz is faced with the decision of whether to consider the other people who need the drug just as badly as his wife. Heinz ought to act not according to his particular feelings toward his wife, but considering the value of all the lives involved" (Kohlberg, 1969, p. 380).

At the postconventional level, moral judgments are made on the basis of *principles*. Conflicts between rules and their underlying principles are resolved in favor of the principles. As an example, some of the civil-rights demonstrations of the 1960s were illegal, but the underlying principle of justice overrode those particular conventions, and led to civil disobedience. A minority of adults over age 20 reach the postconventional level of moral judgment (Kohlberg, 1976).

Kohlberg's model of moral development is intriguing; it is also "moralistic," or so it appears to many critics (e.g., Simpson, 1974). In particular, the stage sequence suggests that higher stage judgments are better—that anyone who reasons at the lower stages is less morally mature. The danger in this conception lies is dismissing large groups of people as less moral in a psychological sense when they have not had the role-taking opportunities to pro-

The March on Washington, August 1963. Many of the civil-rights demonstrations of the 1950s and 1960s were technically illegal. The principle of justice overrode this technicality for many participants, however, leading to civil disobedience.

(Photo by Flip Schulke/Black Star)

gress through the stages. "We claim that each higher stage of reasoning is a more adequate way of resolving moral problems judged by moral-philosophic criteria" (Kohlberg, 1976, p. 46). By implication, high-school and college students, housewives, and residents of underdeveloped cultures are doomed to less adequate moral judgment because, in Kohlberg's model, they are unlikely to reach postconventional moral stages.

Cognitive and Moral Stages

Kohlberg's theory is a special case of cognitive-developmental theory applied to moral domains. It is of particular relevance in the study of adolescence because it concerns changes in judgment that take place between preadolescence and young adulthood. Moral judgment, as a type of reasoning, is related to stages of logical reasoning discussed in the previous chapter. For example, those who have not progressed beyond concrete-operational thought are limited to preconventional moral reasoning. Those who have attained only rudimentary formal operations are limited to conventional moral reasoning (Cauble, 1976; Tomlinson-Keasey & Keasey, 1974).

Research has supported Kohlberg's assertion that stages of moral and cognitive development are related. For example, students in 4th through 7th grades were given tasks to assess their level of cognitive development; these tasks included the pendulum and chemicals problems discussed in Chapter 5. Their level of moral judgment was assessed with Kohlberg's interview in a pretest; they were retested following instruction designed to stimulate thinking at Stage 3 in Kohlberg's scheme. Students at the formal-operational level showed more Stage 3 thinking to begin with, and benefitted far more from instruction, than students in the concrete-operational stage, as shown in Figure 6-1. Students using formal operations increased their Stage 3 usage by 37 percentage points with instruction, in comparison to a 2 percentage-point increase shown by students using concrete operations. Similar increases in Stage 4 usage with instruction have been shown for students who were further along in their stage of cognitive development (Walker & Richards, 1979).

This does not mean, however, that everyone who has reached full formal operations shows high-level moral judgments; cognitive stages are prerequisites, but they are not guarantees. Aristotle, in fact, recognized the distinction between intelligence and morality more than 2,000 years ago. "When we are speaking of a man's character we do not describe him as wise or understanding, but as patient or temperate" (*Ethics*, Book I).

FIGURE 6-1
**Percentage of Stage 3
moral judgments by
cognitive level, before
and after instruction.**

(From Walker, 1980.)

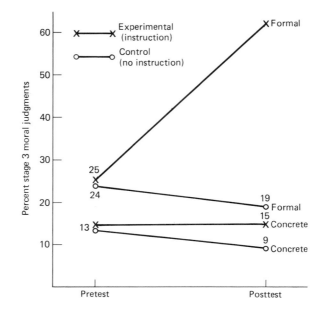

**Moral Stages and
Development**

Few of us are neutral about moral issues; witness the long history of legal dispute and public debate over the issue of abortion. Because Kohlberg's research and theory inevitably suggest moral education, the formal characteristics of the stages and of stage movement deserve careful attention.

The stages outlined in Table 6-2 appear to be qualitatively different from each other. Examples of reasoning offered by real respondents to the moral-judgment interview can be reliably assigned to a stage by trained coders, which suggests that the stages represent recognizably different types of reasoning. Although the Kohlberg coding scheme is difficult to learn and has been constantly revised over the last few years, coders agree on stage assignment about 70–85 percent of the time (Kurtines & Greif, 1974).

The Defining Issues Test of Moral Judgment The Kohlberg moral judgment interview must be individually administered and laboriously coded to yield a score representing stage of moral judgment. James Rest and his colleagues have devised a much simpler method of assessing moral judgment, called the Defining Issues Test (Rest, Cooper, Coder, Masanz, & Anderson, 1974). The Defining Issues Test uses the same situations as Kohlberg's dilemmas, but instead of asking open-ended questions about the dilemmas, it presents a series of questions from which the subject must choose the most important. It can therefore be scored quickly and objectively, and it minimizes individual differences in verbal expressiveness. Some of the questions the subject must choose from on Heinz's dilemma are

Isn't it only natural for a loving husband to care so much for his wife that he'd steal?

Is Heinz willing to risk getting shot as a burglar or going to jail for the chance that stealing the drug might help?

What values are going to be the basis for governing human interaction? (Rest et al., 1974)

The Defining Issues Test yields a score reflecting the amount of principled—or postconventional—choices an individual makes. The percentage of use for each of Kohlberg's other stages can also be calculated. Research indicates that there is a strong relationship between Kohlberg's and Rest's assessments of moral judgment, but that they are not identical (Rest et al., 1974; Froming & McColgan, 1979).

Cross-sectional Studies of Stages   All of Piaget's studies of moral judgment, and many of the studies on Kohlberg's theory, have been cross-sectional in nature. Individuals in different age groups have been assessed for their level of moral judgment; differences among age groups are assumed to represent developmental changes in moral and cognitive maturity.

Groups of people who are presumably more "advanced" do use more principled reasoning in Kohlberg's interviews (Kohlberg, 1969) and make more principled choices on the Defining Issues Test (Rest, Davison, & Robbins, 1978). College graduates made a majority of principled choices on this test, in comparison to less than one-fourth of the junior high-school students tested. Senior high-school students and college students fell in between these two groups in percentage of principled choices.

Longitudinal Studies of Stages   The best evidence for a sequence of stages is longitudinal evidence, in which the same people are retested at intervals for their level of moral reasoning. Since the late 1950s, Kohlberg and his colleagues have been assessing moral judgment in the same group of boys at 3-year intervals, starting from the time they were preadolescents (Kohlberg, 1969). Indeed, these boys (now young men) have shown rather consistent sequential stage movement.

Adolescents have shown gains in principled choices on the Defining Issues Test in short-term longitudinal studies. Junior and senior high-school students retested after 2 years made gains in higher-stage judgments at the expense of lower stages. A majority of the students advanced in their stage of moral judgment, although a few (9 percent) showed a downward shift in moral stage (Rest, 1975).

Cohort Analyses   Moral judgment may be particularly susceptible to cohort effects, changes in moral reasoning that are attributable to time of birth, because of the historical and cultural events a given birth cohort experiences. Consider Kohlberg's longitudinal sample of young men who were in their early teens in the 1950s; they have experienced such events as the Vietnam War, student protests, the civil-rights movement, and Watergate. These events have involved moral components, such as fairness. Changes in moral judgment might conceivably be a by-product of cultural change experienced by this birth cohort.

Rest presented evidence, however, that cohort effects are minimal on the Defining Issues Test, as Figure 6-2 shows. Three

FIGURE 6-2
Assessment of age and cohort effects on moral judgment principled reasoning (P-score). Cohort effects are minimal.

(From Rest, Davison, & Robbins, 1978. Copyright © 1978 by the Society for Research in Child Development, Inc.)

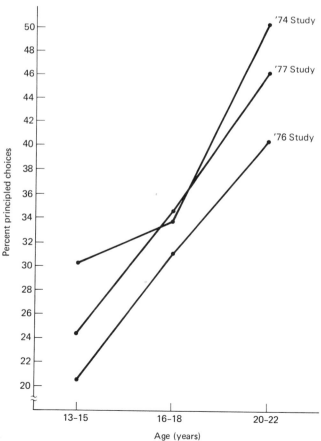

groups of students of different ages were tested at three separate times, allowing a separate assessment of age and cohort effects. There was the usual increase in moral judgment stage with age, but no major differences for the three birth cohorts at either time (Rest et al., 1978).

The Issue of Sequentiality

Kohlberg has steadfastly contended that the six stages of moral judgment occur in an invariant sequence. In this view, moral stages represent more than personality types. Rather, an individual moves through the stages successively; a person who reaches Stage 4 will of necessity have passed through Stages 1, 2, and 3. The theory permits neither skipping stages nor regression.

For technical reasons, a researcher should not use the same group of subjects to examine sequentiality as were used to construct the stage types in the first place. Unfortunately, Kohlberg has used this approach. Also, a 3-year interval between assessments makes data interpretation difficult. Boys who showed no stage advance in a 3-year period would not refute sequentiality because they might be "stuck" at a particular stage for some time. Similarly, boys who advanced by more than one stage would not disprove sequentiality because they might have gone through the intervening stages in the interval between testings. The only possibility that would pose problems for the interpretation of invariant sequence would be those subjects who regressed, that is, who showed lower-stage judgments at the later testing (Kuhn, 1976).

Regression In fact, Kohlberg and Kramer (1969) found just such a pattern of regression among several participants in the longitudinal study, between the end of high school and their mid-college years. After reaching Stage 4 (law-and-order orientation), one-fifth of the middle-class adolescents temporarily regressed to Stage 2 before moving on to Stage 5 (social-contract orientation). What are we to make of this regression? Some would suggest that it refutes the sequential-stage hypothesis. "The downward shift seems to indicate that the stage sequence is flexible. Thus, this longitudinal study provides no clear evidence for either the invariant developmental sequence or the reorganization of stages as postulated by Kohlberg" (Kurtines & Greif, 1974, p. 463).

An alternative view was provided by Turiel (1974). He interviewed college students using Kohlberg's dilemmas, as well as using questions on social and conventional norms. Turiel interpreted the moral relativism in this age group as a transitional phase between Stages 4 and 5, when an individual moves from conventional to postconventional morality. He argued that it was similar to

Stage 2 in content alone, and not in underlying structure. Many of these students expressed the view that both moral and conventional values are arbitrary. One 21-year-old male, for example, expressed it this way:

If there is a God—the Jewish people, for example, have a God who says not only don't kill and don't commit adultery and don't steal, but wear fringes on your garments. You are supposed to do that. Wear fringes to signify the presence of God. The religion says God recognizes that one is more important than the other—in the original Ten Commandments. But if there is a God and he is telling you what is right, then he can prescribe all kinds of conduct. If it all comes from God, maybe it is just as important to wear fringes on your garments as to abstain from killing. But if society is just claiming to have or adhere to a divine or some kind of a priori or supernatural, or any kind of superhuman code, and I don't see any basis for it, it doesn't matter to me if they say the code prohibits killing or the code prohibits going nude. (Turiel, 1974, p. 25)

When Turiel reinterviewed these students 2 years later, the previously transitional students had progressed to the next higher stage of moral reasoning. He argued that what looked like regression was merely the normal confusion of a transitional phase, and cited the new interviews as evidence (Turiel, 1974).

Kohlberg (1973) has himself reconsidered the data on regression; he refined his coding scheme and reanalyzed the college students' responses. The later analysis indicated that college "regressors" were actually in transition to Stage 5, as Turiel had suggested. Kohlberg did not, however, provide data on the reliability of this new coding scheme. If the statements are so similar to Stage 2 thinking that Kohlberg himself was fooled about their structural nature, reliability of the new scheme is an important question.

Meanwhile, Deanna Kuhn (1976) assessed the short-term sequentiality of Kohlberg's moral stages by testing 50 children twice, at 6 month intervals. Examination of data after 6 months revealed no stability; children declined in stage as well as increased. After a 1-year interval, however, Kuhn found more regular stage advance. Among her 50 subjects, 32 increased in stage, 13 showed no change, and only 5 declined. Given the difficulties of "proving" stage progressions in developmental research, this study provides a strong suggestion of sequentiality in Kohlberg's moral stages but indicates that an interval of at least 1 year is needed to show the progression. Presumably the instability observed in shorter intervals reflects transitional thinking. We encountered a similar problem when examining Piaget's account of the transition from concrete to formal operations.

A study of students who were 13 years old when first tested for moral stage provides further clarification of the regression issue.

When they were reinterviewed 3 years later, very few of the students who were originally classified in the lower stages (Stages 1, 2, or 3) had regressed, whereas about one-fourth of the students classified in the higher stages (Stages 4, 5, or 6) had regressed (Holstein, 1976).

Taken as a whole, these studies on regression suggest that there is some downward shift in moral judgment for some adolescents. The majority of individuals, however, show stepwise progress in their moral development. The greatest instability in stage classification is at the higher stages of moral judgment. Much of the instability of stage classification at the higher stages is probably due to the flawed coding scheme developed by Kohlberg and his colleagues. Problems with the coding scheme even led Kohlberg, who developed strategies for classifying replies to dilemmas into stages in the first place, to misclassify some adolescents as regressors. Rest's more objective scoring methods for the Defining Issues Test corroborate the finding that some adolescents do show downward stage movement, or regression. The percentage of students who regress (9 percent) is overshadowed, however, by those who advance (58 percent) or remain at their same stage (14 percent) when they are retested (Rest, 1975).

The Structured Whole in Moral Development

A structured whole refers to generalized stage usage, that is, consistent application of the structures at a given stage. According to this principle, a person judges most moral issues at one stage, with the remaining judgments in adjacent stages. Moral judgments that skip all about in the stage sequence do not represent structured, unitary thinking. Consistency in judgment should apply even on different types of moral dilemmas. Heinz's dilemma concerned the value of human life versus property and the role of law. Another of Kohlberg's dilemmas (Table 6-3) involves a father who breaks a promise to his son. We would expect people to judge these very dif-

---

TABLE 6-3
One of Kohlberg's Dilemmas: The Broken Promise

Joe is a 14-year-old boy who wanted to go to camp very much. His father promised him he could go if he saved up the money for it himself. So Joe worked hard at his paper route and saved up the $40 it cost to go to camp and a little more besides. But just before camp was going to start, his father changed his mind. Some of his friends decided to go on a special fishing trip, and Joe's father was short of the money it would cost. So he told Joe to give him the money he had saved from the paper route. Joe didn't want to give up going to camp, so he thought of refusing to give his father the money.

Source: Kohlberg, 1976.

ferent moral situations at the same stage in order to endorse the structured whole.

Kohlberg (1976) reported that adolescents and adults who are presented moral dilemmas make about half of their judgments at one dominant stage in his scheme. The remaining half of their judgments are distributed in the two adjacent stages. Although we might hope for more than half of one's judgments at the dominant stage, Kohlberg presented an explanation for the observed pattern that is consistent with a structured whole.

An individual's response profile typically represents a pattern composed of the dominant stage he is in, a stage he is leaving but still uses somewhat and a stage he is moving into but which has not yet "crystallized." (Kohlberg, 1969, p. 387)

Allinsmith (1960) did not use Kohlberg's dilemmas, but he used similar verbal situations with a moral component. In one, a boy steals money while no one is watching from a man who is asleep in the park. Intensity of guilt in one type of transgression was unrelated to guilt in others. Adolescent and preadolescent subjects might write guilty responses to the situation of theft in the park, but not to a situation involving a boy's disobedience to his mother's orders. Guilt, however, may be relatively independent of moral judgment.

Another study (Tomlinson-Keasey & Keasey, 1972) did use seven of Kohlberg's dilemmas and found that preadolescent respondents showed very little consistency in moral judgment from one dilemma to the next. The predominantly white students tended to give high-stage judgments to a dilemma on whether to return a runaway slave and to the story of the promise-breaking father. There was no consistency to responses on the other five dilemmas, however. St. Clair (1976) found a similar lack of consistency on Kohlberg's dilemmas among college students.

Turiel conceives of the structured whole not as a consistent pattern of response from a given subject but rather as "ideal types" that represent stages.

Stages are structured wholes not so much because they reflect a unitary form of individual functioning but because they refer to qualitatively different forms of thought. Consequently, the stages define "ideal types" which are representative of forms of thought rather than people. (Turiel, 1969, p. 115)

Stages do refer to forms of thought and not to people, but the structured-whole concept implies that these forms of thought are used *by* people in a consistent manner.

Research on Piaget's formal operations suffered from a similar lack of consistency across situations, as outlined in Chapter 5. If the general stage interpretation is correct, there are two possible sources of such inconsistency. First, the tasks designed to measure the concept might be at fault. Second, adolescents might become more consistent in reasoning as they move into adulthood. Longitudinal studies, preferably using subjects from a variety of backgrounds, are needed to assess the nature of inconsistency in judgments across the life span. Unfortunately, few such studies are in progress as of the early 1980s.

Moral Dilemmas, Revisited The dilemmas used to measure moral judgment have relied heavily on weighty issues such as human life, mercy killing, and slavery. These tasks may obscure some of the thinking of adolescents by being so remote from their lives. One reseacher simply asked adolescents in 7th, 9th, and 12th grades to write a realistic moral dilemma, with no examples provided. Students wrote dilemmas on a wide range of issues, from alcohol use to civil rights, from smoking cigarettes to stealing (Yussen, 1977). In general, it appears that dilemmas that spontaneously occur to adolescents involve issues closer to their own lives. It is conceivable that their judgments would be more consistent on dilemmas of this type.

Heinz's dilemma, in fact, appears rather implausible. Answers that adolescents give to an implausible dilemma may be less thoughtful because it is a fanciful situation. In *Crime and Punishment*, Dostoevski's brooding novel about a poor young student's psychological turmoil over a murder he has committed, the student Raskolnikov poses a dilemma to his friend Sonia. He asks which she would choose to die: Luzhin, the scoundrel who attempted to brand her as a thief, or Sonia's tubercular stepmother and her children. Sonia rejects Raskolnikov's dilemma because it is too implausible: "How could such a thing depend on my decision?"

People do seem to act and reason differently when they are confronting their own life dilemmas. Consider a young man who was given Kohlberg's moral judgment interview as a senior in college. At that time, he scored in the highest level of moral judgment, the level of absolute principles; he advocated without hesitation the moral "rightness" of Heinz's stealing the drug to save a life. In his own life, however, he confronted a dilemma in which fairness and justice were issues. He was having an affair with a woman who was married, and whose husband had not been told of the affair. The young man acknowledged that this situation constituted a moral violation. The young man's dilemma was resolved when the husband discovered the affair on his own, but the young man was shaken in the process.

What I learned was I became much less absolute. I was always aware of the kind of situation in which truth was not absolute. If a person comes up to me with a gun in his hand, in that situation I never thought that the truth was that absolute. But with interpersonal situations that dealt with psychological realities and with psychological feelings, with emotions, I felt that the truth should win out in most situations. Then after that situation, I became more relativistic about it. As you can tell, right now, I have not worked out a principle that is satisfactory to me that would resolve that issue if it happened again tomorrow. (Gilligan & Murphy, 1979, pp. 94–95)

Five years later, when the young man was 27, he was retested on the moral judgment interview, and his score had fallen back to the transitional level. Reflecting back on the affair with the woman whose husband was being deceived, he described his moral bewilderment as resulting from "an incredible amount of immaturity on my part." He elaborated:

The justice approach was really blinding me to a lot of issues. And, in a sense, I was trying to make it a justice issue, and it really blinded me to a lot of the realities of the problem. And now, being in a situation where, you know, married for a few years . . . it's a very different perspective to have on it. I think that the moral issue was simply the matter of honesty and truth in the relationship. But even if that had been fulfilled, we would have been left with the interpersonal dilemma of life choices, of what kind of relationship you want in your life. It could have been just as easy that [she] told her husband. So what? [You are] still left with the choice. And morality won't do you one bit of good in that decision. (Gilligan & Murphy, 1979, p. 96)

This young man illustrates a developmental change that many people seem to go through in the realm of moral judgment (Gilligan & Murphy, 1979). Real-life dilemmas have changed this young man's perspective even on hypothetical ones.

MORAL JUDGMENT AND MORAL BEHAVIOR

We often assume that a person's level of moral behavior is a character trait—a relatively enduring moral stance. We describe people as "honest," "good," or "altruistic," and assume that the descriptions accurately reflect their tendencies when confronted with a moral situation. We also tend to assume that our own behavior is a consistent reflection of our character. And yet, inconsistency of behavior in situations with moral overtones seems more the rule than the exception.

The same individual who cheats on one occasion but not on another, who lies in one context but is truthful in another, who steals at one time but helps a friend generously and unselfishly at another, may still readily construe himself as basically honest and moral. (Mischel & Mischel, 1976, p. 106)

In the 1920s, Hartshorne and May conducted a now-classic series of studies on "character." They concluded that very little consistency is evident in situations involving honesty. Some young adolescents would cheat in one situation, and yet return change to a storekeeper who made a mistake (Hartshorne, May, & Shuttleworth, 1930).

Cheating

Cheating has been a favorite target of psychologists' studies; and the results are depressing, if not surprising. Grinder (1962) designed an ingenious apparatus to measure cheating among preadolescents (aged 11–12 years). His "ray gun" was presented as a test of marksmanship—rather like the electronic games for shooting asteroids one finds in college-town bars. A score between 0 and 5 was possible with each pull of the trigger; but the devilish apparatus was preprogrammed so that after 20 shots, one would score 31. In order to win a marksman's badge, the shooter had to score 35. "Sharpshooter" and "expert" badges required 40 and 45 points, respectively. Since students tabulated their own scores, however, cheating was both possible and (supposedly) undetectable. Grinder found that fully 70 percent of his subjects cheated in order to win a badge. Furthermore, 40 percent of them cheated by more than 10 points to reach the "expert" category. His subjects were among a group whose parents had been interviewed several years earlier in a study of child-rearing techniques (Sears, Maccoby, & Levin, 1957). He thought that those children whose relationship to their parents was characterized by "warmth" might be more likely to resist the temptation to cheat. This optimistic prediction was not supported, however. No obvious relationship emerged between parental warmth and resistance to temptation.

Academic Cheating The ray gun is a clever test, but it might be argued that cheating to get a badge is not a very serious matter. What of academic cheating? Studies on this topic find a similar high level of cheating. One study, for example, presented 5th graders with two types of math tests, on one of which cheating was less likely to be detected. Students corrected their own papers while the teacher was away, but they did it on specially treated carbon paper that revealed changed answers to the experimenter. More cheating occurred, among both boys and girls, on the test that was not likely to result in detection (Johnson & Gormly, 1972).

It appears that many, if not most, adolescents cheat at one time or another. Although cheating appears not to be a trait that shows consistency from one situation to another, we might ask if people who are higher in their stage of moral judgments are less *likely* to cheat than those at lower stages.

To test this hypothesis, a group of researchers (Schwartz, Feldman, Brown, & Heingartner, 1969) administered four of Kohlberg's moral dilemmas, along with a cheating test, to 35 undergraduate males at the University of Michigan. The cheating situation was a vocabulary test including 12 very difficult and obscure words; the highest score obtained by a control group with no access to answers was 6. The test group, however, had the answers printed on the back of their tests. "Cheating" was operationally defined as scoring above 6 on the test. There was also a monetary incentive to cheat: Students were told they would receive 20 cents for each correct answer. Of those students above the median in moral judgment, only 17 percent cheated, whereas over half of those below the median cheated. Thus although nearly one-fifth of those high in moral judgment cheated, there appears to be a tendency for higher moral judgment to be associated with more honorable behavior.

Kohlberg (1969) has argued that one should not expect stage of moral judgment to determine behavior in these pseudomoral situations. His stages are cognitive and judgmental, which means they reflect how an individual evaluates a moral situation. Behavior in any given situation one encounters is determined by several factors, only one of which is stage of moral judgment. Students may not even think about contrived cheating tests in moral terms.

Obedience

Stanley Milgram designed a study to test the limits of obedience to authority. Briefly, Milgram (1965) had subjects come to a laboratory at Yale University, ostensibly to participate in a study of the effects of punishment—in the form of electric shocks—on learning. A confederate of Milgram's served as "learner," although his "teacher" subjects were deceived into believing that roles were assigned by chance and that the "learners" were also participants in the experiment. Milgram had shown that a majority of people could be induced by an authority figure to deliver potentially dangerous shocks to another human being—despite protests of pain.

Most of us view the administration of severe electric shock to another person as a morally abhorrent act. If there is a relationship between moral judgment and moral behavior, we would expect to find it in this situation. In one study of this relationship, college men were given a moral judgment interview as well as a test of their moral conduct in the Milgram shock situation (Podd, 1972). Although 32 of these students scored at the highest moral level, they were no more likely to refrain from administering the maximum shock ("danger—severe shock") than the lower-stage students. This finding is both important and depressing. It indicates that even individuals who are more "moral" in their level of judgment can be induced by an authority figure to inflict pain on their fellow human beings.

In fairness, however, it should be pointed out that the powerful Milgram situation has characteristics that entangle subjects in ways that are difficult to overcome by refusing to carry out the experiment. Deference to the legitimate authority leads many people to obedience despite their moral reservations. Consider the following subject, who had just administered what he thought was a shock of 195 volts.

"You see he's hollering. Hear that. Gee, I don't know." The experimenter says, *"The experiment requires that you go on." "I know it does, sir, but I mean—huh—he don't know what he's in for. He's up to 195 volts!"*

[210 volts delivered]

[225 volts delivered]

[240 bolts delivered] "Aw no. You mean I've got to keep going up with the scale? No sir. He's hollering in there. I'm not going to give him 450 volts!" (Milgram, 1974, p. 74)

In fact, this subject *does* proceed through the sequence to 450 volts under orders from the experimenter.

Prosocial Behavior   The studies described above, on cheating and on administration of electric shocks, involve negative behavior and its relationship to level of moral judgment. These studies collectively suggest that the relationship between moral judgment and refraining from negative behavior is negligible. Perhaps people who reach higher levels of moral judgment are more likely to engage in prosocial behavior, however, even if they do not reduce their negative social behavior.

Individuals over a wide age range from adolescence to adulthood were recruited for a study on this relationship through newspaper advertisements: "Good pay for little work—Subjects wanted for psychological experiments" (Krebs & Rosenwald, 1977). The first 31 persons who responded to the ad were given Kohlberg's moral judgment test. They were then told that the researcher had been unable to schedule a room for the remainder of the psychological tests; therefore, participants were asked to take the tests home, fill them out, and return them by mail in stamped and preaddressed envelopes. As Figure 6-3 shows, the participants who were higher in stage of moral judgment were more likely to return the completed

FIGURE 6-3
The relationship be-
tween moral judgment
and prosocial behavior.
Students at higher
stages of moral reason-
ing were more likely to
return their question-
naires on time.

(From Krebs & Rosenwald,
1977.)

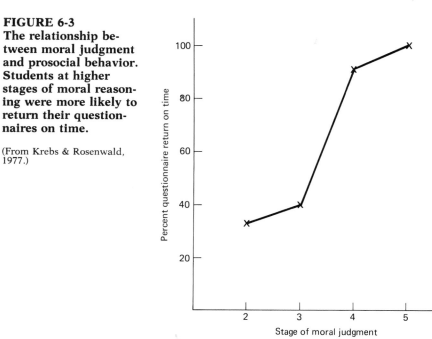

tests to the experimenters. One might conclude that "trust" and "obligation" were more salient aspects of the situation for the people in the higher stages of moral judgment.

On a more general level, moral behavior may be related to situational and personality factors as well as to level of moral judgment. Elms and Milgram (1966) contacted 40 subjects from the shock experiment: 20 who had been fully obedient and 20 who had defied the experimenter. The obedient subjects scored significantly higher on the California F Scale, a measure of authoritarianism. Hogan (1970) reported a similar relationship between F-Scale scores and moral judgment.

The Good Samaritan The parable of the Good Samaritan suggested a study of moral behavior to Darley and Batson (1973). The parable goes as follows:

A man was going down from Jerusalem to Jericho, and he fell among robbers, who stripped him and beat him, and departed, leaving him half dead. Now by chance a priest was going down the road; and when he saw him he passed by on the other side. So likewise a Levite, when he came to the place and saw him, passed by on the other side. But a Samaritan, as he journeyed, came to where he was; and when he saw him, he had compassion, and went to him and bound up his wounds, pouring on oil and wine; then he set him on his own beast and brought him to an inn and took care of him. (Luke 10:20–34)

Darley and Batson asked 47 students at the Princeton Theological Seminary to participate in a study of "religious education and vocations." All students were initially given personality questionnaires in one building, after which they were to give a talk in another building, either on the Good Samaritan parable, or on job opportunities for seminarians. Some participants were told they were late for the talk and had to rush across campus; others had ample time. Darley and Batson had hired an actor and stationed him along the students' route. As each passed, the shabbily dressed actor was slumped in an alleyway, with head down and eyes closed, coughing and groaning. This man's plight was about as close to that of the man on the road from Jerusalem to Jericho as one could construct in Princeton, New Jersey, in the 1970s. The results were surprising: 60 percent of these seminarians passed by the man without offering any assistance. Furthermore, the Good Samaritan speechmakers were no more likely to stop than other students. Some of them, in fact, stepped over the man on the way to deliver their speeches. Students who most frequently helped were those not in a hurry. Darley and Batson concluded that the study confirmed the notion that "ethics becomes a luxury as the speed of our daily lives increases" (Darley & Batson, 1973, p. 107).

EFFECTS OF SOCIAL ENVIRONMENT ON MORAL DEVELOPMENT

If ethics can be described as a "luxury" in Princeton, New Jersey, consider the Ik, a group dwelling in Kidepo Valley between Kenya and Uganda, described by anthropologist Colin Turnbull. Although the Ik were a nomadic group, they were forced to settle in Kidepo, which is unsuited for hunting and gathering; and they were forbidden to hunt in the nearby Kidepo National Park. With no knowledge of farming, starvation of the entire group became a real possibility. A smug Western concept of goodness seems out of place when applied to the starving Ik.

Their very word for "good," marang is defined in terms of food. "Goodness," marangik, is defined simply as "food," or, if you press, this will be clarified as "the possession of food," and still further clarified as "individual possession of food." Then if you try the word as an adjective and attempt to discover what their concept is of a "good man," iakw anamarang, hoping that the answer will be that a good man is a man who helps you fill your own stomach, you get the truly Icien answer: a good man is one who has a full stomach. There is goodness in being, but none in doing, at least not in doing to others. (Turnbull, 1973, p. 112)

The relationship between moral judgment and moral conduct appears to be negligible, especially in situations involving negative human conduct such as cheating. However, we may still ask if there are characteristics of the social environment that help to enhance moral judgment and moral behavior.

Milgram's obedience situation provides an example of social effects on behavior. People find it difficult to resist an authority figure's supposed superior competence, the social agreement they have entered into, and the social norms of interaction that include accepting another's "definition of the situation." One is tempted to compare the obedience experiment with related, real-life phenomena. In Nazi Germany, for example, ordinary citizens complied with the definition of the situation imposed by the powerful authority figure Hitler embodied. Unquestioned obedience was the sad result. More recently, ordinary American soldiers participated in a massacre of Vietnamese men, women, and children at My Lai during the Vietnam War. High-level members of Nixon's White House staff also exhibited a failure of moral judgment that led to Watergate. We can see from these events that a malevolent social situation can command the darker side of human nature. Let us turn to studies that examine the effects of the social environment on adolescents' judgments and behavior in more normal situations.

Role-Taking Opportunities

Kohlberg (1976) has argued that stage of moral judgment is advanced by increased opportunities for role-taking. Each of Kohlberg's stages requires different role-taking abilities. For example,

The Watergate experience. People find it difficult to resist an authority figure's supposed superior competence and "definition of the situation." Sadly, this phenomenon can lead to unquestioned obedience and a failure of moral judgment, as shown by some high-level staff members of the Nixon Administration during Watergate.

(United Press International Photo)

the Stage 2 instrumental relativist judges right actions as those that are personally valuable; putting oneself in another's place is a way of judging the other's intentions. Similarly, an individual at the Stage 4 law-and-order orientation considers the consequences for the group or society for any moral decisions; role-taking involves viewing an action from the perspective of the generalized other—from people of all positions or roles (Selman, 1976). Social environments that provide practice in role-taking, and greater peer-group participation, might therefore lead to faster movement through the stages—and ultimately to higher stage attainment.

Different types of institutions provide different role-taking practice. Among students in the institutional environment represented by schools, higher social participation in organizations, with the attendant popularity and leadership ratings, is associated with a higher level of moral judgment (Keasey, 1971). On the other side of the coin, American orphanages represent environments with chronically low social participation, and individuals living in them have quite low scores on the moral maturity scale (Kohlberg, 1976).

Role-Playing Studies One way of testing the effects of social participation experimentally is to give students opportunities to take other people's perspective in moral situations such as Heinz's drug-stealing dilemma (Arbuthnot, 1975). Introductory psychology students who were involved in such "role-playing" with opponents who made higher-stage judgments increased in moral judgment. Furthermore, they maintained the higher-stage thinking for at least 1 week. A variety of such role-taking discussions have been successful in raising the level of moral judgment for a short period of time. They include discussions on the film *Fail-Safe*, in which New York City is bombed by the American government to avert a nuclear war after an accidental bombing of Moscow (Lorimer, 1970); discussions of short stories and case studies that contain a moral component (Keefe, 1976); discussions headed by a group leader who presents more sophisticated moral reasoning than the students in the group (Bono, 1976); and role-playing in the situations presented in Kohlberg's moral dilemmas (Turiel, 1969). These studies support the contention that developmental changes in moral judgment result in part from the adolescent's exposure to a higher "moral environment"; the effect is enhanced when the adolescent engages in active role playing within that environment. Young adolescents scoring high on perspective-taking ability were more likely to have reached higher stages of moral development; perspective-taking ability appears to be a prerequisite for reaching as far as Stage 3 in moral development (Walker, 1980).

**Parent Influences on
Moral Development**

Parents are in a position to have the strongest effect on their children's moral environment, although peers are increasingly important in adolescence. The importance of the parents' role is exemplified by the emphasis on socialization in most accounts of moral development (e.g., Hoffman, 1980).

Presence or absence of a parent might have an effect on many forms of social development, including moral judgment. In a study of father absence, Hoffman (1971) gave morality tests to 53 7th graders whose fathers were absent for at least 6 months prior to the study, and to an equal number whose fathers were present. Unfortunately, Hoffman did not report the reasons for father absence, which might have a bearing on moral development.

The tests included "guilt" stories for the students to complete (e.g., a child cheats in a swimming race and wins), as well as moral dilemmas. Boys whose fathers were present wrote stories showing significantly more guilt, and they reasoned significantly higher in moral judgment. In addition, teachers reported that the father-absent boys were more aggressive. None of these relationships held for the girls in Hoffman's study. Hoffman concluded that "father absence has adverse effects on moral development in boys" (1971, p. 403). A variety of theoretical perspectives emphasize the importance of the same-sex parent for both identification and moral development.

College women whose fathers were absent were compared with women from intact families on level of moral judgment. Overall, there was no difference between level of moral judgment for father-present and father-absent women. However, among those whose fathers were absent, there was an age effect. The younger the women had been when father absence occurred, the lower their level of moral judgment (Parish & Copeland, 1981).

Studies of the relationship between parents' and children's moral judgment further support the stronger influence of parents on the moral level of sons than of daughters. A study of moral judgment among parents and adolescent children revealed no relationship between moral level of parents and daughters, in either early or late adolescence. Among sons and parents, moral level was significantly related for the younger adolescents, aged 10–15, but not for older adolescents, aged 16–20 (Haan, Langer, & Kohlberg, 1976).

Modeling Parents influence the behavior of their children by providing models of correct behavior in situations having moral overtones. Although Bandura and McDonald (1963) did not test the effects of *parental* modeling, they found that *other* adults who modelled moral judgments strongly affected the judgments of children (aged 5–11). Another test of adult models (Cowan, Langer, Heavenrich, & Nathanson, 1969) showed essentially the same strong effect on moral judgments. It seems reasonable to conclude that parents' behavior would be at least as strong as that of adult strangers in influencing moral judgments, but studies of parental modeling, surprisingly, are unavailable.

Disciplinary Measures Techniques of discipline used by parents are often assumed to influence moral development. For example, physical punishment might produce lower levels of moral judgment and behavior than techniques of discipline emphasizing reasoning or threats of withdrawal of love. Highest levels of moral development might be elicited by parents who reason, present alternatives, and allow their children some freedom of choice in behavior. As we shall see, evidence for these hypothesized relationships is tentative.

Hoffman and Saltzstein (1967) examined the effects of discipline on moral development among a large group of young adolescent boys in Detroit. They considered three types of discipline: power assertion, including physical punishment; love withdrawal; and reasoning, in which the consequences of the child's behavior for other people were explained. Moral development was assessed on paper-and-pencil tests, as well as through ratings by teachers and peers. Hoffman and Saltzstein found that reasoning was associated with higher levels of moral development, and power assertion with lower levels, when these techniques were practiced by mothers. Love withdrawal appeared to be unrelated to moral development. These results are suggestive, but they are far from conclusive. The relationships outlined did not hold for fathers' discipline techniques. Furthermore, they did not hold among lower-class boys. Apparently only middle-class mothers' discipline exerts these influences. Note also that girls were not tested in this study.

Discipline was also examined among two groups of men in Milgram's shock experiment. A group of men who had obeyed fully—delivering maximum shocks—reported that their parents had used extremely mild punishment or none at all. Standard spankings and some cases of intense physical punishment were reported by a group of subjects who had refused to deliver shocks (Elms & Milgram, 1966). Thus, physical punishment and power assertion were associated with *higher* levels of moral conduct in this study.

A study with a very large number of participants also provided information that further clouds the relationship between moral judgment and moral behavior. In the late 1960s, nearly 1,000 students in the Bay Area of San Francisco were given moral-judgment questionnaires, including five of Kohlberg's dilemmas. Students reasoning at the higher, postconventional level reported that they had had rather unpleasant upbringings. Mothers of principled males had "teased and made fun of them" in a conflicted relationship; principled females had mothers who were disappointed in them, were quick to point out their own sacrifices for their daughters, and were least likely to comfort them when they were upset (Haan, Smith, & Block, 1968). The relationship between principled moral judgment and earlier socialization techniques used by parents was not the sort predicted earlier. In fact, the socialization techniques depicted in this study were very unpleasant.

It appears, therefore, that any conclusions on the relationship between moral development and parental discipline must be highly tentative. The effects of disciplinary techniques depend on many factors; one important one is undoubtedly the child's interpretation of the parents' motives. Discipline, whatever the technique, occurs within the context of a relationship; and the nature of that relationship may be even more important than the type of discipline.

SEX DIFFERENCES IN MORAL DEVELOPMENT

Two contradictory predictions have been offered about sex differences in moral development. One holds that girls are more "socialized," and as a result, exhibit more desirable social behavior in a moral sense. The other prediction, following Freud, holds that girls develop less strong consciences because of the dynamics of family interaction. As we just saw, the relationship between moral development and parent measures is less clear for girls than for boys. Let us examine some of the evidence about moral development in those studies that have included both males and females.

Sex Differences in Moral Judgment

The reader may have noticed that most of the studies of moral development were studies of males. It is particularly noteworthy that Kohlberg's longitudinal study, which established both the qualitative stages and the developmental sequence, included no females. Some studies from Kohlberg's research tradition have included women, however, and have indicated that the modal stage for women is Stage 3, in contrast to Stage 4 for men (Haan et al., 1968; Holstein, 1976).

Carol Gilligan offered an interesting explanation for the observed average differences in level of moral judgment for women and men. In Chapter 3, we encountered the notion that women's identity concerns in adolescence are more likely than men's to center around interpersonal issues. Gilligan extends this identity concern into the realm of moral judgment.

The very traits that have traditionally defined the "goodness" of women, their care for and sensitivity to the needs of others, are those that mark them as deficient in moral development. The infusion of feeling into their judgments keeps them from developing a more independent and abstract conception in which concern for others derives from principles of justice rather than from compassion and care. (Gilligan, 1977, p. 484)

Consider a resolution of the Heinz drug-stealing dilemma from a feminine perspective.

While the morality of Heinz's theft is not in question, given the circumstances which necessitated it, what is at issue is his willingness to substitute himself for his wife and become, in her stead, the victim of exploitation by a society which breeds and legitimates the druggist's irresponsibility and whose injustice is thus manifest in the very occurrence of the dilemma. (Gilligan, 1977, p. 513)

One of the women interviewed by Gilligan using the Heinz dilemma remarked, "I don't think that exploitation should really be a right."

Early adolescence finds girls ahead of boys in moral judgment, but by late adolescence, the boys have caught up or even surpassed the girls in stage of moral judgment (Haan, Langer, & Kohlberg, 1976).

When women and girls are tested with Kohlberg's interviews, interpretation of the data is difficult because the main characters in the dilemmas are males (Kurtines & Greif, 1974; Gilligan, 1977). Perhaps Kohlberg's finding that women more often stop at Stage 3 is a function of the characters in the stories, rather than women's moral maturity. One study, in fact, tested a large number of adolescent males and females with the dilemmas varying by gender of the characters. Adolescents showed higher levels of moral judgment with same-sex characters; furthermore, the girls were more influenced by the character's gender than the boys (Freeman, 1975). Another study, however, found that the protagonist's sex had no effect on level of moral judgment among a group of high-school and college students (Garwood, Levine, & Ewing, 1980).

Sex Differences in Moral Behavior

Grinder (1962) tested an equal number (70) of boys and girls on the ray-gun apparatus and found no sex difference on cheating. To get the "expert" badge, 28 boys and 29 girls cheated by more than 10 points. The lack of sex differences in Grinder's study may reflect equal achievement pressures. Some psychologists argue that males and females begin to differ in the degree to which they are subject to achievement pressures late in their high-school careers. In this view, career-oriented males "wake-up" to the realities of pressure to achieve when they are faced with college admissions and job critiera in their senior years; one result is more pressure to cheat to get better grades. One study tested 7th- and 12th-graders in a potential cheating situation. Sure enough, although more 7th-grade girls than boys cheated, senior boys cheated more than girls (Feldman & Feldman, 1967).

On the other hand, males were able to resist cheating more than females in a college study (Jacobson, Berger, & Millham, 1970). Female students who scored high on a personality test of "self-satisfaction" were especially likely to cheat on the tedious task of matching digits and symbols.

These studies of sex differences, taken together, are a mixed bag. They suggest that a confusing pattern emerges because cheating is related to situational factors (such as achievement pressures) and to personality factors (such as self-concept), which may differ for the two genders; these factors undergo some regular changes in the course of the life cycle, which complicates the picture even more.

IDENTITY AND MORAL JUDGMENT

Perhaps the central theme in the psychology of adolescence is the search for identity, which culminates in a crisis in late adolescence or early adulthood. Resolution of an identity crisis requires a series of commitments, both to an occupational role and to an ideological framework, as we saw in Chapter 3. Capacity for postconventional moral judgment may be one of the benefits of ideological commitments. Younger adolescents are certainly aware of ethical issues, but they are aware of them, according to Kohlberg, on a preethical level. True ethical principles require commitments that resolve the identity crisis.

Two experiences may be particularly important in moving to postconventional moral judgment.

The first experience is the experience of leaving home and entering a college community with conflicting values in the context of moratorium, identity questioning, and the need for commitment. [And the second is] one of new responsibility only for the self; it is primarily an experience of attained freedom to make one's own choice for oneself. (Kohlberg, 1973, pp. 195–196)

Among Kohlberg's longitudinal subjects, no men who went directly from high school to jobs or into the army developed postconventional thinking. Furthermore, no high-school student developed postconventional thinking. Even moral discussion groups—which, as we saw earlier, often lead to stage advance—were unable to move high-school students from conventional to postconventional reasoning. Discussions did work, however, in moving 40 percent of college freshmen and sophomores to postconventional reasoning.

Podd (1972) tested the relationship between identity status and moral judgment more directly by administering identity-status interviews as well as moral dilemmas to 134 junior and senior males at SUNY, Buffalo. He found that half of the students who had resolved the identity crisis showed postconventional moral reasoning versus only 15 percent of other students (either in moratorium, identity foreclosure, or identity confusion). Podd's study suggests a close relationship between commitment to an identity and higher levels of moral judgment, but it should be pointed out that the number of students showing postconventional thinking in this study is noticeably higher than Kohlberg has reported.

A relationship between college attendance and moral maturity has an elitist ring to it. It is possible, of course, that value conflicts and increased freedom that students find in college communities facilitate moral development. This view is consistent with the theoretical emphasis on role-taking opportunities and other social contexts for moral-stage advance. Recall, however, the young man who dismissed his high-level moral absolutism as a college senior by attributing it, at age 27, to "an incredible amount of immaturity on my part" (Gilligan & Murphy, 1979, p. 96).

SUMMARY

1. Piaget assessed moral judgment by presenting dilemmas and found two types of morality. *Heteronomous morality*, typical of young children, is a morality of absolute rules and adult authority. *Autonomous morality*, typical of adolescents and adults, is a morality of flexible rules and subjective subtleties. Research suggests that adolescents begin to judge behavior in terms of the intentions of the actor, and not simply in terms of the consequences of acts.

2. Kohlberg elaborated upon Piaget's moral-judgment research and identified three developmental levels. Young children tend to judge moral issues in a personalistic or *preconventional* way. Right actions are those that avoid punishment, placate authorities, or benefit the actors. At a developmentally higher level, moral judgments are made on the basis of expectations of others, in the family or larger social group. This moral stance is referred to as the *conventional level*. Finally, the *postconventional*, or principled, level is reached when moral judgments transcend the authority of persons or conformity to groups. Rules have meaning only in terms of underlying principles, such as justice

and reciprocity. Kohlberg's approach applies cognitive-developmental theory to moral issues. Thus, stages of moral judgment are correlated with stages of cognitive growth.

3. The moral-judgment interview which Kohlberg devised is time-consuming to administer and difficult to score. An alternative assessment device is the Defining Issues Test, a questionnaire which can be administered easily and scored objectively.

4. Cross-sectional and longitudinal studies of moral development indicate that Kohlberg's stages are qualitatively different from each other. Research on the sequentiality of moral stages is less impressive, but there is general support for orderly development.

5. Moral thinking is not consistent enough from one dilemma to another to provide sufficient support for a "structured whole." Piaget's stage of formal operations suffers from a similar lack of consistency.

6. Kohlberg's moral dilemmas concern weighty issues such as mercy killing and slavery. Adolescents who are asked to provide their own moral dilemmas choose more mundane topics such as smoking cigarettes and getting drunk. Adolescents may view Kohlberg's dilemmas as implausible, and they may not take them seriously as a consequence.

7. Level of moral judgment is only marginally related to behavior in situations with moral overtones. Most students, for example, report cheating at one time or another, regardless of moral judgment. Moral behavior is probably related to situational and personality characteristics, as well as to level of moral judgment.

8. Level of moral judgment appears to increase in response to higher "moral environments," such as role-playing groups in which high-level moral judgments are presented systematically. Adolescents who have the ability to take another person's perspective score higher in moral judgment.

9. Parents may have minimal influence on the moral levels of their children, according to research. For example, adolescents whose fathers are absent do not differ in moral level from adolescents whose fathers are present. Similarly, disciplinary techniques show no systematic relationship to moral level of adolescents. The nature of the parent–adolescent relationship may be more important than the method of discipline.

10. Few systematic sex differences have been observed in moral development, despite the fact that a predominance of studies have

included only male characters in the moral dilemmas. The modal stage of moral judgment among women is Stage 3, one stage lower than the modal stage among men. One possible reason for this difference is the greater degree of interpersonal focus among women, which is scored at a lower level than the instrumental, or legalistic focus used more often by men.

11. College students whose identity status reflects greater commitment exhibit higher levels of moral judgment than their low-commitment peers. The increased freedom and the value conflicts characteristic of college communities may facilitate moral development.

OUTLINE

7. SOCIAL INTERACTION IN ADOLESCENCE

In this chapter we discuss social interaction with parents, peers, and dating partners. As a prelude to this discussion, consider the photograph in Figure 7-1. On the most general level, the photograph features a young woman and a young man, with several other adolescents in the background. There is clearly some form of social interaction taking place, but it is not clear exactly what the nature of the interaction is. Because the interaction is ambiguous, the photograph can be used as a stimulus for eliciting information about people's understanding of social situations. Such a technique reveals, for example, that adolescents and young adults are likely to view ambiguous boy–girl interactions in romantic terms. Here is a story written by a 19-year-old female college student about the picture in Figure 7-1.

Bob and Janet have been introduced before but this is their first real introduction. Bob noticed Janet sitting across the room and decided to become more familiar with her. They are first engaging in the preliminaries.

Next Bob will move on to the secondary stage, by walking her to her next class or walking her home with the end result— him asking for a date.

The girl, Janet, will at first feel unsure of how she really feels about Bob. She'll feel impressed at his interest in her but then will become a little shy.

The guy will first feel nervous at having to ask her for a date, but once she accepts—he'll feel good, maybe even "cocky."

This student's story illustrates some of the issues treated in this chapter, especially issues involved in stages of heterosexual relationships, and issues reflecting an individual's interpersonal cognitive system; however, we must first chart the major advances in social development in adolescence.

**FIGURE 7-1
Example of a photograph used to probe understanding of social situations.**

(Photo by Sybil Shelton/Peter Arnold, Inc.)

In this chapter, we examine three major aspects of social interaction in adolescence. First, we look at adolescents' relationships to their parents. One of the tasks of adolescence, as we have seen in previous chapters, is the establishment of autonomy from parents. The social relationships between parents and adolescents can be discussed with this framework in mind. Second, we examine the influence of the adolescent's peer group on attitudes, values, and behavior. Many researchers have examined group structure in adolescence, as in the friendship groups often known as cliques; we discuss adolescent groups and their role in the development of friendship. Third, we discuss interaction with members of the opposite sex—the phenomenon of dating. In addition, we discuss the psychological implications of norms associated with dating in adolescence.

Social interaction, of course, is a continuous process throughout the life cycle. There are, however, some developmental shifts in social interaction. The emphasis of the social world of the infant is a dependency relationship to one primary caretaker. During childhood, the social emphasis is on a strong attachment bond to parents as well as on nonfamily interaction with groups of peers during the school years. During adolescence, the balance of power between parents and peers in social influence appears to even out. This developmental shift is followed, later in adolescence, by an emphasis on heterosexual interaction. These themes of adolescent social interaction guide our discussion in the chapter.

RELATIONSHIPS WITH PARENTS

Obviously, there is no one pattern of interaction with parents shown by adolescents as a group. The variety of parent–adolescent relationships is as large as that in any other type of interpersonal situation. Some adolescents seem to have harmonious relationships with their parents, without experiencing any major disagreements or blow-ups. Other adolescents bicker with their parents over all issues, great and small.

Autobiographical material submitted by a male college student illustrates one common, but unfortunate, pattern of interaction. In this patten, the child feels that the parent is omnipotent; in later adolescence, it becomes very difficult to alter this unrealistic view of one's parents. Will, the author of the case in point, described his feelings.

Until I was in the tenth or eleventh grade, I thought my father was perfect. That is not to say I didn't have disagreements with him, but they were disagreements with an important stipulation: he was always right. It wasn't that he beat me or something until I admitted to him that he was right—he rarely physically punished me. I just always felt that although we might have a difference of opinion, it was ordained that he was in the right, or rather, that I was in the wrong.

I guess the reason I thought my father was perfect for such a long time is that whenever we do anything together, he always gives advice and I always follow it, so it took me a long time to discover that there is more than one correct way to do everything. When I don't follow his advice, it leaves me feeling anxious, like I've done something wrong in opposing him. I also notice an interesting occurrence when we have disagreements: I stop thinking. As soon as he says, "Why did you . . .?" or "Why don't you . . .?" my mind simply shuts down. (Goethals & Klos, 1976, p. 126)

Social Interchanges

One generalization that can be made with regard to relationships between two or more people is that they are interactive; that is, they involve social interchanges (Cairns, 1979). The behavior of one party influences, and to some extent controls, the behavior of the other party. Reciprocal influence between adolescents and parents can be seen in the mode of discipline within a home, established in large part by parents, which influences the behavior of the adolescent. The adolescent's behavior, in turn, elicits parental discipline. As a consequence, the nature of the relationship between the adolescent and parent is affected.

Family Role Relationships

Research on social interaction has been heavily influenced by Parsons and Bales (1955), who introduced the notion of role specialization within family interaction. An instrumental role, usually played by the father within the family, and an emotional-expressive role, usually played by the mother, characterize some instances of family interaction. Content of a decision-making task may influence patterns of family interaction along instrumental and emotional-expressive lines. This hypothesis was tested in a study of 64 family triads consisting of mother, father, and adolescent son or daughter (Henggeler, Borduin, Rodick, & Tavormina, 1979).

These researchers reasoned that some tasks are more instrumental (e.g., "Where should the family go on its next vacation?"), while others are more emotional-expressive (e.g., "Our biggest family problems should be _____ "). They further reasoned that these tasks might differ in the amount of conflict generated. Measures of conflict that could be easily quantified were chosen, such as number of attempted interruptions and amount of simultaneous speech. Indeed, the instrumental tasks did generate more conflict, using these measures, than did the emotional-expressive tasks among the parents and their adolescent offspring.

The above study also yielded data on patterns of dominance and on parental style. Across all tasks, mothers and fathers showed approximately equal levels of dominance, and both were dominant over their adolescent children. Parents who were chosen for the study were "well-adjusted," and given that, it is interesting that they were rated as moderately warm across tasks, including those which generated conflict. The researchers noted that these well-adjusted families were able to interact with some conflict and yet still maintain their warmth and patterns of dominance. It may be that families are better able to cope with various problems when they can survive conflict without loss of affection (Henggeler et al., 1979).

Styles of Parental Authority The healthy development of autonomy from parents varies as a function of the type of parental authority ordinarily found in the home (Elder, 1963). *Permissive parents*, who allow adolescents virtually unlimited freedom to make their own decisions without parental constraint, tend to have adolescents who show the most autonomy; adolescent autonomy is particularly likely to be present in permissive households where some discipline is combined with explanation. *Democratic households* are characterized by group discussion of issues and problems and group decisions about courses of action. Democratic parents appear to have children who are compliant, in comparison to parents who use other types of authority.

Autocratic parents, who simply tell their children what to do, appear to produce the least amount of autonomy. This type of parental authority does not allow much room for independent thinking by adolescents. Autocratic parents, who cling to a set of rules in which the adolescent has no voice, and who use physical punishment as a means of discipline, tend to have dependent and, at the same time, rebellious adolescent offspring (Douvan & Adelson, 1966). An authoritarian family appears to limit an adolescent's growth.

We would guess that it is the boys and girls who, as adolescents, show this limited growth in autonomy who later make up most of that part of the adult world which has never left home, psychologically, and much of the time, physically as well, marrying in the home town, visiting the parents weekly—shielded, for the most part, from the perils and pleasures of change. (Douvan & Adelson, 1966, p. 172)

There appears to be a curvilinear relationship between parental restrictiveness and adolescent rebellion. Parents who are either highly restrictive or highly permissive are more likely to have rebellious adolescents (Balswick & Macrides, 1975; Kandel & Lesser, 1972).

Type of parental authority influences the adolescent's development of autonomy; additionally, parental behaviors have a strong influence on the amount of time spent with parents and with peers. Support has been found for the general hypothesis that quality of adolescents' interactions with adults affects their involvement with their peer group (Iacovetta, 1975). Such a result was found in a study of over 600 male high-school seniors who answered questionnaires in their home rooms about quality of adult–adolescent interaction and about frequency on interaction with peers. The majority of these high-school seniors who reported that their interaction with adults was of low quality spent large amounts of time with their peers. Seniors with high-quality interactions with adults spent less time with peers.

Family Interaction and Puberty We saw in Chapter 2 that as adolescents undergo the physical changes of puberty, they become different stimulus objects for others. People react differently to a larger, more adult appearance. In turn, the behavior of adolescents changes to match these new reactions. One investigation showed the effect of adolescent boys' physical maturation on social interchanges within families (Steinberg & Hill, 1978). Family triads consisting of a mother, a father, and an adolescent boy, aged 11–14, were asked to discuss a family issue, such as planning a vacation, and arrive at a family decision. The boys had been rated for degree of physical maturation. Findings indicated that the more physically mature boys were more assertive within the family; they used power plays, such as interruption, when dealing with their parents.

The research on puberty stresses the interactive nature of family role relationships. As the adolescent matures physically, parents change their behavior toward their offspring. In effect, puberty signals the role transition from child to adult. In addition to the effects of the physical changes of puberty itself, changes in expectations of parents, and other adults, modify the behavior of the adolescent in any social interchange.

The Generation Gap

One question that we must ask about relationships between adolescents and their parents is this: To what extent is conflict an expectable occurrence between adolescents and their parents? One form that adolescent–parent conflict may take is a "generation gap," a major schism between adolescents and parents in values, attitudes, and behavior. Presumably, the underlying reason for such a schism is a difference in either age, cohort, or both, at a time when adolescents must move in the direction of establishing autonomy from their parents. We now turn to an examination of data bearing on the existence of a generation gap.

A *generation gap* implies differences in values, taste, style, attitudes, and behavior of two generational groups by virtue of membership in different generations. The term is often used to designate such differences between members of the same family, and in particular, to refer to differences between adolescents and their parents (Weiner, 1971).

A generation gap between parents and their adolescent offspring might result simply from age differences at a time when adolescents must face squarely the autonomy issue. Longitudinal research tells us that the concerns of adolescents and middle-aged adults are different (e.g., Levinson, 1978; Vaillant, 1977). Adolescents and their parents also differ in important ways other than age. They are also members of different cohort groups. As we learned in Chapter 1, a *cohort* refers to a group of people who are born at about the same time, and who share a similar cultural and historical experience and perspective. For example, people of college age born in 1950 faced the pressures brought on by the Vietnam War, such as the possibility of being drafted, or of losing a boyfriend to the draft. They also experienced an unprecedented degree of rebellion in this country. Individuals born in 1960 were much less likely to be involved in campus protest and rebellion and were not subject to involuntary military service. These different cohort experiences may be particularly relevant to a discussion of conflict between generations over adult authority and its legitimacy.

The existence of a generation gap should appear in research as a discontinuity between age groups in behaviors and standards (Bengston, Furlong, & Laufer, 1974). Research in the area of attitudes among adolescents and their parents actually reveals little evidence for a generation gap. In fact, there is surprising consistency between the two groups (Hamid & Wyllie, 1980).

One of the ways of measuring attitude consistency is through the administration of the same questionnaire to both adolescents and their parents. One such questionnaire, the Contemporary Topics Questionnaire, contains 36 statements on such topics as sex, drugs, war, and racism. Respondents are asked to agree or disagree with each statement. For example, one item is, "A person's appearance is his own concern, and others should tolerate whatever that person wears." Another item is, "Laws dealing with drugs, such as marijuana, are in dire need of revision." Although adolescents show a somewhat different pattern of attitudes on these topics than their parents, the differences are not dramatically different (Orloff & Weinstock, 1975). Adolescent respondents agree with their parents on approximately 80 percent of the items on this questionnaire. Interestingly enough, however, there is a tendency for adolescents to overestimate the differences in attitudes between themselves and their parents, and tendency on the part of parents to underestimate the differences (Lerner & Knapp, 1975).

It would appear that adolescent rebellion against parents is much less widespread than talk of a generation gap would suggest. Most adolescents gradually go about the business of establishing autonomy from their parents (Offer & Offer, 1975). Most parents, on their part, show a reasonable amount of respect for their children's needs to grow toward independence (Douvan & Adelson, 1966). Adolescents may differ greatly from their parents in matters of taste, but they are likely to share with them a set of fundamental values (Coleman, 1980).

Attributions of Parent and Adolescent Characteristics Groups of adolescents and their parents have rated the "average teenager" and the "average adult" on attitude scales. These ratings allow researchers to determine what sets of characteristics are attributed to adolescents and adults and to determine if the two groups differ in their attributions. Both parents and children rated adolescents about the same, as a close inspection of Table 7-1 shows. Parents, however, were slightly more positive about adolescents than were the adolescents themselves. Parents gave adolescents a higher rating on all dimensions, except tidiness and gratefulness, than adolescents did. Furthermore, adults were rated more positively by both groups, and especially so by adolescents (Coleman, George, and Holt, 1977). It would appear from the results of this study that if a generation gap in attitude exists, it is experienced mainly by adolescents themselves as a negative self-rating.

The term "generation gap" has probably been overused in recent years. Adolescents can be expected, in their normal course of development, to spend time with their peers while they establish in-

	ADOLESCENT RATING		PARENT RATING	
TABLE 7-1 **Parent and Adolescent Attributions of Characteristics toward the Two Age Groups.**	ADOLESCENT	ADULT	ADOLESCENT	ADULT
Hardworking–lazy	2.25	4.34	2.92	4.29
Quiet–Noisy	1.34	2.92	1.76	3.38
Tidy–Untidy	2.78	3.96	2.38	3.70
Patient–Impatient	1.88	3.46	2.01	2.71
Honest–Dishonest	2.96	4.05	3.76	3.46
Reliable–Unreliable	2.75	3.74	3.58	3.45
Selfish–Unselfish	2.55	3.84	3.17	2.71
Grateful–Ungrateful	3.34	4.25	2.88	3.05

*Higher scores indicate more positive evaluations.
Source: Coleman, George, & Holt, 1977.

dependence from their parents. What was a normal developmental change in adolescent–parent relationships may have been mistaken for a generation gap.

Developmental Changes in Adolescent–Parent Relationhips

In adolescence, social influence shifts from a family orientation to an orientation in which the peer group exerts considerable influence. A large group of preadolescents and adolescents, students in grades 4 though 10, were asked questions about their family and peer relationships (Bowerman & Kinch, 1959). For example, they were asked with which group—family or peers—they would prefer to associate. From the 4th to 10th grade, there was a dramatic shift in social orientation from family to peers (Figure 7-2).

This shift in orientation occurs at about the 8th or 9th grade, when peer orientation becomes stronger than family orientation. This generalization is supported by additional research suggesting a developmental shift in social orientation in several areas of behavior (Floyd & South, 1972). One item on the 20-item scale used to measure social orientation concerned norms of dress "I prefer to wear the kind and style of clothing that my parents suggest, regard-

FIGURE 7-2
Association preference by grade in school. Percentage of students who preferred to associate with peers increased, while percentage who preferred to associate with parents decreased.

(From Bowerman & Kinch, 1959.)

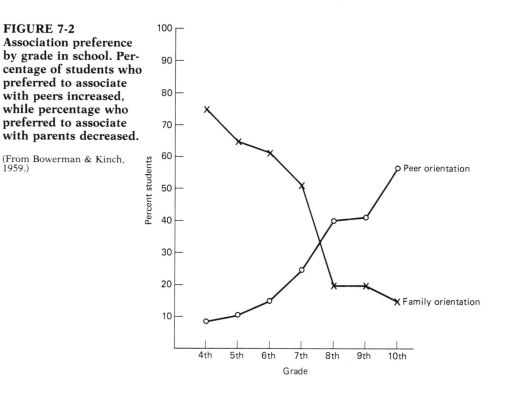

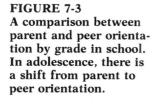

FIGURE 7-3
A comparison between parent and peer orientation by grade in school. In adolescence, there is a shift from parent to peer orientation.

(From Floyd & South, 1972.)

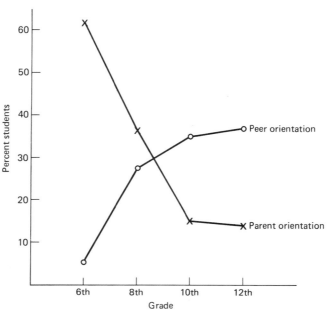

less of what type of clothing my friends and schoolmates think are best." Figure 7-3 shows the shift in social orientation from family to peers between 8th and 10th grades.

During adolescence, attitudes toward parents become less favorable, on the average. As the adolescent's opinion of parents declines, willingness to endorse misconduct by peers increases. Endorsement of peer misconduct is assessed in dilemmas such as the following:

You are out with some friends on Halloween night. They suggest soaping some windows. What would you really do in this situation? Would you tell your friends not to do it, or let each one do what he wants? (Bixenstine, De Corte, & Bixenstine, 1976, p. 228)

As the number of favorable attitudes toward parents declines with grade in school, endorsement of peer misconduct in these hypothetical dilemmas increases.

Although adolescents show more and more autonomy from parents (Curtis, 1975), adolescents may be differentially influenced by parents or by peers depending on the type of situation they are evaluating. The major investigations of parent and peer influence have used the Cross-Pressures Test, a questionnaire with dilemma-like situations requiring choices with conflicting peer versus parent expectations. In one such dilemma, a student must decide whether a hypothetical girl, Nell, should tell on a peer she observed breaking a window. The questionnaire asks the student to respond to the following question:

Can you guess what Nell did when the principal asked her if she saw who broke the glass?

_____ *She told him that she didn't see it broken.*

_____ *She told him who broke the glass. (Brittain, 1963)*

Results from high-school students in the South on the Cross-Pressures Test indicate that adolescents respond depending on the content area (Brittain, 1963, 1967). In general, the more important the situation is perceived to be, the more likely adolescents are to comply with the assumed parental value choice. Other studies have corroborated this finding (Sebald & White, 1980). It is in the more trivial content areas, such as matters of dress, that adolescents' choices reflect peer compliance. Parents have a particularly strong influence in the area of educational plans; much more similarity exists between the plans and aspirations of adolescents and their parents than between adolescents and peers, even best friends (Kandel & Lesser, 1969).

The original impetus for research into parent versus peer orientation was the notion of a developmental shift from parent to peer orientation during the adolescent years. The research reported in the preceding section required adolescents to provide choices that were classified by researchers as either parent or peer oriented. It is conceivable that an adolescent's decision about whether to tell the principal who broke a glass door has little to do with feelings of social influence or social preference. Indeed, the assumption that one choice is parent-oriented is questionable in the absence of more information about the parents' value systems. A more direct measure of an adolescent's orientation toward parents and peers is provided by an inventory of feelings and attitudes about these individuals themselves. This type of measure avoids the pitfall of assuming a seesaw model of social orientation—if one is up, the other must be down. On the Inventory of Feelings, younger adolescents showed a stronger relationship to parents than they did to friends. Older adolescents, 11th-graders, indicated an equally strong set of feelings toward both parents and peers (O'Donnell, 1976). This finding certainly indicates a developmental shift *toward* a peer social orientation, but it does not assume the necessity of a shift *away* from parents.

Parents, Peers, and Drug Use In one area, peers have a strong influence on adolescent choices. This area of influence concerns use of

Teenagers at an arcade in Seattle, Washington. Arcades featuring electronic games, such as Pac-Man, have become increasingly popular with adolescents all over America. Peers have the greatest influence over how a teenager decides to spend leisure time; parents today exert very little influence over these decisions.

(Photo copyright © by Jeffry W. Myers/Freelance Photographer's Guild)

drugs, such as marijuana. Parents have little to do with adolescents' decisions about the use of leisure time in general. This conclusion is derived from a study of 600 students in grades 9 through 12 in Atlanta. These students reported that their peers were much more important in determining use of leisure time (Noe & Elifson, 1976). High-school students also reported that their peers were much more important influences in their decisions about initiating use of marijuana than were their parents (Brook, Lukoff, & Whiteman, 1980; Kandel, 1974).

The above studies are highly suggestive of a link between marijuana use and peer influence, but they rely heavily on overt reports by adolescents. A study using a large number of college students measured parent versus peer orientation as an independent variable. The same number of students were parent-oriented as were peer-oriented (46 percent of the 766 students surveyed were classified in each orientation on the basis of attitude surveys; 8 percent were not clearly oriented either way). The students were then asked a simple question, "Have you ever used marijuana?" Their answers are shown in Figure 7-4 and indicate a strong association between social orientation and use of marijuana. Those who are oriented toward their parents are not likely to have used marijuana; those with a peer orientation are likely to have been users at some time (Stone, Miranne, & Ellis, 1979). When the adolescent's social-

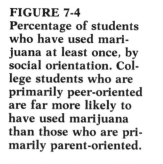

FIGURE 7-4
Percentage of students who have used marijuana at least once, by social orientation. College students who are primarily peer-oriented are far more likely to have used marijuana than those who are primarily parent-oriented.

(From Stone, Miranne, & Ellis, 1979.)

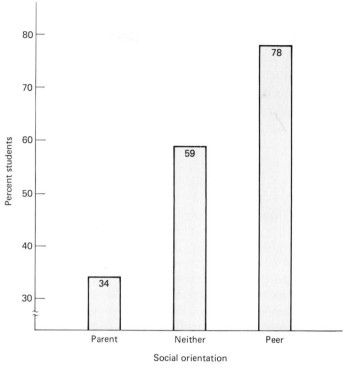

influence orientation is known ahead of time, as in this study, behavior in the content area of drug use can be predicted with a high level of accuracy.

Compliance in Specific Situations   Other attempts have been made to predict the types of situations which will call forth parent versus peer compliance. Kandel and Lesser surveyed a large number of adolescents and their parents in Denmark and the United States. As they stated, "It is misleading to speak of separate adolescent cultures or of general peer versus parental influences. The particular content area under discussion must be specified" (Kandel & Lesser, 1972, p. 183). In both Denmark and the United States, adolescents turned to their parents when they needed advice on problems, and they turned to their peers for companionship and recreation. These results corroborate the finds on drug use that were discussed in the previous section.

Conformity in Adolescence   *Compliance* refers to selection of a course of action based on the assumed wishes or value orientations of either parents or peers. A related phenomenon is *conformity*, matching one's behavior to the behavior of others because of group pressure, either real or implied. In everyday situations that an adolescent might face, this is usually referred to as "going along with the crowd." For example, the adolescent who helps to soap windows on Halloween night because "all the other kids were doing it" is exhibiting conformity.

Conformity has also been studied in the laboratory. Solomon Asch studied the effects of group pressure on perceptual judgments in a series of classic studies in the 1950s (Asch, 1951, 1956). Asch's technique required the use of seven confederates, six of whom stated an obviously incorrect judgment prior to the real subject's turn. In one judgment, shown in Figure 7-5, the confederates stated that Line 2B was the same length as Line A. About three-fourths of the college students who participated in Asch's study made one or more errors by going along with the incorrect group judgment.

Richard Crutchfield (1955) designed an apparatus to allow testing individuals without the necessity of using confederates. Subjects were led to believe other people were making judgments in the experiment, when in reality the judgments were preprogrammed into the apparatus. These judgments could then be attributed to any reference group the experimenter wished.

The Crutchfield apparatus was used to test conformity among young students in four grade levels—1st, 4th, 7th, and 10th (Allen & Newtson, 1972). Previous judgments, which were unanimously incorrect as in the Asch situation, were attributed to either the peer group (other students in the same grade), or to adults (a group of teachers). Conformity was assessed for perceptual judgments, including the lines of Figure 7-5; for opinions (e.g., "Kittens make good pets"); and for delay of gratification (e.g., "I would rather have 50¢ today than $1 tomorrow"). This experiment, therefore, was an examination of conformity to adults and to peers from the 1st to the

FIGURE 7-5
Example from Solomon Asch's perceptual-judgment task. Subjects are asked to pick the comparison line that is closest in length to the standard line, after several "confederate" students have made an incorrect choice.

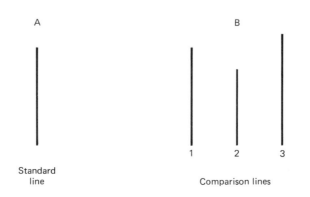

10th grade. In this experiment, a student could be conforming to both reference groups, to neither, or to only one of them. It is unnecessary to assume a seesaw model of peer versus adult influence—if one is up, the other must be down.

The results of this experiment demonstrated a trend toward greater independence of judgment with age. Conformity to both adult and peer judgments decreased with age. While adolescents may respond with answers that comply with adults' presumed wishes in hypothetical situations, they appear to be more willing as they grow older to state their own autonomous judgments in situations which are matters of opinion.

Conformity can also be examined in the situations discussed earlier, such as the Halloween misconduct dilemma. More than 500 students in 3rd, 6th, 9th, 11th, and 12th grades were presented hypothetical situations in which a suggested course of action was attributed to peers (Berndt, 1979). One situation was a variant of the Halloween dilemma.

You are with a couple of your best friends on Halloween. They're going to soap windows, but you're not sure whether you should or not. Your friends all say you should, because there's no way you could get caught. What would you really do? (Berndt, 1979, p. 610)

Willingness to conform to situations involving peer misconduct is greatest during middle-adolescence.

(Photo by Hugh Rogers/Monkmeyer Photo Service)

Other dilemmas in this experiment explored conformity to peer opinions in highly prosocial situations as well. For example, one dilemma involved peer pressure to help your brother after school on an afternoon when you wanted to visit a sick child. Neutral situations were also included, such as items about deciding on places to eat. Thus, independent assessment of the student's tendency to conform to different types of behavior was possible.

Not much consistency was found in the trend to conform to peer pressure by grade level for the prosocial or neutral items, although overall there was more conformity in these situations than in antisocial ones. The age trend was clear, however, for the antisocial items. Peer conformity to antisocial behavior showed an increase between 3rd and 9th grades, followed by a decline in conformity among the 11th-12th grade group. Thus in situations involving antisocial behavior, where sanctions are greater, two generalizations are possible. First, there is less conformity to peer pressure in these situations than in prosocial or neutral situations. Second, developmental trends are more evident, with peer pressure peaking at about age 15, and declining thereafter. Middle adolescence appears to be the time of greatest susceptibility to peer pressure in situations involving antisocial behavior.

The "Launching Center"

When older adolescents are preparing to leave home, they have reached a point in the family cycle when the family is serving as a "launching center" (Kimmel, 1980). College students who are only part-time residents at home, on occasional weekends and during vacations, illustrate the launching-center aspect of the family cycle particularly well. This phase represents a culmination of developmental changes that occur in relationships between adolescents and their parents.

A short-term longitudinal study (Sullivan & Sullivan, 1980) investigated the separation that occurs between adolescent sons and their parents. The psychological reactions of 104 white males who left home to board at college were compared to the reactions of 138 white males who continued to live at home while commuting to college. These young men were pretested while they were still in high school and then retested during their first semester of college. Both groups of men—boarders and commuters—were from families that can be described as launching centers. The boarders, however, had made a more complete break with their families; for them and their families, the psychological effects of separation might be expected to be greater.

These students were asked about their perceptions of their own and their parents' feelings about affection, communication, and independence. For example, the affection questions concerned the degree to which the student believed his parents (a) told their friends about him, (b) hugged or kissed him, (c) got on his nerves, and (d) enjoyed talking to him; and the degree to which he perceived that he (e) enjoyed talking to them, (f) got on their nerves, (g) felt embarrassed by them, and (h) felt uncomfortable being alone with them. Questions were administered twice: in the spring of the last year of high school and in the fall of the first year of college.

There were some differences between boarders and commuters as far as these psychological reactions were concerned, especially in the area of affection. The boarders, those who had made a more complete break with their families, felt that they and their parents showed more affection after the separation. They also experienced more independence, relative to the commuter group. Thus, separation between adolescents and parents seems to be a positive step, with positive psychological reactions, at least for those adolescents who go on to college. Incidentally, the separation from adolescent children may have positive effects for parents as well. Research indicates that it is in the postparenthood phase of the family cycle, the phase in which children have left the parents' home, that marital satisfaction is greatest (Deutscher, 1964). It should be noted that the adolescent-separation study cited above (Sullivan & Sullivan, 1980) did not randomly assign students to the boarder or commuter groups. Differences between these two groups cannot be attributed with certainty to this factor alone. Boarders, for example, had higher SAT test scores, and were more likely to attend 4-year colleges. Many other unassessed factors may also have contributed to the difference.

Those students who decided to remain at home while they attended college may have been more dependent to begin with than their boarder counterparts. Types of discipline customarily used in the homes may have differed systematically. Although adolescents' place of residence during the launching-center phase of the family cycle appears to be associated with psychological responses to separation, we cannot be certain that this is the explanatory factor.

PEER INTERACTION IN ADOLESCENCE

Sullivan's Interpersonal Theory

The developmental history of social interaction has been described nowhere more eloquently than in Harry Stack Sullivan's (1953) interpersonal theory. In Sullivan's paradigm, the major theme of personality is management of anxiety, an emotion that arises out of difficult social interaction. Adolescence is a time of stressful social interaction because the individual's major need systems, which Sullivan calls *dynamisms*, often come into conflict.

Interpersonal Dynamisms   Each individual has three major inter-personal dynamisms: security, intimacy, and lust. The first dyna-mism, *security*, involves feelings of self-worth in interactions with other people, particularly those significant others who are impor-tant in several areas of our lives, like parents. This sense of inter-personal security includes feelings of self-esteem and self-worth. To feel secure is to feel valued and needed because of one's good qual-ities. The second dynamism, which Sullivan called *intimacy*, is a need for emotional sharing with significant others. One needs to feel that strong emotions can be freely admitted without posturing and without fear of rejection. A third dynamism, which is of major im-portance in adolescence, is *lust*, the frankly sexual pressure associ-ated with the genital region of the body.

The major need governing social interaction in infancy and early childhood is the security dynamism. According to Sullivan's paradigm, needs for feeling valued and warmly loved by parents are particularly stong in that era of life. Because children in infancy and early childhood are wholly dependent on others, the potential for anxiety based on insecurity in interpersonal relationships is great. Later childhood represents a time of life when the peer group assumes a greater role in the individual's interpersonal life. The childhood era is often marked by the formation of groups of same-sex friends, who have strong influences on interpersonal security. Children in this era learn the process of social judgment, whereby interpersonal popularity is based on judgments of "pretty, average, or ugly," "good sport or bad sport," "bright, average, or dumb," among others. *Social accommodation* is a form of social learning in which the child begins to understand the ramifications of these la-bels for social behavior. The children labelled "ugly" and "dumb" on the playground are treated very differently from the "pretty" and "bright" individuals, in the social world of children.

While security was the theme of early childhood, intimacy be-comes the theme of preadolescence, in Sullivan's paradigm. Inti-macy, the interpersonal need for emotional sharing, blossoms in the *chum relationship*, a particularly close relationship with one mem-ber of the peer group of the same age and sex. For the first time, the preadolescent experiences sensitivity to what matters to another person, a special friend isolated from the larger same-sex group. Preadolescence is the time of intense friendships, which have a spe-cial role in the development of emotional intimacy. In an empirical study of the chum relationship among 6th grade boys, Mannarino (1976) found that those students with a chum were significantly more altruistic than a group of students without a chum. Patterns of friendship in other cultures also indicate the importance of same-sex friendship in adolescence. Among a group of Indians in Guatemala, called the Chinautleco, friendship "reaches its highest intensity at that transitional stage in life in which young men achieve adult status without its emotional rewards. Most adolescents and young men have 'best friends' with whom they share secrets and ambitions and plan love affairs" (Brain, 1976, p. 40).

During adolescence, there is a shift from same-sex intimate friendships to opposite-sex intimate friendships. Following puberty, the lust dynamism emerges as a major need to be integrated with security and intimacy in a close relationship with a member of the opposite sex.

Many adolescents have difficulty integrating these three dynamisms. The lust and security dynamisms often clash because of "genital phobia," stemming from earlier ridicule of any genital manipulation, especially ridicule from parents. Embarrassment and awkwardness result from the clash between lust and intimacy. Many adolescents experience insecurity over impending loss of virginity because of clashes between lust and security or intimacy. Anxiety over one's potential for smooth sexual performance is an emotion that many adolescents find difficult to share, especially with the person with whom sex is contemplated. Avoiding the integration of lust, intimacy, and security in one special relationship, many adolescents turn to masturbation as a way of satisfying the lust dynamism as best they can under the circumstances. And even masturbation is not a wholly satisfactory solution to the dilemma of integrating the major dynamisms. Masturbation itself is often condemned in cultures that impose restrictions on sexual expression. As Sullivan described it, "That's very neat, you see; it means that adolescence is going to be hell whatever you do, unless you have wonderful preparation for being different from everyone else—in which case you may get into trouble for being different" (Sullivan, 1953, p. 270).

Stages of Adolescent Group Development Research on the social structure of adolescent groups is consistent with Sullivan's interpersonal approach to social development. Size, structure, and dynamics of peer groups were examined in a field study of Australian adolescents, aged 13–21 (Dunphy, 1963). Questionnaires, diaries, and interviews supplemented data from field observations. Stages of group-structure development, similar to those outlined by Sullivan, are presented in Figure 7-6. A first stage can be described as isolated unisexual cliques, groups of three to nine members of the same sex who rarely interacted in any organized fashion with individuals outside of their own cliques. These cliques included the intense in-

FIGURE 7-6
Stages in the development of adolescent groups.

(From Dunphy, 1963.)

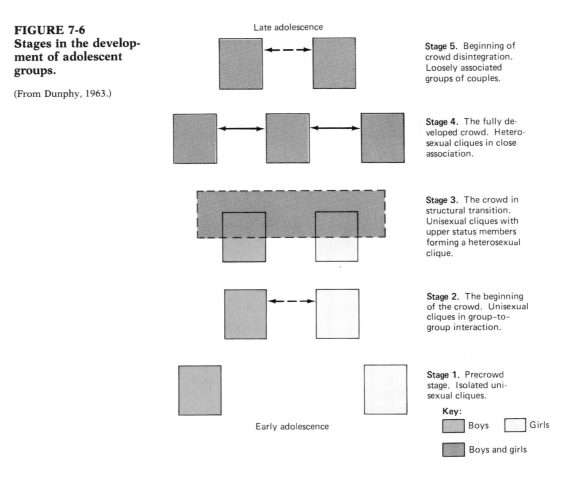

Late adolescence

Stage 5. Beginning of crowd disintegration. Loosely associated groups of couples.

Stage 4. The fully developed crowd. Heterosexual cliques in close association.

Stage 3. The crowd in structural transition. Unisexual cliques with upper status members forming a heterosexual clique.

Stage 2. The beginning of the crowd. Unisexual cliques in group-to-group interaction.

Stage 1. Precrowd stage. Isolated unisexual cliques.

Key:

⬛ Boys ⬜ Girls

⬛ Boys and girls

Early adolescence

timate relationships which Sullivan called chum relationships. The second stage of group interaction still involved these unisexual cliques, which now interacted with each other, forming larger groups of individuals called *crowds*. An essential characteristic necessary for membership in these first two stages of group development was conformity: Failure to conform resulted in exclusion from the group (Dunphy, 1963). Conformity was required in matters of importance to the group, such as matters of dress, of expressed values, and of recreational activities, such as drug use. As others have pointed out, "studies of cliques suggest that the game of inclusion and exclusion is both fevered and deadly at adolescence" (Douvan & Gold, 1966, p. 495).

Despite the prevalence of inclusion and exclusion as social processes in adolescent groups, individuals who are excluded do not

Isolated cliques in early-adolescence usually consist of three to nine members of the same sex who rarely interact in any organized way with individuals outside their clique.

(Photo copyright © 1979 by George Zimbel, Island Documentaries, Ltd./Monkmeyer Press Photo Service)

appear to be noticeably different from their popular counterparts in terms of their extracurricular activities. Eighteen social isolates, who were not selected by any of their peers as "best friend," were compared to 18 over-chosen adolescents, and to 18 who were chosen an average number of times. There was no significant difference for any activity among the three groups. These adolescents were isolated with respect to friendship choice, but not with respect to the activities engaged in (Horrocks & Benimoff, 1967).

A third stage of adolescent group development found in Dunphy's study emphasized leadership. Those members of the group who assumed upperstatus roles began to break out of the unisexual constraints of the group to initiate heterosexual interaction. The result was the formation of heterosexual cliques from the membership of the unisexual cliques. Gradually, other members of the cliques moved toward heterosexual interaction, following the lead of the more mature members of the group. "In the adolescent peer group, the leader is the person who plays the most advanced heterosexual role. He moves the group to participate in heterosexual activities and encourages members to develop more mature heterosexual roles" (Dunphy, 1963, p. 242).

By the fourth stage of adolescent group development, cliques had become heterosexual. Interaction was now common across clique lines as well, resulting in a heterosexual "crowd" formed from cliques in close association. The fifth and final stage was the disintegration of the crowd. Interaction was most commonly in terms of loosely associated groups of couples.

This pattern of group development, from unisexual cliques including chum relationships, to heterosexual cliques, and finally to intimate heterosexual relationships, follows the theoretical sequence of psychological development that Sullivan outlined for adolescence. Both Sullivan's theoretical view and research suggest the psychological importance of group membership in adolescence. The adolescent "needs to establish an identity and inner definition of self that is legitimized and corroborated by the responses of some relevant public" (Douvan & Gold, 1966, p. 491). This psychological need is met by membership in cliques.

The Interpersonal Cognitive System

Sullivan's interpersonal theory calls attention to the importance of changes in interaction with peers during adolescence. The increased importance of friends should be reflected in, among other things, the adolescent's psychological understanding of friends which has been called the adolescent's "interpersonal cognitive system" (Barenboim, 1977). Adolescents between the ages of 10 and 16 were asked to describe people whom they knew well. The proportion of psychological statements that they used increased with age (Figure 7-7). There appears to be a rather dramatic increase in the ability to make psychological inferences between the ages of 10 and 14. Only about 13 percent of 10-year-olds used psychological constructs in their descriptions, compared to about 70 percent of 12- and 14-year-olds, and an even larger proportion of 14- and 16-year-olds (Barenboim, 1981). It is also during this age range that children become more adept at perspective-taking (Elkind, 1980), and show mature understanding of subjectivity, or the lack of agreement on criteria for such judgements as "attractive" (Rothbaum, 1979). In middle adolescence, individuals become aware of the subjective nature of values and attitudes, and begin to search for others who share their own system of values and attitudes.

Friendship Formation The interpersonal cognitive system in adolescence seems to favor same-sex friendships. A large part of adolescent social interaction occurs with members of the same sex. This generalization is supported by research with college freshmen at the University of Rochester, who were asked to keep records over a 2-week period in the fall semester and a 2-week period in the spring semester of all their social interactions which lasted 10 minutes or more. A majority of their interactions (56 percent) were with mem-

FIGURE 7-7
Developmental changes in the ability to make psychological inferences. In describing people they know well, older adolescents used a higher proportion of psychological statements.

(From Barenboim, 1981.)

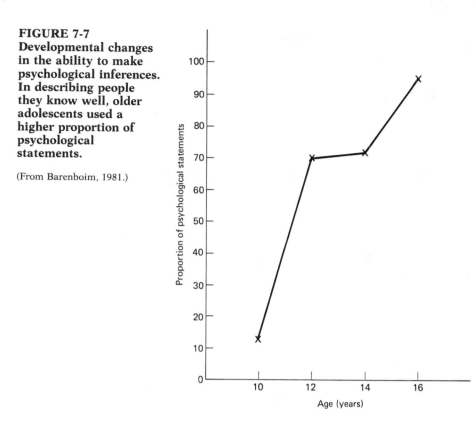

bers of the same sex only, while only 19 percent were with members of the opposite sex only. The remaining 25 percent of their interactions were in mixed-sex groups (Wheeler & Nezlik, 1977).

In one interview study of friendship within a university, information was obtained on 132 friendships (Bloom, 1971). Of those friendships, only 15 percent were opposite-sex friendships. The major reason these students gave for their friendship was affinity. Common interest was another typical reason. Information obtained from 500 students at another college led to similar conclusions: Intimate same-sex friendships were formed because of factors such as attitude similarity, intimate accessibility, and reciprocal candor (Knapp & Harwood, 1977). Other studies demonstrate the power of similarity in friendship formation, particularly similarity of attitudes (Byrne, 1961).

Developmental History of Friendship in Adolescence In early adolescence, friendships revolve around shared activities and interests, rather than psychological commitment (Coleman, 1980). In middle-adolescence, emotional sharing represented by sensitivity, empathy, and other "psychological" factors become more important. These aspects of adolescent friendship appear to be particularly strong among girls (Douvan & Adelson, 1966; Coleman, 1980; Richey & Richey, 1980). Good looks and attractive personality characteristics are assets to the middle-adolescent in being a popular member of the peer group. For boys, athletic prowess is an added bonus. Late-adolescents settle into a relatively more secure form of friendship. Close same-sex friendships become more relaxed; but in general, late-adolescents begin a shift toward more heterosexual interests, including close friendships with members of the opposite sex.

Social Class   Social pressures on adolescents overwhelmingly favor friendships along social-class lines. The most convincing demonstration of a relationship between adolescent friendships and social class comes from a careful field study of 735 adolescents of both sexes in "Elmtown," a pseudonym for a midwestern town studied in the 1940s (Hollingshead, 1949). The majority of high-school cliques involved members who occupied the same social class and the same grade in school (Figure 7-8). More than 60 percent of clique memberships involved students from the same social class. One Elmtown high school girl described social-class pressures on friendship that she and her best-friend Gladys felt.

I don't want to run any of the kids down, but there are certain girls here who are just not my type, and they're not Gladys' type; they'd like to run around with us, but we don't let them. Pauline Tyron and her bunch would like to run around with us, but we turn our backs on them because they run around all night, cut school, and hang out down at the Blue Triangle. There are some kids we'd like to go around with, but they don't want us to go with them. Gladys and I would like to go around with "Cookie" Barnett and her bunch, but they snub us if we try to get in on their parties, dances, or date the boys they go with. (Hollingshead, 1949, p. 209)

The same-sex friendships favored by the interpersonal cognitive system of early- and middle-adolescence give way in late-adolescence to opposite-sex relationships fostered by the American norms of dating and becoming a member of a couple. Once adolescents begin to date, their interpersonal interests change dramatically (Douvan & Adelson, 1966). They may now find that they have little in common with nondating members of the peer group. Overall, there appears to be a shift in late-adolescence away from strong same-sex friendships toward opposite-sex relationships and dating.

FIGURE 7-8
Distribution of cliques by social class and school grade for adolescents in "Elmtown."

(From Hollingshead, 1949.)

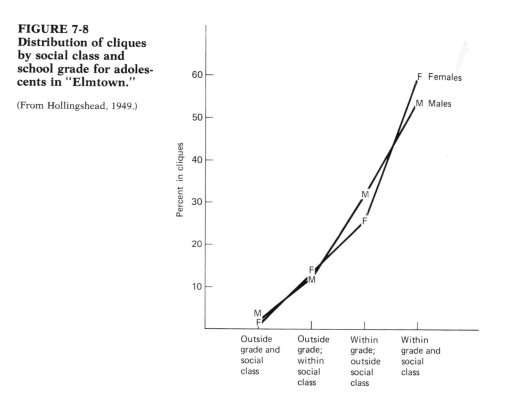

DATING AS ADOLESCENT SOCIAL INTERACTION

As the interpersonal cognitive system develops in adolescence, there is a shift toward romantic interpretations of situations involving male–female communication (Broderick & Weaver, 1968). For example, more than 3,000 adolescents, aged 10–17, were asked to interpret four cartoons of such situations. One cartoon showed a boy and girl sitting on a bench. Adolescents were asked, "What is happening now? Why? What will happen next? How will the girl feel then? How will the boy feel then?" Figure 7-9 shows the percentage of boys and girls whose stories focus on the pair as a romantic unit. For both sexes, there is a shift toward a more romantic interpersonal cognitive system with age. About 35 percent of the 10- to 11-year-olds focused on the pair as a romantic unit, compared to about 68 percent of the 16- to 17-year-olds. Adolescent boys were somewhat more likely to view the situation as romantic than were girls. Other studies have also shown adolescent males to be more "romantic" than females (Knox & Sporakowski, 1968; Rubin, Peplau, & Hill, 1981).

FIGURE 7-9
**Percentage of adoles-
cents' stories that focus
on romantic involve-
ment of a couple sitting
on a bench.**

(From Broderick & Weaver,
1968.)

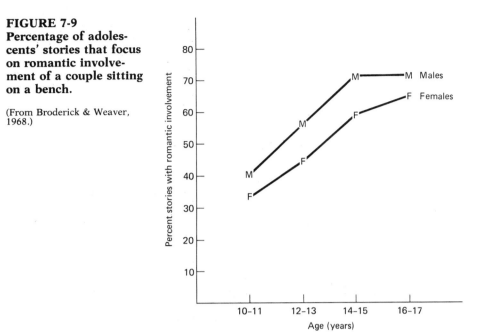

Unfortunately, there is some evidence that in the adolescent interpersonal cognitive system, self-doubt also increases, as reflected in feelings of social inadequacy. A 17-year-old boy provided the following interpretation to the bench cartoon:

The boy is trying to become acquainted with the girl and is gradually moving closer to her. The girl seems to be in a position to talk to strangers, and the boy seems to be a little uneasy and probably uncomfortable. The girl is telling herself to act as calm as possible and to try not to show her anxiety over the fact that the boy considers her pretty enough to talk to. The boy definitely is very nervous and is hoping that he can make a good impression with the girl. He is probably concerned over the fact that she might not consider him handsome and won't want to talk to him. (Broderick & Weaver, 1968, p. 622).

As adolescents become involved in dating, fears of social inadequacy and rejection surface. The major themes in this young man's interpretation of the cartoon are anxiety, nervousness, and concern over physical attractiveness.

**Historical Changes in
Heterosexual
Interaction**

One of the functions of society, as Margaret Mead (1959) has pointed out, is to regulate the behavior of young people between the time they reach sexual maturity and the time they get married.

Contemporary American society permits heterosexual interaction without much prior commitment. Dating has come to represent any paired association between members of the opposite sex prior to marriage (Lowrie, 1951). Dating is a term that could be applied to casual arrangements for fun and recreation, as well as to serious relationships in which the partners plan to marry.

In earlier American history, dating as a casual recreational activity did not exist. Rather, there was a system of courtship, in which partners were assessed in terms of their suitability for marriage (Kett, 1977). If a man asked permission of a colonial father to call on his daughter, he was in effect asking permission to marry her if they found each other suitable. There are several important differences between the colonial regulation of premarital courtship and the prevalent contemporary system of dating. First, it was the father's prerogative to limit access to his daughter. He could exercise veto power over her potential suitors, screening out those he deemed inappropriate marriage prospects for her. Second, the colonial norms of heterosexual interaction did not allow casual relationships. Courtship was viewed as serious by all parties concerned. Marriage was the logical end to a courtship that had not encountered any major snags. Third, colonial daughters might find themselves married with households of their own to take care of after only one or a small number of brief courtships. Life expectancy was shorter in colonial America, and one had to get on with the business of raising a family before it was too late.

Soon after the turn of the century, and coincident with the rise of the automobile as a common form of transportation, norms of premarital heterosexual interaction changed. Dating replaced courtship as the primary form of premarital relationship at about the time of World War 1 (Dornbusch, Carlsmith, Gross, Martin, Jennings, Rosenberg, & Duke, 1981; Hansen, 1977; Mead, 1959). Paired association became more casual at that time, with no necessary commitment beyond recreation.

Functions of Dating The single aim of courtship—finding a suitable marriage partner—was replaced by a series of other functions for dating relationships. Among these functions are the amusement and competition that has been described as the "thrill of the chase" (Waller, 1937). This dating function is found where there are large numbers of adolescents who are clearly understood to be postponing marriage.

Within the context of social norms for pair bonding, dating also allows young people to attend social functions, such as parties, dances, and sports events, without the embarrassment of having to

Prior to this century, the single aim of courtship was to find a suitable marriage partner. Today, dating serves a variety of functions: companionship, attending social functions without commitment, prestige and status, sexual experimentation, and fun. Moreover, dating provides adolescents with the opportunity to learn about the opposite sex and to develop criteria for evaluating potential marriage partners.

(Photo by Bruce Anspach/EPA Newsphoto)

go "stag." No emotional attachment to the date is necessary in such a casual arrangement; no commitment to the partner is implied. Dating can also be a place for identity seeking, and for sexual experimentation. Finally, dating conveys status in the peer group (Hansen & Hicks, 1980). Being out on dates has important symbolic value in the peer group. "The idea of having a date, and of other people knowing about the date, is often more exciting than the date itself" (Elkind, 1980, p. 439).

Diverse functions of dating were examined by asking high school and college students aged 16–21, to select their most important reasons for dating from a list of eight reasons provided by researchers. The weighting of reasons for dating among these 985 males and 994 females is shown in Table 7-2. These data indicate that male and female adolescents tend to attribute very similar meanings to dates. Notice that the rankings for the two groups are nearly identical. Female adolescents are somewhat more likely than males to cite the "educational" function of learning to adjust as a reason for dating; and male adolescents are somewhat more likely to cite the "sexual" and "prestige" functions (Lowrie, 1951). Studies with more recent cohorts have confirmed the similarity in dating interests of male and female adolescents (Hansen, 1977).

Stages of Dating

It is reasonable to suppose that several dates with the same person suggest a serious relationship. Stages of dating do show a

TABLE 7-2 **High-School and College Students' Reasons for Dating**	PERCENTAGE OF STUDENTS CITING REASONS (AND RANK IN IMPORTANCE)			
	MALES		FEMALES	
Affection	27.2	(1)	24.8	(2)
Gain poise or ease	20.3	(2)	25.4	(1)
Mate selection	13.9	(3)	15.7	(3)
Get to social events	12.9	(4)	11.1	(5)
Learning to adjust	8.5	(5)	13.2	(4)
Fun	8.1	(6)	8.0	(6)
Necking/Sex	6.0	(7)	0.5	(8)
Prestige/Status	3.1	(8)	1.3	(7)

Source: Lowrie, 1951.

movement away from superficial reasons for dating to more psychologically meaningful reasons (Herold, 1974).

Stage 1 of date selection, termed *filtering*, indicates a focus on physical appearance by both males and females. This superficial basis for dating is shown by young adolescents' answers to the question, "What do you think makes a girl popular with boys?" A majority (56 percent) answer that physical appearance is the key (Douvan & Adelson, 1966). Even more striking are adolescents' answers to questions about desirable characteristics in a date for themselves. High-school students were asked which they would rather go out with, the best-looking, the most brilliant, or most active student (represented by being either a star athlete or a cheerleader). Boys expressed an overwhelming preference for the best-looking dates, by a margin of more than two-to-one for either of the other choices. Girls also preferred the best looking dates, but not as strongly as the high-school boys. They were about as likely to want to go out with a star athlete as with the best-looking boy. Neither high-school girls nor boys expressed much interest in dating the most brilliant student (Coleman, 1961).

In Stage 2, or *narrowing*, physical appearance is not viewed as critically as it was earlier, but is still important. Of more importance are personality and social sophistication (Hansen & Hicks, 1980). Still, adolescents in Stage 2 of dating have developed very little sense of emotional give-and-take.

Stage 3, *evaluating*, is the final stage of dating and focuses on an evaluation of the person's deeper psychological traits, such as honesty, reliability, and stability. Both male and female students express a preference for dating someone who is pleasant, dependable, considerate, and who has a sense of humor (Hansen, 1977). Having a sense of humor becomes progressively more important as the relationship progresses (Hansen & Hicks, 1980).

Sara Davidson captures the essence of these three stages of date selection in a brief passage from her book, *Loose Change: Three Women of the Sixties.*

Looking back, I can see that at sixteen I had a willowy, beautifully proportioned body but at the time I was only aware of what I considered its unnatural elongation. When . . . I grew to be 5'10", I calculated that 90 percent of the men in the world were inaccessible to me because they were shorter. I daydreamed of going to Sweden to have an operation on my legs that would diminish me by three inches. When friends offered to fix me up, my first question was always "Is he tall?" followed by "Is he cute?" (Later I would ask, "Is he bright?" and still later, "Is he sensitive?") (Davidson, 1977, pp. 24–25)

Dating Adjustment

Herold (1973) has constructed a dating adjustment scale to determine the degree to which adolescents are confident of their dating ability, and satisfied with dating itself. The Dating Adjustment Scale (Table 7-3) yields a score that appears to be valid. That is, dating adjustment is closely related to actual dating experience, such as frequency of high-school dating, and emotional involvement in dating. Interestingly, adolescents who began dating early had a somewhat lower dating adjustment score, among both men and women. In one study at a midwestern university, females had higher dating adjustment scores than their male counterparts, and also dated more frequently (Herold, 1979). This may be explained, however, by the fact that the school in question had a 2.5:1 male-to-female ratio.

The traditional view of courtship as a means to mate selection has given way to a view in which dating has a social value in its own right. In the contemporary view, dating is a fundamental aspect of adolescence. Adolescents who do not measure up in this system, by their own evaluations can be said to be relatively less well adjusted. Those adolescents who are better adjusted are the ones who have had more dating experience.

Although the interpersonal cognitive system of many adolescents leads them to view dating as full of difficulties, dating itself is still seen as a very desirable activity. In contemporary American society, dating is crucial in the "career of passing from adolescence to adulthood" (Place, 1975, p. 157). Dating seems to imply overall social adjustment. Adolescent boys and girls who date are more likely to be members of organized social groups, have a greater number of leisure-time activities, and are even more likely to hold jobs than their nondating counterparts (Douvan & Adelson, 1966).

TABLE 7-3
Items on the Dating Adjustment Scale

1. It is easy to meet persons of the opposite sex here at this University.
2. On dates I *often* worry that I might do or say something that would embarrass me.
3. I lack confidence in my ability to get dates.
4. There are sufficient opportunities to meet potential dates here.
5. I often feel that I am a failure at dating.
6. In general I feel satisfied with my dating.
7. There are lots of available potential dates on this campus.
8. I *often* feel ill at ease when dating.
9. Because of the unfavorable sex ratio here it is futile to try to find a good date.
10. I rarely worry about getting a date when I feel the need for one.
11. I usually feel self-conscious on dates.
12. I never worry about boring my date.
13. It's not much sense trying to get a date at this time of the year because all the good ones are taken.
14. On dates I usually worry about whether or not I'm making a good impression.
15. There are very few individuals on this campus who are worth dating.
16. I have no problem feeling relaxed on dates.
17. I often worry about my future dating life.
18. I wouldn't call my dating experience a perfect success but I'm pretty well content with it.
19. Since coming to University my dating experience has been a *great* disappointment to me.
20. The good parts of my dating experience more than compensate for the bad.
21. I wish there were a better way of getting dates than there is.

Source: Herold, 1973.

Dating adjustment as a reflection of overall social adjustment was examined by a group of researchers who asked the question, "Do men and women who do not date much also have difficulty in same-sex relationships?" To address this question, the researchers (Himadi, Arkowitz, Hinton, & Perl, 1980) questioned 3,800 undergraduates at the University of Arizona about their frequency of dating. They then selected 24 students who dated the least and 24 who dated the most for further study. These students kept a record of all their social interactions for 1 week, and also participated in standardized interactions with other students, which provided an assessment of their social anxiety.

Figure 7-10 presents data from this study for male and female students separately. Among the male students, strong evidence was obtained for the notion that dating adjustment is similar to overall social adjustment. Male students who dated frequently had far more interactions with different people, of both sexes, during the week-long monitoring period than did the males who dated least frequently. The low-daters also showed more social anxiety in the standardized interactions, and particularly so with members of the opposite sex.

FIGURE 7-10
Dating adjustment and overall social adjustment(HDF = high dating frequency; LDF = low dating frequency). Male undergraduates who date infrequently are rated as socially anxious with both males and females. Female undergraduates who date infrequently are rated as socially anxious with males but not with other females.

(From Himadi, Arkowitz, Hinton, & Perl, 1980.)

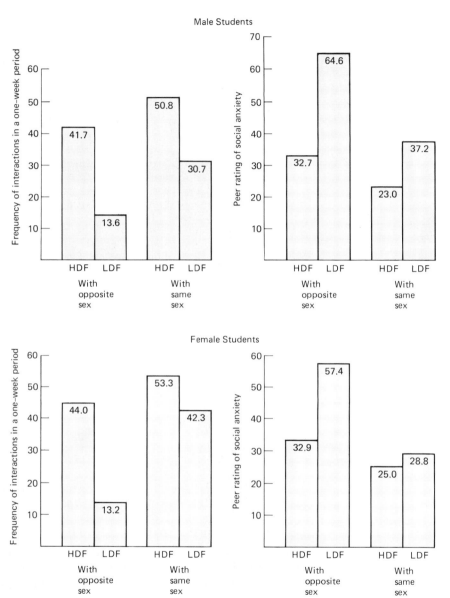

Female students who dated infrequently were anxious with members of the opposite sex in the standardized interaction, and they interacted infrequently with men during the week-long monitoring. However, their social interaction with members of the same sex was not statistically different from the women who were frequent daters.

The Initiation of Dates   Male and female college students who said that they dated infrequently were observed in standardized inter- actions with a member of the opposite sex in a similar study (Lipton & Nelson, 1980). When these students role-played conversations about eating in a fast-food restaurant or inviting a classmate to a party, they had difficulty initiating conversations in comparison to students who dated more frequently. Dating adjustment may reflect social skills in a general way: Those students who are socially adept are more likely to enjoy active social lives with members of the op- posite sex; those who are able to initiate conversations easily with members of the opposite sex may be more likely to be successful in the initial phases of the dating process.

Asking for and accepting dates is actually a complex process. An individual must assess the likelihood of actually getting a date with a potential partner based on several factors, including physical attractiveness of the date in comparison to oneself, and probability that the person will accept a date. Female undergraduates, aged 17–22, participated in a study of one aspect of the date-initiating phenomenon (Shanteau & Nagy, 1979). These students were shown photographs of several male students who were potential dates. They were told that the men had been given photographs of them also, which they had used as information for estimating how likely it was that they would go out with the female students. Thus, a fe- male student might be given a photo of an attractive male student with the notation "Tom/Fairly Likely," meaning that good-looking Tom said it was fairly likely that he would accept a date with the girl in question.

The female students in this study, in the age range of late ad- olescence, appeared to combine the probability estimates with at- tractiveness in a multiplicative fashion, as indicated in Figure 7-11. Potential dates who were low in both attractiveness and in likeli- hood of acceptance were viewed as highly undesirable dates; men high on both characteristics were seen as highly desirable dates, more so than through a simple additive combination of the factors. Incidentally, when female students were given photographs alone, without any statement about whether the male student would ac- cept a date, they tended to pick men of intermediate attractiveness as the most desirable dates (Shanteau & Nagy, 1979).

Dating and Sexual Role-Playing

The norms associated with dating, including age norms, are complex. Adolescents are viewed by adults as too young for dating until they are 15 or 16. Adolescents themselves view the age of 16 as best for the first date (Place, 1975). In fact, however, the majority of adolescents begin dating before the age of 15; in a large-scale survey

FIGURE 7-11
Preference for dates based on attractiveness and on probability of date-acceptance. Potential dates low in both attractiveness and probability of acceptance are viewed as highly undesirable, while those high on both characteristics are viewed as highly desirable.

(From Shanteau & Nagy, 1979.)

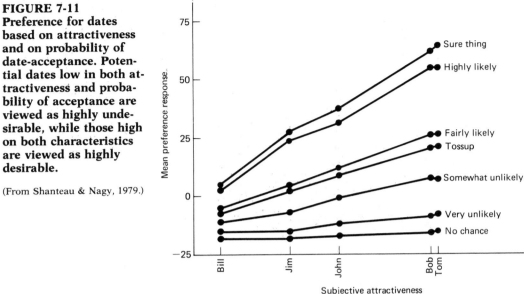

of American adolescents, 56 percent of boys and 56 percent of girls began dating before age 15 (Bayer, 1968).

Norms regulate the behavior of participants when they are on dates. Many researchers have noted the expectancies of dating behavior, which vary by gender, which we may call norms of *sexual role-playing*. For example, it is expected that the boy will ask for a date, and it will be left to the girl to accept or reject his bid. Parents of many adolescent girls still expect the boy to call for her at home and to introduce himself to them. One adolescent girl expressed this sentiment in an interview: "I expect him to come to the door when he takes me out. My parents expect it. If he wants to make points with my parents, he'd better come to the door" (Place, 1975, p. 168). Although many arrangements for heterosexual interaction in adolescence have become informal, few adolescents escape the sexual role-playing requirements of the formal date at some point.

Nonverbal Aspects of Sexual Role-Playing David Givens has described some of the nonverbal aspects of sexual role-playing, involved in flirtation and seduction. Givens (1978) distinguished five phases of heterosexual involvement: attention, recognition, interaction, sexual arousal, and resolution.

Consider an adolescent couple who are strangers to each other and who find themselves at the same table in the school cafeteria. During the *attention phase*, they are aware of each other, and their awareness can be seen in their nonverbal behavior. Their eyes may meet briefly, but each quickly looks away. Their appearance may reveal clues about their "availability": Cologne, make-up, and type of clothing all contain clues about readiness for interaction. The pair unconsciously attend to aspects of each other's behavior. Nervous preening, such as hair-adjustment and face-patting, may indicate interest. They exhibit some nervousness, such as yawning, scratching, and an increased tempo of behavior. According to Givens, this collection of signs indicates an appeal for an affectionate response.

No bids for interaction are made during the attention phase; the pair have not yet "recognized" each other for purposes of interaction. *Recognition* may occur during the second phase. Males hesitate to approach a female without some indication of interest on her part. It is this sign of interest that he will be looking for in the recognition phase. If she gives him a blank stare, and especially if she exhibits discouraging behavior such as subtly showing her tongue, her signals indicate disinterest, and he will not initiate any interaction. On the other hand, she may provide availability signals, such as head tosses, chest protrusion, smiling, raising her eyebrows, or batting her eyelashes, which will encourage him to pursue an interaction. For the male's part, he may behave in a similar fashion to communicate his interest in her. Both members of the pair may show submission postures, according to Givens. These include handclasping, grasping the neck, and rotating the feet inward in a pigeon-toed fashion. These signals are "read," unconsciously, as indications of affectionate interest.

The pair may finally become involved in a genuine *social interaction* in a third phase. Here verbal contact of some sort is virtually essential, but the topic of conversation is irrelevant. There will likely be a lot of tension in the early stage of interaction. People feel vulnerable when they begin conversations of this type because of the possibility of being rejected. Whatever the two finally discuss, their tempo of interaction is likely to increase, their mutual gaze will increase, and finally, their anxiety will decrease. "Do you like the string beans?" he might ask. "Yes," she says, "although they are a little overcooked." Such an innocuous exchange of comments can serve as a way into a more important interaction. Such exchanges are sometimes referred to as "breaking the ice," so that the real interaction can begin.

Givens also described two advanced stages of heterosexual interaction—sexual arousal and resolution—but these phases may be postponed until future interactions. The first three phases, however, are characteristic of early phases of dating: the flirtation and initiation leading to more formal dating interactions. The story to the picture that opened this chapter describes some of the anxiety that attends the early phases of heterosexual interaction.

Sexism and Dating Norms Some aspects of traditional dating norms may be susceptible to charges of sexism in American society. For example, the traditional norm was for the male to provide transportation on the date and to cover the expenses of the couple's entertainment. Sexual role-playing norms allowed the female to go along with this arrangement and to get an evening's free entertainment as part of the bargain. Norms of sexual role-playing also allowed the male to expect a certain amount of "reciprocation in units of sexual access" (Husbands, 1970). The boy, therefore, was expected to try some sort of overtly sexual activity. It was the boy who was expected to kiss the girl and to initiate more advanced forms of sexual interaction, such as petting. The girl might play an active role in encouraging his advances in these games of sexual role-playing. As a young female interviewee pointed out, "If I like him, I'd just move over to him and give him the opportunity of kissing me" (Place, 1975, p. 169). It was the role of the girl to set limits on sexual interaction on the date. These norms were understood by both participants. A contemporary trend toward more informal interaction between adolescent males and females has eliminated some of these aspects of sexism on dates, but they have not altogether disappeared.

Sexual Role-Playing in Anthropological Perspective In the United States, heterosexual interaction has typically been initiated by the male; dates are usually suggested and arranged by him, and sexual contact has been at his initiation. In adolescence, interest in the opposite sex is expected both by peers and by parents. Adolescents may go out in groups to discos or to other group events. They may go to movies, or especially, to drive-ins. Official norms prohibit sexual intercourse but permit kissing and petting. A gradual escalation of sexual activity by dating couples, from kissing and caressing to heavy petting and intercourse, takes place in the modal relationship as it becomes more emotionally intimate. Parents may offer their approval or disapproval of mate selection, but in most segments of American society, parents have little say in their children's choice of friends. An examination of some of the elements of sexual role-playing in other cultures may help to place these aspects of heterosexual interaction in perspective.

In Nyansongo, a community in Kenya, sexual role-playing shares some of the elements described for Americans. "For most individuals, liaisons are not approved by older people and must be carried on privately" (LeVine & LeVine, 1963, p. 59). Both boys and girls have ceremonies in early adolescence signifying their maturity; afterward they may begin their heterosexual activity, usually around the age of 14 or 15. Sexual role-playing involves the girl feigning a reluctance about having sex even when she is willing.

One purpose of norms regarding heterosexual interaction is to regulate the period between sexual maturity and marriage, since in most cultures there is a gap between these two events. A group of people living in the western highlands of New Guinea, the Mae Enga, regulate heterosexual interaction in this period with a set of fearful beliefs about the consequences of sex. The belief that menarche gives women the power to pollute males is one strong regulator of behavior. Sex with a menstruating woman, they believe, can "sicken a man and cause persistent vomiting, turn his blood black, corrupt his vital juices so that his skin darkens and wrinkles as his flesh wastes, permanently dull his wits, and eventually lead to a slow decline and death" (Meggitt, 1964, p. 207). Males must learn magic to counteract the sexual ruin women bring on, and until they do they limit their interaction with the opposite sex. Adolescence, among these people, is relatively chaste.

The rituals of courtship in the United States involve a set of norms guiding behavior in the dating situation. With considerable variation, norms regulate courtship in other cultures as well. A field study of the Paluaungs of Burma in the early 1900s revealed a symbolic language for courtship, involving food metaphors (Milne, 1924). Upon meeting an acquaintance one might ask, "What have you eaten?" Unmarried people answer such a question with a symbolic reply. "I have eaten mustard leaves" means something like "I have wanted to talk to you." "I have eaten mushrooms," however, is a very rude answer. "I have eaten the flowers of the cotton plant" means the equivalent of "I want to go to bed with you." All of these replies form a language of flirtation, which is not taken seriously by the young people involved. Sexual role-playing in our own country is often stilted with pat questions and answers in a similar way. Rona Jaffe described one such scene in her novel about college relationships, *Class Reunion*. The description of a college mixer is provided from the perspective of the character Annabel.

That dance had been like a cement grinder; all those people, no time to talk. But they were there to meet people—how else could you? You had to find out as many names as possible, and ask those dumb questions about their majors and their backgrounds, quick before someone else cut in, and then if you didn't like a boy's looks or pedigree you wouldn't even go out with him and you'd never find out if he was nice or not. That was so superficial. Well, it wasn't as if she were going to marry any of them—she had four years of college ahead of her and plenty of time to think about getting serious. (Jaffe, 1979, p. 31)

It is interesting to note that not all cultures have chosen the same aspects of interaction between unmarried people for close supervision. In the Trobriand Islands (in the 1920s), young bachelors lived in their own special houses and often invited in a group of young girls to live with them—a sort of group marriage without any duties or obligations to each other; however, even for a couple about to be married, sharing a meal was prohibited. "Such an act would greatly shock the moral susceptibility of a native, as well as his sense of propriety. To take a girl out to dinner without having previously married her . . . would be to disgrace her in the eyes of a Trobriander" (Malinowski, 1929, p. 64).

Explanations for the variation in norms regulating premarital heterosexual interaction are fairly complex. The period between sexual maturity and full adult status differs a great deal from society to society, as we saw in Chapter 2. In highly technological societies, this period tends to be lengthy, a time for training and role experimentation. Dating and courtship are matters of individual choice, rather than parental discretion.

The status of women in the economic system is a factor in norms of heterosexual interaction cross-culturally. Cultures in which parents are compensated for the loss of a daughter at marriage often have harsh norms regulating their behavior. In these instances, the girl's virginity at marriage makes her a more highly prized commodity in the marriage market, and restrictive norms are often carefully enforced. Young women in the Indian state of Uttar Pradesh are subject to restrictive norms; when a girl marries in her late teens, "she is put 'on display' every afternoon huddled on the courtyard floor" (Minturn & Hitchcock, 1963, p. 265).

Parental availability for watching over children might help to determine the degree of restrictiveness in norms of heterosexual interaction. Several societies where caretakers are readily accessible tend to have permissive norms, whereas societies in which caretakers are not readily available have restrictive norms (Broude, 1975). Restrictive norms may serve the function of regulating important aspects of child and adolescent behavior when parents and other caretakers are not available to do so directly.

Much of the sexual role-playing illustrated by an anthropological approach to adolescent heterosexual interaction is an expression of the larger social system it represents. In the United States, "falling in love" and "going steady" go far beyond mere sexual expressions. Sexual role-playing is a fundamental part of gender-role expectations, which we discussed in Chapter 4.

SUMMARY

1. Relationships between adolescents and their parents involve *reciprocal influence*, where the behavior of one party to a social interchange influences and controls the behavior of the other party.

2. Reciprocal influence is apparent with respect to parental discipline. Authoritarian discipline, including physical punishment, is associated with dependency and rebelliousness in adolescents. Highly-permissive discipline may also lead to dependency. With physical maturation at puberty, adolescents become more assertive in social interchanges with parents.

3. Research reveals few dramatic differences between attitudes and values of adolescents and their parents, contrary to the implications of the term *generation gap*. Adolescents, however, tend to overestimate the differences that do exist. Adolescents also attribute more positive characteristics to adults than they do to adolescents. Perhaps the adolescent perception of a generation gap occurs as a result of negative self-ratings by adolescents themselves.

4. Adolescents shift their primary social orientation from parents to an orientation in which peers exert considerable influence. During this time, adolescent attitudes toward parents become less favorable, and their willingness to endorse peer misconduct increases.

5. Adolescents are likely to comply with assumed parental values in important areas, such as educational plans, while peers exert influence in more trivial areas, such as matters of dress. Peers are particularly strong, however, in influencing decisions about recreation and drug use.

6. Evidence from research suggests that adolescents show increasing autonomy with age; they become somewhat less likely to conform to either parents or to peers as they grow older.

7. Adolescents appear less likely to conform to antisocial behavior than to prosocial or neutral behavior; conformity to antisocial behavior peaks in middle-adolescence at around age 15.

8. Separation from parents has positive psychological effects for both adolescents and their parents. Male adolescents in launching-center families with a greater degree of separation show more independence from, and affection toward, their parents.

9. According to Sullivan's theory, the major interpersonal need systems of security, intimacy, and lust come into conflict in adolescence.

10. Research on stages of adolescent group development is consistent with Sullivan's interpersonal theory. Isolated cliques of same-sex members become integrated with each other in group-to-group interaction. Upperstatus members then begin forming heterosexual cliques, which subsequently also engage in group-to-group interaction. The crowd finally disintegrates in late-adolescence into loosely associated couples.

11. Psychological reactions to friends and friendship change during adolescence as the interpersonal cognitive system matures. Adolescents become increasingly aware of the subjectivity of values and attitudes and look for others whose values are similar to their own. The interpersonal cognitive system of adolescence favors same-sex friendships and friendships within social-class groupings.

12. The interpersonal cognitive system favors romantic interpretations of ambiguous boy–girl situations in late adolescence. Studies have shown adolescent boys to be at least as if not more "romantic" in their interpretations as girls. Doubts about social adequacy and physical attractiveness also surface as dating becomes a more real possibility.

13. Dating as a form of heterosexual interaction entered the American scene around the turn of the century, replacing more formal courtship. Dating implies a casual heterosexual relationship with no necessary commitments between people who are understood to be postponing marriage. Dating has gradually become a major part of adolescence, serving diverse functions such as recreation, identity seeking, and sexual experimentation.

14. Three stages of dating have been isolated. Physical attractiveness is the focus of Stage 1, *filtering*, prevalent in early adolescence. Superficial personality traits are prevalent in Stage 2, *narrowing*. Deep psychological traits, such as honesty, reliability, stability, and sensitivity, form the basis of date selection in Stage 3, *evaluating*.

15. Those adolescents who date frequently and who are emotionally involved in dating have higher dating adjustment scores. Adolescents who date are better adjusted socially than their non-dating counterparts; daters are more likely to be members of organized social groups and are more likely to hold jobs.

16. Expectancies for dating, which vary by gender, are called norms of *sexual role-playing*. Traditional dating norms, in which the male makes arrangements for a date and pays for entertain-

ment, are examples of sexual role-playing. Sexual role-playing is also included in the complex set of norms involved in initiating a heterosexual encounter.

17. Norms of heterosexual interaction regulate the period between sexual maturity and marriage. Different cultures regulate heterosexual interaction in accordance with their own cultural values and beliefs.

18. Cross-cultural variation in norms for heterosexual interaction is in part a function of length of the period between sexual maturity and full adult status; other factors include level of technological development, status of women, and parental availability for supervision.

OUTLINE

THE SEXUAL REVOLUTION
    Liberalized Attitudes
    Increased Participation in Sexual Behavior

DEVELOPMENTAL ASPECTS OF SEXUALITY
    Development of Interpersonal Intimacy
    Incidence of Coitus in Early Adolescence
    Sexual Intercourse in Late Adolescence

FACTORS INFLUENCING SEXUAL BEHAVIOR
    Sexual Behavior and the Peer Group
    Sex Within a Relationship
    Sex and Moral Judgment
    Puberty and Self-Perception
    Social Characteristics Influencing Sexual Behavior

GENDER AND SEXUAL ROLE-PLAYING
    The Double Standard
    Sexual Role-Playing in Anthropological Perspective

SEXUAL ACTIVITIES
    Masturbation
    Adolescent Homosexuality

DIFFICULTIES WITH SEX RESEARCH IN ADOLESCENCE
    Sample Representativeness
    Response Reliability

SUMMARY

8. ADOLESCENT SEXUALITY

First-person accounts of sexual experiences highlight that aspect of development in a more dramatic and personal way than do charts, tables, and summary statistics. Here is a concise description of adolescent sexual encounters provided by a 17-year-old girl.

Boys would use lines. Most of the guys would get together and start talking about who they had made it with and how they'd come on or something like that, and where. Mostly, I suppose, it was at the drive-in. You'd go to the drive-in and park in the back. You'd sit close to the person and all of a sudden he'd put his arms around you and he'd be reaching down inside your blouse. You'd push his hand away. He wouldn't actually say anything, but he'd think he was really cool, you know.

They'd put their arms around you and they'd slowly drop it to your shoulder and slowly into your blouse. You'd jerk his hand away, and you'd smile or something like that and you'd turn back to the movie and he'd start doing it again. And you'd say, "no," "come on," "stop," or something like that. And he'd say, "What's wrong? There's nothing wrong with it." And he knew you dug it, and you knew he really wanted to.

So it would just get around to it again. This time he'd go further, and he'd undo your bra and that would start it. You'd start kissing and he'd start feeling you. Not that many words, except if you were really a prude. I felt a lot about the guys and saying all they want to do is go out with me for sex or something like that, but at the same time I dug it and thought it wasn't bad for me. But after a while I wanted to go further and further. And then I started getting really paranoid and feeling guilty. I'd start thinking of my father and if he was watching us—like I'd actually feel him watching us even if he wasn't anywhere around. That would make me feel so guilty that I would immediately stop. And the guy would say, "Okay, if you don't want to, I won't make you." They were always cool about it. They would say, "If you don't want to—I only will if you want to." And then I'd say, "I don't want to." (Sorensen, 1972, p. 176)

This 17-year-old's description of sexual relationships in adolescence foreshadows the academic treatment of the topic in this chapter. We discuss some of the factors involved in sexual decision-making—decisions about the types of sexual activities to engage in, when, and with whom sex is to occur. Although we discuss a range of sexual activities in which adolescents partake, the focus is on heterosexual intercourse.

Much attention has been devoted to the issue of a sexual revolution in the United States. Factors involved in a sexual revolution, and research bearing on this issue, are also discussed. Finally, we consider the extent to which sexual roles guide and influence the behavior of young people. The scenario offered by the 17-year-old girl suggests clearly understood gender expectations, with the boy making sexual overtures that the girl rebuffs. In this connection, we examine the existence of a double standard in the sexual behavior of young men and women. Descriptions of norms that guide the sexual behavior of adolescents in several other cultures help to place sexual role-playing in a larger perspective.

THE SEXUAL REVOLUTION

Several commentators on the current social scene have described the trend toward liberalized sexual norms as a "sexual revolution." Nudity and sex in the movies are much more widely accepted. People are discussing sexual lifestyles much more openly than in the recent past. Sexually explicit language is present in literature and in the media in a way that was neither legally nor socially acceptable just a few years ago. Bob Greene, a Chicago columnist, wrote a piece entitled "Beyond the Sexual Revolution" for *Newsweek* magazine in 1975.

In Chicago recently, there was a well-publicized opening-night party for a new private club. The operators of the club, sensing the mood of the times, provided all of the elements of chic decadence that have become socially acceptable. There were naked twin boys, painted silver, wearing jewels in their navels, and waving feathered fans to cool the guests. Behind the buffet table, reclining next to the food, there was a young woman, also painted silver, nude from the waist up, wearing a fish tail from the hips down. The waiters wore glittery T-shirts and rhinestone earrings . . . If there is one moment that deserves to stand forever as the official end of the sexual revolution in America, perhaps it should be the precise instant when the silver fan boy dipped his feather in the direction of James Rochford, the police chief of Chicago.

Liberalized Attitudes

These observations suggest, at the very least, a change in attitudes with regard to sexual matters. Several studies of sexual attitude support this conclusion (Reiss, 1966; Simon, 1969; Whatley & Appel, 1973; Croake & James, 1973). Members of older generations currently hold attitudes that are less permissive than members of younger generations (Freeman, 1972; LoPiccolo, 1973; Orloff & Weinstock, 1975). In a Gallup poll of nearly 1,200 adults in 1969, 30 percent of women and 54 percent of men in the age group 20–29 felt premarital coitus was "not wrong." Only 13 percent of the women and 23 percent of the men in the 40–49 age group endorsed this standard (Alston & Tucker, 1973). In the general population in 1969, 21 percent of Americans judged premarital sex "not wrong"; by 1979, 55 percent of the general population held this standard (Reinhold, 1979).

A shift in attitudes toward sexual behavior is just one of the elements of a sexual revolution. A second element is an increase in sexual participation, reflected in incidence of premarital intercourse. (*Incidence* refers to the percentage of persons who have ever had the experience, on at least one occasion.) Earlier participation in sexual activities is a third element; younger adolescents who participate in advanced forms of sexual behavior would demonstrate this aspect of a sexual revolution. A fourth element of liberalization concerns changes in patterns of sexual behavior, including willingness to engage in more exotic forms of sexual expression, such as oral–genital contact, sodomy, and group sex.

Increased Participation in Sexual Behavior

Not all researchers agree on the extent of liberalization in sexual behavior. Many recent studies, however, strongly suggest that the liberalization in attitudes discussed above is being matched in behavior. A measure of this change is provided by the *Redbook* report on female sexuality. *Redbook* magazine published a questionnaire about sexual behavior in October 1974. The response was overwhelming, with more than 100,000 replies, an unprecedented response rate for a published survey. Premarital sexual intercourse had been experienced by 81 percent of the respondents. The survey also suggested earlier participation in sexual activities; nearly half (49 percent) had had intercourse at age 17 or younger (Tavris & Sadd, 1977). Several competent studies point to the conclusion that more adolescents are experiencing advanced forms of sexual behav-

FIGURE 8-1
Incidence of premarital
intercourse in college
men (M) and women (F)
from 1938 to 1975.

(From Hopkins, 1977; King,
Robinson, & Balswick, 1977.)

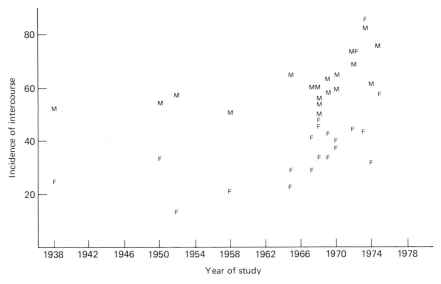

ior now than at any other time in the country's history. Between 1970 and 1978, the number of unmarried individuals under 25 who were living together increased by a whopping 800 percent (Reinhold, 1979).

Increased participation in sexual activities is further demonstrated by comparing reported incidences of premarital intercourse over the last four decades. Such a comparison reveals that young people reported more sexual experience beginning in the decade of the 1960s, as can be seen in Figure 8-1. The noticeable increase in reported incidence of premarital intercourse accelerated even further in the decade of the 1970s (Jessor & Jessor, 1975; King, Balswick, & Robinson, 1977; Jessor, Costa, Jessor, & Donovan, 1981).

While these data may not support the contention of a full-fledged revolution in sexual behavior, they certainly indicate a dramatic liberalization in standards and behavior over the past few decades. Liberalized standards are a part of the cultural context in which sexual socialization and sexual decision-making take place.

DEVELOPMENTAL ASPECTS OF SEXUALITY

It is probably not a surprise that sex is an important topic for discussion and for thought among adolescents. A study of more than 4,000 Americans, aged 8–99, showed that thoughts about sex occurred more often among adolescents and young adults than any other age group (Cameron & Biber, 1973).

Development of Interpersonal Intimacy

Unstructured interviews with 91 teenagers in a longitudinal study in New York revealed a developmental sequence of increasing levels of intimacy. Interpersonal interaction progressed from same-sex friends, to mixed-sex friends, to dating, and subsequently to advanced forms of dating, including steady dating and sexual affairs (Chess, Thomas, & Cameron, 1976). We encountered a similar developmental progression in social interaction in Chapter 7.

Several factors appear to be involved in such a developmental progression. The changing status of interpersonal interaction undoubtedly reflects the motivational pressures of physical maturation. Physical changes following puberty are themselves orderly, as we saw in Chapter 2, and make the individual a different stimulus object. The different pattern of reactions elicited from others influences one's sexual identity, and one's selection of sexual standards and behavior. A study of adolescent sexual behavior based on a random sample of nearly 2,000 unmarried British teenagers, aged 15–19, underscores this point. Interviews with the adolescents in this survey revealed five stages in the developmental sequence of sexual behavior, which are described in Table 8-1. The percentage of boys and girls with experience at each stage parallel the increasing levels of intimacy described earlier for the smaller sample of New York teenagers. Reactions from other people are crucial in determining the level of intimacy chosen by those adolescents. "At the age of fourteen a boy may be discouraged by parents from taking a girl out even if he wanted to; but by the age of nineteen he is expected by adults and his own friends to be showing an interest in the opposite sex" (Schofield, 1965, p. 48).

**TABLE 8-1
Stages of Sexual Experience and Percentages of Boys and Girls, Aged 15–19, at Each Stage**

STAGE	PERCENT OF BOYS	PERCENT OF GIRLS
I. Little or no contact with the opposite sex. May have been out on a date but has never kissed.	16	7
II. Limited experience of sexual activities. Has experienced kissing and may have experienced breast stimulation over clothes, but has never experienced this under clothes.	35	46
III. Sexual intimacies which fall short of intercourse. Has experienced breast stimulation under clothes and may have experienced genital stimulation but has no experience of sexual intercourse.	29	35
IV. Sexual intercourse with only one partner.	5	7
V. Sexual intercourse with more than one partner.	15	5

Source: Schofield, 1965.

Loss of Virginity For many adolescents, dating relationships ultimately reach a point of intimacy at which sexual intercourse seems a logical conclusion. First experience of intercourse is an important psychological, as well as physical, event in a person's life history. The transition from virgin to nonvirgin has some of the psychological characteristics of a rite of passage, a change in psychological status. "I felt I had to prove to myself once and for all that I could, and perhaps because I wanted to," is the description of motivation behind first sexual intercourse provided by one adolescent boy (Schofield, 1965, p. 66).

Certainly most adolescents have devoted a lot of thought to sex before their first experience of intercourse. Nevertheless, loss of virginity is usually not a premeditated, planned event; rather, it "just happens," as one behavior in a logical sequence within a relationship. The following description is provided by a girl who had her first intercourse at age 16:

I'll never forget that evening. We were at a friend of a friend's house—they were real rich, twelve bedrooms and all that bit. We were just sitting in one of their many bedrooms during the party. And we were talking about an hour. And then we just kind of got into things. I don't know—it was the way we felt about each other and everything. I didn't even need any lessons or anything. It just came natural. We talked about it before, but we never made any specific time or anything like that. I was scared all along, and I kind of sat down and thought everything over a lot, and it didn't seem terribly wrong if two people really loved each other. (Sorensen, 1972, p. 194)

A large majority of boys and girls reported that their first experience of sexual intercourse was unpremeditated (Schofield, 1965).

Emotional reactions to first experience of intercourse are not universally positive. Fewer than one-half of the boys and fewer than one-third of the girls in two major studies of adolescent sexuality reported being happy after their first experience (Schofield, 1965; Sorensen, 1972). Other studies show a similar high level of unpleasant reactions to first coitus (Hessellund, 1971; Hunt, 1974; Jessor et al., 1982). Boys report more enjoyment of the first experience and less shame. About the same percentage of both boys and girls (7 percent) said they actively disliked it (Schofield, 1965). Nevertheless, about a third of the girls and a quarter of the boys had sex again within a week of their first experience (Schofield, 1965).

Many adolescents feel that their first sexual experience enhances emotional closeness to their partners. A teenage girl provided the following description of her rationale for intercourse:

He kept telling me that this sort of thing is all right for two people who are in love and plan to get married. I thought about it and agreed. I just sort of

thought, "Well, he does love me and he wants to marry me, so why not?"
(Schofield, 1965, p. 66)

A large percentage of all sexually experienced adolescents feel that their relationship was strengthened by sexual intimacy. About half of the boys and three-fourths of the girls have intercourse with their first partner on at least one subsequent occasion (Schofield, 1965; Sorensen, 1972).

The traditional gender difference, in which women tie their sexual experience more closely to emotional commitment than men, was found in a study employing a representative sample of adolescents, aged 14–18, in Illinois, and a sample of students at a 4-year college. These data are presented in Table 8-2 and show that females experience intercourse for the first time with partners to whom they are emotionally attached far more often than men. This gender difference suggests that first intercourse may have different psychological meaning for males than for females. Boys may be more likely to desire sexual experience to demonstrate maturity and peer-group normality. Girls, on the other hand, may be more likely to view sex as a demonstration of close attachment and as a means of interpersonal communication.

In the decade of the 1970s, the average age at first intercourse was between 16 and 18 for boys, and around 18 for girls (Jessor et al., 1981; Schalmo & Levin, 1974). Average age is somewhat misleading as a statistic, however, because the variability around age at loss of virginity is very large. It is more convenient to discuss sexual intercourse in terms of incidence, which refers to the percentages of individuals who have ever engaged in the behavior in question.

TABLE 8-2 **Relationship to First Coital Partner Among Males and Females**		MALES	FEMALES
	PERCENT WHO REPORT THAT FIRST COITAL PARTNER WAS:		
	Pick-up or casual date	26	4
	Frequent date, no emotional attachment	16	1
	Date with emotional attachment, but not love	23	14
	Person with whom in love, but no plans to marry	17	22
	Person plan to marry	14	59
	(Prostitute)	4	—

Source: Simon, Berger, & Gagnon, 1972.

Incidence of Coitus in Early Adolescence

Few adolescents of either gender have experienced sexual intercourse by the age of 13. In subsequent periods of adolescence, not surprisingly, incidence of intercourse increases. The Kinsey reports indicated that among young adolescents who ultimately attended college, 2 percent of the girls and 10 percent of the boys had sexual intercourse. These percentages, and comparable data from more recent studies, are presented in Table 8-3; these data are discussed in some detail in the next few paragraphs.

Robert Sorensen's study is one of the earliest large-scale surveys specifically concerned with adolescent sexuality. Sorensen attempted to obtain a representative national sample by selecting 839 households in which there were adolescents present. From these households, 331 cases were eliminated because of parental objection, and another 115 were eliminated because the adolescents themselves refused to participate. Thus only 47 percent of the original sample are included in the data presented in Sorensen's report. Sorensen's data are likely to overrepresent the most sexually aware and liberal adolescents, individuals who are willing to answer questions about their sexual activities, and whose parents have specifically endorsed that willingness. As Table 8-3 shows, incidences of intercourse reported by adolescents in the Sorensen study are remarkably high. The adolescents questioned in that survey are probably not lying; rather, their data must be interpreted in terms of the method of sampling, which is likely to be biased in favor of more liberal respondents.

TABLE 8-3
Incidence of Intercourse among Teenagers from Several Studies of Sexual Behavior

| STUDY | DATE OF DATA COLLECTION | AGES OF ADOLESCENTS | | | |
| | | AGE 13–15 | | AGE 16–19 | |
		MALES	FEMALES	MALES	FEMALES
Kinsey et al. (1948, 1953)	late 1940s early 1950s	10	2	42	18
Schofield (1965)	early 1960s	11	6	30	16
Vener & Stewart (1974)	1970	24	11	34	25
Miller & Simon (1974)	1971	9	7	21	22
Sorensen (1972)	1972	44	30	72	57
Vener & Stewart (1974)	1973	33	17	36	33
Jessor & Jessor (1975)	1969–1972	—	—	27	38

Sources: Hopkins, 1977; Schofield, 1965.

The remaining studies whose data are summarized in Table 8-3 suggest a trend toward earlier sexual experience in adolescence. The studies also strongly suggest a breakdown in the double standard with regard to sexual behavior. Vener and Stewart's figures from 1973 show very little difference in incidences for males and females; Shirley and Richard Jessor report a slightly higher incidence of intercourse among adolescent girls than boys in the age range 16–19; these data were obtained in 1969–1972.

These studies of adolescent sexual behavior lead to the following conclusions: First, as one might expect, all the studies show a greater degree of sexual activity among older adolescents. Second, the studies, which were done from the late 1940s to the mid-1970s, show a trend toward earlier experimentation with intercourse among adolescents. Finally, reported differences in incidence of intercourse between male and female adolescents have diminished or even undergone a slight reversal; the sexual *behavior* of adolescents no longer seems to be governed by a double standard.

Sexual Intercourse in Late Adolescence

College students, representing late adolescence, have provided the most extensive data on sexual behavior among young people. Table 8-4 presents incidence of premarital intercourse from several college studies. The pre-1970 studies indicate that the number of males who engaged in coitus from the late 1930s to the late 1960s remained fairly constant; just over half of all college males reported experiencing sexual intercourse. During this same time range, reports of coital experience among college women showed more fluctuation. The trend, however, was in the direction of a gradual increase in reported sexual experience, but never reaching the 50 percent level.

The studies that are summarized in Table 8-4 suggest several interesting trends in the sexual experience of college students. Overall, the studies provide evidence from several different areas of the country that there has been an increase in the sexual experience of young people. The shift toward greater numbers of young people engaging in sexual intercourse was particularly dramatic in the 1970s.

Regional differences may be important in explaining some of the variation in incidence reflected in Table 8-4. Regional variation may result from differences in the actual behavior or from differences in willingness to share private moments with sex researchers. Whatever the explanation, predictable regional variation occurs in reports of sexual experience. For example, Christensen and Gregg (1970) surveyed the sexual behavior of college students in three areas that have different sexual standards: Mormon (restrictive),

TABLE 8-4
Incidence of Intercourse among Males and Females during the Late Adolescent (College) Years

STUDY AND PUBLICATION DATE	DATE OF DATA COLLECTION	MALES	FEMALES
Bromley & Britten (1938)	1930s	52	25
Kinsey, Pomeroy, & Martin (1948)	1940s	54	—
Kinsey, Pomeroy, Martin, & Gebhard (1953)	1940s	—	33
Christensen & Gregg (1970)	1958	51	21
Ehrmann (1959)	1950s	57	13
Freedman (1965)	1960s	—	22
Robinson, King, & Balswick (1972)	1965	65	29
Bauman & Wilson (1974)	1968	56	46
Christensen & Gregg (1970)	1968	50	34
Lewis & Burr (1975)	1967–1968	60	29
Schulz, Bohrnstedt, Borgatta, & Evans (1977)	1964–1968	65	56
Luckey & Nass (1969)	1960s	58	43
Diamant (1970)	1969–1970	59	47
Kaats & Davis (1970)	1969–1970	60	41
Robinson, King, & Balswick (1972)	1970	65	37
Bauman & Wilson (1974)	1972	73	73
Lewis (1973)	1972–1973	63	34
Jessor & Jessor (1975)	1970–1973	82	85

Source: Hopkins, 1977; adapted from Tables 2 and 3.

midwestern (moderate), and Danish (liberal). In 1958, incidence of intercourse followed an orderly pattern for both men and women in these groups, with higher incidences in the more liberal groups. By 1968, the incidences for men were virtually unchanged in these three normative climates, while the figures for women were higher in each group. This study shows a trend toward equality in the reported sexual behavior of college men and women. It also shows that the normative context in which behavior occurs has an important effect on its expression. And it suggests an overall increase in sexual activity among older adolescents in the United States from the late 1950s to the late 1960s.

Two studies published in the 1970s (Jessor & Jessor, 1975; Lewis & Burr, 1975) provided widely differing estimates of sexual experience among college students. Lewis and Burr, who collected

A college-age couple necking on the banks of the Charles River in Boston. The trend in sexual activity among older adolescents is clear: There has been a dramatic increase in premarital sex among this group in recent years, doubtlessly a product of the fast-changing sexual norms that are a by-product of the social upheaval of the late 1960s and early 1970s.

(Photo copyright © 1972 by Lisl/Photo Researchers, Inc.)

their data in 1967–1968, reported virtually the same incidence of intercourse among females as Kinsey and his colleagues had, and a modest increase among males. The Jessors, in contrast, reported the highest percentages yet—85 percent for females and 82 percent for males. These data, in comparison to earlier studies, suggest a remarkable change in the sexual behavior of college students. The 3–5-year difference between the data collections in the two studies may reflect a fast-changing climate of sexual norms, a product of the late 1960s and early 1970s. A study by Bauman and Wilson (1974) supports this conclusion. They administered questionnaires to students randomly selected from the registrar's files of a southern university in 1968 and 1972. In this range of time, there was an increase in reported incidence of coitus of 17 and 27 percentage points, for males and females, respectively.

The trend in sexual activity in late adolescence is fairly clear. Between 1938 and the mid-1960s incidence of premarital intercourse was relatively stable for college men and women—around 55 percent for men and 25 percent for women. Among both males and females, there was an increase in sexual activity starting in the mid-1960s. Through 1965, none of the surveys showed coital incidence for females as high as 40 percent; after 1965, 9 of 14 surveys revealed an incidence this high. For males, four of five pre-1965 surveys found an incidence below 60 percent; in studies done after

1965, 9 of 13 reported incidences of 60 percent or greater for college men. These data, from the spectrum of research into late adolescent sexual behavior, support a conclusion of a major shift toward more permissive norms regulating sexual activity for both males and females. Regulatory norms on most college campuses in the 1970s specify sexual experience, certainly for males and quite possibly for females as well. Students at an Ivy League college, who were interviewed in 1969–1970, expressed the view that virginity, and not sexual experience, constituted the deviant condition (Komarovsky, 1976). One of the sexually inexperienced male students in a 1972–1974 study of dating couples in the Boston area expressed it this way: "You tell somebody you're a virgin at 22 and they don't believe you" (Peplau, Rubin, & Hill, 1977, p. 107).

FACTORS INFLUENCING SEXUAL BEHAVIOR

Sexual behavior is a component of complex interpersonal interaction. The patterning of behavior within that interaction entails a set of personal decisions: "How far shall I go in this sexual interaction?" "Should I stop short of intercourse?" "If I decide to have intercourse, shall I limit this behavior to one close relationship?" "Shall I tell my friends about my sexual experience?" "My par-

Peer-group influence is strongest during the adolescent years, with adolescents adopting the standards and behavior that characterize their reference group. As adolescents approach the college years, peer-group influence increases in the areas of sexual behavior and standards.

(Photo copyright © 1979 by Roger B. Smith/Editorial Photocolor Archives, Inc.)

ents?" "Shall I limit myself to one form of sexual encounter, such as heterosexual intercourse?"

These decisions have important psychological components. The act of first sexual intercourse may have meaning far beyond its pleasureable physical aspect. More than two-thirds of the 13- to 19-year-old adolescents in one study disagreed with the statement that "the most important thing in a sexual relationship is just the sheer physical pleasure of having sex" (Sorensen, 1972, p. 50). For many young people, sex is a form of escapism, from the pressures of growing up, from problems with parents, from plain loneliness. In particular, adolescents often use sex as a way of making a statement to their parents. They may wish to hurt their parents, or to let them know that they are physically mature. It is almost as if exercise of this physical capability implied social maturity. Two other psychological meanings attached to adolescent sexual behavior seem particularly important: the affirmation of normality within the peer group and the implicit statement of readiness for interpersonal intimacy. A 15-year-old boy expressed the importance of emotional closeness in the following terms:

It's like getting inside a girl's head. It isn't that you just know a girl better after you've had sex with her. It's that you open up with each other, and you trust each other, and you find yourself saying things that maybe you never even thought out for yourself before. I get to know a girl a lot better after we've balled, better than I used to think I had a right to know anybody. (Sorensen, 1972, p. 51)

The decisions surrounding sexual behavior, whether they are arrived at rationally or haphazardly, are influenced by several important factors in the adolescent's life, such as the peer group and the nature of the relationship in which sex occurs.

Sexual Behavior and the Peer Group

The influence of the peer group is strong during adolescence. In the area of sexuality, adolescents tend to adopt the standards and behavior that they think characterize their reference group. Among college students, peer group influence on sexual behavior and standards increases during the college years (Mirande, 1968).

Perceived sexual behavior of friends was examined in a study of college students at the University of Wisconsin. One of the strongest factors associated with sexual behavior of the respondents was friends' sexual experience. For each additional friend out of five who was perceived as sexually experienced, the incidence of premarital intercourse was 12–14 percent higher, among both men and women (Schulz, Bohrnstedt, Borgatta, & Evans, 1977). A majority of the 13-

to 19-year-olds in a large-scale survey of sexual behavior endorsed the statement, "When it comes to sex, a lot of young people these days do the things they do just because everyone else is doing it." However, a smaller percentage (26 percent of the boys and 14 percent of the girls) believed that their own sexual behavior had not been influenced by peer-group expectations. Even if they do not think they have been pushed into having sex by their friends, adolescents tend to match their level of sexual experience with the perceived experience of their close friends. A survey of British teenagers revealed that only 7 percent of the boys and 5 percent of the girls thought their friends had less sexual experience than they themselves did (Schofield, 1965).

Peer-group influence is also seen in young people's reactions to their first sexual encounter. In a survey of more than 1,000 undergraduates, aged 17–24, Carns (1973) found that a large number of students told five or more friends about their first coitus. Perceived peer-group norms appear to be a stronger factor among adolescent boys than among girls. Males told their friends about their sexual experiences quicker than the girls, and they also were more likely to tell several friends; more than half of the males, but less than one-fourth of the females, told five or more friends about their sexual experience (Carns, 1973).

Sex Within a Relationship

The developmental sequence of sexual behavior described above suggests that increasing levels of sexual intimacy occur within relationships that have become progressively closer. Sexual intimacies become legitimized by commitment to a partner (Ehrmann, 1959).

Research in the 1970s and 1980s suggests that more advanced levels of sexual behavior are permissible than in earlier decades, but adolescents still require commitment to the relationship. A very small percentage of male and female adolescents experience intercourse on a first date. With increasing levels of commitment to a relationship, the percentage of students who report experiencing coitus increases; the highest percentages, among both men and women, occur in relationships in which marriage is under consideration (Collins, 1974).

Standards of Sexual Behavior Four standards regulating premarital sexual intercourse can be isolated (Reiss, 1967). The standards differ for the two genders as a function of the nature of the relationship. A *single standard* calls for abstinence from sexual intercourse for both genders before marriage, the traditional conservative standard. The *double standard* sanctions sexual experience prior to marriage among men, but forbids it for women. The double standard, which we return to later in this chapter, is the basis for much of the sexual role-playing that characterizes heterosexual relationships. The two remaining standards are permissive with regard to premarital sexual experience. A standard of *permissiveness with affection* limits premarital sex to relationships characterized by some degree of emotional commitment; *permissiveness without affection*, the most liberal standard, allows or even encourages sexual experimentation prior to marriage.

The predominant standard among young people in the United States in the 1980s appears to be permissiveness with affection, although a good deal of variation is evident. Sexual behavior is an expression of emotional closeness among both men and women. This conclusion is supported by surveys of the sexual behavior and dating relationships of nearly 2,500 undergraduates from four geographical areas. These students endorsed the standard of premarital intercourse within the context of a committed relationship for both males and females (Lewis & Burr, 1975).

Other studies of dating relationships have confirmed the standard of permissiveness with affection among young people (Harrison, Bennett & Globetti, 1969; Christensen & Carpenter, 1962; Avery & Ridley, 1974). One of the couples in a longitudinal study of dating relationships in the Boston area illustrates this standard.

Before they met, Sandy was a virgin, while Tom had had coitus with three different women. Three weeks after their first date, Tom told Sandy that he loved her. She was in love, too, and their relationship grew quickly. In a few months they were spending weekends together at one of their dorms. They slept in the same bed, but did not have intercourse. Although Tom was very attracted to Sandy, he was slow to initiate intercourse. "I didn't want to push it on her," he said. "I felt that we shouldn't have sex until our relationship reached a certain point. Sex is something I just can't imagine on a first date." Just before becoming engaged, Tom and Sandy first had intercourse with each other. For Tom, "Sex added another dimension to our relationship; it's a landmark of sorts." (Peplau, Rubin, & Hill, 1977, p. 98)

Conclusions about a standard of permissiveness with affection are further clarified by data from a longitudinal study of undergraduates at the University of Wisconsin at Madison, who entered college in 1964 (Schulz et al., 1977). Figure 8-2 shows the incidence of premarital intercourse by courtship status (excluding 9 percent of the sample of 2112 responses who had experienced coitus prior to college). These results imply that the nature of the emo-

FIGURE 8-2
Incidence of premarital intercourse by courtship status among college men (M) and women (F).

(Reprinted from *Social Forces,* 56, September, 1977. "Explaining Premarital Sexual Intercourse Among College Students" by Schulz, Bohrnstedt, Borgatta, & Evans. Copyright © 1977 by the University of North Carolina Press.)

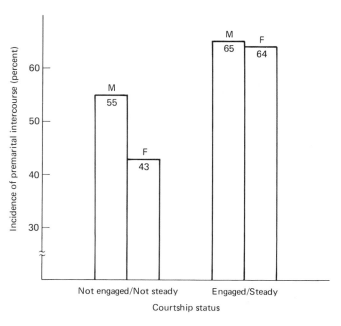

tional relationship is a stronger determinant of sexual behavior among women than among men; however, the sex difference disappears for close relationships. This may indicate the elimination of the double standard in close relationships in favor of a standard of permissiveness with affection. It should be noted, however, that an alternative interpretation of these data is that men and women may construe relationships differently. Women may be more likely than men to view themselves as "going steady," and might especially consider a relationship steady if there were a sexual component. In addition, women may be more embarrassed than men about reporting sexual involvement in a relationship with minimal emotional commitment.

Sexual decision-making takes place within the context of a social encounter, and usually within the context of a relationship. The decision to have sex for the first time with a casual date or during a transitory encounter is reported fairly frequently by adolescent boys, and much more rarely by girls. The predominant standard governing premarital sexual behavior appears to be more permissiveness with affection for both males and females. Although emotional closeness may be a more important factor in sexual decision-making among adolescent girls than boys, there are no differences in standards governing sexual behavior for the two genders in close relationships.

Sex and Moral Judgment

Standards that govern adolescent sexual behavior are norms or rules pertaining to social conduct. The standard that an adolescent chooses, and the justifications offered for the standard, reveal something about the person's understanding of the world. Standards of sexual conduct may be viewed in terms of level of cognitive and moral judgment (as discussed in Chapters 5 and 6). As Miller and Simon pointed out,

A violation of fundamental gender-role expectations is a violation of the moral order. Sexual behavior, then, is more than just gender-significant behavior, it is also moral behavior. Compared to the sexual, there are few other forms of behavior where the stigma attached to a flawed performance or a violation of moral standards is so enduring and encompassing. (Miller & Simon, 1980, p. 392)

Sexual standards and moral judgment have been assessed and compared among college students, using moral dilemmas and questionnaires about sexual attitudes. Kohlberg's moral dilemmas, used to assess level of moral judgment, were administered to 160 college students, along with questions about premarital sexual standards. Those students operating at lower levels of moral judgment chose standards of traditional morality or the double standard—permissiveness for males but abstinence for females. Students at a moderate level of moral judgment were more likely to choose a standard of permissiveness with affection. Nonexploitative permissiveness without affection, the most liberal standard, was often chosen by students at the highest level of moral judgment (Jurich & Jurich, 1974). Sexual standards differ in their logic and in their conceptualization of the rights and responsibilities people have in their interactions with each other; these facets of sex perhaps explain the influence of cognitive moral judgment on sexual decision-making.

Judith and Anthony D'Augelli (1977) have also studied the relationship between moral judgment and sexual standards and have isolated three types of relationship reasoning that are systematically associated with moral judgment and sexual philosophy. The first level of relationship reasoning they have labelled *egoistic:* Individuals view their relationships in terms of cost–reward analysis, with the optimal relationship being the one that provides the most immediate benefit. A 17-year-old girl in Sorensen's study, describing her first intercourse, illustrates egoistic reasoning.

We were just friends at first. It was really strange, because I was on a thing where I liked him but I didn't show it to him because I didn't think he liked me, as a girl friend anyway. I was so lonely at the time; I thought, "I'm so horny, if I do find a boyfriend, I want to go to bed with him." So we had dinner at my house and we got drunk. Not really drunk, because I knew what I was doing. But I wanted to go to bed with him and he wanted to go to bed with me, so we did. (Sorensen, 1972, p. 220)

In the second level of relationship reasoning, called *dyadic reasoning*, members of the dyad make decisions about their behavior based on their perceptions of what their partner expects. Expectations about the role requirements of being in a relationship are important in decision-making. The musings of a 16-year-old girl illustrate this type of relationship reasoning.

I think [love is] giving yourself to somebody—really giving—and caring for that person more than yourself. It's a kind of a loss of all self-concern at one point. It's like I feel I have to give myself in all ways, and you don't become attached at all to what you might feel. You just give whatever you can to them—you think of them before anything else—before yourself . . . At first when you get it you become a little frightened, because you don't know how far you're getting into it. (Sorensen, 1972, p. 233)

The final level of relationship reasoning isolated by D'Augelli and D'Augelli is *interactive reasoning*. Here decisions are based on mutual agreement about responsibilities and norms within the relationship, to the point of creating norms that are specific to the couple. A male college student illustrates this position.

Having sex can be part of building a relationship . . . If they both agree, then sex is right. I feel that what I'm doing now is acceptable to my partner and me and that's what counts. (D'Augelli & D'Augelli, 1977, p. 58)

These three levels of relationship reasoning are analogous to Kohlberg's three levels of moral judgment. They form a sequence of progressively more sophisticated reasoning, taking into account the perspective and role requirements that are involved in interaction with another person. Relationship reasoning lends a cognitive component to the sexual decisions that a person makes, and influences the behavior engaged in with the partner (D'Augelli & D'Augelli, 1977).

Sex Guilt   Violations of perceived moral standards are often judged as "wrong" or "bad." In the sexual arena, such feelings are summarized by the label *sex guilt*. Sex guilt appears to be an important factor in determining the extent of sexual experience. In fact, the best predictor of a couple's sexual experience is the amount of sex guilt expressed by the male. Couples in which the male expressed high sex guilt were less likely to have engaged in sexual intercourse (D'Augelli & D'Augelli, 1977). Undergraduate men and women who have high sex guilt are less likely to have experienced sexual intercourse, and are also less permissive in their attitudes about acceptable sexual practices (Mosher & Cross, 1971).

Puberty and Self-Perception

Physical changes at puberty focus a great deal of one's attention on the body. "There is an intensification of body awareness during adolescence, based upon the fact that the body is a primary 'symbol of self' in which feelings of personal worth, security, and competence are rooted" (Maddock, 1973, p. 327). Hormonal changes that accompany puberty and development of secondary sex characteristics alter to some extent the developing individual's sexual feelings.

Nevertheless, heterosexual intercourse for the large majority of adolescents does not occur until several years after puberty. Puberty is certainly a signal of maturation of the reproductive system, but it is not a reliable predictor of either dating behavior or sexual experience (Dornbusch, Carlsmith, Gross, Martin, Jennings, Rosenberg, & Duke, 1981; Miller & Simon, 1980).

Physical Attractiveness One of the physical factors that is associated with sexual experience is physical attractiveness. Incidence of coital experience, for example, was found to be much higher among college women who were rated as high in physical attractiveness than among those low in attractiveness (Kaats & Davis, 1970). These findings have been corroborated for both males and females; more attractive men and women of college age have more sexual experience than their less attractive counterparts (Curran, Neff, & Lippold, 1973). Male and female college students who have remained virgins view themselves as less attractive than do their counterparts with sexual experience (Jessor et al., 1981).

Social Characteristics Influencing Sexual Behavior

Social-background characteristics, such as social class, education, and religiosity, might be expected to influence sexual behavior in adolescence. Social-background characteristics presumably exert their influence through values that contribute to development of a sexual philosophy.

Social Class Kinsey and his colleagues (Kinsey, Pomeroy, & Martin, 1948; Kinsey, Pomeroy, Martin, & Gebhard, 1953) were among the first researchers to document an association between social class and sexual experience. These well-known sex researchers used educational level as the most convenient expression of social level.

They found that men and women from lower social strata—individuals whose ultimate educational attainment was lower—were more sexually experienced. Less advanced forms of sexual activity, such as petting, were frequently engaged in by adolescents who were from upper social levels, whereas sexual intercourse was far more frequent among lower social strata. Incidences for both forms of sexual activity were considerably higher for boys than they were for girls. Kinsey delineated separate codes of sexual morality by social level which applied to adolescents in the 1940s and 1950s.

In the upper level code of sexual morality, there is nothing so important as the preservation of the virginity of the female and, to a somewhat lesser degree, the similar preservation of the virginity of the male until the time of marriage . . . the lower levels see no sense in this. They have nothing like this strong taboo against pre-marital intercourse and, on the contrary, accept it as natural and inevitable and a desirable thing. Lower level taboos are more often turned against an avoidance of intercourse, and against any substitution for simple and direct coitus. (Kinsey, Pomeroy, & Martin, 1948, p. 379)

Sexual philosophies, such as those Kinsey described, varied with social class during the 1940s and 1950s. Current evidence, however, suggests that the relationship Kinsey found between sexual behavior and social class no longer holds. By 1965, Reiss found no evidence for the Kinsey pattern of increased permissiveness among lower social class adolescents.

The association between social class and sexual experience that Kinsey reported may have been a product of the sexual philosophies of the time. Included in the sexual scenario for that era was a belief that middle- and upper-class males would seek out lower-status females for sexual gratification, while preserving a virginal pool of same-status females for future marriage partners. In addition to Kinsey's work, Hollingshead's (1949) classic study in "Elmtown" affirmed this pattern for an earlier decade. Ehrmann's (1959) data also supported this popular notion, showing that boys engaged in more advanced forms of sexual behavior with girls of same and lower classes. Ehrmann also observed that girls were more likely to engage in advanced levels of sex with boys of same or higher classes. Such a double-standard sexual philosophy appears to have been undermined in recent decades, with a corresponding change in reported sexual experience among teenagers.

Instead of recruiting "bad girls," males are probably finding available partners among their own peers to an extent that they have not in the past . . . The emotional vs. sexual distinction which qualified the relationships of male adolescents with different females in the past is less salient (as females are no longer specializing along good girl—bad girl lines), such that coitus is possible for substantial numbers of females. In consequence, males are denied easy access to exploitative relationships. (Miller & Simon, 1974, p. 65)

Implied in this reorganization of sexual philosophies is a pattern of sexual experience that is more nearly equal among the various social classes. Incidence of sexual intercourse has increased among girls of higher social status, approaching the incidence found among lower social status girls. Higher-social-status boys are also reporting more sexual experience than in the past, while lower-social-status boys are reporting less.

In fact, sexual experience in college was *more* likely among higher-socioeconomic-status students in the early 1970s (Simon, Berger, & Gagnon, 1972). The percentage of students who had any coital experience in college is shown in Table 8-5. Notice that each indicator of sexual behavior is greater among the high socioeconomic status students, both male and female.

Education   Data from adolescents in a carefully selected sample in Illinois in 1971 indicate that incidence of coital experience was unrelated to social class of origin (Miller & Simon, 1974). In other words, parents' occupational and educational levels did not predict the adolescents' behavior. Rather, the educational level of the adolescents themselves is associated with sexual experience. Incidence of premarital intercourse is higher among students who do not go on to college (Jessor et al., 1981). A larger number of young people from lower social statuses are now going to college. But change in the make-up of the college population by social status of one's family appears to exert little influence on sexual experience. Rather, sexual behavior among college-age adolescents reflects a change in the norms of sexual expression for the population at large.

TABLE 8-5
Socioeconomic Status and Sexual Experience in College

SOCIOECONOMIC STATUS INDEX	PERCENT WITH ANY COITAL EXPERIENCE IN COLLEGE		PERCENT WITH MORE THAN RARE EXPERIENCE IN COLLEGE		PERCENT WITH THREE OR MORE COITAL PARTNERS IN COLLEGE	
	MALE	FEMALE	MALE	FEMALE	MALE	FEMALE
Low	38	20	28	8	28	0
Low-middle	77	48	43	32	43	6
High-middle	66	42	34	32	22	12
High	80	54	58	40	54	17

Source: Simon, Berger, & Gagnon, 1972.

Religiosity Sexually inexperienced adolescents are more likely to describe themselves as religious than those who have sexual experience. Among adolescents in one study who were still virgins, 76 percent described themselves either as "very" or "somewhat" religious, compared to 55 percent of adolescent nonvirgins (Sorensen, 1972). Adolescents who attend church are less likely to have had sexual intercourse than nonchurchgoers (Libby, Gray, & White, 1978).

GENDER AND SEXUAL ROLE-PLAYING

Sexual role-playing refers to the stylized patterns of behavior that males and females engage in with respect to sexuality. Sexual role-playing includes the stereotyped roles assigned to males and females in the sexual scenario. Boys are expected to try for sexual contact, girls are expected to set limits. A 13-year-old girl described such a scene.

The parties we used to go to, everybody would be making it with each other—just kissing and touching each other. I could see it, you know? And I wanted to do that, too. So I did. And someone put his hand on my breast or something like that and I felt really good. I felt really guilty. I would want him to go on and at the same time I'd say, "No, no." He'd say, "Aw, come on, you'd really like to," and I'd say, "No I don't. No I don't." (Sorensen, 1972, p. 163)

The Double Standard

One aspect of sexual role-playing is the double standard, which refers to different regulatory norms for males and females. The double standard in sexual role-playing implies that the girl's reluctance is more likely than the boy's to be the inhibiting factor when a couple abstains from sexual intercourse. Just such a pattern was found in a major study of more than 200 dating couples. Among these college-age couples, 18 percent had not had intercourse. When asked the reason for this decision, nearly two-thirds of the men said the girlfriend's reluctance was responsible; only 11 percent of the women said their boyfriend's reluctance was the factor (Peplau et al., 1977).

Although both men and women use strategies of seduction when they want to influence a partner to have sex, men are more likely to use this direct strategy than women. Men are viewed as initiators of sexual activity, while women are viewed as limit-setters in the ballet of sexual role-playing (McCormick, 1979).

Sexual role-playing is also reflected in the sexual experience members of a couple bring to a relationship. The double standard suggests that prior experience on the part of the woman would lead to a higher probability that the couple would have sex than prior experience of the man. This result was also found in the study of dating couples in Boston, as shown in Table 8-6. The couple almost certainly had sex if the woman was experienced. In terms of sexual role-playing, the attitudes and experience a girl brings to the relationship determine the level of sexual activity chosen by the couple—she sets the limits.

The double standard asserts itself in the decision-making process about the level of sexual behavior a couple will engage in. Girls are more likely than boys to require a love relationship as a background for advanced forms of sexual behavior (Ehrmann, 1959; Barták & Mellan, 1971; Croake & James, 1972; Peplau, 1976; Schulz et al., 1977). A description of the modal sexual initiation of a boy and a girl by two respected sex researchers highlights this aspect of sexual role-playing.

For both males and females, modal experience of first coitus occurs prior to marriage. The modal male will have sexual relations with an initial partner for whom he feels neither love nor emotional attachment. The modal female, however, will be in love with her first partner and planning to marry him. The male and his partner will have coital relations a few times or perhaps never again; the female and her partner will have coitus more often and may, in fact, eventually marry. While the "scoring" ethic appears to organize much of the initial premarital coital behavior of males, the female usually enters into such relations in the service of the most conventional of goals—to secure an enduring dyadic relationship with a partner whom she hopes will eventually make her his bride. (Miller & Simon, 1980, p. 396)

While sexual role-playing continues to lend different psychological meanings to sex for adolescent boys and girls, differences in actual behavior are disappearing. Almost one-fourth of the 10th-graders in a small Rocky Mountain town studied by Jessor and Jessor (1975) were nonvirgins. There was virtually no gender differ-

TABLE 8-6
Percentage of Couples Having Sexual Intercourse Based on the Prior Experience of Members of the Couple

	MALE SEXUALLY EXPERIENCED	
	Yes	No
FEMALE SEXUALLY EXPERIENCED — Yes	94%	100%
FEMALE SEXUALLY EXPERIENCED — No	67%	50%

Source: Peplau, Rubin, & Hill, 1977.

ence, with 21 percent of the males and 26 percent of the females reporting experience with sexual intercourse. Among college students, the same convergence in experience for the two sexes is observed, with 82 percent of the males and 85 percent of the females reporting coital experience. As these researchers remarked, "whatever the reason, the data suggest that the traditional male–female asymmetry in rates of premarital sexual activity may be in the process of disappearing" (Jessor & Jessor, 1975, p. 482).

Sexual Role-Playing in Anthropological Perspective

In the United States, heterosexual interaction has typically been initiated by the male; dates are usually suggested and arranged by him, and any sexual contact has been at his initiation. In adolescence, interest in the opposite sex is expected both by peers and by parents. Much of the sexual role-playing illustrated by an anthropological approach to adolescent sexual behavior is an expression of the larger social system it represents. In the United States, "falling in love" and "going steady" go far beyond mere sexual expressions. On Dobu Island, off the southern shore of eastern New Guinea, the social system is arranged in a series of villages. There is little trust with anyone outside the village. However, sexual liaisons and marriages must take place between young people of two different villages, even though there may be a great deal of hostility between the villages. Young adolescent males are barred from their own houses following puberty. The typical adolescent male spends each night sleeping with an unmarried girl in her own house but sneaks out before daylight. He may spread his sexual favors widely until he is finally trapped.

Marriage is set in motion by a hostile act of the mother-in-law. She blocks with her own person the door of her house within which the youth is sleeping with her daughter, and he is trapped for the public ceremony of betrothal. . . . When he is trapped at last, it is usually because he has tired of his roaming and has settled upon a more constant companion. Nevertheless he is never thought of as being ready to undertake the indignities of marriage, and the event is forced upon him by the old witch in the doorway, his future mother-in-law. (Benedict, 1934, pp. 133–134)

Sexual role-playing is a fundamental part of gender role expectations, which we discussed in Chapter 4.

SEXUAL ACTIVITIES

We have examined some of the factors that influence adolescent sexual behavior. Advanced forms of heterosexual behavior are more likely to occur in relationships involving a commitment, and the decisions appear to follow a rough developmental sequence. In addition, cognitive and moral-judgmental factors appear to be related to sexual decision-making. It is time now to look at some sexual activities other than heterosexual intercourse. In the sections that follow, we review some of the research on masturbation and homosexual behavior among adolescents.

Masturbation

Accurate historical data on incidence of masturbation are difficult to obtain because the ideology associated with this form of sexual expression has changed so much. Both Jewish and Christian religious traditions condemn the act as unnatural and immoral. Medical advice on the subject has changed dramatically in the past several decades. Two physicians published a popular manual of advice entitled *What a Boy Should Know* in 1909, which contained the following on masturbation:

Whenever unnatural emissions are produced . . . the body becomes "slack." A boy will not feel so vigorous and springy; he will be more easily tired; he will not have so good "an eye" for games. He will probably look pale and pasty, and he is lucky if he escapes indigestion and getting his bowels confined, both of which will probably give him spots and pimples on his face . . .

The results on the mind are the more severe and more easily recognized . . . A boy who practices this habit can never be the best that Nature intended him to be. His wits are not so sharp. His memory is not so good. His power of fixing his attention on whatever he is doing is lessened . . . A boy like this is a poor thing to look at . . .

The effect of self-abuse on a boy's character always tends to weaken it, and, in fact, to make him untrustworthy, unreliable, untruthful, and probably even dishonest. (Hunt, 1974, pp. 69–70)

Masturbation among males was held responsible for, among other ailments, pimples, stooped shoulders, fatigue, insomnia, neurasthenia, weak eyes, digestive upset, stomach ulcers, loss of weight, genital cancer, impotence, and insanity. Girls did not escape the medical evils of masturbation; they were said to be subject to hysteria, dizziness, deformed figure, jaundice, paroxysm, dessication, frigidity, sterility, exhaustion, pain, and perhaps even death as a result of the practice (Kinsey et al., 1948; Kinsey et al., 1953). The 1940s and 1950s witnessed the transformation of medical opinion to the view that harmful effects were not a result of masturbation per se, but to *excessive* masturbation. Manuals advising adolescents and their parents in the 1960s warned of psychological effects of masturbation, such as guilt, rather than physical deformities which would result. Dr. Benjamin Spock's (1976) revision of his classic manual for parents included the following advice to parents of adolescents:

Some conscientious adolescents feel excessively guilty and worried about masturbation, even when it's just a thought, and need reassurance. If a child seems to be generally happy and successful, doing well in school, getting along with his friends, he can be told that all normal young people have these desires and that a great majority do masturbate. This won't take away all his feeling of guilt, but it will help. (p. 413)

Adolescents are more likely to be advised in the 1980s that *failure* to masturbate is unusual. Even fundamentalist religions now tolerate masturbation (Gold & Petronio, 1980).

Cumulative incidence of masturbation to orgasm in Kinsey's sample of males and females is presented in Figure 8-3. For this earlier generation of sex-survey respondents, the figures show, about 92 percent of men reported masturbation by age 20, in contrast to only 40 percent of women by that age. Ultimately, a majority of women in Kinsey's sample reported masturbation to orgasm.

In addition to incidence, males and females in Kinsey's samples differed on psychological factors relating to masturbation. About half of the females had some type of sexual fantasy during most of their masturbatory experiences. More of the males, about three-fourths, had fantasies during most of their masturbation ses-

FIGURE 8-3
Cumulative incidence of masturbation to orgasm for various age groups of males and females in Kinsey's national samples, statistically adjusted by census figures to represent the population at large.

(From Kinsey, Pomeroy, & Martin, 1948; Kinsey, Pomeroy, Martin & Gebhard, 1953.)

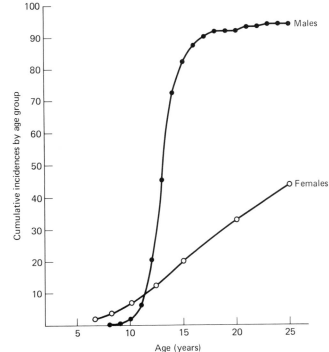

sions. Kinsey's figures for males were replicated almost exactly in another careful study during the same era (Finger, 1947).

More recent data show that masturbation is an almost universal experience for adolescent boys and very frequent among girls. A study of college undergraduates at the University of Connecticut revealed that 92 percent of the males and 72 percent of the females had masturbated (Abramson & Mosher, 1975). Current data also suggest that many females as well as males make use of fantasy when masturbating (Hunt, 1974; Sorensen, 1972).

It is interesting to note the influence of religion on masturbatory behavior, given the strong stand against this behavior taken by Judeo-Christian tradition. Religion appears to be a restraining influence only among girls. The same large number of males report masturbatory experience, regardless of religious conviction. Females are more affected by religion, as shown in Figure 8-4. Female churchgoers report less masturbatory experience than non-churchgoers, especially if they attend church regularly (Hunt, 1974).

The more permissive atmosphere of the 1980s is not easily captured by incidence figures. Kinsey was not overstating the issue when he described boys' psychological responses to masturbation. "Millions of boys have lived in continual mental conflict over this

FIGURE 8-4
Percentage of males (M) and females (F) who have ever masturbated, by religiosity, all faiths.

(From Hunt, 1974.)

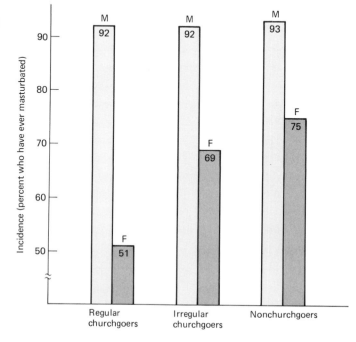

problem" (Kinsey et al., 1948, p. 513). Modern adolescent boys and girls say that they enjoy masturbating, and they also experience it without feeling very much guilt, anxiety, or concern (Sorensen, 1972).

Adolescent Homosexuality

Surveys of adolescent sexual behavior have provided much less information about incidence of homosexuality than about heterosexual experience. In Schofield's (1965) study of adolescents, interviewers did not press for answers about homosexuality as they did in other areas of sexual life. "Despite the widespread readiness of teenage boys to talk about most sexual matters, questions about homosexual activities often caused embarrassment, particularly if the boy is still involved in some way. Consequently we decided not to press these questions" (Schofield, 1965, p. 60).

Incidence of Adolescent Homosexuality Sorensen's study of adolescent sexuality did include a series of questions about homosexuality. Male adolescents in his study reported more homosexual experience as they grew older, as Figure 8-5 indicates. Among younger adolescents, 5 percent of the boys and 6 percent of the girls had had

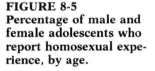

FIGURE 8-5
Percentage of male and female adolescents who report homosexual experience, by age.

(From Sorensen, 1972.)

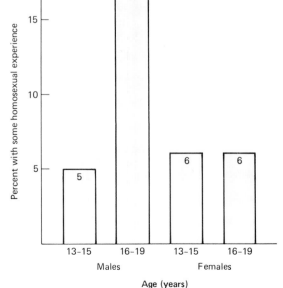

one or more homosexual experiences; among older adolescents, however, 17 percent of boys had had homosexual experiences, compared to 6 percent of girls (Sorensen, 1972).

Origins of Homosexuality During adolescence, close same-sex friendships are common and often very important to the psychological development of young people. Some of these friendships include homosexual behavior, such as mutual masturbation; however, there is no clear evidence that such experimentation is linked to adult homosexuality. Some of these individuals may subsequently adopt homosexual lifestyles, while others go on to adopt heterosexual lifestyles.

Early attempts to understand the development of homosexuality often focussed on the family and suggested that childhood experiences predisposed individuals to be either homosexual or heterosexual. There is no scientific evidence for this family-predisposition view of homosexuality (Bell & Weinberg, 1978).

A few studies have been done to see if homosexual and heterosexual individuals differ in their early experiences; these studies are aimed at isolating factors that contribute to the adoption of one sexual orientation or another. In one study, 28 homosexual males and 22 heterosexual males were asked about sexual activity in four age periods: childhood, preadolescence, adolescence, and early adulthood. Homosexual men reported more sexual experiences with other males in childhood and preadolescence, but often shifted to both male and female partners in adolescence and early adulthood. Data from this research show that at each age level, a minority of homosexual men had sexual experience exclusively with members of their own gender (Manosevitz, 1972).

A study of male and female bisexuals confirmed the notion that individuals with homosexual orientations are a diverse group with respect to sexual experience. In interviews conducted in 1973–1975, 78 male and 78 female bisexuals discussed their sexual biographies. Many males and a majority of females had had no homosexual experience prior to adulthood (Blumstein & Schwartz, 1977). In addition, the stereotyped family setting for the development of homosexuality—a weak or absent father and a strong, overwhelming mother—was rare.

It does appear that boys are more likely to have early homosexual experience than girls are. In a sample of 305 boys, 52 percent reported some prepubertal homosexual experience compared to 34 percent heterosexual experience (Elias & Gebhard, 1969). Level of prepubertal homosexual and heterosexual experience was roughly

A homosexual-adolescent couple participating in Gay Pride Day in New York City. There is no single cause or route to homosexuality, as there is no single cause or route to heterosexuality. Adolescence is an important time for the development of an individual's sexual and affectional preferences. While most homosexual adults developed their sexual orientation prior to age 20, both heterosexual and homosexual adults can change their sexual orientation and lifestyles subsequent to adolescence.

(Photo copyright © by Michael Hanulak/Photo Researchers, Inc.)

equivalent among the sample of 127 girls, 35 percent homosexual and 37 percent heterosexual. This prepubertal experience includes sex play and masturbation as well as full sexual contact.

In many of the studies of homosexuals, both male and female, some individuals indicate that they "knew" that they were homosexual from childhood or adolescence, some even before they had had any sexual experience (Manosevitz, 1972; Thompson, Schwartz, McCandless, & Edwards, 1973). About one-fourth of a group of lesbian respondents said that they had become aware of their homosexual orientation before the age of 10.

Taken together, these studies provide some interesting clues about sexual orientation, but they do not completely clarify the issues. It would appear that the stereotyped family situation is only weakly associated with homosexual decision-making, if at all. Early sexual experience is associated with homosexuality, especially among males, but it is not known why this is the case. The association does not demonstrate causation.

There is likely to be no single cause or route to homosexuality, and no single cause or route to heterosexuality. Adolescence is an important time in the development of one's sexual and affectional preferences. It is during adolescence that the culture encourages dating, that individuals start to wonder about and want to "fall in love," that adolescents fantasize about what it feels like to have sex. Initial commitments may be made to homosexual or heterosexual lifestyles during adolescence. Many homosexual adults, though not all, developed their sexual orientation before age 20. Further, researchers have demonstrated that people can change their sexual lifestyles during adulthood. Some heterosexuals change their sexual orientation after adolescence, and some homosexuals do as well.

DIFFICULTIES WITH SEX RESEARCH IN ADOLESCENCE

There are special difficulties attached to the conduct of research on the topic of sexual behavior. Many people, young or old, are reluctant to discuss their sexuality in interviews or in questionnaires—out of embarrassment or guilt or fear of betraying abnormality. Research on the sexual behavior of young people must also contend with ethical issues of informed consent. Studies conducted through school systems must have the approval of parents as well as adolescent respondents. As we discussed earlier, Sorensen's random sample became a biased sample because of a large refusal rate among adolescents as well as parents. This set of difficulties raises two important issues with regard to adolescent sex research. The issues are sample representativeness and response reliability.

Sample Representativeness

The manner in which a sample of adolescents is chosen for sex research is important for interpreting their responses. Objection by parents to participation of their children in projects about youthful sexual expression is a serious problem. Fully 39 percent of the adolescents chosen for study in Sorensen's probability sample were lost due to parents' objections. It seems likely that more "liberated" parents would allow their offspring to answer questions about sexual matters. It may also be argued that children of these liberal parents would themselves be more liberal in their behavior and attitudes.

The most extensive body of data on the sexual behavior of young people comes from studies of college students. There are very good reasons for studying college students. Academic researchers have easy access to them; parental permission is not required; and they are highly literate, which makes questionnaire research easy. And yet, extensive use of college students in sex research poses a problem of representativeness. The complex of psychological, economic, motivational, and political reasons for attending college may vary systematically with attitudes and behavior in the sexual domain. Kinsey showed that incidence of coitus was in general higher for adolescents at all ages who ultimately did not attend college. Miller and Simon (1974) found that incidence of coitus was twice as high among their adolescent respondents who did not plan on college. Jessor and his colleagues (1981) also reported more sexual experience among noncollege adolescents.

Furthermore, many sex researchers on college campuses select students from their own classes. For example, one study of sexuality in the 17–22 age range used volunteers from introductory psychology classes at the University of Connecticut (D'Augelli & Cross, 1975). Another study sampled only students from sociology classes during class time (Lewis & Burr, 1975). Samples from social-science courses at one southern university provided the data for another study (Robinson, King, & Balswick, 1972). These research projects have relied heavily on students in the social sciences; it is impossible to say with certainty that they are representative of young people in general, or even of college students on their own campuses.

The college data may be misleading for other reasons. Women and men who do not go to college may marry earlier, on the average, than college students. The young people who are college educated, therefore, have more years to engage in premarital coitus (Kerckoff, 1974). Another subtle factor may also add bias: It appears that firstborns are somewhat more likely to engage in premarital coitus than laterborns (Touhey, 1971). Achievement-oriented firstborns are proportionately overrepresented in the college ranks. Their data may add a birth-order artifact to the reported incidence of intercourse among college youth.

Response Reliability

Norms and expectations of a given cultural group help to determine the level of sexual activity of members of that group. Adolescents may modify their behavior to conform to their expectations of what is typical or usual among the peer group, thus imposing a social-desirability effect whereby they match their behavior to what is seen as a socially desirable, normative standard. Research shows a clear relationship between a person's behavior and estimates of the behavior of others. For example, incidence of sexual activities is generally in the same direction as one's expectations about the level of activity of the peer group (Collins, 1974).

Social-desirability effects raise the possibility of a self-fulfilling prophecy. With all the discussion in the media about liberalized sexual behavior, sexual activity may escalate because of the liberalized climate of expectations. It is in this way that "prolonged reporting of a sexual revolution may itself become something of a change agent" (Simon, Berger, & Gagnon, 1972, p. 221).

Terminology of Sexual Behavior Response reliability hinges on the clear understanding of adolescent respondents about the terminology of sexual behavior. While sex researchers may find terms such as "virginity" and "sexual intercourse" unambiguous, evidence suggests that adolescents may have different interpretations of sexual terms. Even college students have disagreed about the "sexual events and/or behaviors constituting 'loss of virginity' " (Berger & Wenger, 1973). Among the possibilities for female loss of virginity, 41 percent of college students agreed that a woman could lose her virginity by bringing herself to climax during masturbation. Another 17 percent felt that female virginity was lost when the vagina was penetrated by something other than a penis, and 5 percent said that full penetration of the vagina by a penis did *not* constitute loss of virginity. The data on male loss of virginity are almost as perplexing. Bringing a woman to climax was the index chosen by 13 percent; 2 percent said loss of male virginity occurred when "he ejaculates by self-manipulation"; and 23 percent said a man was still a virgin if he penetrated a woman's vagina but did not ejaculate.

The term "sexual intercourse" may be equally ambiguous, at least to young adolescents. Many young adolescents reported that the term meant "socializing with the opposite sex." Naturally, these young people were certain that they had had sexual intercourse (Vener & Stewart, 1974). The critical questions asked in sex-research projects include the following: "Have you ever had sexual intercourse with a girl (boy)?" (Sorensen, 1972). "Have you ever engaged in sexual intercourse with someone of the opposite sex?" (Jessor & Jessor, 1975). One researcher asked his respondents if they were "virgins," providing the responses "yes" and "no" for circling (Touhey, 1971).

Exploratory research on the phrasing of questions about sexual behavior has highlighted the difficulties. For example, one girl was asked, "Are you a virgin?" She replied, "Not yet." As the researchers remarked on this interchange, "Individuals often answer a question in different terms and at another level from that in the mind of the person who constructed the questionnaire" (Schofield, 1965, p. 240).

In short, difficulties with sex research among adolescents require that we evaluate trends carefully when charting this important behavior. It is helpful to look at the entire spectrum of research, as we have tried to do in this chapter, without relying too heavily on one or a few studies of sexual behavior.

SUMMARY

1. Patterning of sexual behavior in adolescence is a fundamental part of psychosocial development. The psychological overtones of adolescent sexuality are important for understanding this period of the life cycle. Sexual activity serves important purposes other than physical gratification, including a demonstration of maturity and a declaration of independence from parents. These purposes are reflected in the psychological pressures of sexual decision-making.

2. The sexual revolution has been discussed a great deal in recent years. Although there has been a marked liberalization in sexual standards and behavior among young people, there has not been the complete overthrow of norms regulating behavior that is implicit in the term revolution. An analysis of sexual role-playing in the current American scene suggests that elements of a double standard still exist, even though no such standard appears in the latest figures on incidence of premarital intercourse. Boys are still more likely to initiate sexual contact, and girls are still more likely to set the limits of a couple's sexual activity.

3. Nevertheless, there has been a liberalization in sexual behavior in adolescence. More adolescents are engaging in advanced forms of sexual behavior than ever before. This increase in sexual participation has been particularly evident among adolescent girls, leading to an intergender convergence in indexes of sexual activity, such as premarital intercourse. In addition, adolescents appear to be beginning their sexual careers earlier than in past generations. More and more younger adolescents are becoming sexually experienced in the 1980s.

4. For most adolescents, sexual activity follows a rough developmental sequence. Degree of emotional commitment present in a relationship is a factor in determining the level of sexual activity. Girls seem to require a stonger commitment than boys, as can be seen by their lower level of sexual activity in casual relation-

ships. However, boys and girls appear to be equally likely to want to fit sex into relationships where emotional commitment is present. As a result, the predominant sexual standard in the United States, among young people, is "permissiveness with affection."

5. Level of cognitive and moral development affects the manner in which a person reasons about any phenomenon, including intimate relationships. A sequence of reliable stages of relationship reasoning has been isolated. The sequence of stages, in turn, underlies a person's sexual philosophy and is an important factor in sexual decision-making. Other major contributing factors to one's chosen standards for sexual conduct include perceived standards adopted by members of the peer group, the prevailing sexual ethic of one's socioeconomic stratum, and one's self-evaluation based on judgments of physical attractiveness.

6. The cultural ideology about masturbation has changed dramatically over the past several decades. Masturbation is no longer viewed as a medical and psychological calamity, as it was in earlier generations. A large majority of both male and female adolescents report that they sometimes masturbate, and they do it without feeling very much guilt, anxiety, or concern.

7. A minority of adolescents report that they have had homosexual experiences. Somewhat more adolescent males than females report such experiences. Firm evidence about the origins of homosexuality is lacking. Predisposing family interaction appears only weakly associated with homosexuality, if it is associated at all. There is probably no single factor associated with sexual orientation.

8. Psychosexual milestones, such as loss of virginity, continue to be significant events in the lives of adolescents and young adults. The pressures that one feels for engaging in sexual activity, or for abstaining, continue to exert a powerful influence on the psychological development of the individual. Aspects of adolescent sexuality continue, therefore, to form an important part of the psychological domain of the period.

OUTLINE

9. YOUTH CULTURE AND POLITICAL SOCIALIZATION

There is a literary genre of "on-the-road" novels about the restlessness of youth. Jack Kerouac, a writer of the 1950s "beat generation," became a major figure in this literary tradition with the publication of *On the Road*.

The greatest ride in my life was about to come up, a truck, with a flatboard at the back, with about six or seven boys sprawled out on it, and the drivers, two young blond farmers from Minnesota, were picking up every single soul they found on that road—the most smiling, cheerful couple of handsome bumpkins you could ever wish to see, both wearing cotton shirts and overalls, nothing else; both thick-wristed and earnest, with broad how are you smiles for anybody and anything that came across the path. I ran up, said "Is there room?" They said, "Sure, hop on, 'sroom for everybody."

I looked at the company. There were two young farmer boys from North Dakota in red baseball caps, which is the standard North Dakota farmer-boy hat, and they were headed for the harvests; their old men had given them leave to hit the road for a summer. There were two young city boys from Columbus, Ohio, high-school football players, chewing gum, winking, singing in the breeze, and said they were hitchhiking around the United States for the summer.

"We're going to LA!" they yelled.

"What are you going to do there?"

"Hell, we don't know. Who cares?"

(Kerouac, 1957, p. 26)

The restless-adolescent theme of on-the-road novels reaches its apex in the meanderings of Sissy Hankshaw, the large-thumbed heroine of Tom Robbins' *Even Cowgirls Get the Blues*.

A teenage hitchhiker on-the-road in New Jersey. Adolescent restlessness typifies one subgroup of youth culture that seeks identity through the rejection of parental authority and the postponement of the responsibilities and commitments of adulthood. It is easy to label this sort of behavior as "copping-out," but in reality, such behavior can serve an important psychological motivation: The need to form a bridge between the freedoms of adolescence and the commitments of adulthood.

(Photo copyright © by Ed Lettau/Photo Researchers, Inc.)

When I was younger, . . . I hitchhiked one hundred and twenty-seven hours without stopping, without food or sleep, crossed the continent twice in six days, cooled my thumbs in both oceans and caught rides after midnight on unlighted highways, such was my skill, persuasion, rhythm. I set records and immediately cracked them; went farther, faster than any hitchhiker before or since. As I developed, however, I grew more concerned with subtleties and nuances of style. Time in terms of m.p.h. no longer interested me. I began to hitchhike in something akin to geological time: slow, ancient, vast. Daylight, I would sleep in ditches and under bushes, crawling out in the afternoon like the first fish crawling from the sea, stopping car after car and often as not refusing their lift, riding only a mile and starting over again. I removed the freeway from its temporal context. Overpasses, cloverleafs, exit ramps took on the personality of Mayan ruins for me. Without destination, without cessation, my run was often silent and empty; there were no increments, no arbitrary graduations reducing time to functional units. I abstracted and purified. (Robbins, 1976, pp. 53–54)

Sal Paradise, the hero-narrator of *On the Road*, and Sissy Hankshaw are fictional representatives of a type of youth culture. They represent individuals who seek an identity by "opting out" of the mainstream of American life. They adopt a different set of attitudes and values to guide their behavior. Many observers of adolescent subcultures believe that this behavior is in the service of an important psychological motive. "The essential task is a psychological metamorphosis—a kind of cocoon work—shucking parental authority and making ready to accept the responsibilities for a spouse and family" (Prince, 1974, p. 265).

In this chapter, we examine the psychological metamorphosis represented by various youth subcultures. The discussion takes us through a historical review of youth movements, particularly those involving protest against elements of the larger society. Political socialization is an important theme in our discussion of youth protest. We also encounter the concept of *generation units*, the idea that specific segments of the population respond differently to the cultural and historical events that they experience at a unique moment in time. Within this context, we encounter several of these groups, or generations units, such as hippies of the 1960s, political radicals of the 1970s, and the Jesus People of the 1980s.

YOUTH CULTURE AND GENERATIONAL DIFFERENCES

As we saw in Chapter 1, age effects, cohort effects, and period effects are obstacles to interpreting research in developmental psychology. We must acknowledge in this chapter that these obstacles are particularly great when we encounter youth culture and political socialization. *Youth culture*, in fact, refers to a subculture of the larger society in which young people are the primary members. Regulatory norms, values, and attitudes of the subculture are perceived as being different from those of the larger society, and particularly from those held by members of older generations. Differences between youth culture and the rest of the culture may be due to differences in age, or to historical contexts in which childhood and adolescent socialization took place.

Cohort Effects

A cohort is a group of people who were born at about the same time, and who therefore have different cultural and historical events which help to shape their lives. Consider the three birth cohorts illustrated in Figure 9-1. The cohort born in the year 1924 spent their late childhood years in the Great Depression of the early 1930s. Their 18th birthdays occurred in 1942, during the Second World War. A large number of the young men of this cohort served in the armed forces during the war, either voluntarily or through conscription. Many women in this cohort also worked in the war effort, in active service roles or in the domestic labor force. The interpersonal hardship brought about by separation affected both men and women in this cohort; at the same time, there was little active youthful protest or opposition to America's entry into the war after the Japanese attack on Pearl Harbor in December, 1941.

FIGURE 9-1
Illustration of three birth cohorts. Individuals born in 1924 experienced adolescence during the Depression and during preparation for World War II; those born in 1944 experienced adolescence during the Civil Rights Movement; those born in 1964 experienced adolescence during the post-Watergate era.

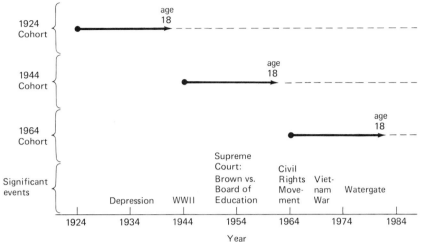

The 1944 birth cohort reached age 10 in 1954, the year of the landmark Supreme Court decision ordering desegregation of public schools, *Brown versus Board of Education of Topeka.* The Civil Rights Movement was an historical event which characterized most of the adolescent years of this birth cohort, whose members reached their majority in 1962, the year after the Cuban Missile Crisis, and the year before the assassination of John F. Kennedy. Many members of this birth cohort became active in protest movements in the turbulent 1960s and 1970s—decades of lunch-counter demonstrations, freedom rides, and peace marches.

Individuals born 20 years later, in 1964, passed their 10th birthdays in the year that Richard Nixon became the first President of the United States to resign from that office, following the disgrace of the Watergate revelations. They reached age 18 in 1982.

Psychological and behavioral differences among these three groups that can be traced to their experience of these unique historical and cultural phenomena are called *cohort effects.* The 1924 birth cohort, in their late teen years, were not very likely to use marijuana. The prevailing cultural ethic with respect to this drug was decidedly negative, even among the younger age groups. By contrast, the 1944 birth cohort experienced a different set of cultural ideas with respect to drugs when they were teenagers in the 1960s. Many members of this cohort actually smoked marijuana; even among those who did not, there was far greater tolerance than in the 1924 birth cohort. These differences are an illustration of cohort effects.

FIGURE 9-2
Differences between 1961 and 1970 student cohorts' opinions covering the level of provocation necessary before use of nuclear weapons.

1. Under present circumstances; that is, wage a preemptive war.
2. If the communists attempt to take over any other country, no matter how small.
3. If the communists interfere with important rights of the U.S., such as access to Berlin.
4. If the communists attack an ally of the U.S. with conventional weapons.
5. If the communists attack the U.S. with conventional weapons.
6. If the communists attack an ally of the U.S. with nuclear weapons.
7. If the communists attack the U.S. with nuclear weapons.

(From Starr, 1974.)

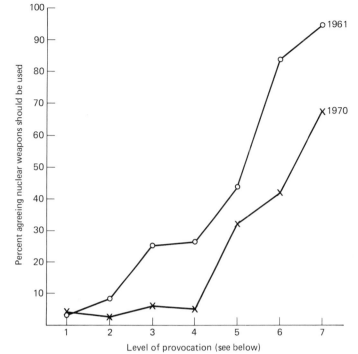

Finally, consider cohort differences encapsulated in the brief span of time between the early 1960s and 1980s. College students were asked an identical set of questions in 1961 and 1970 about the level of provocation necessary to justify the use of nuclear weapons by the United States. As the replies in Figure 9-2 show, more students from the 1961 college cohort than those from the 1970 college cohort were willing to use nuclear weapons (Starr, 1974). For example, nearly 90 percent of the 1961 group thought nuclear weapons should be used in retaliation for a Communist attack on an ally of the United States, compared to about 40 percent of the 1970 group. Sociohistorical experiences which have differed for the two cohorts presumably account for much of this difference, rather than age, since all the students were between 18 and 22. For the 1970 college cohort, it was probably the Vietnam War that increased the reluctance to use nuclear weapons. Many members of the 1980s college cohort are involved in an organized antinuclear movement.

Age Effects

Age effects involve psychological and behavioral differences between people who are at different points in the life cycle. Individuals in the 1944 birth cohort have decreased in frequency and incidence of marijuana use as they have moved into different stages of the life cycle. Cessation of marijuana use altogether is associated with age-related status changes, such as marriage and parenthood (Henley & Adams, 1973).

Knowledge of a person's age alone is actually ambiguous information with respect to cohort and age effects (Cutler, 1977). For example, if we know that a group of students were 18 years old in the year 1982, we presume that they had experienced the phenomenon of puberty, that they had some interest in sexual expression, that they had a minimum amount of educational training, and so on. In fact, we assume that any 18-year-old would have had some similar experiences that impinge in important ways on psychological development. We do not, however, assume that all 18-year-olds had these similar experiences at exactly the same age or to the same degree. Some of them may have begun dating at age 13, others at age 16. Some may have considerable dating experience, others very little. Despite this variation, these developmental events are age-related, and are similar from cohort to cohort.

Even though some developmental events are age related, "each birth cohort represents the unique intersection of history, events, and individuals; and the aggregate biography of successive birth cohorts can be quite different, especially in terms of political socialization and political orientations" (Cutler, 1977, p. 295). Adolescents who were 18 years old in 1982 were born in 1964. Their political socialization may have been influenced very little by the Vietnam War because of their young age at the time of the war; however, the Watergate scandal, which occurred during their elementary school years, may have produced an unusual view of government among members of this cohort in the United States.

As we mentioned in Chapter 1, cross-sectional studies, in which different age groups are studied at the same time, cannot separate the differential contributions of age and cohort effects. Unfortunately, most of the research on generational conflict under the heading of "youth culture" is cross-sectional.

Period Effects

Period effects are largely ignored in psychological research because their effects are so hard to estimate. A *period effect* concerns psychological and behavioral differences that can be traced to the time of the investigation itself. If a test of mood had been given to a sample of the population on January 20, 1981, the day American hostages were released by Iran, it would doubtless have revealed a distortion of mood in comparison to more ordinary days. Such a shift in mood would likely have occurred across age groups, at least beyond the childhood years. When factors coincident with time of measurement influence behavioral and psychological characteristics, we refer to these factors as period effects.

Because of the discrepancy between the sociohistorical events experienced by parents and the sociohistorical events their children experience, potential for conflict persists throughout the overlapping stages of their respective life cycles. Kingsley Davis, in a classic paper on generational conflict, described the effect of social change on the potential for conflict with the following:

Social change adds another source of conflict, for it means that the parent, when at the stage where the child now is, acquired a different cultural content from that which the child must now acquire at that stage. This places the parent in the predicament of trying to transmit old content no longer suited to the offspring's needs in a changed world. (Davis, 1940, p. 525)

According to this model, the potential for conflict is greater when the pace of social change is greater. We encounter this notion again later in the chapter.

Clearly, adolescents and their parents do not differ from each other on every single issue; furthermore, important differences exist even within a cohort. Response to the Vietnam War provides a good example. Although there was an active protest movement, a good

Vietnam War protesters at a rally during the early 1970s. The active counterculture of youthful antiwar protesters during the Vietnam era was not as large nor as cohesive as some thought. Maybe one-fourth of the student population and even fewer nonstudents were actively engaged in rebellious activities during this period.

(Photo copyright © by Christina Armstrong from Rapho/ Photo Researchers, Inc.)

many young people supported American involvement in Southeast Asia. The active counterculture of youthful antiwar protest was not as large and cohesive as some observers have suggested. Although 25 percent of the students at one large midwestern university were "highly rebellious" during the Vietnam War protest era, a majority (55 percent)) engaged in no rebellion at all (Frankel & Dullaert, 1977). Detailed reviews of student activism in the 1960s and 1970s lead to similar conclusions (for example, Gallatin, 1980). Student protest may simply be more visible than the behavior of the majority of students.

It is valuable to recognize, for example, that youth has long been viewed as a problematic time of life, and that innumerable precedents exist for the process, familiar to us, by which small groups of influential adults single out the experiences of small groups of young people and pronounce those experiences as archetypical, uniquely important, and harbingers of all future tendencies. (Kett, 1977, p. 4)

At this point, it is useful to examine some of the "innumerable precedents" to which Kett alluded. The student protest movement of the 1960s and 1970s was not a novel phenomenon, although it did differ in some important respects from earlier student protest. A brief history of student protest will be helpful before we undertake an analysis of the phenomenon.

HISTORY OF STUDENT PROTEST IN THE UNITED STATES

Eighteenth- and 19th-Century Protest

Organized student rebellions began on American college campuses in the 1700s. There was continuous rebellion on the Yale campus from 1760 until the college's President, described by students as "a Tirant and a sovraign," resigned in 1766 (Kett, 1977). Harvard College students tended to rebel and riot over quality of food served in the dining commons, beginning with a riot over bad bread in 1766, followed by the Bread and Butter Rebellion of 1805 and the Cabbage Rebellion of 1807 (Eisenberg, 1970). Among the worst student riots were those in response to faculty attempts to control the behavior of the "set of pretty wild fellows" at the University of Virginia. In the 1830s, the faculty passed antiriot laws and tried to establish control over student military organizations. Two students horse-whipped Professor Harrison at a riot in 1839, and a student murdered Professor Nathaniel Davis in 1840 (Kett, 1977).

Twentieth-Century Protest

Most of the protest on American college campuses in the 18th and 19th centuries was nonpolitical. Political youth movements in the early part of the 20th century were typically spin-offs of adult political movements (Altbach & Peterson, 1972). Organizations of students, usually located on college campuses, received backing from adult political organizations. The Intercollegiate Socialist Society (ISS), founded in 1905, is a case in point: By the time it changed its name to the League for Industrial Democracy in 1919, there were 60 chapters and a membership of 2,200. It ultimately became the Student League for Industrial Democracy (SLID) in the 1920s. The Young People's Socialist League (YPSL), formed in 1907, was the youth affiliate of the regular Socialist Party, and had 4,200 members in 112 chapters in 1913.

Student political groups continued to form during the 1920s, but they were largely fragmented and enjoyed little popular student support. In the 1930s, however, the first mass student movement began to take shape, rallying around the antiwar issue of the time, an echo of the sentiment of adult society in the United States. "The generation gap, so much a part of the political rhetoric of the sixties, was absent during the thirties. Politically active students were generally affiliated with adult political groups and usually took their cues from the adult movement" (Altbach & Peterson, 1972, p. 19). There was little sentiment in the 1930s for active involvement in a war unless there was a direct invasion of the United States. When the student newspaper at Brown University polled more than 15,000 students on 65 college campuses, about half said they would bear arms "only in case of an invasion of the United States" (Altbach & Peterson, 1972).

Many student groups were united under the umbrella of the American Student Union from 1935 to 1939, a leftist group that adopted an American version of the Oxford Pledge. (The Oxford Union, a political debating group at Oxford University, had passed a resolution stating that no one should fight "for King and country" under any circumstances.) An ASU-sponsored strike against war brought 25,000 participants in 1934 and 150,000 in 1935 (Draper, 1972). The ASU had a membership in 1938 of 20,000 students in 150 colleges and 100 high schools. It waned in popularity when Stalin and Hitler agreed on a Nazi–Soviet nonaggression pact and went out of existence altogether when the United States entered World War II following the Japanese invasion of Pearl Harbor in 1941.

At the 1937 convention of the ASU, according to Draper (1972), the following six student issues were decided upon, in order of their importance:

1. An antiwar, and antiReserve Officer Training Corps (ROTC) stance
2. Violations of academic freedom
3. Economic aid to students

4. Reforms of college boards of trustees

5. Aid to labor movements

6. Antifascist activity

There is a remarkable similarity between these issues, and lists of student demands in protests of the 1960s and 1970s. In fact, the American Student Union left a liberal–radical tradition on several American campuses, particularly Wisconsin, Berkeley, Michigan, Harvard, and Columbia (Birnbaum & Childers, 1972).

The years of World War II found no appreciable student protest movement. The return of student political organizations after the war was along traditional lines. The National Student Association, formed in 1948, was a loose federation of student governments, which had little grass-roots support. It maintained an anti-Communist, Cold-War stand throughout the 1950s. Even though the Korean War was not popular on college campuses, there was no real antiKorean War student movement.

The trend away from adult domination of student groups began in the late 1950s. The Student League for Industrial Democracy changed its name in 1959 to Students for a Democratic Society, or SDS. In 1961 the Student Nonviolent Coordinating Committee was formed to coordinate the civil-rights struggles of young blacks, and later whites as well. The date of the modern activist protest move-

Charlotte, North Carolina: February 9, 1960. Black students engage in a now-historic sit-in at Woolworth's lunch-counter. Demonstrations such as this that placed principles above technical legality were instrumental in leading to the civil-rights legislation of the mid-1960s. This particular protest led to more immediate gains: On July 3, 1960—5 months following the initial protest—this lunch-counter and all others in Charlotte were opened to members of the black community.

(Photo copyright © 1980 by Bruce Roberts/Photo Researchers, Inc.)

ment of high-school and college students can be pinpointed; it was February 2, 1960, when four "well-dressed Negro college students staged a sitdown strike" at a Woolworth's lunch counter in Greensboro, North Carolina. Before the civil-rights legislation of the 1960s, eating facilities in many parts of the country were segregated, as well as schools, transportation, lodging, and other facilities. The lunch-counter demonstration in Greensboro began an activist youth movement to secure equal treatment of blacks and whites in integrated facilities. The movement included such tactics as economic boycotts, marches, civil disobedience, and sit-ins.

Political Events and Youth Movements

Youth involvement in the Civil Rights Movement and the Antiwar Movement was in part a response to the political climate in the country. "Youth movements represent ways dissatisfied young people organize to bring about change in society" (Braungart, 1980, p. 563). Table 9-1 shows the relationship between political events and student movements in the United States since 1900. In the postVietnam era, there has been a shift away from radicalism toward behavior more directly related to personal concerns. Certainly the fact that the United States is no longer engaged in an unpopular war explains part of this shift. Another contributing factor may be the downward shift in the nation's economy, including inflation and the job squeeze. Unemployment is a problem for the economy as a whole, but it is particularly acute among teenagers and new entrants into the job market. The shift away from radicalism and toward personal concerns can thus be viewed as a reaction to current political and economic events. One might predict, however, that the shift away from radicalism would be more characteristic of young whites than of young blacks, who have historically had less chance of entering the job market, and who would therefore profit less from a traditional mainstream effort to enter the job market. The British riots of 1981 began in predominantly nonwhite inner-city areas, such as Southall in London. Minority youth were hardest hit by economic conditions in England as well as the United States.

Overall, there are significant differences between the alienation scores of black and white high-school students. On inventories used to measure alienation, blacks score higher than whites. Higher scores among blacks also tend to be associated with behavioral measures of alienation, such as underachievement, classroom disruption, and absenteeism (Allen, 1975). Blacks and whites show different developmental patterns of alienation as well. As they pro-

TABLE 9-1 Relationship between Political Events and Youth Movements	TEMPORAL LOCATION	DECISIVE POLITICAL EVENTS	YOUTH MOVEMENTS
	1900–1929	Economic growth and cultural liberalism Industrialization, United States develops favorable balance of trade and becomes world industrial power World War I Isolationism Prohibition Women's suffrage "Roaring twenties"	Youth culture challenges Victorian social and sexual mores
	1930–1940	The Great Depression Poverty Election of FDR—"New Deal" Government economic programs Growth of national socialism in Germany	Youth join antiwar movement Sign Oxford Pledge Campus strikes
	1941–1949	World War II Truman administration Atomic bomb Returning GIs Global reconstruction, United Nations	Little youth movement activity
	1950–1959	The Cold War—Eisenhower years Growth of "military-industrial complex" Dulles foreign policy Recession McCarthyism 1954 Supreme Court desegregation decision House Un-American Activities Committee	"The silent generation"

	1960–1968	Kennedy-Johnson years
		"New Frontier"
		Civil rights demonstrations
		Peace Corps, poverty programs
		Vietnam escalation
		Assassinations of Kennedy brothers and Martin Luther King
		"Great Society" programs
		Ghetto riots and campus disruption
			New Left
			New Right
			Civil rights and
			    Black Power
			Protest demonstrations,
			    strikes, violence

	1969–1976	Nixon-Ford Years Emphasis on "law and order" Voting Rights Act Vietnam War ends Kissinger foreign policy Inflation, job squeeze	Women's rights Ecology movement Charismatic religious movements Quiet seventies

TEMPORAL LOCATION	DECISIVE POLITICAL EVENTS	YOUTH MOVEMENTS
	Growth of multinational corporations	
	Watergate	
	OPEC and Middle East oil embargo	
1977–1979	Carter administration	"No-Nuke" movement
	Conciliatory, practical, informal mood in White House	Gay liberation
	Emphasis on government reorganization	
	National energy crisis	
	Inflation, job squeeze continues	
1980–1982	Early Reagan administration	"Solidarity" protests in
	Economic retrenchment	Washington against
	Social programs cut	economic programs

Source: Braungart, 1980.

gress through high school, there is a tendency for whites to feel less, and blacks more, alienated (Allen, 1975).

In summary, although there has historically been an activist segment of American youth involved in protests, these protests were not of a political nature in the 18th and 19th centuries. The formation of political groups on college campuses was adult-dominated

British riots of 1981, such as the one pictured here, occurred in predominantly nonwhite areas of the city where minorities were the hardest hit by the prevailing economic malaise. Whatever the motivation, youth movements share a commonality: A way for young people to organize in order to effect a change in the existing political and social order.

(Wide World Photos)

through the 1950s. The first large-scale, political-activist student movement in the United States came in the 1960s, beginning with lunch-counter sit-ins in 1960.

Generation Units

Cohort effects, as stated in the preceding section concern groups of people born at about the same time. *Generation units,* however, are subgroups from a larger cohort. These subgroups have a different experience of the historical context in which they grow up. In the ante-bellum South of the United States, for example, blacks and whites born in the year 1800 were members of the same cohort. They had a very different experience of the sociohistorical events of the time, however. Subgroups from the same cohort constitute generation units.

Generation units, then, are subcultures of the population, who are born at the same time, and who also have roughly similar experiences *within* a generation (Mannheim, 1952/1972). The concept of generation units is particularly useful in discussing youth subcultures, which by definition involve a generational segment of the population. As examples, consider some of the varieties of young people, who celebrated the 1980 Fourth of July in Washington, D.C. (Bruske & Sager, 1980). Thousands of young rock fans came to hear a free concert by the Beach Boys at the Washington Monument. Meanwhile, members of the Community for Creative Non-Violence served hot dogs and potato salad to members of another generation unit, the Washington "street people." Near the White House, 2,000 people, mostly young, staged the 13th-annual marijuana smoke-in; 100 of these young people clashed with yet another generation unit, members of the Revolutionary Communist Party who were selling red flags near the Lafayette Park smoke-in. The existence of these diverse groups within roughly the same cohort implies different psychological responses to current sociohistorical events; in addition, the types are recognizable from one locale to another.

Generation units are a product of three main characteristics of society: (1) new participants are always emerging to take part in the cultural process; (2) at the same time, former participants in this cultural process are disappearing; and (3) it is possible for members of one generation or birth cohort to participate in only a limited set of historical and cultural events that are present during their life cycles (Mannheim, 1952/1972). "Youth experiencing the same concrete historical problems may be said to be part of the same actual generation; while those within the same actual generation which work up the material of their common experiences in different specific ways, constitute separate generation-units" (Mannheim, 1952/1972, pp. 119–120).

**Explaining
Generation Units:
Political Socialization**

The development of different generation units within the same cohort is the focus of the remainder of this chapter. We examine several factors that may contribute to differences among generation units. We also discuss examples of specific generation units within modern American society, such as hippies of the 1960s, activists of the 1970s, and religious cultists of the 1980s.

Generation-Unit Differences We are ultimately interested in why young people experience the world in which they grew up so differently as to become members of different youth subcultures. The outcome we are interested in is a generation unit; and we would like to know the influence of observable factors on the generation-unit outcome.

Research and theory on generation units has focused primarily on youth movements, particularly political activism among young people. In one study, students at Syracuse University were asked in a 25-minute interview about their candidate support in the 1972 presidential election. Political positions of the 373 Syracuse students were compared to those of 134 local Syracuse residents in the same cohort. Political positions of these two groups of young people differed; youth politics is *not* a homogeneous phenomenon. The *determinants* of political positions differed for the two groups. Family variables, especially parents' political position, were strong determinants of youth politics for both groups. Unlike the college youth, those who were not in college were more heavily influenced by factors such as income level, and by their confidence in government institutions. This research underscores the fact that college and noncollege youth, although members of the same cohort, are likely to be members of different generation units.

Even within a college population, young people are far from uniform in their political activities and beliefs. More than 1,200 students who participated in one study of student politics illustrate the political diversity found among young people. There were students holding a variety of political persuasions, from the left-oriented Students for a Democractic Society, to the moderate-to-left Young Democrats, to the moderate-to-right Young Republicans, to the right-oriented Young Americans for Freedom. In addition, a substantial number of the students were apolitical, not subscribing to any particular political philosophy (Braungart & Braungart, 1979).

**POLITICAL
SOCIALIZATION**

The outcome of decisions among young people about political positions is a result of many factors. Political socialization refers to the ways in which a person's political attitudes, values, and behavior are influenced by agents of socialization, such as parents, peers, schools, and the media. In this section we are concerned with influences on the political choices of young people. Differences among generation units can serve as a guide for this discussion. First, we examine research on agents of political socialization, particularly parents. We also discuss the relationship between generation units and individual characteristics, such as personality and cognitive stage. Finally, this section considers influence in the larger society itself, such as rate of technological development and youth access to the labor market.

Parental Influences on Political Behavior

Political Socialization by Parents It is not clear exactly how parents exercise their role as agents of political socialization. Most observers agree that the process is an indirect one; parents rarely exercise deliberate political influence on their children. On the other hand, parents represent one of the most influential agents of political socialization, especially where political-party preferences are concerned. During the early childhood years, when the foundations of a political ideology are presumed to be laid, parents have the greatest influence as agents of socialization by virtue of the amount of time children are exposed to them.

Although parents may not directly inculcate a political ideology into their children, there are many possible indirect influences. One such indirect type of political influence concerns the emotional and disciplinary climate within the home. A large group of college students in the San Francisco area were asked about their perceptions of their parents and the child-rearing practices that had been used in their upbringing (Block, Haan, & Smith, 1972). Students who engaged in neither political protest nor social-activism programs reported the least emotional involvement on the part of their parents. They said that their parents discouraged their sexual expression, and that they used anxiety as a means of behavioral control. Students in the generation unit involved in sororities and fraternities gave the most positive description of their parents; they were most highly differentiated in terms of sex-role socialization. The most highly-active students, in social-service work and in protest activities, gave somewhat negative descriptions of their parents but reported that they were encouraged to develop independence and personal responsibility. Since the students in the San Francisco study were from comparable backgrounds in terms of parental education and occupation, and in religious affiliation, these child-rearing styles may reflect a central factor in the political activities of different generation units.

Parents and Political Parties A common index of political influence is political-party affiliation of adolescents and their parents. Several studies indicate a strong relationship between parents' and children's political-party identification. Sixth-, 9th-, and 12th-grade students indicated that parents were the single most influential agents in political party choice (Figure 9-3). The students in this study could name more than one source of influence for political orientation. Parents were named most often, by almost 60 percent of the students, while same-sex peers were second, named by 44 percent. Teachers and opposite-sex peers were named by fewer than one-quarter of the students as influential agents in political-party identification (Woelfel, 1978).

The most carefully designed study of adolescent and parent political-party identification is that of Jennings and Niemi (1974). They conducted interviews with a representative national sample of 1,669 seniors in 97 high schools, as well as auxiliary interviews with mothers of one-third of the students, fathers of one-third, and both parents of the remaining one-third. They found a strong relationship between party identification of parents and their adolescent offspring. Two-thirds of the parents who were Democrats had children who chose that party affiliation. Similarly, more than half the

FIGURE 9-3
Percentage of high-school students naming various socializing agents as influential in political-party identification.

(From Woelfel, 1978.)

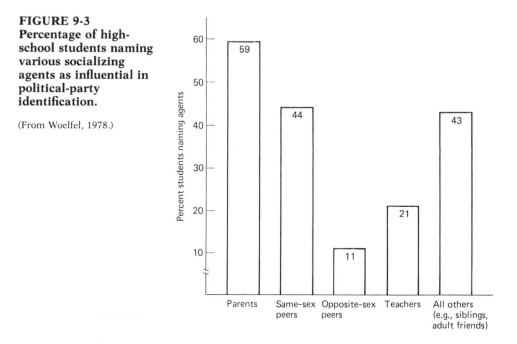

Republican and Independent children chose the party of their parents (Jennings & Niemi, 1974).

Although the association between parents and their adolescent offspring's party identification is fairly substantial, it does not come about through conscious influence. More than one-third of the parents were unable even to identify the party preferences of their children (Jennings & Niemi, 1974). Furthermore, party identification has very little to do with positions taken on national issues, for either parents or adolescents. For example, there is little relationship between party preference and attitudes toward school prayer or attitudes toward industrial unions (Schwartz, 1977).

Furthermore, an association between parent and adolescent political-party identification does not mean that the parents caused their children to identify with a given party. The fact that approximately 60 percent of adolescent-parent pairs agree on party identification is interesting, but this fact does not go beyond demonstrating an association (Beck, 1977). Perhaps both parents and adolescents were influenced by other agents of socialization, such as television.

Two major points can be made about the development of political ideology: First, liberal parents tend to have children who are more politically active; 57 percent of the college-age children of liberal parents have engaged in political activities, versus only 17 percent of conservatives' children (Thomas, 1971). Second, when students do engage in political activism, either for liberal or conservative causes, they tend to mirror their parents' political stance. This relationship can be seen in college students' participation in two political action groups from different parts of the political spectrum. Table 9-2 shows that members of SENSE (Students for Peace) tend to be children of Democrats or Socialists, and members of YAF (Young Americans for Freedom, a right-wing student group) tend to be children of Republicans. Among the SENSE students, 68 percent were children of Democrats or Socialists while 71 percent of the YAF students were children of Republicans. Other researchers have also found a tendency for leftist students to have liberal parents,

TABLE 9-2 Distribution of Student Activists by Political Affiliation of Parents

POLITICAL AFFILIATION OF PARENTS	SENSE (STUDENTS FOR PEACE)	YAF (YOUNG AMERICANS FOR FREEDOM)
Democrat, Socialist	68%	29%
Republican	32	71

Source: Westby & Braungart, 1972.

and rightist students to have conservative parents (e.g., Kraut & Lewis, 1975).

Conflict with Parents   Despite the considerable agreement between adolescents and parents on political ideology, much attention has been given to conflict between generations as a source of student protest. The bulk of the evidence, however, favors the interpretation that students and their parents agree on many political issues (e.g., Douvan & Adelson, 1966; Kandel & Lesser, 1972; Gallatin, 1980). A study of a group of junior high-school students, aged 13–15, found no evidence for a relationship between domestic disagreement and political disagreement between parents and children (Eckhardt & Schriner, 1969).

The adolescent years may in fact be the years when most clashes occur between parents and children, even though the conflict is not of serious magnitude in most instances. Over time, however, parents and children appear to converge in their political views. Students in Jennings and Niemi's (1975) study of adolescent politics were interviewed as high-school seniors in 1965 and again in 1973. These young people, by their mid-20s, had moved closer to their parents in political views. Parents and their children were asked four questions assessing political trust and cynicism; as Figure 9-4 shows, the two generations moved closer together in attitudes during the 8-year time period. It is also interesting to note that *both* generations moved in the direction of increased cynicism. Both adolescents and their parents agreed with the statement that "government wastes a lot of money," and that "quite a few people running the government are crooked." While both groups became more cynical, the gap between the two was closed during the 8-year time span.

Peer Influence on Political Behavior

In Chapter 7, we examined the differential influence of parents and peers on adolescent value systems. Very little research has been carried out on peers as agents of political influence (Silbiger, 1977). One of the few investigations of this topic is that of Sebert, Jennings, and Niemi (1974), whose data support our conclusions in Chapter 7: It appears that in the political arena, as in other areas, parents and peers exert their influence on specific issues. Jennings and Niemi asked high-school seniors in 13 schools (located in 10 states in the East) to fill out questionnaires on political attitudes and values. They were also asked to name the five senior-class members of their own sex with whom they "went around most often." We can therefore estimate the degree of agreement in political atti-

FIGURE 9-4
Parent and youth re-
sponses to items assess-
ing political trust and
cynicism.

(From Jennings & Niemi, 1975.)

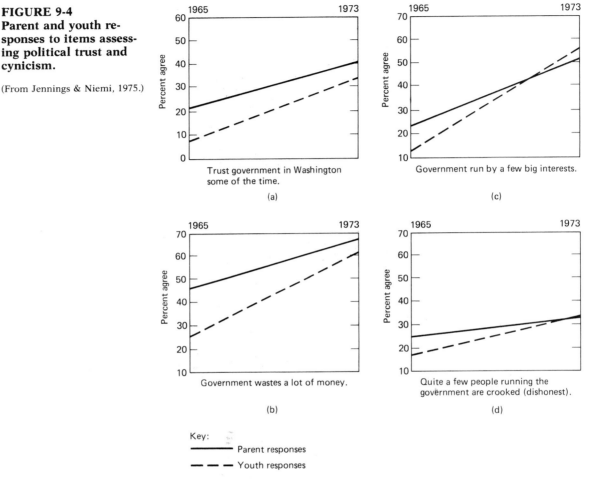

tudes between friends in the senior class. Correlation coefficients, which indicate the amount of agreement, are presented for students and their peers, as well as students and their parents, in Figure 9-5. Parents and students agreed most on party identification, which we saw earlier. Parents and students also agreed on the 1964 presidential vote more than students and peers. The remaining three issues, however, showed less agreement. For two of these issues, political efficacy and the 18-year-old vote, the students agreed with peers more than they did with parents.

Overall, although empirical studies of peer influence on political development are sparse, the data that do exist suggest that peers can influence political thinking, even as late as the college years (Beck, 1977).

FIGURE 9-5
Degree of agreement between students and parents and students and peers on selected political issues.

(From Sebert, Jennings, & Niemi, 1974.)

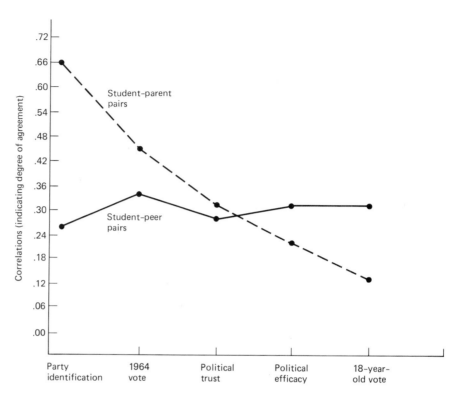

Other Socialization Agents

Schools and Teachers The political character of high-school students is not dramatically influenced by the school curriculum (Jennings, Ehman, & Niemi, 1974). This conclusion holds true even with respect to students' political knowledge. Teachers themselves exert little influence as agents of political socialization. Civics teachers who had had seniors in classes were interviewed about their political positions. The data indicate that teachers and their students seldom agree, and they agree much less often than students agree with their parents (Jennings, Ehman, & Niemi, 1974).

Although students' political knowledge and attitudes may be relatively independent of teacher influence, other aspects of political development may come under more teacher–school influence. It is in school, under the direction of teachers, that most students acquire political concepts, such as "the role of government for the individual and the society," "law and democracy," and "majority rule."

In fact, the role of schools and teachers in the political socialization of elementary and high school students is surprisingly under-researched. The relationship between parents' and adolescents' political views can be studied through correlations. However, because schools are institutions and not individuals, this technique is inappropriate when school influence is examined. Still, it seems reasonable that schools and teachers do exert some influence on adolescent political socialization through providing information about governmental procedures, and through subtly influencing attitudes, such as the value of democratic political orientations (Patrick, 1977). Although this phenomenon lacks firm empirical support, "circumstantial evidence of the influence of schools in the United States may be found in the higher support for democratic norms among better educated citizens" (Beck, 1977).

Mass Media   We have few measures of the influence of mass media on adolescents' political socialization. Students and their parents differ in the frequency of their use of various media, specifically with regard to issues of public policy and of politics. High-school seniors use the mass media for political information far less often than their parents (Jennings & Niemi, 1974). Parents report greater frequency of media use for political information than adolescents for each of four types of media: newspapers, television, radio, and magazines. The implication is that in posthigh-school years, individuals consult the media more frequently for political information.

Nevertheless, many researchers now believe that adolescents get more of their political information from the media than they do from any other source (Chaffee, Jackson-Beeck, Durall, & Wilson, 1977). Young people are also likely to say that the media, and television in particular, have had an impact in shaping their political opinions. Television appears to exert relatively more influence on political opinion formation among elementary school than high-school students, and more among poor people than wealthier people (Chaffee et al., 1977).

FACTORS ASSOCIATED WITH GENERATION UNITS

Personality Characteristics

Generation units, such as political activists and hippies, may involve different personality configurations. Radical activists of the 1960s were likely to hold basic values for academic, as opposed to vocational, training; hippies, on the other hand, were more alienated, experiencing a sense of estrangement from mainstream American society (Keniston, 1968).

Activist students have been studied in most detail, the result of increased attention during the protests for Civil Rights and against the Vietnam War. Studies suggest a particular personality profile for activist students in comparison to nonactivists (Table 9-3). This profile of traits—impulsive, determined, self-confident, and idealistic, as well as alienated—seems ideally suited to the pro-

**TABLE 9-3
Personality Profile of
Activists**

1. Spontaneous, impulsive, uninhibited, restless.
2. Strong-willed, assertive, determined.
3. Self-confident, self-centered, exhibitionistic.
4. Idealistic, altruistic, romantic, nonmaterialistic.
5. Alienated, estranged, distrustful.
6. Intellectually oriented.
7. Creative–expressive.
8. Community-service oriented, nonjock.

Source: Braungart, 1980.

test mode. The generation-unit model we have been discussing implies that such a profile of personality traits may be associated with a particular mode of upbringing at a particular time in history.

**Cognitive
Development and
Political Knowledge**

Political attitudes and behavior probably change throughout the life cycle. Political awareness certainly increases during the elementary-school years (Jennings & Niemi, 1974); however, changes in political orientation continue through adolescence, and may be influenced by advances in cognitive development.

Adolescence is the life-stage when capacity for formal thinking occurs, which should manifest itself in greater sophistication in political matters. In fact, a shift toward more sophisticated political thinking does occur during adolescence, as a study of students in

Hippies, such as the ones pictured here in 1969, represented one type of generation unit. The hippie youth movement manifested its deep estrangement from the mainstream of American society through a subculture characterized by distinctive types of dress, behavior, and drug-orientation. Popular singers and slogans of the period are represented here on the bedroom walls.

(Photo by Bonnie M. Freer/ Photo Researchers, Inc.)

Grades 6 and 12 demonstrated (Gallatin, 1980). These adolescents were asked, as part of intensive interviews, "Do you think it would ever be possible to eliminate poverty?" One 6th-grader replied

I don't, well, if they got the person to really work hard that there might not be anyone that would, uh, be poor and that, but if there was someone that would just be retired, he could just lay around the house because he's already put in his years of work and that.

Interviewer: *Do you think it would ever be that there wouldn't be any poor people?*

6th-grader: *Maybe, in the future, if they could enforce the law that all lazy people and that should work. (Gallatin, 1980, p. 350)*

This preadolescent's concept of the government's role in social policy is naive and simplistic: Eliminate poverty by enacting a law that all lazy people should work. By contrast, a 12th-grader's reply to the same question is far more broad and less personalistic.

Yes because this is the most highly advanced, richest country in the world. And the world knows because we're putting money over here, overseas there, or we're putting money over there. Money in Africa, putting a hell of a lot of money in Asia, the Southeast, I don't see why we should be putting money there while we still have poor here. I'd say we could put in a little money but why do we have to buy airplanes. We've done a hell of a lot for the foreign countries, as they say, so I don't think we should. (Gallatin, 1980, p. 351)

This high-school senior has some trouble keeping to the point in his reply, as does the 6th-grader, but his thinking is somewhat more abstract than the younger respondent's. Movement away from simplistic and concrete views of government characterizes adolescent political development.

All student replies in this interview study were categorized for sophistication in political thinking, and three levels were isolated: Level I is "confused, simplistic, punitive, and concretely pragmatic" thinking, while Level II is a transitional stage with rudiments of political concepts, still somewhat personalized and fragmented. Level III, the most sophisticated level found among these adolescents, is more abstract and conceptual, based on political ideals (Gallatin, 1980). The percentages of simplistic and conceptual thinking at each grade level are presented in Figure 9-6; there is a clear developmental shift toward greater sophistication in political thinking among the students in this cross-sectional study. Among 6th-graders, almost 60 percent of political thinking was simplistic, compared to 11 percent conceptual. By 12th grade, the balance of power in thinking has reversed, with 19 percent simplistic thinking compared to 41 percent conceptual (Gallatin, 1980).

**FIGURE 9-6
Simplistic and conceptual political thinking from grades 6 through 12.**

(From Gallatin, 1980.)

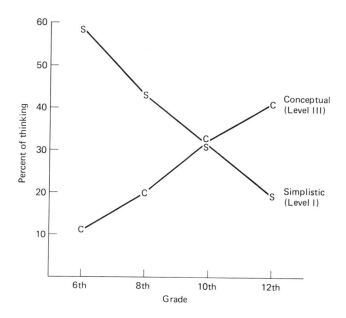

The same cognitive–political developments were found a decade earlier (Adelson & O'Neil, 1966). Age trends associated with the various levels are roughly the following: Level I, simplistic, up to 12 years old; Level II, transitional, 12–16 years old; and Level III, conceptual, developing at around age 16–18.

Movement away from a personalistic understanding of politics is a striking feature of development in adolescence. Concepts such as *government* and *society* are too abstract for children and younger adolescents to grasp. Consider the following replies to the question "What is the purpose of government?"

11-year-old: *They want to have a government because they respect him and they think he's a good man. (Adelson & O'Neil, 1966, p. 297)*

Presumably this youngster feels that government's role (="they") should be viewed in relation to the merits of its citizens, one by one (="him"). Contrast this reply with that of an older adolescent to the same question:

13-year-old: *So the people will have rights and freedom of speech. Also so the civilization will balance. (Adelson & O'Neil, 1966, p. 297)*

Adolescence appears to favor three major developments in political thinking. First, there is a decline in authoritarianism, the view that those in authority are right and must be obeyed. Second, growth in political knowledge co-occurs with growth in general cognitive capacities. Finally, development of a political and social ideology and an increased understanding of community needs favor the decline of personalism in political thinking (Adelson & O'Neil, 1966).

Level of Moral Development

Moral Judgment and Activism   Research on the 1960s activist generation unit suggested a relationship between level of moral judgment and radical behavior. Specifically, students who were arrested for sitting-in at Berkeley during the Free Speech Movement in 1965 were found to be overrepresented in either preconventional stages of moral judgment, or principled stages of moral judgment (Haan, Smith, & Block, 1968). Moral judgment was measured using the standard dilemmas designed by Kohlberg, which we discussed in Chapter 6. In another investigation of the relationship between moral judgment and political ideology (Fishkin, Keniston, & MacKinnon, 1973), 75 students on eight large college campuses in the United States were given moral-judgment dilemmas, as well as a scale to measure radicalism versus conservatism. (The eight campuses were Yale, Harvard, Oberlin, UCLA, UNC, Texas, Iowa, and Michigan). Figure 9-7 shows that conventional moral judgment is associated with conservatism; radical orientations were more likely to occur among students whose judgments were preconventional or principled. Students in Stage 4 of Kohlberg's scheme for moral judgment scored highest of all the participants in conservatism.

FIGURE 9-7
Relationship between radicalism–conservatism and moral judgment among college students in May 1970.

(From Fiskin, Keniston, & MacKinnon, 1973. Copyright © 1973 by the American Psychological Association. Adapted by permission of the authors.)

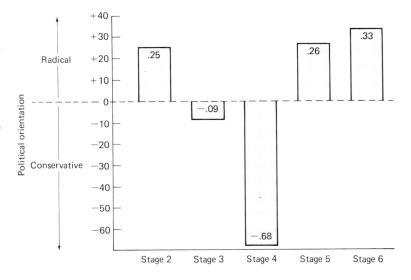

Students in the lower and in the higher stages of moral judgment scored in the radical end of the political-orientation scale. It was the preconventional students who were more likely to subscribe to radical violence as a political stance.

Even though these findings are in accord with other investigations, such as those of Haan, Smith, and Block (1968), they must be interpreted with caution. It should be noted that the study described previously (Fishkin et. al, 1973) was conducted during one of the most unusual times in American college history—May 1970— the month that saw major campus protests against the United States invasion of Cambodia, and against the killings of students at Kent State and at Jackson State by National Guard troops. Because it was conducted at such an unusual time, the study is susceptible to strong period effects and the data must be viewed cautiously.

Other studies have found only a slight indication of any relationship between moral judgment and potential radicalism. For example, in one study, there was no relationship at all between the two among 7th-graders, and only a slight tendency for high-school seniors who had reached postconventional moral judgment to have a higher radicalism score (Merelman, 1977).

Radicals a Decade Later

There have been a few scattered attempts to trace changes in the political development of radical students of the 1960s and 1970s. One such attempt was a follow-up of a few of the students arrested in the Berkeley Free Speech Movement. Among the 15 students who could be located who were still living in the San Francisco area, there has been a striking reduction in political activity in the eleven intervening years. These former radicals had become more conventional in their political orientations. However, a major weakness of this study is that no comparative data were collected on a random sample of Berkeley students. A shift toward conventionalism may or may not characterize the majority of college students 10 years later. We therefore have no indication of ordinary and expectable age effects.

Even if 1960s activists become more conservative in their political orientations, they may remain a distinct subgroup of their cohort. A generation-unit analysis would suggest that activists should, in fact, be distinct in some ways. In one of the few studies with data bearing on this issue, a group of white students at Florida State University who had sat in for integration in 1960–1963 were compared to students in two control groups: a group of FSU students who had been active in conventional student-government politics, and a group who had not been involved in any type of political activity. The student activists did remain a distinct generation unit, in terms of occupations (e.g., teaching and human-service careers), organizations, and marital lifestyles (Fendrich, 1974).

Social Structure and Technology

Political protests and other forms of youth behavior are often considered to be responses to technological development. One psychologist offers a whole catalogue of social ills associated with progress.

The fragmentation of the extended family, the separation of residential and business areas, the breakdown of neighborhoods, zoning ordinances, occupational mobility, child-labor laws, the abolition of the apprentice system, consolidated schools, supermarkets, television, separate patterns of social life for different age groups, the working mother, the delegation of child care to specialists—all these manifestations of progress operate to decrease opportunity and incentive for meaningful contact between children and people older or younger than themselves. (Bronfenbrenner, 1974, p. 54)

Advanced technological societies, such as the United States, have undergone major changes in social organization. In this section, we examine the effects of some social-structural factors on the formation of generation units, particularly those involved in expressions of alienation, such as political protest.

Demographic Factors The demographic landscape has undergone considerable change as American society has evolved from an agricultural economy to an industrial economy. Most American males entered the labor force in the 19th century sometime after the age of 7, but before puberty (Kett, 1977). By the age of 15 or 16, these adolescent males were fully incorporated into the adult labor force. The composition of the labor force reflected, in part, the pattern of population distribution by age. In 1800, the median age was 16; by 1980, it had reached 30. Advanced industrialization, however, made younger workers a threat to older ones, who excluded the young from the labor force through labor laws requiring work permits, and compulsory-education laws.

Generation units involved in youth protest may be expressing their estrangement from the larger society. "The problem of student unrest," one observer flatly noted, "is rooted in the prolongation of adolescence in industrial countries" (Berger, 1971, p. 101). A cross-cultural example provides some support for this notion. Young people in the 1960s who lived on Israeli collective farms were not involved in the protests that characterized Western societies such as the United States and France. "The striking absence of adolescent

Young people who lived on the collective farms of Israel in the 1960s were not involved in the protests and social unrest that characterized many western societies, such as the United States and France. The key reason: the societal need in Israel for the labor of the young in order to perpetuate and maintain the economy of the collective.

(Photo by van de Poll/Black Star)

unrest in Israeli collective farms is in part explicable in terms of the need for the labor of the young, upon whom the collective depends for its existence" (Eisenberg, 1970, p. 1690).

With increased technological development, more young people are brought together in urban areas, at the same time they are being excluded from the labor force. Figure 9-8 shows the proportion of the population of the United States living in cities from 1870 to 1970. Increased urbanization, which this figure dramatically documents, provides an opportunity for large numbers of young people to share alienation from society.

A direct effect of industrialization on the adolescent age group was to make it nonessential to the economy. Unlike modern teenagers, 19th-century adolescents were economic assets. Children in Massachusetts in the 1870s provided an average of 25 percent of family income (Kett, 1977). Now economic forces operate to keep this same age group out of the labor force altogether. It should be noted, however, that exclusion from the labor force also served to protect children and adolescents from abuses of labor exploitation. One unintended result of this protective legislation may be an increase in youthful alienation.

Unemployment statistics for teenagers indicate the extent to which they are excluded from the labor force in modern American

**FIGURE 9-8
Percentage of the population living in cities in the United States, by year.**

(From Starr, 1974.)

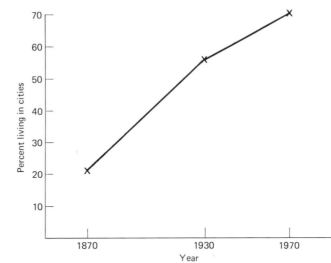

society. Figure 9-9 indicates that unemployment is a major problem for the current teenage cohort, and particularly for black teenagers. The unemployment rate hovered around 25 percent for black teenagers through the 1960s, in comparison to a rate of 10–15 percent for white teenagers, and around 5 percent for white adults. Unemployment was around 35 percent for black teenagers in the 1970s,

**FIGURE 9-9
Annual average unemployment of adult and teenage blacks and whites in the United States from 1960 to 1979.**

(*The Washington Post*, June 29, 1980. Copyright © 1980 by *The Washington Post*.)

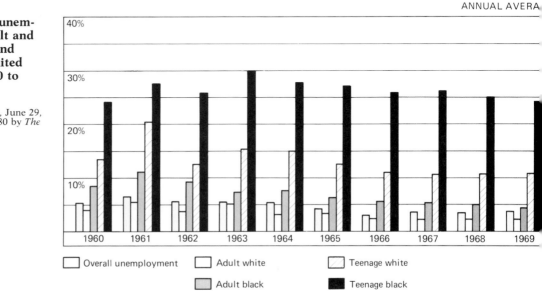

compared to around 15 percent for white teenagers and 5–8 percent for white adults.

One might predict that a sizeable number of these young people, excluded from institutional participation, would react to their estrangement through active protest. Participation in protest against the system bears a paradoxical relationship to demographic factors, however, such as social class and family income. It was the children of wealthier, upper-middle-class families who were most visibly engaged in protest against the Vietnam War (Westby & Braungart, 1972). One possible explanation of this paradox is that the young people who are represented in the high teenage-unemployment statistics may be more likely to protest against the *domestic* political situation, in riots, such as those which occurred in Miami in May of 1980 and in England in the summer of 1981.

Rapid Rate of Development Not only has the United States become one of the world's most industrialized nations, it has also undergone this tremendous social change rapidly. Technological societies are thought to be most conducive to alienation and political protest among youthful members of society, as we have seen. The *rate* of social change is also viewed as a contributing factor to protest-prone generation units. Kingsley Davis viewed the rapid rate of social change as a cornerstone of parent–youth conflict: "Within a fast-changing social order the time-interval between generations,

UNEMPLOYMENT

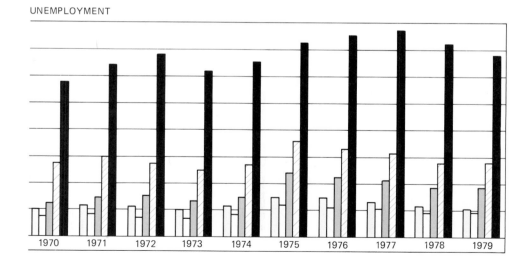

ordinarily but a mere moment in the life of a social system, becomes historically significant, thereby creating a hiatus between one generation and the next" (Davis, 1940, p. 523). Parent–youth conflict, alienation, and probability of protest appear to be greater where rapid social change is characteristic: nonstable societies, such as Pakistan; immigrant families in this country; and revolutionary epochs, such as the late 18th century.

Modernization and Identity Problems   Parent–youth conflict is only one potential link between student activism and rapid social change (Elder, 1980). Rapid social change can produce an entire complex of characteristics, which has been described as an "alienating society" (Keniston, 1965). Adequate role models are absent in such a society; young people have few guides for the establishment of their identities, a crucial task of the adolescent years.

It is a paradox of modern society that the technological development that has reduced the drudgery of daily life may also have contributed to conditions favorable to psychological discontent, especially identity problems among young people. Identity problems arise from five major sources in modern, technological societies. The first is the *problem of employment,* to which we have already alluded. Modern societies have successfully excluded the majority of young people from the labor force, removing the opportunity to define heir identities in terms of a work role. *Generational discontinuity,* a second source of identity problems, creates the potential for outright conflict between parents and children; in addition, it robs young people of traditions that help to define a secure identity.

A third source of identity problems is *social mobility.* In a high-developed society, people move from place to place and from status to status with relative ease and frequency. Identity must be adjusted from situation to situation, rendering identity an image rather than a personal reality. People learn to play roles without becoming psychologically involved. Friends become replaceable commodities. As one moves about geographically and sociologically, the danger increases of becoming alienated from one's own self and society (Klapp, 1969). Fourth, identity is threatened by the *bureaucratic and dehumanizing nature of work roles* in a technological society: One becomes a "cog in the machine" rather than a proud participant in creating a product.

Finally, a fifth source of identity problems is *prejudice and discrimination,* which plague pluralistic and technological societies. Minority groups are often assigned unsatisfactory identities by people who would prefer to see them excluded from desirable positions in the labor force. Blacks, women, Jews, Irish, Chinese, Mexicans—

all have been victims of imposed identities at one time or another in the economic system in the United States. Minority youth from former colonies in the British Empire who have immigrated to England often find that they are unsuited for high-level positions in the economic system, and their senses of identity and integration within the society suffer as a result.

Modernization, with all its positive contributions to contemporary life, has helped to foster identity problems leading to alienation, protest, nonconformity—in short, leading to participation in youthful generation units beyond the mainstream of society. Modernization is only one contributing factor to the development of youthful generation units, however. As we have seen, different styles of parental socialization, different climates within the family, different demographic characteristics all contribute to the formation of separate generation units.

NONPOLITICAL GENERATION UNITS IN ADOLESCENCE AND YOUTH

Any subcultural categorization of youth groups can be viewed as an example of a generation unit. In fact, most adolescents appear to make the transition from childhood to adulthood as members of the mainstream generation unit. They are not in any great conflict with their parents or with society as a whole. They are not addicts or cultists. They are, for the most part, satisfied with their lives, even happy to be in the adolescent stage of the life cycle. A visible and interesting segment of the youthful population, however, become members of generation units that stand apart from the larger society. We now turn to a discussion of two generation units that represent aspects of "youth culture" that are not primarily political: religious cults and countercultural groups.

Religious Cults

At the outset we must distinguish between the spiritualistic framework offered by most organized religions, and the total abandonment to a world-view represented by cults. Most religions offer their followers a religious philosophy and a set of values and beliefs that help them to understand and to organize their lives. Religious cults, on the other hand, require a near-total submission by their adherents to the cult and the cult leader. Cults are often aimed predominantly or exclusively at young people.

If the young people who become members of religious cults do so in response to lack of ritual and lack of cultural symbolism in modern American society, they certainly get these things in the Hare-Krishna cult. At a minimum, rules involve abstaining from eating meat, fish, or eggs; abstaining from drugs and alcohol; chanting 16 rounds on their prayer beads daily; and abstaining from gambling and illicit sex. Adherents must also shave their heads, wear saffron robes, get up at 3:45 a.m. to read scripture, and then do an assortment of activities until 10:00 a.m., including prayer, lessons, reading, and street chants (Judah, 1974).

This Hindu religious sect was imported into the United States from India in 1965. More than 90 percent of its members are under the age of 25, mostly middle-class whites. Identity seems to be a central problem for the young people who choose the Hare-Krishna cult. "In many cases they are youths who have left home feeling some doubt about their parents' ability to see their problems or give them guidance" (Judah, 1974, p. 475).

Studies of religious-cult members indicate that they often experience a sense of low self-esteem. One group of cult members in their late teens and early 20s, members of the Coffee House Ministry, were compared to a group of mainstream Protestants in the same age cohort. The cult members scored high on self-derogation, answering "yes" to such items as, "I certainly feel useless at times" and "I feel I do not have much to be proud of." After they became cult members, their self-derogation decreased dramatically, indicating the psychological benefit they derived from their association with the group (Freemesser & Kaplan, 1976). Apparently, members of this generation unit had a psychological profile which was distinct from that of other young people in their birth cohort.

"Jesus People" are members of several different Christian counterculture groups, including Street Christians, Gods' Forever Family, and Jesus Freaks. Members of the Jesus-People generation unit are not necessarily in an organized social movement but rather subscribe to Christian fundamentalism as a means of reaching a goal of self-expression and self-identity. Identification with the movement enables young people to reduce the loneliness and alienation they feel from the larger society, as well as to obtain spiritual guidance.

Many religious cultists have reported a preoccupation with drugs before they became involved in the movement (Bengston & Starr, 1975). For one college dropout, who had been a drug dealer at the University of North Carolina, the Meher-Baba cult was a generation unit he could use as a stepping stone back into society.

When I left Chapel Hill, I had been thrown out. Like everybody was just trying to do me in. The administration, the police. They took me down to a cellar, you know, interrogating me. It was really something. After Meher-Baba I went back up there, and I talked to the dean, who a year before had made very serious efforts to have me put in prison. He was shaking my hand, saying, "Oh, it's so good you're back, you're just the kind of boy we need." That was an experience! He did everything but give me a scholarship. (Anthony & Robbins, 1974, p. 505)

Popular religious cults among young people have run the gamut from Christian fundamentalism to Eastern philosophy, and even witchcraft and the occult (Greeley, 1969). Several of the more visible religious cults are highlighted in Table 9-4.

Religious enthusiasm is not a new phenomenon, of course, nor is it limited to young people. But involvement in religious generation units among some adolescents in recent years can be distinguished from earlier involvement, such as in the Student Christian Volunteer Movement.

It is significant that religious enthusiasm among youth in the early 1800s led them toward maturity, while today the comparable enthusiasm of the "Jesus freaks" seems only to reinforce the latter's status as adolescents—that is, as

TABLE 9-4 **Religious Cults of** **Recent Years that** **Recruited Many Youth** **Followers**	SUFISM *Principal Leader:* Pir Vilayat Inayat Khan *Goal:* To experience joy "as a consequence of being freed from the limiting powers of the body, and the mind." HARE KRISHNA *Principal Leader:* Swami A. C. Bhaktivedanta *Goal:* To purify the self "under the guidance of a spiritual master and in obedience to the scriptures." MEHER BABA *Principal Leader:* Meher Baba, Father of Compassion (né Merivan) *Goal:* "Love and service"—no methods, mantras, yoga, or ritual prescribed. DIVINE LIGHT MISSION *Principal Leader:* Guru Maharaj Ji (né Balyogeshwar Param Hans Satgurudev Shri Sant Ji Maharaj) *Goal:* "Knowledge of one's true self, the true nature of one's soul"—no creed, no dogma, nor moral codes, only total submission. UNIFICATION CHURCH *Principal Leader:* Sun Myung Moon *Goal:* "Right-wing fundamentalism, antiCommunism, messianic doctrine for Moon and South Korea." *College-based Affiliate:* Collegiate Association for the Research of Principles (CARP) OTHERS THE WAY INTERNATIONAL THE CHURCH OF SCIENTOLOGY HAPPY, HEALTHY, AND HOLY THE BLACK HEBREW ISRAELITES

cultural outsiders who assume a detached stance toward conventional institutions and beliefs. (Kett, 1977, p. 81)

Countercultural Generation Units

Apparent dropouts from mainstream American society, such as hippies, may also be searching for an identity. Countercultural lifestyles are sometimes referred to as *antinomian movements* (from "anti" = against, plus "nomos" = Greek for law, thus "opposition to established values"). Antinomian movements allow their participants to improvise new roles and new ways of defining the self; the movements may be viewed as psychological mechanisms for personal anchorage and orientation (Adler, 1974). Communes provide an example of an antinomian movement.

Ethnographic observation of eight rural communes in the western United States showed that young members rejected most conventional standards. Children, for example, were included in drug use and were allowed free sexual expression. Hippies in these communes subscribed to the notion that society ruins the natual beauty of childhood. As one member put it, childhood "is a natural acid trip from which maturity brings you down" (Berger & Hackett, 1974, p. 168).

The community of Isla Vista, adjacent to the University of California at Santa Barbara, provides a particularly good example of a countercultural generation unit. In 1970, the population of Isla Vista was 11,000, of whom 80 percent were between the ages of 16 and 24. An ethnography of the community of Isla Vista revealed rejection of conventional standards in dress, hair styles, manners and morals (Wieder & Zimmerman, 1974). Complete antinomianism was the rule among the residents, as interviews revealed.

I think this system is completely fucked and the whole American ethic is fucked . . . There's nothing, no words can describe it, how much I abhor America and American government. I would really dig the whole system as we have now being completely destroyed and having a better one put up. (Wieder & Zimmerman, 1974, p. 143)

For this young respondent, as for many other residents at Isla Vista, the conventional system did not provide appropriate supports for his self-identity. Membership in a countercultural group helped to provide those supports. Rejection of American materialism seemed to be a rather common response to the historical moment of the 1960s and 1970s. By the 1980s, membership in dropout generation units was a much rarer phenomenon. The remnants of one countercultural movement, the Rainbow People, have an annual reunion, held in 1980 at the Monongahela Forest in West Virginia. Among the Rainbow People are a subgroup whom one member described as "Bliss Ninnies": "They're the ones who walk around and think love always come from peace and gentleness" (Darling, 1980, p. D3).

Like Sal Paradise and Sissy Hankshaw setting out on the road, many young people have used generation units of the counterculture to find themselves. It is not necessary to be a psychologist to understand that identity search may be one function of countercultural generation units. Belle Vass, a West Virginia coal-miner's wife, understood it: "You know what I think it is," she said of the Rainbow People, "I think it's a bunch of people searching. I hope they find what they're looking for" (Darling, 1980, p. D3).

SUMMARY

1. One major obstacle to explaining youth culture is the distinction among age effects, cohort effects, and period effects. Age effects are psychological and behavioral differences among people due to age differences. Cohort effects are differences that can be traced to different experiences by virtue of being born at different historical times. Period effects concern differences due to the events occurring at the time data are collected. These three effects are often difficult to estimate, and especially so in cross-sectional research.

2. Student protest is not a new phenomenon. Riots and protests occurred on college campuses in the United States at least as early as the 1700s. Most students protests were apolitical until the beginning of the 20th century. At that time, student political groups were typically affiliated with adult groups. Not until the 1950s did large-scale student political-activist groups form independently of adult-dominated organizations.

3. Social and political events have an influence on youth movements. In recent years, students have shifted away from activism and toward more personal concerns. This shift may be due, in part, to economic trends.

4. Generation units are subgroups from a larger cohort that have different psychological reactions to the historical context in which they grew up. Generation units form because new cohorts are continually being born; old cohorts are continually dying out; and any one subgroup of the population has a limited set of events to experience.

5. Political socialization refers to the way in which political attitudes, values, and behavior are influenced by agents of socialization, such as parents, schools, and the media.

6. Parents are highly influential agents of political socialization, particularly with respect to political-party affiliation, in spite of the fact that parents do not consciously socialize their children's politics. Adolescents and their parents agree on many political issues, and they move closer together in political attitudes in the postadolescent years.

7. The media, especially television, have a strong influence on political knowledge in adolescence. Other socialization agents play a less important role in political development. Peers, school curricula, and teachers appear to have a relatively minor influence on political socialization.

8. Political activists, generation units that have received much attention by researchers, may have distinct personality profiles. Traits attributed to activists include impulsivity, assertiveness, self-confidence, idealism, and alienation.

9. Political thinking undergoes three major changes in adolescence: (1) decline in authoritarianism; (2) growth in political knowledge, with greater understanding of political abstractions, such as *society;* and (3) decline in personalism. There is a stage-like growth in adolescent political thinking.

10. There is scant evidence for a relationship between moral judgment and political activism. Activists appear less likely to endorse conventional moral judgments. The few longitudinal follow-ups of former radicals indicate increased conventional political behavior with age. Even so, activists retain their distinctiveness as a generation unit in their occupations and lifestyles.

11. Generation units within youth culture may develop because adolescents have been systematically excluded from adult society. Age trends, such as increases in the median age of the population, have forced adolescents out of the labor market; schools have become compulsory institutions. Increased urbanization places adolescents in close proximity, enabling them to share their alienation. These social-structural factors facilitate the development of youth subcultures.

12. Modernization has increased identity problems of young people through the problem of employment (lack of work role); gener-

ational discontinuity (lack of tradition); social mobility; the bureaucratic and dehumanizing nature of work roles; and prejudice and discrimination. The resulting alienation intensifies the formation of generation units; alienation can thus be expressed in countercultural activities.

13. Examples of recent generation units that may be responses to cultural alienation are religious cults, such as the Hare-Krishna sect; political groups, such as the Weather Underground; and countercultural dropouts, such as hippies.

OUTLINE

10.
JUVENILE DELINQUENCY

This chapter begins with the case history of a teenager who joined a gang and engaged in delinquent behavior. The case is abstracted from a longer case study of Juan Hernandez (Ralston & Thomas, 1974).

THE CASE OF JUAN HERNANDEZ

Juan Hernandez is a 17-year-old adolescent who lives in the Puerto Rican section of a large city. Juan was conceived before his parents were married, but they married as soon as the pregnancy was discovered and tried to hide the illegitimacy. Juan's mother died of leukemia when he was 6 years old. He then went to live with his grandparents for a few months, until his father remarried.

Juan was never a good student. Throughout elementary school, he was a discipline problem. He did as little academic work as possible, just barely managing to get passing grades. The inner-city schools Juan attended were racially mixed. In his perception, his teachers favored the white children, tolerated the blacks, and liked the Puerto Ricans least.

Eventually, Juan attended a junior high school in the inner city, and his misbehavior escalated. He began to cut classes or skip school altogether, and he learned how to forge his own excuses to cover absences. He had secured a firm reputation as a troublemaker by the time he entered high school; he claimed that one young teacher resigned because he and his friends made her life in school so miserable. Juan failed nearly every subject in high school. In 10th grade, he scored 90 on an IQ test, a low-normal score. However, as soon as he reached the age of 16, Juan dropped out of high school and began a series of low-paying jobs, such as stock clerk, gas-station attendant, and window washer.

Juan's relationships with his relatives during adolescence were far from ideal. He described his father as "a weak, stupid man who lets people step all over him." Juan said that he felt nothing for either of his mothers—his real mother, who died when he was 6, or his stepmother, who died when he was in 8th grade.

Before Juan dropped out of school, he had flirted with gang membership. He and some friends formed a gang, got into a fight at school, and were suspended for a week. Later, after he had dropped out of school, Juan came to the attention of a gang of Puerto Rican toughs called the Knights. He attracted their attention by stealing hubcaps in "their" neighborhood, but he was subsequently invited to join them. With the Knights, Juan became involved in rolling drunks, fighting with other gangs, and stealing cars. At age 17, Juan had an income of several hundred dollars a week, primarily from auto theft with the Knights.

Juan's father, Manuel Hernandez, has ceased to care much about what happens to him. Manuel predicts that it is only a matter of time until Juan ends up in jail, "where he belongs." Juan's former teachers agree with Manuel's assessment: Juan appears to be

A street-corner gang. Members of some juvenile gangs become involved in delinquent behavior and crime. The need for peer acceptance appears to be a strong factor in the motivation for such behavior. Indeed, such juveniles are overwhelmingly more influenced by same-sex peers than their families. Other contributing factors include socioeconomic status and ethnic-group affiliation.

(Photo by Jeffrey Sylvester/ Freelance Photographers Guild, Inc.)

one of the casualties of the social system of the inner city, an adolescent who could not be reached or helped by the schools.

How are we to explain delinquent behavior? It would be comforting to believe that we could isolate a set of early experiences that lead to juvenile delinquency with a high level of probability; we might then be able to intervene in high-risk cases to reduce the amount of juvenile crime. Indeed, several factors are often mentioned as being associated with juvenile delinquency. Among these are gender, socioeconomic status, and ethnic group.

A profile of the "typical" juvenile delinquent who comes to the attention of the juvenile-justice system in the suburbs has been provided by authorities in the Washington, D.C., area: "He is a 15-year-old white male who commits amateurish burglary of a home in his own neighborhood, often during the day and most frequently during the summer" (Boodman, 1980). Juveniles who become delinquent are also often depicted as coming from broken homes, or from families in which there is a great deal of instability, such as Juan Hernandez's family.

It is probably too late to help Juan Hernandez and the thousands whose predicament he illustrates. The case illustrates the state of research and knowledge on juvenile delinquency. We do not know to what extent adolescent delinquent behavior and adult delinquent behavior are determined by early experiences. We do not know which early experiences are crucial in determining specific delinquent behavior patterns, although extensive research has identified some factors associated with a higher probability of delinquency.

This chapter concerns some of the issues raised by Juan Hernandez's case. We first discuss the distinction between official delinquency and delinquent behavior. Juan Hernandez is not yet an *official delinquent*, which means he has not yet been apprehended by authorities in the juvenile-justice system. *Delinquent behavior,* on the other hand, is any behavior that a juvenile engages in which would be a chargeable offense according to the legal system. The distinction is a very important one. We are concerned primarily with deliquent behavior in this chapter, rather than the more misleading phenomenon of official delinquency; however, it is important that we examine the data on "official" versus "hidden" delinquency to see if the types of offenses committed differ. In connection with this discussion, the types of offenses that juveniles may be charged with under the legal code bear close examination.

In this chapter, we also examine major explanatory models that attempt to account for the phenomenon of juvenile delinquency. Among these are the faulty-family model, with its contention that stress and strain in family interaction give rise to psychological problems; one symptom of these problems is delinquent behavior. Sociological models of juvenile delinquency focus on the sociocultural environment, and posit so-called subcultures of delinquency. These models are examined in terms of overall delinquent behavior as well as official delinquency.

Few studies of juvenile delinquency—either official or hidden—have used a longitudinal research design. The few that are available may provide particularly useful information about the effect of early experience on later behavior. Longitudinal studies help to identify precursors of delinquency because they rely less on hindsight in their evaluation.

Finally, we examine research and theory on factors associated with juvenile delinquency. Among the major factors examined are family relationships, socioeconomic status, race, education and IQ, and gender.

DELINQUENT BEHAVIOR VERSUS OFFICIAL DELINQUENCY

The term "delinquency" is derived from a Latin word meaning "to leave undone." Hence the definition of *delinquency*, according to *Webster's New World Dictionary*, is "failure or neglect to do what duty or law requires." This definition, in principle, could apply to individuals of any age group; but in practice, the term is usually preceded by the word "juvenile," so as to limit its application to adolescents (and in exceptional cases, to children). In practice, delinquency usually refers to acts committed by juveniles in willful violation of rules or statutes. Any act that could place the juvenile who committed it in jeopardy of adjudication (that is, action by law-enforcement agencies) if it were to be detected is *delinquent behavior*. Delinquent behavior includes instances of undetected or hidden delinquency, as well as the cases of official juvenile delinquency. Official delinquency refers only to those cases that come to the attention of the juvenile-justice system and enter into the record books. A 17-year-old who smokes marijuana during a high-school lunch break—and is not caught—is engaging in "hidden" delinquent behavior. A 15-year-old who is arrested and booked for smashing the windows in his parents' bedroom after a family argument has become an "official" delinquent.

Delinquent Offenses

Many forms of behavior will place a juvenile in jeopardy of legal action if detected. However, the types of behavior that are illegal vary from state to state, as do the age limits for "juvenile" classification (Goldstein, 1976). In Table 10-1, juvenile offenses are listed in order of the frequency with which they occur in various state statutes. Many of these offenses are *status offenses;* this means that the offenses are subject to legal action only if committed by a juvenile, a person in a special age status. An adult committing the same offenses would not be charged with a violation of the legal code. "Habitual truancy," "incorrigibility," and "being beyond the control of parent or guardian" are examples of status offenses. Approximately 25 percent of juvenile court cases are for juvenile status offenses (Haskell & Yablonsky, 1982).

Table 10-2 shows the total number of actual arrests of persons 21 years of age and younger in 1978. In 1978, there were nearly

TABLE 10-1 **Juvenile Offenses** **Ordered by Frequency** **with Which They Occur** **in Various State** **Statutes**	1. Violation of a law or ordinance 2. Habitual truancy 3. Association with known thieves, vicious or immoral persons 4. Incorrigibility 5. Being beyond control of parent or guardian 6. Growing up in idleness or crime 7. Deporting self so as to injure or endanger self or others 8. Absence from home without parent's or guardian's consent 9. Immoral or indecent conduct 10. Habitual use of vile, obscene, or vulgar language 11. Visits to a known house of ill repute 12. Patronizing or visiting policy shop or gaming place 13. Habitual wandering about railroad yards or tracks 14. Jumping train or entering car or engine without authority 15. Patronizing saloon or dram shop where intoxicating liquor is sold 16. Wandering streets at night while not on lawful business 17. Patronizing public poolroom or bucket shop 18. Immoral conduct around school 19. Engaging in an illegal occupation 20. Engaging in occupation or situation dangerous or injurious to one's self or others 21. Smoking cigarettes or using tobacco in any form 22. Frequenting a place whose existence violates law 23. Being found in a place permitting activities for which an adult may be punished 24. Addiction to drugs 25. Disorderly conduct 26. Begging 27. Use of intoxicating liquor 28. Making indecent proposals 29. Loitering, sleeping in alleys, vagrancy 30. Running from state or charity institutions 31. Being found on premises occupied or used for illegal purposes 32. Operating a motor vehicle dangerously or while under influence of liquor 33. Attempting to marry without consent, in violation of law 34. Sexual irregularities

Source: Vedder & Somerville, 1975. Courtesy of Charles C. Thomas, Publisher, Springfield, Illinois.

TABLE 10-2
Total Number of Arrests of Persons under the Age of 21 in 1978,* by Category of Crime

OFFENSE CHARGED	GRAND TOTAL ALL AGES	NUMBER OF PERSONS ARRESTED			PERCENT OF TOTAL ALL AGES			
		UNDER 15	UNDER 18	UNDER 21	UNDER 15	UNDER 18	UNDER 21	UNDER 25
TOTAL	**9,775,087**	**728,198**	**2,279,365**	**3,909,507**	**7.4**	**23.3**	**40.0**	**56.6**
Murder and nonnegligent manslaughter	**18,755**	244	1,735	4,519	1.3	9.3	24.1	43.4
Forcible rape	**28,257**	1,102	4,517	9,266	3.9	16.0	32.8	53.9
Robbery	**141,481**	13,086	48,088	79,933	9.2	34.0	56.5	75.4
Aggravated assault	**257,629**	11,508	41,253	79,368	4.5	16.0	30.8	49.1
Burglary	**485,782**	93,652	250,649	346,122	19.3	51.6	71.3	83.9
Larceny–theft	**1,084,088**	194,680	454,994	636,749	18.0	42.0	58.7	71.8
Motor vehicle theft	**153,270**	20,146	77,534	106,970	13.1	50.6	69.8	82.5
Other assaults	**445,020**	28,496	82,425	148,132	6.4	18.5	33.3	51.8
Arson	**18,114**	5,129	8,760	11,013	28.3	48.4	60.8	72.1
Forgery and counterfeiting ..	**73,269**	1,680	9,991	22,768	2.3	13.6	31.1	53.4
Fraud	**249,207**	7,084	18,874	46,312	2.8	7.6	18.6	39.2
Embezzlement	**7,670**	185	909	2,088	2.4	11.9	27.2	46.8
Stolen property; buying, receiving, possessing	**112,317**	10,997	37,490	60,949	9.8	33.4	54.3	70.8
Vandalism	**223,391**	66,586	127,973	160,947	29.8	57.3	72.0	82.5
Weapons; carrying, possessing, etc.	**149,957**	5,504	23,689	49,114	3.7	15.8	32.8	51.6

Prostitution and commercialized vice	**89,365**	659	4,212	25,567	0.7	4.7	28.6	63.0
Sex offenses (except forcible rape and prostitution)	**65,666**	4,427	11,842	20,291	6.7	18.0	30.9	47.1
Drug abuse violations	**596,940**	20,771	141,186	301,135	3.5	23.7	50.4	73.4
Gambling	**53,066**	300	2,137	6,067	0.6	4.0	11.4	22.0
Offenses against family and children	**54,014**	1,230	2,871	9,819	2.3	5.3	18.2	37.6
Driving under the influence .	**1,204,733**	513	27,494	174,592	(†)	2.3	14.5	32.1
Liquor laws	**357,450**	9,761	127,069	253,507	2.7	35.5	70.9	81.2
Drunkenness	**1,117,349**	4,195	43,210	164,280	0.4	3.9	14.7	29.0
Disorderly conduct	**679,112**	34,978	124,307	259,746	5.2	18.3	38.2	57.9
Vagrancy	**46,896**	1,960	6,578	15,067	4.2	14.0	32.1	55.4
All other offenses (except traffic)	**1,788,794**	96,735	341,579	652,740	5.4	19.1	36.5	55.8
Suspicion	**21,650**	1,987	6,154	10,601	9.2	28.4	49.0	67.4
Curfew and loitering law violations	**78,972**	20,723	78,972	78,972	26.2	100.0	100.0	100.0
Runaways	**172,873**	69,880	172,873	172,873	40.4	100.0	100.0	100.0

* 1978 estimated population 207,060,000.
† Less than one-tenth of 1 percent.
Source: United States Department of Justice, Uniform Crime Reports, 1979.

331

4 million arrests of persons below the age of 21. In the table, the arrests are broken down by category of crime. For example, motor vehicle theft accounted for 77,534 arrests of persons under the age of 18. All of the arrests in Table 10-2 fall under the category of official delinquency.

Self-Reports of Delinquent Behavior

If only official juvenile delinquency is studied, a distorted picture of adolescent behavior emerges. At the same time, official delinquency is relatively easy to examine because of official reports and statistics. However, approximately 90 percent of delinquent acts go undetected and never enter into the official statistics (Empey & Erickson, 1966).

One technique for estimating the extent of delinquent behavior is to ask adolescents to respond anonymously to questionnaires about delinquent offenses. A study using this technique (Kratcoski & Kratcoski, 1975) sampled 248 11th- and 12th-grade students of both sexes; students were asked to place a check beside those behaviors they had engaged in at least once. Table 10-3 shows the percentages of males and females who reported participation in several types of delinquent behavior. Two conclusions are readily apparent from these data: Adolescents report a high incidence of delinquent behavior, and boys are more likely to report that they have engaged in most classes of delinquency than are girls.

In a similar study conducted in a Catholic, coeducational high school in Oakland, California (Hindelang, 1971), 763 students filled out self-report questionnaires about their delinquent behavior. Every one of these students admitted at least one act of delinquency in the past year. A total of 8,315 delinquent acts was reported by the male students, and 4,527 by the female students. Adolescents engage in more delinquent behavior than one would suspect from an examination of the official statistics.

The prevalence of hidden delinquency among adolescents in ordinary suburban high schools raises an important question: Is the delinquent behavior of official delinquents more serious than the wrong-doing of hidden delinquents? We turn now to an examination of this issue.

TYPES OF DELINQUENCY

Delinquency is often divided into three major categories. *Crimes against persons* is one of the most serious categories. This category includes assault and is a category that applies to criminal behavior of adults as well as juveniles. The second category, *crimes of theft,* includes burglary, shoplifting, and purse-snatching. These acts are

		PERCENT OF	
TABLE 10-3 **Percentage of Boys and Girls Who Report That They Have Committed Delinquent Acts**	TYPE OF DELINQUENT ACT	MALES (N = 104)	FEMALES (N = 144)
	Driving without a license	75	63
	Skipped school without legitimate excuse	78	72
	Had a fist fight with another person	90	38
	Ran away from home	17	24
	Defied parents' authority	70	74
	Driven too fast or recklessly	59	37
	Taken little things (worth less than $2) that did not belong to you	73	53
	Taken things of medium value ($2–50)	48	22
	Taken things of large value ($50 or more)	16	3
	Used force to get money from another	17	5
	Taken part in gang fights	31	10
	Taken a ride in a car without the owner's knowledge	24	10
	Bought or drank beer, wine, or liquor	88	90
	Used or sold drugs	35	40
	Had sex relations with another person of the same sex	5	2
	Had sex relations with a person of the opposite sex	77	51
	Beat up kids who hadn't done anything to you	29	8
	Gambled for money or objects	79	31
	Broken into a building with intent to steal	20	3
	Sent in a false fire alarm	10	6
	Set fire to building or other property	8	3

Source: Kratcoski & Kratcoski, 1975.

also criminal among adults as well as juveniles. The third major category, the *status offenses*, comprises behaviors that are subject to adjudication only when performed by juveniles. Examples are buying beer, running away from home, and skipping school.

A few studies have selected participants in a way that allows us to compare frequency and type of delinquent behavior among adolescents who have never been in court for juvenile offenses, and those who have become official delinquents. One such study (Empey & Erickson, 1966) sampled four groups of white male teenagers: 50 who had never been in court; 30 who were in court only once; 50 who were on probation; and 50 who were incarcerated for delinquency. Each of these boys was interviewed and asked about 22 juvenile offenses. These 180 adolescents reported committing thousands of offenses, over 90 percent undetected. The large number of admitted offenses is especially striking because this study did not employ an anonymous questionnaire; the boys admitted the offenses in an open interview. Although there was a high incidence of delinquency overall, the frequency of self-reported delinquent behavior differed among the groups. The boys who had never been to court or who had been in juvenile court only once reported significantly fewer delinquent acts than the boys who were more familiar to the juvenile authorities, either as probationers or as incarcerated delinquents. This important finding bears further examination. On the face of it, this finding suggests that the juvenile-justice system manages to snare the adolescents who more frequently engaged in delinquent activities. It might be, however, that the official and undetected delinquents differ in their willingness to admit delinquent behavior in a face-to-face interview. Those on probation or in institutions have already suffered the consequences of their delinquent acts, in contrast to the boys whose delinquency went undetected, or unpunished. The latter groups might be more reluctant to reveal their delinquencies for fear of subsequent punishment.

Anonymous and Nonanonymous Disclosure

The role of anonymity is self-disclosure of delinquency was examined directly in another study (Kulik, Stein, & Sarbin, 1968). Adolescent boys, both official delinquents and regular high-school students, were given an opportunity to report their delinquent behavior. In the first part of the session, they filled out anonymous questionnaires, indicating for each of 52 possible delinquent acts the extent of their involvement (from "never committed it" to "often committed it"). Next, the boys were given a set of intervening tests, including a Teenage Difficulties Scale. These tests were *not* anonymous. Finally, in the third part of the session, the boys were again asked to fill out the delinquency questionnaire, this time with their names attached so that the researchers could relate their delinquent behavior to their test scores. The results of this investigation of anonymity indicate that boys in both the high-school sample and the official-delinquent sample admitted more delinquent behavior when the questionnaires were anonymous. Differences were statistically significant in three of the five categories of delinquency surveyed by these researchers: "delinquent role violations," such as school disobedience; parental defiance; and total delinquent behavior. In each case, however, the official-delinquent group admitted more delinquent acts than the high school sample (Kulik et al., 1968).

This study is useful for clarifying the data on official and hidden delinquency. It would appear that those boys who are apprehended for delinquency have had a history of more delinquent behavior. At the same time, a great deal of delinquent behavior, among both official and hidden delinquents, goes undetected.

Seriousness of Delinquent Behavior

In addition to a greater frequency of delinquent behavior among official delinquents, there is a tendency for their delinquency to be more serious, as shown in Figure 10-1. For example, assaultiveness accounts for a larger percentage of delinquent behavior among the official-delinquent group than among the high-school sample—8.6 percent versus 2.5 percent. Status offenses, such as pa-

FIGURE 10-1
Percentage of total delinquent behavior accounted for by assaultiveness and status offenses among high-school and official-delinquent samples.

(From Kulik, Stein, & Sarbin, 1968.)

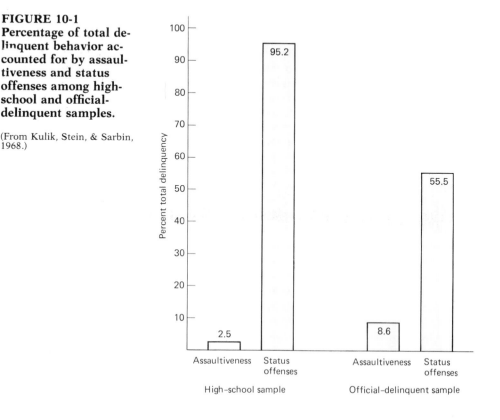

rental defiance and use of alcohol, account for a high percentage of the delinquency of high-school students (Kulik et al., 1968).

Patterns of delinquent behavior appear, from the above studies, to be different for official delinquents, in comparison to those who had not entered in the statistics for engaging in delinquency. Although there is a good deal of hidden delinquency, individuals who have not been identified as delinquents are less likely to engage in delinquent behavior than are their official-delinquent counterparts. And if they *are* involved in delinquent behavior, it is less likely to include serious delinquent acts such as assault.

EXPLANATORY APPROACHES TO DELINQUENCY

A great deal of research on delinquency has focussed on differences between delinquent and nondelinquent subgroups of the adolescent population. In this section we examine studies from a sociological tradition—studies of subcultures that may be more likely to produce delinquent adolescents, and studies of the differences between delinquent and nondelinquent adolescents. Later, we examine some of the factors which appear to be associated with individual variation in delinquent behavior, such as family relationships and educational commitments.

The conclusion that the overall patterns of delinquent behavior differ between official delinquents and others suggests a methodological approach for isolating factors associated with delinquency. Specifically, longitudinal studies that focus on delinquency status as a classifying variable provide some promising leads for explaining delinquency. Sheldon and Eleanor Glueck adopted this approach in their large-scale, longitudinal study of delinquency in the Boston area, covering the years 1948–1965.

The Glueck Study

The Gluecks carefully matched 500 delinquent boys with an equal number of boys not identified as delinquent. The boys were matched for residence in underprivileged areas, age, ethnic origin, family size, and overall tested intelligence. These 1,000 boys, all of whom were white, had spent their early years in underprivileged areas of Boston. The boys averaged 14 years of age when first taken into the study. Extensive background studies were conducted in an attempt to find childhood precursors of delinquent careers. Follow-up investigations lasted until the participants were 31 years old, yielding valuable data on adult outcomes of delinquent and nondelinquent careers.

The Gluecks used as their operational definition of official delinquency "repeated acts of a kind which when committed by persons beyond the statutory juvenile court age of sixteen are punishable as crimes" (Glueck & Glueck, 1968, pp. 49–50). Note that this definition excludes status offenses, or isolated contacts with police. In fact, 22 of the "nondelinquents" had been convicted of status offenses as juveniles.

Results of the Glueck Study   Glueck and Glueck (1968) found evidence of greater family disorganization among the boys with official-delinquent careers. Family members exhibited such negative habits as alcoholism and criminality to a greater degree than did the families of nondelinquent-career boys. There was more separation and divorce in the delinquent group. The delinquent homes were characterized as having less supervision for the boys and as having fewer rules, such as set meal and bedtimes. Both groups involved large families; they had been matched for family size. As we have seen from studies of self-reported hidden delinquency, the "nondelinquent" group was probably not as law-abiding as the Gluecks would have us believe; in fact, 37 of them (8.3 percent) were later found to have appeared in court as juveniles. Nevertheless, there does appear to be a relationship between family instability and disharmony on the one hand, and delinquent behavior on the other. We return to this issue later in the chapter.

The Gluecks found little evidence for any differences in physical characteristics between the two groups. All the boys were given a series of physical and mental examinations. While it was reported that the delinquents tended to be more sturdily built and more "masculine," the physical examinations revealed no differences in physical health. Neurological problems were found in a surprisingly large number of the boys; 64 percent of the delinquents and 73 percent of the nondelinquents had such problems. Note that the nondelinquent group had the greater incidence of these problems during their adolescent years.

The official delinquents seemed to be plagued by school problems. Among the delinquent group, 41 percent were 2 or more years behind the proper grade, compared to 21 percent of the nondelinquents. Truancy was also very high among the delinquent boys: 95 percent were singled out as truants, compared to only 10 percent of the nondelinquent boys. In interviews with the project psychiatrist, the delinquent boys often made negative statements about school, such as: "I hate school because I am always left back." "It is too hard." "I want to go to work." (Glueck & Glueck, 1968, p. 31). More boys in the delinquent group did, in fact, drop out of school before age 16 than in the nondelinquent group—67 percent versus 12 percent. This difference is in spite of the fact that the two groups—delinquent and nondelinquent—were matched for overall intelligence.

In their search for precursors to delinquency, the Gluecks found some seemingly bizarre correlates of official-delinquent behavior. For example, a greater number of delinquents had been struck down by motor vehicles, 14 percent compared to 5 percent of nondelinquents. They had also been involved in more serious accidents of other types. The Gluecks reasonably supposed that this reflected a greater craving for risky adventure on the part of the official delinquents.

Perhaps the most striking correlate of official delinquency was the delinquency status of close friends. Among the delinquent group, 98.4 percent reported having friends who were official delinquents; this compared to only 7.4 percent among the nondelinquent group.

Follow-ups of the Glueck-Study Participants Subsequent follow-ups of the delinquents and nondelinquents in the Glueck study revealed that they continued to show some group differences. The two groups appear to be distinct generation units. Those men designated as delinquents showed greater geographic mobility. Excluding men who were either in institutions or in the armed forces, 35 percent of the delinquent group had moved more than once a year between the ages of 17 and 22; only 6 percent of the nondelinquent group had shown that much household instability. The delinquent group showed a similar level of marital instability: There were more early marriages, more forced marriages, more remarriages, and more children fathered out of wedlock by males in this group.

What of the outcomes of the two groups in terms of adult criminal behavior? Recall that "delinquency" in the Glueck study was defined as behavior subject to criminal penalties if performed by an adult offender. Among the nondelinquent boys, 442 were followed into their adult years in this longitudinal study. Of those 442, 62 (or 14 percent) were convicted of crimes during their adult years, up until the age of 31. In addition to offenses associated with excessive drinking, they were convicted of crimes, such as breaking and entering, abuse of a female child, larceny, assault with a dangerous weapon, lewdness, and disturbing the peace.

The data on the 438 delinquent boys who were followed into adulthood yield two main conclusions. First, they were arrested for far more criminal offenses than their nondelinquent counterparts. Second, they showed a reduction in criminality over the age range studied, as indexed by arrest records. The latter conclusion is based on the data presented in Table 10-4. The table omits arrest for minor offenses, such as violations of parole or probation and petty larceny. Note the general decline in arrest rate between the second and third age groups.

While the original nondelinquent group engaged in some official delinquency in their adult years, boys who were official juvenile delinquents showed a decline in criminal behavior into adulthood. Prior to the 17th birthday, 90 percent of the delinquent boys had committed one or more of the serious offenses listed in Table 10-4. Between the 17th and 25th birthdays, the percentage of serious offenders had fallen to 60 percent, and between the 25th and 31st birthdays, the percentage had declined to only 29 percent (Glueck & Glueck, 1968).

Although we do not have information on the incidence of actual delinquent behavior among the delinquent and nondelinquent males in the Glueck study, we do know that they diverge in their official-delinquent careers. Glueck and Glueck (1968) believed that this divergence was due to the early experiences of the two groups of boys. The primary precursors of delinquency, they argued, are parental and other family influences on the boys. This theoretical

TABLE 10-4
Percent of Males Arrested, Longitudinal-Study Delinquency Group at Three Age Periods (Serious Offenses Only)

OFFENSE	PRIOR TO 17TH BIRTHDAY	17TH TO 25TH BIRTHDAYS	25TH TO 31ST BIRTHDAYS
Homicide	0.2%	2.0%	3.0%
Violent and/or pathologic sex offenses	3.0	5.9	3.0
Robbery	7.8	28.2	21.3
Arson	1.8	0.8	1.1
Extortion	0.0	0.0	0.8
Burglary	68.5	48.6	28.1
Larceny	86.1	63.5	33.1
Receiving stolen goods	3.2	5.6	4.2
Other theft offenses	1.6	2.8	4.9
Abduction/ Kidnapping	0.2	0.6	1.9
Selling narcotics	0.0	0.3	0.4
Serious motor-vehicle violations	4.6	12.1	9.5

Source: Glueck & Glueck, 1968.

orientation, focusing on early experiences in the family, stresses family relationships as critical for explaining delinquency.

The Youth-in-Transition Project

The Glueck study provided valuable information about the delinquent behavior of young men who were classified as official delinquents in comparison with a group of young men who were not so classified. Another major longitudinal study, the Youth-in-Transition project (Bachman, O'Malley, & Johnston, 1978), involved a large group of young men selected at random from 87 different public schools nationwide. When the study began in 1966, the participants were just entering 10th grade. Data are now available on the young men through 1974, 5 years after high-school graduation. The Youth-in-Transition project represents the most complete longitudinal study of a cross-section of male adolescents in which delinquent behavior was included as a research topic. Table 10-5 provides information about the methods of data collection used in this major longitudinal study.

During the initial interview, adolescent males who participated in the Youth-in-Transition project were asked if they had en-

TABLE 10-5
Methods of Data Collection in the Youth-in-Transition Project

DATA COLLECTION	TIME 1	TIME 2	TIME 3	TIME 4	TIME 5
Date	Fall 1966 (10th grade)	Spring 1968 (11th grade)	Spring 1969 (12th grade)	Spring 1970 (grade 12 +1 yr.)	Spring 1974 (grade 12 +5 yrs.)
Procedure	Individual interviews; group-administered tests and questionnaires	Individual interviews and questionnaires; $2 payment	Group-administered questionnaires; $5 payment	Individual interviews and questionnaires; $10 payment	Mail questionnaires; $10 payment
Location	Schools	Neutral site	Neutral site	Neutral site	Respondent's home
Number of respondents*	2,213	1,886	1,799	1,620	1,628
Percentage of original sample (N=2,277)	97.2	82.8	79.0	71.1	71.5

*Probability sample located in 87 schools.

Source: Bachman, O'Malley, & Johnston 1978. Copyright © 1978 by the Institute for Social Research of the University of Michigan. Reprinted by permission.

gaged in each of several delinquent behaviors during the previous 3 years—that is, during their 7th, 8th, and 9th grades in school. In each subsequent interview, they were asked if they had been involved in the same delinquent acts in the intervening year.

The delinquency items that were used in the Youth-in-Transition project are presented in Table 10-6, together with the percentages of respondents who reported that they had been involved in these acts over the five interviews, covering a span of 10 years. Notice that the acts of delinquency covered in the list appear more serious than those in many other surveys, such as the Kratcoski and Kratcoski (1975) survey (Table 10-2), and the juvenile offenses listed in Table 10-1 (Vedder & Somerville, 1975). The Youth-in-Transition items involve extortion, arson, and assault.

TABLE 10-6 **Delinquent Acts Reported by Adolescents in the Youth-in-Transition Project**	PERCENTAGE OF RESPONDENTS WHO REPORTED THE BEHAVIOR ONE OR MORE TIMES DURING THE PRECEDING PERIOD				
	TIME 1*	TIME 2*	TIME 3*	TIME 4*	TIME 5*
Interpersonal Aggression Index					
Hit an instructor or supervisor	8	6	4	7	2
Used a knife or gun or some other thing (like a club) to get something from a person	6	4	4	7	1
Got something by telling a person something bad would happen to him if you did not get what you wanted	28	16	15	16	6
Hurt someone badly enough to need bandages or a doctor	27	19	16	20	11
Taken part in a fight where a bunch of your friends are against another bunch	33	21	21	22	10
Gotten into a serious fight in school or at work	52	32	25	28	15
Hit your father	9	7	6	6	–
Hit your mother	6	5	3	3	–
Theft and Vandalism Index					
Set fire to someone else's property on purpose	7	6	4	4	1

(*continued on p. 342*)

*Reporting intervals were as follows: three years prior to Time 1, 18 months prior to Time 2, 12, or 18 months prior to Time 3, 12 months prior to Times 4 and 5.

Source: Bachman, O'Malley, & Johnston, 1978. Copyright © 1978 by the Institute for Social Research of the University of Michigan. Reprinted by permission.

TABLE 10–6 **Delinquent Acts** **Reported by Adolescents'** **in the Youth-in** **Transition Project** **(Continued)**	PERCENTAGE OF RESPONDENTS WHO REPORTED THE BEHAVIOR ONE OR MORE TIMES DURING THE PRECEDING PERIOD				
	TIME 1*	TIME 2*	TIME 3*	TIME 4*	TIME 5*
Took a car that didn't belong to someone in your family without permission of the owner	9	6	5	6	3
Took an expensive part of a car without permission of the owner	6	7	7	7	5
Damaged school property on purpose	25	19	17	18	4
Took an inexpensive part of a car without permission of the owner	11	10	10	12	6
Took something not belonging to you worth over $50	10	9	9	11	7
Went onto someone's land or into some house or building when you weren't supposed to be there	66	48	47	53	28
Took something from a store without paying for it	50	36	34	41	24
Took something not belonging to you worth under $50	46	37	39	45	35

Our primary interest centers around developmental changes in delinquent behavior over the 10 years covered by the longitudinal study. The highest rates of self-reported delinquent behavior are at Time 1; more boys reported engaging in serious delinquent acts during their early teen years than at any other time. Other researchers have reached similar conclusions. Clark and Wenninger (1962), for example, found that self-reported delinquency was at a peak at age 14 or 15. Gold and Petronio (1980) reported a peak in the seriousness of delinquent offenses at age 15 for both boys and girls.

During the later teen years, in 11th and 12th grades and one year after high school, the boys' reports of delinquency remained rather stable. The biggest drop in self-reported delinquency occurred between Time 4 and Time 5, when most of the young men were about 22 years old. For most of the delinquent acts covered in the survey, the drop in rates of participation fell by one-third or more. These figures on developmental changes in delinquent behavior from a cross-section of the adolescent male population are in general agreement with the trends reported by the Gluecks for lower-class urban boys. This agreement strengthens our confidence in the conclusion that delinquent behavior decreases with age and maturity.

Intraindividual Stability Intraindividual stability of delinquent behavior across time periods does not appear very high. Another way to put this is to say that the most delinquent junior high-school students were not necessarily the most delinquent young men at Time 5, in their early 20s. Developmental history of delinquent behavior appears to vary as a function of other variables, such as subsequent history of marriage and parenthood. Boys who were to become early fathers showed the highest level of interpersonal aggression, such as assault, in their junior high-school years. Over the 10-year period, however, the interpersonal aggression exhibited by these young men declined to a level comparable to that shown by single men and married men with no children. It is possible that parenthood ultimately helps to contribute to the "reform" of previously aggressive adolescents.

The Youth-in-Transition project is a very important contribution to our knowledge about delinquent behavior. It is especially valuable in providing information about the developmental history of delinquency. Indications are that there is an overall decline in delinquent behavior from early adolescence to young adulthood. The transition from childhood to adulthood apparently carries with it a reduction in relatively serious negative behavior.

Subcultures of Delinquency

Recall that all the boys in the Glueck study came from inner-city slums. Many psychologists and sociologists believe that such environments provide conditions in which delinquent behavior becomes more likely. Theories help researchers to focus on factors that might be relevant for explaining a given phenomenon. A brief review of theories in the sociological tradition may help us to isolate factors of particular relevance for research in delinquent behavior.

Miller's Street-Corner Gangs In contrast to the Gluecks' focus on faulty family relationships, many sociologists believe that juvenile delinquency is associated with the social disorganization of inner-city life. A major proponent of this view is Walter Miller, who has studied street-corner gang delinquency. Miller (1958) argued that lower-class culture actually favors illegal acts by juveniles; he based this argument on observations of 21 gangs in a large eastern city slum, including black and white, male and female adolescents.

Adolescents appear to gain status and psychological benefits from behavior favored by their peer group. In Chapter 7, we saw that most adolescents were influenced by both parents and peers, and that the two groups exerted their influence in different areas. Miller felt that members of the street-corner gangs he studied were overwhelmingly more influenced by same-sex peers, and that the family unit exerted very little, if any, influence. Furthermore, gang members gained their status by behaving in ways suggesting toughness, smartness, and autonomy. Delinquent behavior may therefore provide a great deal of status for a relatively small investment of energy (Miller, 1958). In this way, lower-class areas of the inner city provide an environment conducive to generating delinquent behavior. In a later section of this chapter, we examine research bearing on the relationship between social class and delinquent behavior. Miller's theoretical position, as we shall see, has not held up well empirically.

Merton's Modes of Adaptation Robert Merton (1957) also believes that juvenile delinquency may be associated with certain subcultures, but his position is somewhat more formal and theoretical than Miller's. Social structure, according to Merton, includes a set of culturally defined goals. In America, the success-and-money ethic is one of these cultural goals. In addition, a social structure also includes means for reaching its legitimate goals. One avenue to success and money in the United States is through the institution of education. Those with higher levels of educational achievement, on average, are more successful and have higher incomes. However, the institutional means for achieving these cultural goals are not evenly distributed throughout the population. Many people, in fact, are denied access to legitimate means for achieving society's goals.

Merton (1957) postulated five possible adaptations to social structure that have relevance for juvenile delinquency; these adaptations are outlined in Table 10-7. For those individuals who accept the goal of success as legitimate and who have access to legitimate institutional means of achieving that goal, the mode of adaptation is *conformity*. This is the most common situation in a stable society, and the modal response in American society for most adolescents most of the time.

Merton called the second mode of adaptation *innovation*. This mode arises when people accept the success-and-money goals but

TABLE 10-7
Modes of Adaptation to Various Combinations of Legitimate and Illegitimate Goals, and Legitimate and Illegitimate Means of Obtaining Them

MODE OF ADAPTATION	CULTURAL GOALS	INSTITUTIONAL MEANS OF OBTAINING THEM
I. Conformity	+	+
II. Innovation	+	−
III. Ritualism	−	+
IV. Retreatism	−	−
V. Rebellion	±	±

KEY: + = Legitimate
       − = Illegitimate
       ± = Reject Prevailing Values, Substitute Others

Source: Reprinted with permission of Macmillan Publishing Co., Inc. from *Social Theory and Social Structure,*Revised and Enlarged Edition, by Robert K. Merton. Copyright © 1957 by The Free Press, a Corporation.

are denied access to legitimate institutional means for obtaining them. They may therefore turn to illegitimate means for obtaining the goals, such as theft. Among adults, white-collar crime illustrates the adaptation of innovation; among adolescents, many forms of hidden delinquent behavior are in the service of obtaining legitimate goals through illegitimate means.

In the third mode of adaptation, *ritualism*, the goals are rejected even though the legitimate means for securing them are available. This mode of adaptation may occur when individuals fear that they may fail in their efforts to achieve money and success. Ritualists keep their aspirations low in order to avoid disappointment.

The least common mode of adaptation, according to Merton, is *retreatism*, in which both legitimate goals and legitimate means of obtaining them are rejected. This mode of adaptation characterizes runaways, vagrants, vagabonds, and tramps, as well as alcoholics and psychotics, who typify neither the culture's success goal, nor the legitimate behaviors associated with it.

A final mode of adaptation is called *rebellion*. Here the prevailing values are rejected, but other values are substituted for them. If the American success ethic is rejected, there are other values which can be substituted, such as the value of respect for the environment even when it might result in less success and money. One rebels against the prevailing goals and behavioral norms of the culture.

A high level of delinquent behavior should be associated with the modes of adaptation that involve rejection of legitimate institutional means for obtaining success-and-money goals (i.e., innovation and retreatism). According to Merton, the reason is that in

Some adolescent runaways are *retreatists,* **individuals who accept neither the goals of society nor the legitimate means of obtaining them. Many adolescent shelters have been established to aid runaways, such as Covenant House in Boston, where this teen has found temporary shelter.**

(Photo copyright © 1982 by Ed Lettau Studio, Inc./Photo Researchers, Inc.)

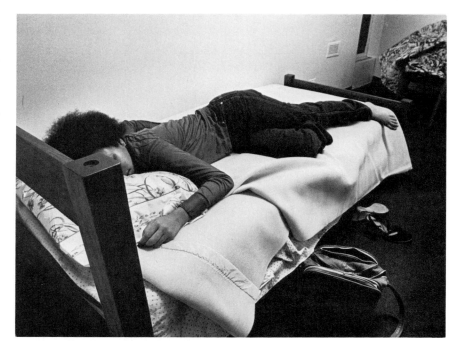

these situations, adolescents who engage in nonconforming behavior, such as delinquency, "are responding normally to the social situation in which they find themselves" (Merton, 1957, p. 255).

Cloward's Delinquent Subcultures   Cloward (1959) elaborated upon Merton's theoretical position by suggesting that two things are implied about the social situation. First, different environments provide different contexts for learning about the values and skills associated with a given mode of adaptation. A delinquent subculture, one in which many members are practiced at deviant behavior, provides a context for learning how to perform a delinquent act, such as burglary. Second, social environments differ in the extent to which they provide opportunities to play a given role. Subcultures of delinquency can thus be viewed as environmental contexts that provide opportunities for learning about and engaging in delinquent behavior. One learns about the legitimate goals of the culture, but one also learns about illegitimate means for obtaining them when other avenues are blocked. Inner-city ghettoes may provide greater access to delinquent roles simply because legitimate avenues to success and money are less likely among the urban poor.

On the basis of such a theoretical typology, two types of delinquent gangs can be specified (Haskell & Yablonsky, 1982). One gang type, called the *violent gang*, includes adolescents who are characterized by emotional disturbance. They may be either retreatists or rebels, having a distinct value system in which they habitually needle, ridicule, and fight with each other. Urban-gang warfare usually occurs among violent gangs. Ordinary *delinquent gangs*, however, include members who generally accept society's materialistic goals, but who must try to achieve them through illegitimate means only because the legitimate means are closed to them. They are individuals, like Juan Hernandez, who have learned illegal behavior in the inner-city context. Such a view might help in understanding the higher arrest rates for juvenile delinquency among blacks than whites.

Drifting into Delinquent Behavior Adolescents in some environments may be more at-risk for engaging in delinquent behavior because their subcultures provide learning situations and opportunities for delinquent behavior. David Matza (1964), in a theoretical extension of the subcultural explanation of delinquency, described a subculture of *drift*. Adolescents as a group are somewhat less subject to conventional norms than adults are; they are expected to postpone commitments and decisions about adult roles. At the same time, most adolescents do subscribe to the goal of success. In the subculture of delinquency, the adolescent also learns that illegal acts *can* be performed, and when goals are blocked, that they *may* be performed. Vacillation between conventionality and delinquency, which Matza called *drift*, was described this way:

The delinquent transiently *exists in a limbo between convention and crime, responding in turn to the demands of each, flirting now with one, now the other, but postponing commitment, evading decision. Thus, he drifts between criminal and conventional action. (Matza, 1964, p. 28).*

Delinquency cannot be said to be a stable trait; rather, it is an act that a person may perform under certain circumstances. The circumstances may be more likely in some environmental contexts, such as inner-city slums.

These theoretical notes on delinquent behavior provide guidelines for our review of empirical research on the phenomenon. Theories that focus on a subculture of delinquency suggest several factors for further investigation. Social class, a summary term for a multitude of factors, is frequently studied. In addition, rural and urban environments, which provide different contexts for learning about and engaging in delinquent behavior, might be expected to influence rates of delinquency. The discussion of legitimate and illegitimate means for obtaining cultural goals suggests that we examine data on educational attainment and race. To the extent that legitimate means are denied to some racial groups, and to the extent that educational attainment is a powerful legitimate means, these factors should influence delinquent behavior. Finally, the literature on sex differences in delinquent behavior demands a search for a reasonable explanation of the disparity of rates between males and females.

FACTORS
ASSOCIATED WITH
DELINQUENCY

Family Relationships

Some researchers, such as Glueck and Glueck (1968), argue for a direct causal connection between broken homes and delinquent behavior. There is a striking relationship between broken homes (from divorce, separation, and death) and official delinquency, over a broad range of studies, as Table 10-8 indicates. Adolescents who become official delinquents, in comparison to adolescents who are not so identified, are consistently more likely to have come from broken homes (Haskell & Yablonsky, 1982). In addition, there is some suggestion that, even among the official delinquents, adolescents from disorganized families are more likely to become recidivists, defined as having some further record of delinquency within 20 months of the first occasion (Ganzer & Sarason, 1973).

Adolescents who are official delinquents also have significantly more negative attitudes toward their parents than a comparison group of adolescents not labelled delinquent. Recall Juan Hernandez's characterization of his father as "a weak, stupid man." In a study of 11- to 16-year-old suburban adolescent males (Duncan, 1978), 18 statements involving attitudes toward parents were pre-

TABLE 10-8
Incidence of Broken Homes among Official Delinquents and among Comparison Groups Not Identified as Delinquent

| | | PERCENT FROM BROKEN HOMES | |
		OFFICIAL DELINQUENTS	NONDELINQUENT CONTROLS
Weeks & Smith (1939)	Boys	41.4	26.7
Shaw & McKay (1942)	Boys	42.5	36.1
Merrill (1947)	Boys and Girls	50.7	26.0
Glueck & Glueck (1950)	Boys	60.4	32.4
Nye (1958)	Boys	23.6	17.6
Koller (1971)	Girls	61.5	12.9

Source: Martin R. Haskell and Lewis Yablonsky: *Juvenile Delinquency*, p. 108. Copyright © 1982 by Houghton Miflin Company. Adapted by permission.

sented. Boys incarcerated for delinquency expressed many more negative attitudes toward parents, 15.8 versus only 4.0 among the nonincarcerated boys. The author of this study quite rightly points out, however, that "it is conceivable that a negative attitude toward parents is one of the numerous results of being incarcerated as a delinquent" (Duncan, 1978, p. 367).

Adolescents who have had trouble with law-enforcement agencies believe that their parents are less positively involved with them, more detached, and more lackadaisical in their enforcement of rules. These conclusions were derived from a study of two groups of white, male adolescents in California (Robinson, 1978). One group of boys was on probation for failure to obey their parents, while boys in the other group were "well-behaved" adolescents. All the boys were in the age group 14–17. Questionnaires about parental behavior were administered to adolescents and to parents in the homes. Each questionnaire contained simple statements calling for a judgment about whether the behavior described was "like," "somewhat like," or "not like" the parent's behavior. As examples, here are two items from the questionnaire.

Hardly notices when I am good at home or at school.
Soon forgets a rule she (or he) has made. (Robinson, 1978, p. 113)

The behavior of parents who had trouble controlling their adolescent children was viewed by their offspring as characterized by less positive involvement, more hostile detachment, and less rule enforcement, in comparison to the views of well-behaved adolescents about their parents. In addition, the views of the parents themselves were congruent with their children's views.

Obviously not all adolescent children who come from broken homes embark on careers of juvenile delinquency. In fact, no firm conclusions about the relationship between family life and overall delinquent behavior—including both official delinquency and hidden delinquency—can be reached from currently available research. However, studies of official delinquency have consistently shown a relationship between indexes of family disorganization, such as divorce and separation, and delinquency. It seems safe to conclude that when there are strained relationships between parents and adolescent children, for whatever reason, the adolescents are more likely to become official delinquents, and that juvenile delinquency is likely to cause some deterioration in family relationships.

Social Class   Many people have traditionally assumed that lower-class adolescents are more likely to engage in delinquent behavior than their middle- and upper-class counterparts. As we saw, this was the fundamental assumption in Walter Miller's approach to explaining delinquency. In the past few years, research has cast doubt on assumptions about the association of social class and delinquent behavior.

Miller (1958) studied metropolitan street-corner gangs. Following this tradition, researchers studied boys in gangs in metropolitan Chicago in an effort to shed some light on the social class issue (Gordon, Short, Cartwright, & Strodtbeck, 1963). Lower-class gang and nongang boys were compared with nongang, middle-class boys with respect to their evaluation of middle-class norms, such as working for good grades in school, saving money, and reading books. No major differences were found between gang and nongang, lower-class and middle-class boys, or between black and white boys in their evaluation of these middle-class norms.

Still, researchers often find an overall association between delinquent behavior, especially official delinquency, and social class. The study of 15- to 17-year-old males in Utah (Empey & Erickson, 1966), which we have already considered, is a case in point. In this self-report study of delinquency, the 180 respondents admitted thousands of delinquent acts, about 90 percent of which went undetected. Breakdowns by social class were available for these boys: 29 percent were lower class, 55 percent middle-class, and 16 percent upper-class. There was a slight tendency for the upper-class boys to commit fewer delinquent acts than the boys in the other two groups. The upper-class boys accounted for 16 percent of the sample but committed only 9 percent of the delinquent acts. The primary association with social class appears to be tendency for the upper-class boys to be less involved in delinquent behavior (Erickson & Empey, 1965).

Arrest Rates Arrest rates for juvenile delinquency *do* show a strong tendency to be higher among lower-class adolescents. For example, data from the California Youth Authority in the 1970s indicate that 56 percent of the males and 61 percent of the females were of below-average socioeconomic status (Haskell & Yablonsky, 1982).

We have referred several times throughout this chapter to the distortions created by concentrating on adjudicated delinquents, and we have tried to introduce as many studies as possible of delinquent behavior by nonadjudicated as well as official delinquents. This approach is particularly important when we consider social-class and race differences in delinquent behavior because of the possibility of bias in arrest rates as a function of class and race.

In an important study of social class and delinquency (Clark & Wenninger, 1962), a large number of adolescents, in grades 6–12, were asked to fill out questionnaires about their participation in various forms of delinquent behavior. Four types of community were used in this research: (1) lower-class, rural-farm community; (2) lower-class, urban community; (3) middle-class, industrial city; and (4) upper-class, urban community. The data obtained from this study indicate that for most offenses, there are no striking differences among the groups in their self-reported delinquent behavior.

Race Most of the research on race as a factor in delinquent behavior has focused on differences between blacks and whites. Studies in which other racial groups are included are infrequent, or have small samples. Our discussion, therefore, will concern black–white differences in delinquent behavior.

One of the most comprehensive studies of racial differences in delinquency surveyed more than 800 13- to 16-year-old males and females nationwide (Williams & Gold, 1972). Interviews were conducted with each adolescent, usually outside the home, about a variety of topics including family, school, and dating, as well as about behavior "that would get teenagers into trouble if they were caught." Teenagers admitted engaging in quite a lot of delinquent behavior (88 percent had been involved in at least one chargeable offense); and most of it—more than 97 percent—went undetected. These findings are in agreement with results from several other studies, as we have seen.

Williams and Gold's data on race differences are of special interest for our present discussion. Data on frequency and seriousness of delinquent behavior were presented by race for males and females separately. These data indicated that white females were no more nor no less frequently delinquent, and no more nor no less seriously delinquent, than black females. Among the males, whites and blacks reported being delinquent with equivalent frequency; however, whites were less seriously delinquent than blacks. Black teenagers appear, from this self-report study, to engage in more delinquency involving property damage, theft, and assault (Williams & Gold, 1972). There was, however, considerable overlap even in serious delinquent behavior.

Victim Reports Both self-reports of delinquent behavior and arrest rates are subject to some distortion. Reports of victims of delinquent behavior are another source of information about rates of de-

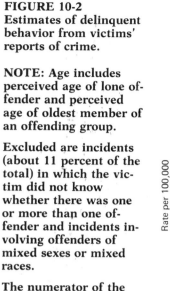

FIGURE 10-2
Estimates of delinquent behavior from victims' reports of crime.

NOTE: Age includes perceived age of lone offender and perceived age of oldest member of an offending group.

Excluded are incidents (about 11 percent of the total) in which the victim did not know whether there was one or more than one offender and incidents involving offenders of mixed sexes or mixed races.

The numerator of the rates of offending for 12- to 17-year-olds includes incidents (about 1 percent of the total) in which the offender was perceived by the victim to be under 12 years of age. The denominator of the rate is the number of 12-to 17-year-olds in the general population.

(From Hindelang, 1981.)

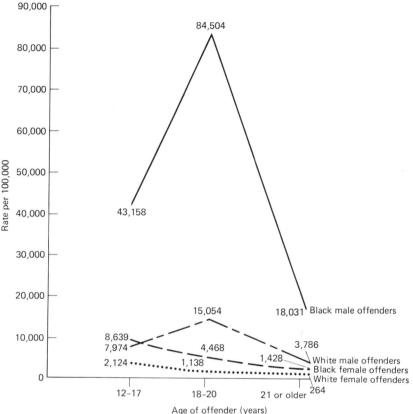

linquency. The National Crime Survey, conducted by the Bureau of the Census, contains estimates of delinquency based on victims' reports (Hindelang, 1981). A nationally representative sample of 65,000 households was surveyed at 6-month intervals between 1973 and 1977. Respondents were asked if they had been the victims of crime in the past 6 months; and if so, they were asked the age, race, and sex of the individuals who committed the crime. As Figure 10-2 shows, there are different patterns of delinquent behavior by race, age, and sex. Females were reported to be perpetrators of crimes far less often than males. In addition, respondents said that they had been victimized by black males more often than white males. Rate of reported criminal behavior among black males was strikingly high: Estimates for the 18 to 20 age group were 85,000 crimes for every 100,000 black males in that age group in the population at large (Hindelang, 1981).

Teenage arrests on Hollywood Boulevard in Los Angeles, 1981. Police officers' judgments as to the disposition of juvenile lawbreakers are frequently based on such external cues as age, dress, and demeanor.

(Photo by Tom Zimberoff/ Sygma)

Victim reports do not exactly coincide with arrest rates because not all crimes are reported, and because not all juveniles are apprehended even if the crime is reported. Furthermore, while victims can probably judge the race of juveniles reliably, they may not be as accurate in their estimates of age.

Arrest rates are higher among blacks (and other racial minorities) than among whites. Arrest rates may not always accurately reflect the rates of commission of delinquent acts. A discrepancy in arrest rates could arise from a tendency on the part of police officers and other juvenile-justice authorities to treat adolescents differently as a function of their race and socioeconomic status. Police officers have a great deal of discretion in deciding what they do with a juvenile caught in a delinquent act, from outright release to arrest and confinement. In making a judgment about what to do with a given juvenile, officers use cues such as age, dress, race, grooming, and demeanor. An observational study of all juvenile officers in one police department for 9 months bears out this conclusion (Piliavin & Briar, 1964). In this police jurisdiction, for this 9-month period of time, a juvenile was more likely to be arrested if he or she were older, black, and dressed in black jacket and jeans. An uncooperative juvenile was especially likely to be arrested. Race was a powerful determinant of a juvenile's outcome with the police. Several of the police officers (18 of 27) admitted to prejudice against blacks. One officer expressed his views this way:

They [blacks] have no regard for the law or for the police. They just don't seem to give a damn. Few of them are interested in school or getting ahead. The girls start having illegitimate kids before they are 16 years old and the boys are always "out for kicks." Furthermore, many of these kids try to run you down. They say the damnedest things to you and they seem to have absolutely no respect for you as an adult. I admit I am prejudiced now, but frankly I don't think I was when I began police work. (Piliavin & Briar, 1964, p. 213)

Intelligence

Studies on the relationship between delinquent behavior, on the one hand, and social class or race, on the other, indicate that overall delinquent behavior varies to some extent as a function of racial and social-class groups. Intelligence also seems to exert an influence on delinquent behavior.

A large number of black and white male adolescents were asked to indicate which acts of delinquency they had engaged in, the method for obtaining information on self-reported delinquency with which we are now familiar. IQ scores were also available for these adolescents. In Figure 10-3, IQ scores have been grouped into percentiles; for each percentile, the percentage of black and white males who admitted two or more delinquent acts is shown. The percentage of blacks and whites who admitted delinquency is very similar. Furthermore, there was a clear relationship between IQ and

FIGURE 10-3
Percentage of black and white adolescents reporting that they had engaged in delinquent behavior, by IQ.

(From Hirschi & Hindelang, 1977.)

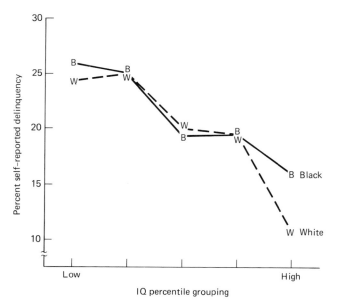

delinquency: Adolescents in the lower IQ percentiles, whether they were black or white, were more likely to admit to delinquent behavior (Hirschi & Hindelang, 1977). The authors of this study speculated that the mechanism linking IQ and juvenile delinquency is probably school performance and adjustment.

Education and Delinquency

Data from the Youth-in-Transition project (Bachman et al., 1978) lend some support to the conclusion that educational attainment is associated with juvenile delinquency. Adolescent males in the Youth-in-Transition project were followed over a 10-year period, as we saw earlier. Throughout this 10-year period, there was a strong relationship between educational attainment and rates of delinquent behavior, as shown in Figure 10-4. Interestingly, educational attainment cannot have been the *direct* cause of different rates of delinquency, for the differences showed up at the very start of the study, before the various levels of education were attained.

FIGURE 10-4
Interpersonal aggression in the Youth-in-Transition project, by educational attainment. Adolescents who became dropouts engaged in more interpersonal aggression, even before they dropped out of school.

(From Bachman, O'Malley, & Johnston, 1978.)

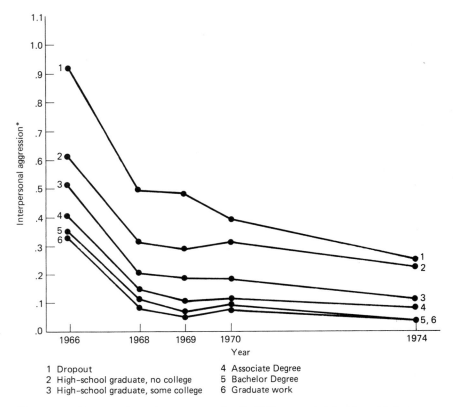

1 Dropout
2 High-school graduate, no college
3 High-school graduate, some college
4 Associate Degree
5 Bachelor Degree
6 Graduate work

*The measures of interpersonal aggression were retrospective. The 1966 measure asked about the past 3 years; the 1968 and 1969 measures asked about the past 18 months; the 1970 and 1974 measures asked about the past year.

The differences by educational attainment were mirrored in both frequency and in seriousness of delinquency: "During junior high school those who later became high school dropouts were involved in serious delinquency more than twice as often as those who later became college graduates" (Bachman et al., 1978, p. 176). These findings are similar to those of Glueck and Glueck (1968) showing that high-school dropouts were more likely to become official delinquents.

One possible reason for the association between education and delinquent behavior, demonstrated by both the Youth-in-Transition project and the Glueck study, is the young adolescent's response to school and the larger cultural meaning of success in school. Our earlier discussion of the success-and-money ethic, with the hypothesis that education is a legitimate means for obtaining the success goal, is relevant here. One student of juvenile delinquency put it this way:

Mass formal education has created serious problems of life goals for adolescents with education disabilities. For academically successful adolescents, school is a bridge between the world of childhood and the world of adulthood. For children unwilling or unable to learn, school is a place where the battle against society is likely to begin. (Toby, 1967/1969, p. 310)

Gender

We began this chapter with the case of Juan Hernandez, an adolescent boy who engaged in delinquent behavior. It seems appropriate to initiate the section on gender differences in delinquent behavior with the case of an adolescent girl, summarized from a longer treatment by Robey (1969).

The Case of Ann Grant Ann came to the attention of the juvenile court after she ran away from home. She was almost 15 years old at her initial encounter with juvenile authorities. Ann's mother had found her in bed with her boyfriend, whom her parents had forbidden her to see. The court placed Ann on probation, and her probation officer referred her to a clinic. During this period, her mother, while going through Ann's purse, found a letter to her boyfriend; Mrs. Grant showed the letter to Ann's father, who dragged her out of bed, slapped her several times, and threatened to resume "discussion" of the matter in the morning. Ann ran away again during the night.

She was returned home by the authorities, and the situation stabilized until Ann's boyfriend attempted suicide. Finally it became necessary to place Ann in a center for problem adolescents, the House of the Good Shepherd. She adjusted well at this facility, where she remained for several months, until her boyfriend appeared one day with a pistol and demanded her release. Following this incident, Ann was placed under the care of her paternal grandmother.

Those are the bare facts of Ann Grant's career as an official delinquent. Closer inquiry reveals a family situation of disharmony and instability. Mrs. Grant was angry toward her husband and refused to participate in sexual intercourse with him. Mr. Grant, for his part, frequently beat his wife, drank heavily, and had several extramarital affairs. Mrs. Grant knew about the affairs. Mr. Grant had had a close relationship with Ann until she reached puberty; at that time he became quite strict about her activities.

Ann was allowed to begin dating at around age 13. Trouble leading to her official delinquency began 2 years later, when she became involved with the emotionally unstable boyfriend who was found in her bed. Ann had asked him to get into bed with her, and that was as far as it went; they did not have intercourse. When Ann's mother walked in, Ann taunted her with, "What do you think of sex now, Mother dear?" It was at this point in the case that Ann's official delinquency began.

Delinquency among Girls Ann's delinquency fits the stereotyped assumption that adolescent girls specialize in certain types of delinquent behavior, showing a different pattern than adolescent boys.

While the young male delinquent shows a wide variety of behavior, the girl, in contrast, possesses a quite limited delinquent repertoire. By and large, her legally defined offenses consist of sexual acting out, vagrancy, running away, and stealing of the kleptomaniac type. (Friedman, 1969, p. 114)

It is likely that official charges of female delinquency involve sexual delinquencies and running away, as we saw in the Ann Grant case. By contrast, self-reports of delinquent behavior indicate that female adolescents do not specialize in these few delinquencies. For example, self-reports of delinquency gathered from more than 750 students at a coed high school in Oakland, California, revealed *patterns* of delinquency that were highly similar for the two sexes (Hindelang, 1971). The mean *frequency* of delinquent acts, however, was greater among males. The ratio of 2:1 male-to-female delinquency seems to be a roughly accurate figure (Kratcoski & Kratcoski, 1975).

Sex ratios in frequency of committing 24 delinquent acts are presented in Table 10-9. These ratios show that males consistently commit more delinquent acts than females. At the same time, adolescent girls commit a full range of delinquent acts, not specializing in any given category. They are far less likely than males, however, to engage in theft of large amounts, gang fist fights, gambling, or promiscuous sexual behavior (Hindelang, 1971).

The stereotype that adolescent girls are more likely to become sexual delinquents is a special case of sexism in American society. In particular, juvenile courts have historically treated females more severely than males, subjecting them to personal indignities involving sexual matters (Schlossman & Wallach, 1978). Consider the case of Annagret Schmitt, culled from court records in Milwaukee in the early 1900s.

Neither the hearing transcript nor the accompanying records provides a precise reason why Annagret was brought into court—a common occurrence, since it was assumed that some form of aberrant sexual expression was behind any specific accusation. Thus Annagret, like every girl who appeared in court, was subjected to a vaginal examination. The only proof of virginity was an intact

TABLE 10-9
Sex Ratios for Several Delinquent Acts, Male Rate Expressed for Each Female Occurrence

OFFENSE	SEX RATIO
Theft less than $10	2.03
Theft greater than $10	4.15
Property destruction (less than $10)	3.13
Property destruction (more than $10)	3.08
Drinking alcohol	1.48
Getting drunk	2.26
Individual fist fights	2.58
Gang fist fights	4.11
Carrying a concealed weapon	3.28
Individual weapon fights	2.70
Gang weapon fights	2.92
Gambling	4.23
Using marijuana	1.80
Sniffing glue	1.58
Using LSD, Methedrine, or Mescaline	1.54
Using Heroin	1.47
Shaking down others for money	3.00
Promiscuous sexual behavior	4.86
Drag racing on street	2.01
Driving under the influence	3.33
Hit and run accidents	1.39
Cheating on exams	1.20
Using false ID	1.56
Cutting school	1.63

Source: Hindelang, 1971.

hymen. To his own surprise the examining doctor concluded that Annagret was still a virgin, but he informed the court that irritation in her clitoral area indicated she was a regular masturbator. The probation officer, a woman, analyzed the situation as follows: "She masturbates, and she has somewhat injured herself in that way, and probably this is the cause of her conduct at home and says things [sic] that are not true . . . [Annagret] most likely is trying to imagine things, and then believes everything is true." . . . Thus, according to the court, Annagret's masturbatory habits explained her penchant for fantasy and justified labeling her a delinquent and placing her under supervision. (Schlossman & Wallach, 1978, p. 73)

Data from self-report studies of delinquent behavior now make it clear that classifying adolescent girls' behavior along sex-related specialties, in contrast to adolescent boys' behavior, has no empirical support. What is clear is that adolescent boys are far more likely to engage in delinquent behavior in the first place, by a factor of roughly 2:1.

This gender disparity in rates of delinquent behavior poses a challenge to the explanatory models of delinquency that we have reviewed in this chapter. Each of the factors that we have cited—family relationships, social class, geographic area, age, education—should apply equally to males and to females. Growing up in broken homes or in urban ghettoes should not logically be more harmful to the psychological development of adolescent boys than of adolescent girls. As we saw in Chapter 4, however, adolescence is an important stage for sex-role consolidation. It is a stage in which important divergences between males and females take place; among these are the stereotypes associated with gender. It is certainly possible that sex-role consolidation in adolescence is a process heavily influenced by environmental contexts, such as family situation and socioeconomic status.

Although a gender disparity is one of the most reliable findings in the area of delinquent behavior, it is one of the least researched. It is particularly regrettable that the two mammoth longitudinal studies of delinquency reported in this chapter—the Glueck study and the Youth-in-Transition project—failed to include adolescent girls in their samples.

SUMMARY

1. There is an important distinction between delinquent behavior and official delinquency. *Delinquent behavior* refers to any act of a juvenile that would be a chargeable offense according to the juvenile-justice laws. *Official delinquency* refers only to those acts involving adolescents actually apprehended for delinquent behavior. The disparity between these two categories, acts per-

formed but not resulting in legal action, is referred to as *hidden delinquency.*

2. The legal code includes some acts, such as truancy and incorrigibility, that apply only to juveniles; these acts are called *status offenses.* Each state has a somewhat different set of laws for regulating juvenile behavior.

3. Anonymous reports by adolescents reveal a large proportion of hidden delinquency. Approximately 90 percent of adolescent delinquency, most of it relatively minor, goes undetected. About one-quarter of all court cases are for status offenses.

4. Comparisons of anonymous and nonanonymous, self-reported delinquency on questionnaires show that anonymity encourages adolescents to report more delinquent behavior.

5. Both anonymous and nonanonymous questionnaire results suggests that adolescents apprehended as official delinquents have had a history of more frequent and more serious delinquent behavior.

6. Longitudinal studies, in which the same individuals are studied at regular intervals, provide information about antecedents of delinquent behavior and about adult outcomes of individuals who engaged in delinquent behavior in adolescence. The Glueck study, comparing 500 official-delinquent and 500 nondelinquent males from their early teens through age 31, led to the conclusion that boys who became official delinquents had come from homes characterized by greater family disorganization. Officially delinquent boys had far more trouble in school than their counterparts not identified as delinquent, and they were more likely to have officially delinquent friends.

7. Official and nonofficial delinquents in the Glueck study remained distinct groups into adulthood. Far fewer young men from the nondelinquent group established criminal records as adults, in comparison to the delinquent group. However, the delinquents showed less and less criminal behavior in adulthood.

8. Another longitudinal study, the Youth-in-Transition project, included a nationwide cross-section of adolescent males, not identified as delinquent. They were interviewed from 10th grade through 5 years post-high school. A large percentage of these boys reported some participation in relatively serious delinquent behavior, such as assault. Rates of delinquent behavior were highest in early adolescence and lowest when the boys had

become young men. Delinquency did not appear to be a highly stable intraindividual characteristic.

9. Other explanatory schemes for delinquent behavior emphasize subcultural groups, such as street-corner gangs. Subcultures of delinquency are viewed as environmental contexts in which society's goals of success and money may be accepted in the absence of institutional means to achieve the goals. Pressure to achieve the goals through delinquent behavior may be greater in some subcultures. Some subcultures may also provide more opportunities for learning how to perform a delinquent role.

10. Research has focused on factors that tend to be associated with delinquent behavior. Among these factors are family relationships. Officially-delinquent adolescents are more likely to come from broken homes than other adolescents. Officially-delinquent adolescents also have more negative attitudes toward their parents.

11. Another factor is social class. Although arrest rates are strongly associated with social class, self-reported delinquent behavior is much less so. In self-report studies, middle-class and lower-class adolescents report equivalent rates of delinquent behavior.

12. Race differences show a similar pattern to social-class differences: Blacks are more likely to be charged with delinquency than whites, and yet self-reported delinquent behavior is no more frequent for one group than the other. There is a tendency for black male adolescents to report more serious delinquency, however. Victims of delinquency identify black male adolescents as perpetrators with striking frequency.

13. Rates of delinquent behavior are higher among low-IQ groups of adolescents, both black and white. Rates of delinquency also vary by ultimate educational attainment. Adolescents who stop school early are more frequently and more seriously delinquent than those who continue in school.

14. A consistent finding in research on delinquent behavior is the greater rate of delinquency among males. The stereotype that female adolescents are more likely to specialize in sexual delinquency and running away is not supported. However, males are far more likely to be involved in delinquency, by a factor of 2:1. No major longitudinal study of delinquency which includes both males and females has yet been undertaken.

OUTLINE

11. PROBLEMS AND PATHOLOGIES IN ADOLESCENCE

It sometimes happens that perplexing and disturbing behavior develops during adolescence. Such was the case with Jules and with Alma, described in the sections that follow:

THE CASE OF JULES

Jules was an only child who grew up pampered by his mother but severely punished by his father. It seemed to him that his parents diverged even more in their behavior and affection as he reached adolescence, and he became confused and depressed. He had a very high IQ, around 140, but was unable to keep up with school work. He was expelled as he became more and more disruptive and unmanageable in school.

Jules, an amateur photographer, asked his parents for a Polaroid SX 70 instant camera; his parents refused. Jules responded by having a tantrum and threatening to kill himself. His parents then slipped into the roles they had developed for dealing with their son: His father adamantly refused to buy the camera, and his mother said she would if he got straight-A's in school. Suddenly Jules went to his bedroom, stood on the window sill, and shouted, "I'm going to jump!" (Klagsbrun, 1976).

THE CASE OF ALMA

Alma had had a relatively normal early adolescence. She had begun menstruating at age 12 and had successfully progressed through the major stages of puberty. At age 15, however, her mother began to insist that she go to a school with a higher academic reputation, and her father suggested that she begin to diet. Alma, at 5 feet, 6 inches tall, weighed 120 pounds. Alma did begin a diet, which she supplemented with a program of vigorous exercise—tennis, swimming, and calisthenics. As a result, she lost weight rapidly, and her menstruation stopped. A consulting psychiatrist, who provided the information on Alma's case, described her this way:

Alma's arms and legs were covered with soft hair, her complexion had a yellowish tint, and her dry hair hung down in strings. Most striking was the face—hollow like that of a shriveled-up old woman with a wasting disease, sunken eyes, a sharply pointed nose on which the juncture between bone and cartilage was visible. When she spoke or smiled—and she was quite cheerful—one could see every movement of the muscles around her mouth and eyes, like an animated anatomical representation of the skull. (Bruch, 1978, p. 2)

Alma did not view herself as needing treatment. She said, "I enjoy having this disease and I want it. I cannot convince myself that I am sick and that there is anything from which I have to recover." (Bruch, 1978, p. 3).

Alma was diagnosed as having anorexia nervosa, a puzzling eating disorder that occurs more often among girls than boys, and that is virtually restricted to the adolescent and young-adult age group.

Alma and Jules illustrate two forms of pathology in adolescence: anorexia nervosa and suicidal behavior. These pathological reactions are among several that we examine in the course of this chapter. Many observers believe that the rapid physical and psychological changes that occur in adolescence make it a particularly vulnerable period for the development of pathological reactions. Indeed, many of the problems discussed in this chapter appear to have special variations during the adolescent years.

It is important to point out, however, that maladjustment and pathology are not the most common styles of making the transition from childhood to adulthood. Psychological turmoil during the transition from childhood to adulthood appears to be the exception instead of the rule (Offer & Offer, 1975). Nevertheless, trends in recent years toward more frequent behavioral disturbance in adolescence should encourage us to pay more attention to the psychological demands of this age period.

In this chapter, we adopt a problem-oriented approach to adolescent pathology, similar to that advocated by Weiner (1980). We have selected four problems for scrutiny, without pretending that these problems exhaust the list of disturbances that adolescents may face. In Chapter 10, we considered the problem of juvenile delinquency, as one form of adolescent behavioral disturbance, in detail. In the present chapter, we discuss four adolescent pathological problems. First, we discuss adolescent schizophrenia, which differs in some important ways from the disorder in adulthood. Next, we look at adolescent depression and its most severe manifestation, suicidal behavior. Thirdly, anorexia nervosa, illustrated in the beginning of the chapter by Alma's case, is discussed. Finally, we review the problem of substance abuse in adolescence, focusing on drug and alcohol use and abuse.

ADOLESCENT SCHIZOPHRENIA

Schizophrenia is a serious psychological disorder that is characterized by an inability to function in the day-to-day world. Typically, the disorder includes marked impairment in intellectual functioning, bizarre thought processes, such as delusions and hallucinations, and little or no insight into the disorder. Because of the serious consequences to normal human functioning, schizophrenics often require institutionalization or other forms of chronic care.

Schizophrenia is only one diagnostic category for psychiatric problems in adolescence. Schizophrenia accounts for approximately 8–10 percent of cases of psychological problems in adolescence. A comprehensive study of one community—Monroe County, New York—categorized every adolescent aged 12–18 who was an inpatient or outpatient in the community's mental health facilities (including a university medical center, a community mental health center, and community and state hospitals). It is, therefore, one of the most comprehensive studies of the types of psychological problems that adolescents suffer. The results suggest a difficulty in precisely categorizing the psychological problems of adolescents. Thus, the two most prevalent categories, "personality disorder" and "situational disorder," are rather vague and nonspecific. Schizophrenia accounted for 8.5 percent of the sample of adolescents who sought psychological counseling.

Special Aspects of Adolescent Schizophrenia

Up to a point, the situation for schizophrenic adults and adolescents is the same. However, there are some special aspects of adolescent schizophrenia which make it a disorder worthy of special attention in a textbook on adolescence.

First of all, the prognosis for schizophrenia is less favorable when it appears in adolescence than when it occurs in adulthood. Among schizophrenics whose symptoms first appear in adulthood, approximately one-third can be expected to recover, one-third will improve but suffer a relapse, and one-third will remain permanently hospitalized. The comparable figures for schizophrenics whose symptoms first appear in adolescence are one-fourth recover, one-fourth improve, and one-half require permanent hospitalization (Weiner, 1980).

A 5-year follow-up study of 78 adolescent schizophrenics (Annesley, 1961) illustrates this point. Among this sample of adolescents, 19 percent recovered, 23 percent improved, and 58 percent had showed no change in their condition. Furthermore, the prognosis was far less favorable for male than for female adolescents, as shown in Figure 11-1. Twice as many of the adolescent females recovered or improved.

Second, the onset of schizophrenia may be more difficult to detect among adolescents than among adults. Some of the initial signs of the disorder may be mistaken for the expectable changes in behavior or mood which accompany adolescence. Thus, family conflict, school failure, truancy, feelings of hopelessness, and lack of interest in other people may arise as a function of the schizophrenic breakdown, but may be mistaken for adolescent rebellion or turmoil (Weiner, 1970). Consider the case of a 14-year-old girl, in which there was an increasing pattern of withdrawal. Such withdrawal could have been mistaken for behavior changes accompanying normal adolescence, at least in its early stages, although in fact it was associated with a diagnosis of schizophrenia.

A girl, aged 14, was referred because of increasing withdrawal. The family history was negative [i.e., no pathologies were present]. Her home background was stable and affectionate and her early development normal. She was a very

FIGURE 11-1
Prognosis for male (M) and female (F) adolescent schizophrenics, based on follow-up study of 78 patients.

(From Annesley, 1961.)

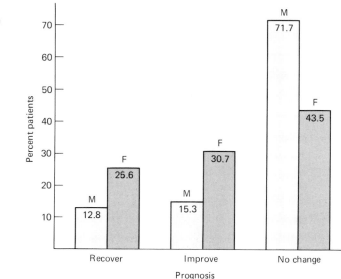

Schizophrenia is a serious psychological disorder characterized by an inability to function in the day-to-day world. The prognosis is less favorable for adolescent than adult schizophrenics, with only one-fourth of adolescent schizophrenics recovering as compared to one-third of adults.

(Photo copyright © by Catherine Ursillo/Photo Researchers, Inc.)

shy child. She adjusted to primary school but broke down at her secondary school after being falsely accused of pilfering. She became increasingly solitary and withdrawn. She was manneristic, giggled to herself and, on occasion, attempted to injure herself. (Annesley, 1961, p. 273)

A final special aspect of adolescent schizophrenia is that there are often behavioral signs of the disorder in earlier adolescence or in childhood, prior to the actual onset of the syndrome (Weiner, 1980). There are indications that adolescents who later develop schizophrenia are somewhat more likely to display a personality orientation of either withdrawal from social contact, or antisocial behavior. In the withdrawn, shut-in type, the adolescent shows little or no interest in activities with other people. This pattern appears to be somewhat more characteristic of preschizophrenic girls than of boys. The antisocial type is likely to be egocentric, unpleasant, and negativistic. This pattern is somewhat more characteristic of preschizophrenic boys (Watt & Lubensky, 1976).

Developmental History of Adolescent Schizophrenia

Schizophrenia that becomes manifested in adolescence or youth can be divided into phases, as shown in Figure 11-2. These phases distinguish between the period before diagnosis (sometimes called the "premorbid" phase), and the period when the disorder is becoming apparent or when outright symptoms have developed.

**FIGURE 11-2
Developmental model of schizophrenic system formation.**

(From Garmezy, 1970.)

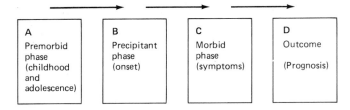

Premorbid Phase Many adolescent schizophrenics who are destined to have the disorder in adulthood show early signs that they may develop the disorder. "From a third to a half of them are easily identifiable as deviant in childhood before they show any clear indications of psychotic disorganization," reported two researchers who undertook a careful documentary study of all mental patients hospitalized during the years 1958–1964, whose admission age was 16–35 (Watt & Lubensky, 1976). In other words, there are some warning signals for a large number of adolescents during the premorbid phase of the disorder.

These conclusions were derived from a careful study of the cumulative school records of all the hospitalized schizophrenics in Massachusetts, drawn from the sample described above. Their cumulative school records contained comments from teachers about behavior in and around the school. The ad lib comments were coded along dimensions of conscientiousness, emotional stability, extraversion, assertiveness, and agreeableness. The same coding scheme was used for a group of matched control students who were not later diagnosed as schizophrenic. The volume of teacher comments, incidentally, was not different for the preschizophrenics and the normals. Compared to the matched control group, preschizophrenic boys were written about as less conscientious, less emotionally stable, and less agreeable, while preschizophrenic girls were written about as more introverted and more passive.

As mentioned earlier, radical disruptions in social interaction usually accompany the onset of schizophrenia. The data on differences between preschizophrenics and control subjects on social dimensions indicate that social interaction patterns are noticeably disrupted in the premorbid phase for a large number of individuals.

Schizophrenia is also accompanied by disordered thinking, often including an inability to operate at a proper level of abstraction, or an inability to use everyday logical operations. There is little or no evidence, however, that signs of disordered thinking appear during the premorbid phase in adolescence, as shown in Figure 11-3. The preschizophrenics and the matched control subjects were

FIGURE 11-3
Longitudinal analysis of IQ scores of preschizophrenic students and matched control students.

(From Watt & Lubensky, 1976.)

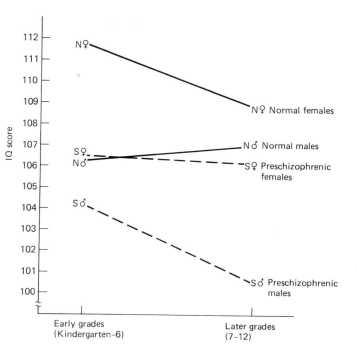

compared in a longitudinal analysis of their IQ scores. Although the control students scored slightly higher, on the average, on these standardized tests of intelligence, there was no reliable pattern of IQ decline over time among the preschizophrenics, as one would expect if thought processes were becoming more and more disordered during the premorbid phase of the illness. Indeed, the preschizophrenic girls were more consistent in their IQ scores during the early and later grades than their matched control group (Watt & Lubensky, 1976).

Precipitant and Morbid Phases Although the onset of schizophrenia may be more difficult to detect among adolescents than among adults, the same clinical signs are used for diagnosis. These include evidence of disordered thinking, disruptions of social skills, and bizarre thought patterns such as delusions. It may be some time before this pattern of symptoms gets officially diagnosed as schizophrenia, as in the following case:

A girl, aged 12, had been deluded for a year. Her father's mother was paranoid. The family history was otherwise negative [i.e., no other family pathology was indicated]. She was late in walking at two years. She was a shy child who did not mix. She made an average adjustment at school until the onset of her illness. Her delusions started at the age of 11.

She was tense, suspicious, believed her food was being poisoned and thought a neighbor had told the police her parents were going to murder her. She heard people in the street saying she was going to die. She was admitted when she became uncontrollable at home, with a diagnosis of paranoid schizophrenia. (Annesley, 1961, pp. 272–273)

The thinking of schizophrenics is less mature than that of their otherwise normal counterparts. Researchers, for example, have asked 17–18-year-old schizophrenics and normal controls to describe an ideal society for an imaginary island. Normal adolescents in this country usually model the society on what they know best—the abstract democratic principles of American society. One female adolescent selected the following ideal society:

Let's see. A president elected by the people and a vice-president. More or less the form of government that we have here in the United States. The house of Congress, the two houses, right? And let's see, the only thing is the people will have more influence; the people will have more say in what the government is going to do. So there will be representatives of the people other than the Congress and the House of Representatives; they will come from each community. (Crain & Starace, 1976, p. 275)

The following visionary society is typical of the more fanciful imaginations of schizophrenic teenagers:

I would declare myself president of the whole island, mainly because no one else has ever thought of it before. And I got the idea first. There would be no words I couldn't stand or stomach; only good words. I would have a movie house and not only TV shows but cartoons, talk shows, movies, soap operas, even cook shows and exercise shows. And I would watch them and not miss one show at all. . . . People of all races would love each other. And my mother would love my father. And there'd be a pink lemonade water fountain and a big soda ocean that goes over the falls, and lots of nice doggies and cats and birds. (Crain & Starace, 1976, p. 277)

Some people might consider the second answer to be the more interesting and creative. Indeed, it is sometimes difficult to distinguish between supernormal creativity and abnormal fancy. The point of the study discussed above is that there is a difference between the types of replies given by schizophrenics and normal control adolescents, not that one should be judged better or duller than another.

Prognosis The prognosis for adolescents who are diagnosed as schizophrenic is poorer than for other major diagnostic categories. In one study, all adolescents aged 12–18 who were admitted to the

Payne-Whitney Psychiatric Clinic during the years 1936–1950 were followed up in adulthood (Masterson, 1956). This long-term follow-up study allows us to compare the prognosis for adolescent psychological disorders. Figure 11-4 shows the comparative percentages of adolescents who had good follow-up adjustments with the diagnosis of schizophrenia and other psychological problems.

The other diagnostic categories included were psychopathic personality, in which the adolescent is capable of willfully delinquent acts without shame, anxiety, or remorse; affective disorders, serious mood disturbances, such as depression; and psychoneuroses, psychological disturbances, such as phobias that make life difficult or unpleasant. Fewer adolescents made "good" adjustments if they were diagnosed as schizophrenic; a good adjustment was defined as having no impairment or minimal impairment in functioning.

In addition, adolescents who were below age 15 during the precipitant phase of the disorder had a poorer prognosis than adolescents who were 15 or older. About a third of the older group made good adjustments, compared to only 10 percent who were

FIGURE 11-4
Percentage of adolescents making "good" follow-up adjustment by diagnostic category. Fewer adolescents diagnosed as schizophrenic made "good" adjustments than those in other diagnostic categories.

(From Masterson, 1956.)

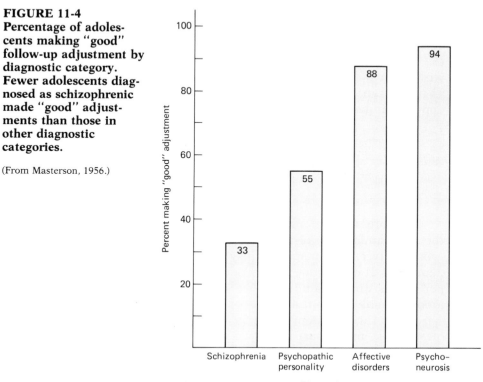

younger than 15. A gradual onset of the disorder as distinct from a sudden, acute onset, was also associated with a poorer adjustment on follow-up.

Presence or absence of a family history of emotional illness appears to be unrelated to outcome in terms of adjustment level on follow-up (Masterson, 1956; Annesley, 1961). Stability in the home is a factor in prognosis, however. Adolescents from more stable home backgrounds are more likely to improve or recover from the disorder, than are adolescents from unstable homes (Annesley, 1961).

Developmental studies of schizophrenia, such as those reviewed above, indicate that symptoms of the disorder first appear during the adolescent period in a significant number of cases. The earlier in adolescence that one is diagnosed as schizophrenic, the poorer the prognosis for subsequent improvement. Schizophrenia is always a perplexing disorder; when it afflicts adolescents, it appears to be particularly debilitating.

DEPRESSION AND SUICIDAL BEHAVIOR

Depression is a mood that everyone experiences to some extent. For most individuals, depression is a transient mood state. Depression as a clinical diagnosis, however, is a serious affective disorder. It involves a marked negative orientation toward the world, in which the individual dwells on a low view of self. The person suffering with clinical depression tends to view the future as bleak, the world as unpleasant, and the self as blameworthy. A woman with clinical depression described the feeling this way:

There is such a terrible nothingness. There is no beauty; there's no love. There's no hope, no joy. And the only thing there is is that terrible fear and an awful desire to die. . . . It's hell when you don't have to die to go to hell. All you have to do is be depressed. (Klagsbrun, 1976, p. 38)

Trends in Adolescent Depression

Depression among adolescents is not a common diagnosis, as the data in Figure 11-5 indicate. Among the 10–14-year-old age group, only 1.5–3.5 percent of psychiatric patients are diagnosed as depressed. It does, however, increase with age during the adolescent period. As among adults, depression is somewhat more common among females than males.

The rarity of depression as a psychiatric diagnosis among adolescents stems in part from two special characteristics of the adolescent period that interact with the symptomatology of the disorder (Weiner, 1980). Adolescents have difficulty in admitting concerns about themselves, and so they may hide the self-depreciation that is

FIGURE 11-5
Percentage of adolescent psychiatric patients diagnosed as depressed, by age and gender.

(From Weiner, 1980.)

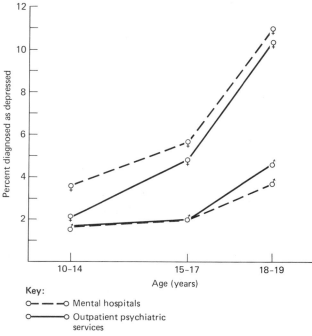

Key:
⊶ — —⊶ Mental hospitals
⊶———⊶ Outpatient psychiatric services

such a strong indication of the disorder among adults. Furthermore, adolescents are more likely than adults to be action oriented. As Weiner put it, "early adolescents are still at a developmental stage in which they are inclined more toward doing things than thinking about them" (Weiner, 1980, p. 455). Depression experienced by adolescents may therefore become expressed in behaviors—in drug use, alcohol abuse, promiscuous sexual behavior, or ultimately, in suicide. Thus, although depression is a relatively uncommon psychiatric *diagnosis* among adolescents, it is not necessarily a rare psychological *experience*. Other symptoms or behavior problems may be more likely to mask the underlying depression among adolescents than among adults.

Many adults experience depression following a loss. The death of a spouse or of another significant person may precipitate a depressive reaction. Loss of self-esteem though failing health or feelings of unattractiveness may also lead to episodes of depression. Among adolescents, too, loss is the most frequent cause of depression (Krakowski, 1970).

Parental loss is one of the most common causes of a serious depressive reaction among adolescents (Toolan, 1975), although loss of a girlfriend or boyfriend may also be a precipitating event. Some authorities (e.g., Weiner, 1980) believe that the complex physical and psychological changes that accompany adolescence may cause some individuals to enter depressive states.

Whatever the cause, depression is a serious negative orientation. A typical depressive reaction in adolescence includes reduced self-esteem manifested by insecurity, inadequacy, helplessness and hopelessness, or by other symptoms, such as isolation and lowered intellectual achievement (Krakowski, 1970).

Adolescent Suicidal Behavior

We have said that adolescents tend to act out their problems rather than to talk about them. Serious depression may precipitate a change from being a pleasant teenager to being an unruly one. This change is a different response than the oppressive moroseness common of depression among older people. Suicidal behavior, however, is one response to depression among either age group—adults or adolescents. Among adolescents who attempt suicide, the suicidal behavior is accompanied by serious depression in approximately 80 percent of cases. Suicide attempts among adolescents are often unplanned and impulsive; the underlying wish is to get help, rather than to die (Grueling & DeBlassie, 1980; Weissman, 1974). Suicidal attempts among adolescents are often impulsive attempts to avoid the overwhelming unhappiness of depression, arising from what is perceived to be an untenable situation.

Trends in Adolescent Suicidal Behavior Suicidal behavior, which includes both suicide attempts and successful suicides, is increasing among adolescents both in absolute numbers and in percentage of the youthful population. The suicide rate is rising worldwide (Grueling & DeBlassie, 1980). Figure 11-6 shows the actual suicide rate among young people aged 15–24. In the 20 years from 1955 to 1975 the suicide rate more than doubled. For males in this age group, the rate tripled. Although the rate of suicide attempts has increased among young people over the last several years, the comparative rate of suicide is lower in adolescence than in older age groups. While approximately 6 percent of successful suicides are committed by adolescents, they account for about 12 percent of the known suicide attempts (Corder, Shorr, & Corder, 1974; Seiden, 1969). It is estimated that each year, about 1 out of every 1,000 adolescents attempts suicide. Suicide is now the second most common cause of death among adolescents (Grueling & DeBlassie, 1980).

The average age of persons who attempt suicide has decreased over the last 10 or 15 years (Weissman, 1974). Suicidal be-

**FIGURE 11-6
Suicide rate (per 100,000
population) for males
(M) and females (F) in
the age group 15–24, by
year.**

(From Klagsbrun, 1976; U.S.
Bureau of the Census, *Statistical
Abstract of the United States,
1980.*)

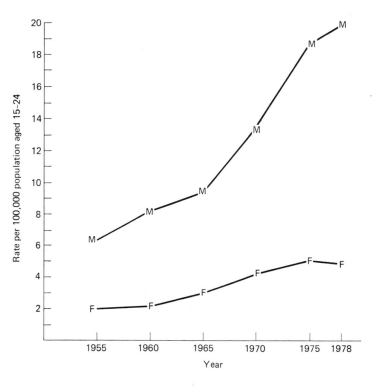

havior is becoming more and more a problem in the adolescent age
group.

Explanatory Factors in Adolescent Suicide   Some authorities argue
that alienation in adolescence increases the probability of suicidal
behavior. Furthermore, this argument goes, young people experience more alienation in complex, highly mobile societies. There is
some support for the notion that alienation is related to adolescent
suicidal behavior. In a study of 200 suicide attempters who called
crisis centers and emergency facilities, the psychological experience
of alienation appeared to be a common mediating factor in suicidal
behavior. In turn, alienation was experienced more by adolescents
with a range of problems typical of the period, such as those listed
in Table 11-1.

  From a sociological point of view, adolescence is a stage of
life when the social structure creates problems for psychological adjustment. Age segregation in the compulsory school system, institutionalized social life, and a perceived lack of alternatives are
social-structural features that may increase the likelihood of

TABLE 11-1 **Adolescent Problems** **That Were Related to** **Alienation among** **Youthful Suicide** **Attempters**	1. Problems of social contact with peers 2. Conflict with parents 3. Broken romances 4. Lower economic status of parents 5. Communication problems with parents 6. Problems of school performance 7. Broken homes

Source: Wenz, 1979.

alienation among adolescents (Wenz, 1979). Cross-cultural studies suggest that strong family ties decrease the pobability of suicide (McAnarney, 1979).

A study of characteristics of suicide attempters who call crisis centers is suggestive, but a more rigorous method is to compare suicidal adolescents with nonsuicidal ones. For example, one such study compared suicidal adolescents in clinics with other adolescent clinic patients who were not suicidal; this comparison holds constant the factor of hospitalization. Both groups of clinic adolescents felt social isolation, and both felt they had little communication with their parents. The suicidal adolescents, however, were more likely to have had a history of suicide in their families or

Concerned officials attempting to dissuade an adolescent from jumping off the Brooklyn Bridge. The psychological profile of adolescents who attempt suicide is one of alienation: hopelessness, depression, lack of investment in the future, and the absence of identification with an adult figure.

(Photo by J. Cowell/Black Star)

among their close friends. They also expressed the psychological syndrome of alienation: absence of identification with any adult figure; lack of investment in the future; hopelessness; depression. Their school involvement was lower than that of nonsuicidal adolescents, and they reported more open and active conflict with their parents (Corder, Page, & Corder, 1974).

Oral questionnaires given to suicidal adolescents, and to control adolescents matched for age, sex, and socioeconomic status, suggest that the family context may be an important contributing factor to adolescent suicidal behavior. Suicidal adolescents' families showed more evidence of family disorganization, such as illness or job loss. Suicidal adolescents were also more subject to rigid discipline, such as restrictions on dating and on friends. Within the family interaction itself, suicidal adolescents more often said that they had no opportunity to express their feelings than nonsuicidal adolescents. A young male college student recently told me that after his parents divorced when he was 13, his mother turned to alcohol. Life at home with his mother, for this young adolescent, became virtually intolerable. "I thought about suicide," he said, "but then I decided to try another way. I knew I couldn't take it anymore at home, so I left." He ultimately went to live with his father and stepmother; without some viable alternative, he, too, might have ended up attempting suicide.

In this context, the suicide attempt can be viewed as a form of communication itself, albeit a high-risk one. One adolescent put it this way: "I didn't know whether I would die or not. I thought things might change . . . and if they didn't, I'd just as soon be dead anyway" (Corder, Page, & Corder, 1974, p. 288).

Between 1958 and 1966, 64 children and adolescents (aged 6–19) attempted suicide and were admitted to a hospital in Fifeshire, Scotland (Haider, 1968). These young people were studied in order to learn more about reasons for suicide attempts in one community. The findings parallel those reported earlier. Disorganized or broken homes were common among the suicide attempters; 56 of the 64 were listed as coming from "disturbed" families that had been broken by death or divorce. Table 11-2 presents a breakdown of the reasons supplied by the young people for their suicide attempts. Again, the most prevalent reason involves faulty communication within the family, such as quarreling with parents, or the strain of family problems. Other researchers have confirmed the higher incidence of faulty communication with families of adolescent suicide attempters (e.g., Hendin, 1976; Hill, 1970).

Adolescence is a time of relative instability for many young people. Changes in one's physical appearance, which had been more

TABLE 11-2
Motivations for Suicide Given by 64 Adolescent and Child Attempters in One Community in Scotland

REASON GIVEN	NUMBER	PERCENT
Quarrel with parents	30	60
Anxiety about sex	7	14
Truancy detected	7	14
Strain of family problems	6	12

Source: Haider, 1968.

or less gradual during childhood, now become dramatic—and often embarrassing. The suicide rate shows its first major increase in incidence in connection with the onset of puberty (Otto, 1972), which is certainly a period of physical instability.

Other life events associated with instability have been implicated as causes for adolescent suicidal behavior, as shown in Table 11-3. "The suicidal risk is thus increased where the individual finds himself in an unstable situation, as between childhood and adulthood, between home leave and military service, between summer vacation and schooling" (Otto, 1972, p. 362).

Thought Processes among Suicidal Adolescents A suicidal person may experience disordered thinking in a variety of ways. Some research indicates that suicidal adolescents are more likely to use rigid and dichotomous thinking than nonsuicidal ones (Lester & Lester, 1971).

Rigid thinking refers to a cognitive orientation in which individuals cannot give up a train of thinking or a way of viewing the world upon which they have settled. There is no flexibility in interpretation, no willingness to seek alternative solutions. This cognitive orientation may make an adolescent's decision to attempt sui-

TABLE 11-3
Indicated Cause of Suicide Attempt among a Sample of Adolescent Attempters

INDICATED CAUSE	PERCENT BOYS	PERCENT GIRLS
Love conflicts	27	39
Family problems	21	35
School problems	6	7
Mental illness	36	14
Military service	10	—
Pregnancy	—	5
	100	100

Source: Otto, 1972.

cide difficult to alter without help from others because the adolescent would find it "difficult to generate new or alternative solutions to debilitating emotional problems" (Levenson & Neuringer, 1971, p. 433).

Dichotomous thinking refers to the tendency to see the world in terms of two basic possibilities, admitting no in-between solutions. From the point of view of the potential suicide, the possibilities may be (a) living a perfect life, or (b) choosing death.

Altered thought processes among suicidal adolescents have been studied by Neuringer and his colleagues. Suicidal individuals were found to have the most pronounced dichotomous thinking, and also the most rigid thinking, in comparison to normal and to emotionally disturbed—but nonsuicidal—subjects (Neuringer, 1961; 1964).

In an experimental test of the question "Is suicide in adolescence linked to diminished problem-solving capacity?" adolescents of both sexes between the ages of 15 and 17 were matched for scores on an "Information" subtest of an IQ test. There were 13 adolescents in each of three groups: suicidal adolescents; emotionally disturbed but nonsuicidal adolescents; and normal adolescents. After being matched for general knowledge, these adolescents were given problem-solving tasks—the arithmetic subtest of the IQ test and a map reading test. Figure 11-7 shows that the suicidal adolescents scored lower on arithmetic problem-solving than adolescents in the

**FIGURE 11-7
Mean WAIS arithmetic subtest score among three groups of adolescents.**

(From Levenson & Neuringer, 1971.)

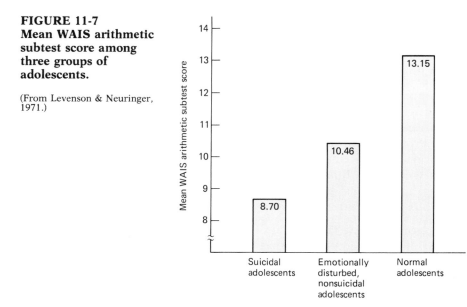

other two groups. In addition, far more suicidal adolescents failed the map-reading test: 9 of 13 suicidal adolescents failed this test, in comparison to 3 of the 26 remaining adolescents (Levenson & Neuringer, 1971).

The conclusion seems warranted that suicidal adolescents experience some changes in their cognitive orientation. These changes may include the tendency to view the self in rigid ways and may even include distortions of the self-concept. If one views one's self or one's situation as worthless or bad, and one cannot see any possibility of change, then a suicide attempt becomes more probable.

Adolescent Suicidal Behavior: Common Misconceptions It is important to know what is true and what is false in the area of adolescent suicidal behavior. Available research and the experience of professionals in crisis centers and in mental health clinics suggest that there are some common misconceptions about suicidal behavior among adolescents. These misconceptions, adapted from Klagsbrun (1976) and Lester and Lester (1971), are presented and discussed below in the hope that they may provide a useful set of guidelines for understanding potential suicidal behavior.

Misconception 1. People who talk about suicide a lot never actually try to kill themselves.
Fact: Repeated threats of suicide provide a signal that an individual is having serious suicidal thoughts. Some professionals believe that threats are an attempt on the part of the adolescent to communicate that something is wrong. Dismissing a threat under the misapprehension that it means the person is not really serious would therefore tell the adolescent that the attempt at communication was a failure; an attempt at suicide could be the next step in the communication process.

Misconception 2. Because there is so much shame and pain associated with a suicide attempt, the adolescent will not attempt suicide a second time.
Fact: Professionals believe that the first attempt is the hardest. Having previously attempted suicide is certainly not an indication that there will be no further attempt. Data indicate that of every five successful suicides, four of the individuals had made one or more previous suicide attempts (Klagsbrun, 1976).

Misconception 3. The return of a cheerful disposition following a period of depression means that the danger of suicide has passed.
Fact: The cheerful mood may simply reflect the relief experienced by a person who has come to a decision to attempt suicide. There is often an improvement in mood prior to a serious suicide attempt.

Misconception 4.   Suicide runs in families.
Fact: Suicidal tendencies are not inherited. As we discussed earlier, however, greater exposure to suicide, either in one's own family or among friends and acquaintances, is associated with suicide attempts in adolescence.

Misconception 5.   Gloomy and oppressive weather is associated with suicidal behavior.
Fact: Although people may experience mood shifts that vary with weather changes, the suicide rate goes up in the spring months, peaking in April and May.

Misconception 6.   Suicide attempts usually occur in the dark of night.
Fact: The peak hours for suicide are between 3 and 6 p.m. Many professionals believe that adolescent suicide attempts are appeals for help. Making an attempt during the daylight hours, when one might be seen, can be viewed in this context.

Misconception 7.   One should not talk about suicide in front of the potentially suicidal person because it will give the person ideas.
Fact: The potentially suicidal person already has the ideas; talking about suicide might actually help the person by focusing on the problems at hand.

Misconception 8.   It was not a case of suicide if there was no suicide note.
Fact: Only a minority—about 15 percent—of known suicide attempts have involved suicide notes. A note is particularly unlikely in the impulsive form of suicide attempts often observed among adolescents.

Misconception 9.   Anyone who attempts suicide is mentally ill.
Fact: Although the suicidal individual is probably desperately unhappy, he or she is not necessarily mentally ill. Terrible unhappiness may be a product of several potential causes, including loss of a loved one, debilitating physical illness, and unbearable family disorganization.

Misconception 10.   Adolescents who are rich and pampered are more likely to attempt suicide. (Alternate form of **Misconception 10:** Adolescents who are very poor are more likely to attempt suicide.)
Fact: The incidence of suicide attempts is about the same across socioeconomic status lines.

Misconception 11.   Once a decision to attempt suicide is made, nothing can stop the person.

Fact: This is one of the most pessimistic and wrongheaded of the misconceptions about suicide. As we have emphasized, suicide may be a desperate bid for communication; it is often preceded by signals. Given this set of circumstances, it is possible to prevent many suicide attempts by recognizing the problems and helping the troubled adolescent to deal with them.

Suicide among older adolescents, those in late high school or college, may be a special case. There is some evidence that a strong motive for suicide among some high-school and college students is escape from achievement pressures. In this regard, it is interesting to note that suicide rates are higher among college students at prestige universities than among young people of equivalent ages in the general population. Suicidal students also have somewhat higher grades than comparison groups of nonsuicidal students (Lester & Lester, 1971).

Preventing Adolescent Suicide   A substantial number of adolescent suicides are impulsive acts; for individuals who appear at risk for this form of suicide, precautions should be taken to keep the means for self-destruction out of access. Hanging, shooting, and poisoning are the most common means of self-destruction (Weiner, 1980.)

Many other suicides are the culmination of a long history of failure to adapt. Although many adolescent suicides are not preceded by warning signals, estimates indicate that such signals are present in one-half to two-thirds of cases (Grueling & DeBlassie, 1980). Therefore, parents, friends, and other caring individuals should look for warning signs of an impending suicide attempt. A list of symptoms that tend to be associated with adolescent suicide attempts are presented in Table 11-4. When such signs are present in an adolescent's behavior and a suspicion of suicidal intent is aroused, resources to help the potentially suicidal adolescent should be sought.

Friends and family provide the most accessible resource for helping a potentially suicidal adolescent. These individuals should be encouraged to discuss the adolescent's feelings openly and frankly. They may help the adolescent to clarify confusing thoughts and feelings; they may help to put these feelings into perspective by simply restating them to the troubled adolescent. This restatement will hopefully reflect the friend's or relative's genuine attempt to understand the adolescent's feelings. The following dialogue is offered as an example by Lester and Lester:

Suicidal adolescent: *"I can't ever seem to get a date, and when I do the girl is a real dog. There just aren't any nice girls around."*

Friend: *"You'd like a girlfriend and you feel lonely without one, but you're*

**TABLE 11-4
Symptoms Associated
with Impending
Suicide Attempt
among Adolescents**

Eating disturbances:
loss of appetite;
loss of weight

Psychosomatic complaints

Insomnia

Withdrawn or rebellious behavior

Neglect of school work

Inability or unwillingness to communicate

Promiscuity

Use of alcohol or drugs

Truancy or running away

Neglect of personal appearance

Sudden changes in personality

Difficulty in concentration

Source: Seiden, 1969.

*afraid you'll never be able to get together with a girl and have a real relation-
ship." (Lester & Lester, 1971, p. 160)*

Family and friends are obviously not appropriate resources
for the potential suicide when they are a major part of the problem.
In these cases, adolescents may be referred to professional thera-
pists or counselors for the help they need. Suicide prevention centers and crisis hotlines are also resources in many communities. On
college campuses, peer counseling is usually available in addition to
the college counseling center or mental health clinic.

ANOREXIA NERVOSA

Anorexia nervosa is a very serious eating disorder that primarily affects adolescent girls. The major feature of the disorder is self-
starvation, with weight loss of 25 percent or more of total body
weight. Although "anorexia" means loss of appetite, young people
with anorexia are usually preoccupied with food and with food-
related thoughts and behavior (Bruch, 1978). Many anorexics also
experience bulimia, a dramatic increase in the sensation of hunger
leading to binge eating, often followed by self-induced vomiting to
avoid any weight gain (Richardson, 1980).

Preoccupation
with Food

The preoccupation with food that many "anorexics" experience is well-illustrated by the case of Opal:

*Her excessive concern with dieting began when she was 15. From then on, her
life centered on maintaining control. After an initial phase of rigid restriction,*

she was terrified by her urges to eat. Opal developed a refined method of control by becoming a gourmet cook . . .

Spending time on cooking made her feel somewhat less depressed and anxious. Opal and her father live in a large house, run by a housekeeper and cook. To help her with the anxiety, Opal's father had a special kitchen and dining room-library built as an addition to the house. She had a collection of cookbooks, over a thousand volumes, specializing in old English cookbooks. The routine she developed kept her free from anxiety for several years. (Bruch, 1978, p. 80)

Many of the case studies of anorexics reveal an excessive concern with cooking and food-related activities (e.g. Norris and Jones, 1979).

The fanatical preoccupation with food is illustrated in a self-portrait (Figure 11-8), provided by Annie, now a Registered Nurse,

FIGURE 11-8
Self-portrait of an anorexic adolescent.

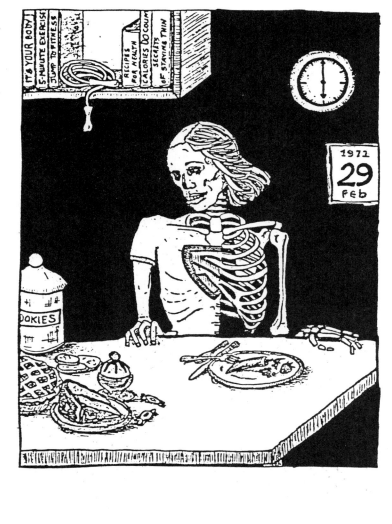

who was an anorexic teenager. Annie explained her portrait this way:

As an [anorexic], I expected my body and the food I took into it to exert a "perfecting influence" on my life. The date, February 29, was created to "make up for" the cumulative imperfections of ordinary days. The books are witness to my relentless, blind pursuit of thinness. I ate a Spartan diet but lusted after rich desserts. A bone-thin body, completely under my command, could more than make up for the imperfections that did not fit my image of myself as a powerful, in-control-of-it-all person. The S on the T-shirt stands for Superwoman. I saw myself split into two equal but opposing forces. There was the me that was, if I could just get to it, perfect and beautiful. There was the me that threatened to overpower all else with its laziness, gluttony, ugliness, and general inferiority. (Ciseaux, 1980, p. 1469)

Annie's portrait and commentary highlight the distortions of self-image and the greatly impaired self-esteem that many anorexics suffer.

Diagnostic Criteria and Incidence

Anorexia nervosa is a *syndrome,* a collection of symptoms characteristic of a disorder, with the diagnostic criteria listed in Table 11-5. The overall incidence of anorexia nervosa is between .24

**TABLE 11-5
Diagnostic Criteria of
Anorexia Nervosa**

A. Age of onset prior to 25

B. Anorexia with accompanying weight loss of at least 25 percent of original body weight

C. A distorted attitude toward eating, food, or weight that overrides hunger, admonitions, reassurances, and threats
For example,
1. Denial of illness with a failure to recognize nutritional needs
2. Apparent enjoyment in losing weight with overt manifestations that food refusal is a pleasurable indulgence
3. A desired body image of extreme thinness with overt evidence that it is rewarding to achieve and maintain this state
4. Unusual hoarding or handling of food

D. No known medical illness that could account for the anorexia and weight loss

E. No other known psychiatric disorder

F. At least two of the following manifestations:
1. Amenorrhea
2. Lanugo (downy hair on the body)
3. Bradycardia (persistent resting pulse of 60 or less)
4. Episodes of bulimia (uncontrolled excessive eating without satiation)
5. Periods of overactivity
6. Vomiting (often self-induced)

Source: Feighner, Robins, Guze, Woodruff, Winoker, & Munoz, 1972.

and 1.6 per 100,000 population; of these cases, between 5 and 15 percent are males. Almost 100 percent of the females who have anorexia become amenorrheic—they stop menstruating. As indicated earlier, "anorexia" is a misleading label for this disorder; the individuals do not have a lack of hunger but rather an unrealistic desire to be thin (Bemis, 1978).

Developmental History of Anorexia Nervosa

Premorbid Phase   Before onset of the disorder, future anorexics are often described by parents and friends as well-behaved, introverted, and conscientious. They are often highly intelligent, shy, and anxious individuals. The first manifestations of the disorder typically appear when adolescents encounter situations where their skills are inadequate. Any major life change will qualify as such a situation, including puberty or entry into college (Bemis, 1978).

Close examination of several case studies indicates that these generalizations apply to a large number of cases (Bruch, 1978; Norris & Jones, 1979). Examination of the backgrounds of 10 anorexic girls, for example, revealed some common personality features. All were described as shy and solitary individuals. All were competitive—with respect to schoolwork, sports, and domestic tasks. The competitive aspect of premorbid anorexics may stem from an insecurity that results in constant comparison to others. Yetta illustrates this form of insecure competition.

Her continuous concern was, "What do they say about me, do they like me, do they think I'm right?" When going out as a teenager she might change as often as three or four times, comparing her outfit to what the others wore and making sure that she was as well or better dressed.

Constant comparison of herself to others interfered with her adjustment at college. While listening to a lecture she would be watching the faces of other students, trying to evaluate whether they understood it better than she did, whether they were concentrating more and would write better examination papers, with the result that she could scarcely follow what was going on and did rather poorly. (Bruch, 1978, p. 52)

While competitive, anorexics are rarely described as overtly aggressive. As their parents said, "Their children had functioned at a well-socialized level until round about puberty when they started withdrawing" (Norris & Jones, 1979, p. 104).

Case Studies   The most extensive case-study reports are those of Bruch (1978). She described the syndrome of anorexia nervosa based on observation of 70 patients. In addition to the physical symptoms described above, Bruch listed three major areas of psychological disturbance that these patients exhibited. First, the anorexics had severe distortions of their body images. They viewed themselves as too plump, despite the fact that they were on the verge of starvation.

Anorexics insist they cannot "see" how thin they are, that all the concern others express is unrealistic because they are just fine, just right, that they look the way they want to look; they even claim they are still "too fat." (Bruch, 1978, p. 81)

Second, anorexics grossly misinterpreted internal cues relating to hunger, often claiming that they did not actually feel empty, or that they reinterpreted the associated cues as fullness rather than emptiness. Tania, for example, had "trained" herself to perceive her internal bodily cues to fit the anorexic syndrome. She would eat a single M&M candy very, very slowly, telling herself that she was getting full from it (Bruch, 1978).

Third, the anorexics felt a deep sense of their own ineffectiveness. They felt that they had little ability to control their own lives. It is this aspect of the psychological matrix of symptoms that Lawrence (1979) called the central paradox of anorexia nervosa. Anorexics are able to exert powerful, almost unbelievable control over food and weight, and yet feel that they have little control over their own lives.

When anorexics talk about control, they invariably mean the power to regulate, command and govern their own lives and actions. They generally fail to do this by turning outwards and engaging with the world on their own behalf. Instead, they exercise self-control, which we might understand as power turned inwards. (Lawrence, 1979, p. 93)

Prognosis Approximately two-thirds of adolescent anorexics show some improvement or recover completely. The outcome for the remaining one-third is chronic illness or death (Bemis, 1978). Among the most important studies of anorexia nervosa are those aimed at isolating factors associated with these outcomes. Early onset of the disorder is the factor most clearly associated with good prognosis. Among the likely factors for poor prognosis are parental conflict, late onset of the disorder, vomiting, laxative abuse, and presence of obsessive-compulsive symptoms (Bemis, 1978).

Family Backgrounds of Anorexics

Adolescents who grew up in upper-middle-class or upper-class homes are more likely to become anorexic than those from lower socioeconomic groups. In addition, parents of anorexics are somewhat older than average. Parents' average ages at the birth of the anorexics among Bruch's (1978) 70 cases were 38 for fathers and 32 for mothers. Also among her cases, there were conspicuously few sons. More than two-thirds of the families had no sons at all.

The set of factors associated with anorexics' families, which we have just described, may produce unrealistic achievement pressures for the children. Bruch suggested that these daughters felt they had to prove something to their families, as payment for their relatively privileged upbringing. As Ida, one of Bruch's patients, put it, "If you are given much, much is expected of you" (Bruch, 1978, p. 26).

Preanorexic children often spend their childhoods as overconformists. The adjectives "passive" and "dependent" are often applied to these children. It is as if the children are attempting to do everything their parents want them to do, be everything they want them to be, without developing a sense of who they are themselves. Self-starvation itself can be viewed as overconformity to the cultural ideal of thinness, especially for females.

There is a psychological dynamic to the development of anorexia, revolving around the issue of self-control. Consider a teenage girl from an upper-middle-class family. She had tried throughout childhood to be the perfect daughter by passively adopting all the behaviors she thought her parents expected of her. She became shy, dependent, and withdrawn, feeling that she had no control over her life, that her life was not her own. She also felt that she had little effect on her parents.

At puberty, she began to change, to mature into a young woman. The fear of leaving the safe haven of childhood is real to many adolescents, and especially so to anorexics. They feel helpless and inadequate to the task of meeting the demands of the status transition from childhood to adolescence. One way out of this control dilemma is to exert powerful and abnormal control as best they can, by controlling their eating and bodily functioning. Paradoxically, the assertion of self-control also begins to control parents in a powerful new way. Parents become alarmed at the development of the disorder. They may restructure the household routine around the anorexic and her special needs. Bruch described this state of affairs succinctly with the following:

When positive self-assertion becomes unavoidable for a child, when an attitude of fitting in is no longer appropriate, the severe deficiencies in the core personality become apparent. The weight loss accomplishes much: the parents are drawn back into being protective, not demanding, toward the child who for the first time experiences that she has power and is in control. Many anorexics explain why they cling to the illness with the simple statement, "If I were well they would not pay attention to me," or "They won't love me anymore." (Bruch, 1978, pp. 94–95)

SUBSTANCE USE AND SUBSTANCE ABUSE

It is during the adolescent years that many people begin to use and abuse drugs and alcohol. In recent years, the youthful population has become more drug oriented than previous generations. In this section, we are concerned primarily with the most popular substances which adolescents use—alcohol and drugs, such as marijuana, hallucinogens, and amphetamines. For an indication of the extent of substance use among adolescents, we first examine questionnaire responses from national samples of high-school students (Johnston, 1973; Bachman, Johnston, & O'Malley, 1980). Figure 11-9 shows the percentage of high-school seniors who have ever tried the substances indicated (namely, alcohol of any kind, ciga-

**FIGURE 11-9
Percentage of high-school seniors who have ever used various drugs.**

(From Johnston, 1973; Bachman et al., 1980.)

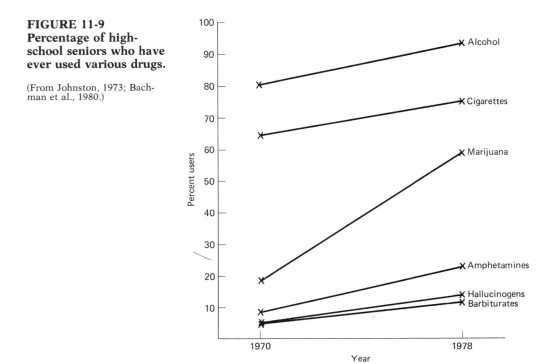

rettes, marijuana, amphetamines, barbiturates, and the class of drugs known as hallucinogens—LSD, mescaline, peyote, psilocybin, PCP). The data are presented for 1970 and for 1978 cohort groups.

Every substance surveyed is used by a larger percentage of high-school students now than just a few years ago. By far the greatest increase in incidence of use is shown for marijuana: Only about one-fifth of the high-school seniors of 1970 admitted using marijuana, whereas about 60 percent of the 1978 graduating class had used this drug. Increases in incidence of use of the other substances is modest but consistent.

Alcohol Use in High School

The incidence of alcohol use in high school is strikingly high, as Figure 11-9 indicates. More adolescents have tried alcohol than any other drug, including cigarettes. Most adolescents have tried alcoholic beverages at least once; indeed, adolescents generally drink moderately and responsibly (Barnes, 1977; Finn, 1979). However, a substantial number of high-school seniors could be considered problem drinkers. For example, seniors were asked the following question in the Youth-in-Transition survey:

More adolescents have tried alcohol than any other drug, including cigarettes. Although most adolescents drink responsibly, a substantial and increasing minority are problem drinkers.

(Photo copyright © 1980 by John Halaska/Photo Researchers, Inc.)

Think back over the last two weeks. *How many times have you had five or more drinks in a row? (A drink is a glass of wine, a bottle of beer, a shot glass of liquor, or a mixed drink.) (Bachman et al., 1980, p. 44)*

Among these high-school seniors, 40 percent had had five drinks in a row at least once; another 5½ percent had drunk this much six or more times in the last 2-week period—about every other day or even more often (Bachman et al., 1980).

Frequent excessive drinking is more common among high-school males than females. More than half of the males (51.4 percent) but less than a third of the females (29.6 percent) had drunk five or more drinks in a row during a recent 2-week period. Excessive drinking was also far more common among white students than among blacks (42.9 percent versus 19.3 percent, respectively).

Over the last few years, there has been a trend toward a greater incidence of excessive drinking among both males and females in high school, and even earlier, in the junior high-school years. Among 7th-graders, 25 percent report getting drunk once a year, while among high-school students generally, 5 percent are drunk as often as once a week. About 1 out of 15 college students get drunk once a week or more (Finn, 1979). Figure 11-10 shows the percentages of male and female students in junior and senior high who reported that they had ever been drunk. The trend toward ear-

FIGURE 11-10
Percentages of students in junior and senior high school who report that they have been drunk.

(From Demone & Wechsler, 1976.)

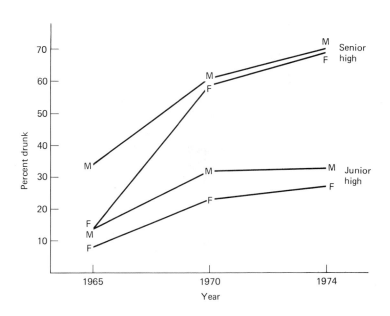

lier experimentation with excessive consumption of alcoholic beverages over the last few years is clear. Furthermore, there is a trend toward intergender convergence in drinking, especially in the senior high-school years (Demone & Wechsler, 1976).

Problems within the family once again seem to be related to youthful drinking. Comparisons between young alcoholics and alcoholics over 30 revealed that the young alcoholics had a higher rate of separation from their fathers before the age of 15; in addition, their fathers were more likely to have been heavy drinkers themselves (Rosenberg, 1969). These comparisons suggest that motivations for problem drinking are different for adolescents than they are for older people in some important respects.

In another search for correlations of drinking with predictive experiences (Moos, Moos, & Kulik, 1976), more than 1,200 college students were classified as abstainers, moderate drinkers, or heavy drinkers. Heavy drinkers were defined as students who "often" drank beer, wine, and hard liquor in senior high school. Questionnaire responses about background and behavior differed among the groups. Heavy drinkers reported behavior in a somewhat negative cluster: They valued academic achievement less (especially the males); they used more common drugs such as NoDoz, laxatives, and tranquilizers; they had poorer general health, reporting more aches and pains, headaches, and anxiety; and they admitted more "impulsive deviance," such as oversleeping, missing classes, breaking school rules, and cheating on examinations. On the positive side, however, the questionnaires suggested that the drinkers were also more likely to have attended cultural activities such as art exhibits or museums; and they engaged in more social activities, such as attending parties (Moos et al., 1976). For some adolescents, alcohol may provide a beneficial "time-out" from the pressures they feel at home and in school (Finn, 1979).

Detecting Adolescent Alcoholism The National Institute on Alcohol Abuse and Alcoholism has estimated that 1 in 10 adolescents is or will be alcoholic. These figures are alarmingly high. As with suicide, there are some signs of problem drinking among adolescents for which concerned friends and relatives can be alert (Table 11-6). Problem drinking in adolescence can be a sign that some serious problems exist for the adolescent. Many adolescents drink to relieve feelings of shyness, loneliness, depression, or anxiety. Problem drinking can be viewed as a symptom of these underlying psychological and interpersonal problems.

TABLE 11-6
Warning Signs of
Problem Drinking in
Adolescence

Falling grades

Deteriorating penmanship

Short attention span

Absence and tardiness from school

Inability to handle frustration

Constant changes in close friendship groups

Irritability with family members and with previous friends

Suspiciousness of friends, students, teachers

Rebelliousness

Giggling and giddiness

Low perseverance

Lying to parents and teachers

Impulsive behavior

Frequent trips to physician or school nurse

Promiscuity

Source: Dykeman, 1979.

Drug Use
in High School

As Figure 11-9 indicates, the order of frequency of drug use during the decade of the 1970s has remained the same: alcohol, tobacco, marijuana. The greatest *increase* in use, however, is for marijuana. More than one-half of all adolescents have tried marijuana by the time they graduate from high school.

By the late 1970s, a substantial segment of the high-school population was using marijuana on a daily basis (Figure 11-11). Almost 10 percent of high school seniors said that, on the average, they smoked four or more marijuana cigarettes a day during the most recent 1-month period (Bachman et al., 1980).

In general, the following assertions seem to apply to illicit drug use among adolescents. The use is more common among boys than among girls; rates of use are higher among whites than among blacks; and there is a steady increase in incidence of drug use from the lower to the upper grades in school. Further, the primary source of drugs for adolescents is the peer group (Gossett, Lewis, & Phillips, 1971; Bachman et al., 1980; Thompson, Smith-DiJulio, & Matthews, 1982).

The above assertions apply to illegal drugs as a class, including marijuana, amphetamines, hallucinogens, and barbiturates. Incidence of use of all these drugs among adolescents has increased over the last decade, although increases in marijuana use are the most striking.

FIGURE 11-11
Frequency of marijuana use among high-school students. Percentages of students supplying various answers to the following question:

During the last month, about how many marijuana cigarettes (joints, reefers), or the equivalent, did you smoke a day, on the average? (If you shared them with other people, count only the amount you smoked.)

(From Bachman, Johnston, & O'Malley, 1980.)

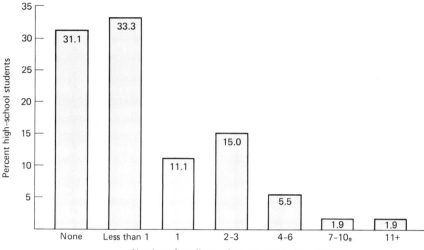

Correlates of Drug Use among Adolescents Much of the research into the phenomenon of adolescent drug use has been a search for factors associated with use. A typical study, for example, is that of Lawrence and Velleman (1974). These researchers gave questionnaires on a variety of topics, including drug use, to 1,416 high-

Adolescents sharing a "joint" at a rainy football game. Although the order of frequency of drug use—alcohol, tobacco, marijuana—has remained the same with adolescents through the 1970s, the greatest *increase* in usage is with marijuana: More than one-half of all high-school students try marijuana prior to graduation.

(Photo by Andre Sacks/Editorial Photocolor Archives, Inc.)

school students outside of New York City. The questionnaires also contained items about parents' habits. High correlations were found between parents' habits and student drug use: Legal parental drug use, such as use of cigarettes, alcohol, and prescription pills, was strongly associated with illegal drug use among the students. This was especially so in the case of the mother. Other factors associated with student drug use in this study were parents' marital problems, including divorce, and use of drugs among peers. In general, drug use among peers is one of the strongest factors associated with adolescent drug use (Thompson et al., 1982).

Parents provide role models for their adolescent offspring with respect to drug use. Adolescents whose parents use or abuse legal drugs, such as alcohol, appear to find general drug use more acceptable as a standard for their *own* behavior (Barnes, 1977). In addition, the emotional climate within the home seems to affect the psychological status of the adolescent. Family disharmony favors the development of emotional difficulties that may become associated with drug use, as well as other adjustment difficulties for the adolescent.

Escaping from emotional difficulties is, however, only one of the possible motivations adolescents have for using drugs. A set of rather desirable personality correlates of marijuana use was found using the California Personality Inventory (Hogan, Mankin, Conway, & Fox, 1970). "In comparison with nonusers, [marijuana users] are more socially skilled, have a broader range of interests, are more adventuresome, and more concerned with the feelings of others" (Hogan et al., 1970, p. 63). Adolescents who use marijuana are more likely to have jobs than nonusers (Thompson et al., 1982); the effect of the working on drug use apparently goes beyond the obvious relationship between having a job and having more money to spend (Steinberg, Greenberger, Garduque, Ruggiero, & Vaux, 1982).

On most surveys, adolescents who use only marijuana score about the same on standard personality profiles as students who do not use drugs. Multiple-drug users generally appear more likely to have personality difficulties. For example, 100 drug users and 100 college students who did not use drugs were given the MMPI—Minnesota Multiphasic Personality Inventory. Multiple-drug users had a higher incidence of abnormal personality profiles, while users of marijuana only were indistinguishable from nonusing college students (McAree, Steffenhagen, & Zheutlin, 1972). Another study indicates that marijuana users are no more likely than nonusers to have impaired parental identifications or other personality-related characteristics, although the likelihood of such characteristics being present in MMPI scores appears to increase with *frequency* of drug use (Brill, Crumpton, & Grayson, 1971).

In a very detailed study of psychological factors associated with drug use (Paton & Kandel, 1978), secondary-school students were classified on the basis of psychological test scores. The sample of more than 8,000 students was divided into low, medium, or high scorers on depression, and low, medium, or high scorers on norm-lessness. Students were then asked how many times they had used several substances, including drugs such as marijuana and amphetamines. The data show a strong relationship between drug use and depression and normlessness. Almost twice as many of the students who scored high on depression and on normlessness said that they had been multiple drug users in comparison to the nonusers. The relationship between depression and drug use was especially evident among adolescent girls. The relationships between psychological states, such as depression, and drug use are suggestive, but it is important to keep in mind that cross-sectional data of this type cannot reveal whether the psychological states *precede* or *follow* the drug use. As in all correlational studies, it is impossible to demonstrate cause-and-effect relationships.

With the increasing prevalence of drug use among adolescents, motivations for getting involved are likely to become more and more related to peer pressure and conformity, rather than to personality pathologies or to inadequate parental role models. As we saw in Chapter 7, use of marijuana is more strongly related to friends' drug use than to any other variable, including parents' values.

SUMMARY

1. Although maladjustment and pathology are not the most common styles of making the transition from childhood to adulthood, they do occur with increasing frequency. Four major problems of adolescence serve as a focus for discussion: schizophrenia, depression and suicidal behavior, anorexia nervosa, and substance abuse.

2. Schizophrenia is a serious psychiatric disturbance characterized by impaired intellectual functioning, disturbed affect, and impaired social interaction. This disorder accounts for 8–10 percent of psychiatric diagnoses among adolescents.

3. Adolescent schizophrenics, compared to adults with the same

disorder, have a poorer prognosis. The onset of schizophrenia is harder to detect among adolescents than adults.

4. Behavioral signs of schizophrenia may appear in childhood or early adolescence, prior to onset of the disorder. Approximately one-third to one-half of preschizophrenic adolescents are identifiable as "deviant" during childhood.

5. The likelihood of making a good adjustment is poorer for adolescent schizophrenics than it is for adolescents with other psychiatric problems. Prognosis is poorer for younger than older adolescents. The seriousness of the disorder is in part a function of the age of onset.

6. Depression is a relatively rare diagnosis among adolescents, although it may be a common psychological experience. Adolescent depressives are less likely than their adult counterparts to admit their strong feelings of worthlessness, and more likely to "act out" their depression. Behavioral manifestations of depression include drug abuse, alcohol abuse, promiscuity, and suicide attempts.

7. Suicidal behavior among adolescents is accompanied by serious depression in about 80 percent of cases.

8. In the last 25 years, suicide rates among adolescents have more than doubled. The increase in suicidal behavior had been especially dramatic among adolescent males. Estimates are that 1 out of every 1,000 adolescents attempts suicide each year; many of them become actual suicides. Furthermore, the average age of persons attempting suicide has decreased in recent years.

9. Many psychologists believe that alienation may be a mediating factor in adolescent suicidal behavior. Several studies have suggested that family problems are also important contributing factors. An attempted suicide may be a radical attempt to communicate to other family members that something is wrong.

10. Suicidal adolescents show some evidence of disordered thinking. They appear to be more rigid thinkers, refusing to consider alternative solutions; and they appear to view the world dichotomously, admitting no compromises between happiness and despair.

11. Several misconceptions have arisen in connection with adolescent suicide, including the notion that those who talk about su-

icide are not likely to try it. In fact, the talk is probably an attempt to communicate a serious problem—an attempt which may culminate in suicide if no help is forthcoming.

12. Anorexia nervosa is a serious eating disorder that primarily affects adolescent girls. Anorexics may literally starve themselves to death, although they are often preoccupied with food-related thoughts. Some anorexics engage in binge-eating, followed by self-induced vomiting to avoid weight gain.

13. Prior to onset of anorexia, individuals who subsequently develop the disorder tend to be well-behaved, shy, and introverted. The disorder is often first observed when adolescents encounter situations for which their interpersonal skills are inadequate. Moving to a new school, beginning college, and attaining puberty are common eliciting events.

14. Bruch has provided the most extensive case studies of anorexics. She found three areas of psychological disturbance commonly accompanying anorexia. First, anorexics have severe distortions of their body images, often seeing themselves as too plump. Second, they often misinterpret their own internal hunger cues, redefining them as feelings of fullness. Third, they express strong feelings of inadequacy and ineffectiveness.

15. Two-thirds of anorexics improve or recover. The remaining one-third suffer chronic anorexia or death. Early onset of the disorder is a major factor associated with a favorable prognosis.

16. Families of anorexics are usually in upper middle-class groups. Anorexic teenagers often feel strong achievement pressures which they are unable to meet. Ironically, they feel they have no self-control, at the same time they exercise intense control over food intake.

17. A larger percentage of adolescents now use alcohol and drugs than in previous years. There is more widespread use of all classes of drugs and alcohol now than just a few years ago.

18. The most frequently used substance among teenagers is alcohol. A substantial proportion of high-school seniors are problem drinkers, especially males.

19. Drinking among adolescents often is associated with family problems, such as parental separation or parental alcoholism.

20. Drug use, like alcohol use, is more common among adolescent boys than girls, and more common among whites than blacks.

21. Drugs are more commonly used by adolescents whose parents have marital problems, including divorce. However, users of marijuana only—as opposed to multiple-drug users—are indistinguishable from nonusers on personality and background questionnaires.

OUTLINE

12. EDUCATIONAL EXPERIENCE

In October 1957, the Space Age was dramatically ushered in with the launching of Sputnik I by the Soviet Union. Critics of American education argued that schooling in the United States was inadequate to the needs of advanced technology, leaving American students behind their Russian counterparts. Americans, it was feared, were losing the space race because they had not been prepared in school to solve the intellectual puzzles required by the highly complex aerospace field. They also feared that the United States would fall behind in other strategic fields, such as medicine and defense.

A panel of experts in the field of education was appointed, and convened in 1959 at Woods Hole, Massachusetts. The Woods Hole Conference duly studied the problem of education in the United States, and recommended sweeping reforms of the educational system, especially in the teaching of science. Many of their recommendations were translated into educational practice in the early 1960s. Rote memorization was minimized in favor of more global conceptualization, particularly in the teaching of arithmetic. Parents complained that they could not comprehend the "set theory" their children were encountering, even in the early grades. Educational theorists, however, were convinced that this form of presentation was more friendly to the young child's level of psychological functioning than the old system, and in the long run would make higher, abstract mathematics more accessible to more students.

In English composition, too, global content and ideas, rather than mechanics of grammar and spelling, were emphasized. Classroom ecology came under closer scrutiny, and the open classroom replaced the more traditional regimentation in educational environments. Open classrooms, in which a student selects an activity and progresses individually, reflected the "discovery" of cognitive stages and the importance of individual readiness.

The United States ultimately won the race to the moon, a national goal made explicit in the 1960 Inaugural Address of President John F. Kennedy. National goals in education appear not to have fared so well. A 4-year study underwritten by the United States Office of Education, and published in 1975, examined the performance of adults aged 18–65 on questions and tasks encountered in everyday life. The results were summarized as follows:

More than 23 million Americans—one of every five adults—cannot read, write or compute well enough to function effectively in today's world. Forty million more possess just the minimal skills necessary for survival. ("A Nation of Dunces," 1975)

Standardized test scores also suggest problems in education. Aptitude tests are distinguished from achievement tests, which measure a person's progress, or achievement, in a given subject matter following educational intervention. Aptitude tests were designed to measure a person's ability for subsequent achievement, and are used as one selection factor by college- and graduate-school admissions boards and some personnel offices. They are not, however, independent of previous educational experience.

Between 1960 and 1980, the average verbal and mathematical scores on the Scholastic Aptitude Test (SAT) declined dramatically (see Figure 12-1). The decline began in 1962, and has continued without reversal since then. No satisfactory explanation has been found for the alarming downward trend in aptitude test scores. However, four factors have received prominent attention: changes in the test itself, changes in patterns of television viewing, changes in the population taking the test, and changes in educational practices.

The College Board, which oversees the administration of the test, has conducted research that indicates that the drop in scores is not due to a tougher test; high-school seniors in 1975 who took parts of older versions of the test did not do as well as students who had originally taken that version. Some critics of modern society have hypothesized that greater amounts of leisure time devoted to television viewing, to the exclusion of recreational reading, might be a factor in the overall decline in verbal abilities. However, patterns of television viewing have probably not changed dramatically between 1960 and 1980, and would therefore not explain the continuous de-

FIGURE 12-1
Decline in average SAT scores for college-bound high-school seniors. Between 1960 and 1980, the average quantitative score (Q) declined 32 points; the average verbal score (V) declined 53 points.

(From *The New York Times*, September 7, 1975; *The Washington Post*, October 5, 1980.)

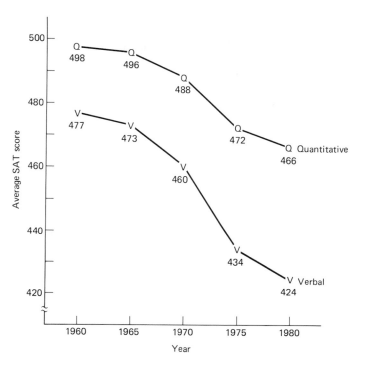

cline in scores, unless the quality of television has also continuously declined.

Students from a wider spectrum of the population are now going to college than in previous years. Larger numbers of individuals from diverse backgrounds are therefore now taking the test. The College Board's analysis of the distribution of scores indicates that this fact does not account for the trend in test scores, however, for there are fewer individuals scoring in the high range on the test, and at the same time, more are scoring in the lower range. Between 1974 and 1975, for example, 20 percent fewer students scored above 600 on the SAT verbal test, and 8 percent fewer students scored that high on the mathematical test (Fiske, 1975). Furthermore, a sample of high-school students who were not going on to college showed a similar distribution of scores; the higher-scoring students are not differentially dropping out of the college-bound population.

Changes in educational practice, which are more difficult to isolate and test, have provided the explanation favored by many observers of the SAT decline. The school system has once again become something of a scapegoat, much as it did following the Sputnik launch in 1957. In fact, the initial decline in scores coincided with the introduction of postSputnik educational reforms in the United States.

Adolescents spend a large proportion of their time in school, and the institution therefore deserves close scrutiny. Critics of the social institution of high school, such as Edgar Friedenberg, say that it has been getting worse for years. The American high school "has always devoted itself to the interests of uniformity more than to individuality; but the uniformities used to be more *external* than they are now. . . . The school today is less a stew pot than a blender. What comes out, when it is functioning effectively, is not merely uniform but bland and creamy; by its very nature inimical to clarity, yet retaining in a form difficult to detect all the hostile or toxic ingredients present in the original mixture" (Friedenberg, 1959, p. 79). A recent graduate of an American high school, David Naimon, described school this way: "The basic motivating force in schools is fear. People are afraid of failure, so people do the minimum to get by and get a grade. . . . There's little emphasis on thinking for yourself—just spitting out random facts" (Morgan, 1980).

In this chapter we are concerned with the educational experience for adolescents. A first issue for discussion is educational attainment. Why do some adolescents drop out of high school, while others go on to graduate from high school and even attend college? What are some of the factors associated with different levels of educational attainment?

A second major issue concerns the effects of education. We are concerned with changes in adolescents as a function of the educational experience, including changes in attitudes and values, and changes in intellectual disposition.

SECONDARY EDUCATION IN THE UNITED STATES

The Woods Hole Conference was not the first attempt to examine the goals and practices of education on a national level. In 1893, Harvard's President Eliot chaired a group called the Committee of Ten, whose function was to take a hard look at secondary education in the United States. The Committee of Ten recommended no sweeping changes in high-school curricula; rather, they approved of the traditional academic orientation of high school (Kett, 1977).

In the 20th century, American business increasingly relied on a labor force that could come to grips with sophisticated technology. More years of formal educational training were assumed to be necessary for members of the labor force. As Kett put it, "Schools served the needs of business in a variety of ways. As the informal machine shop with a dozen journeymen and apprentices gave way to the modern business corporation, education provided a form of certification for young people. A diploma could act as a kind of letter of introduction" (Kett, 1977, p. 153).

In addition to greater emphasis placed on high-school diplomas for occupational certification, there was pressure to keep adolescents out of the labor force through compulsory education laws. The school board in Fall River, Massachusetts, described the educational mood in 1914: "The whole tendency of the times, therefore, is to drive children under sixteen out of work and into school" (Kett, 1977, p. 235). Enrollments in high schools expanded greatly between 1890 and 1920.

Functions of Secondary Education

An influential figure in the study of education in the United States was John Dewey (1966). Dewey felt that schools should integrate young people into work and family roles that they would hold in the larger society. Secondarily, schools should help to promote the intellectual and moral faculties of the individual student.

Observers of the institution of the American high school agree that its major function is to serve as an agent of socialization. "If the nation's youth are to have optimum preparation for their role in society, the question of their education is important at all levels—

High-school enrollments expanded greatly between 1890 and 1920. The driving force behind this expansion was society's desire to keep children under 16 in school and out of the labor force through compulsory education. Turn-of-the-century high schools were more regimented than they are today, as witnessed by this Massachusetts classroom, circa 1898.

(Culver Pictures, Inc.)

kindergarten through college—but particularly at the time of graduation from high school" (Trent & Medsker, 1969, pp. xviii–xix).

The historical trend toward increased education is consistent with the certification and socialization functions of high school. In this century, the percentage of the population aged 5–17 years has remained relatively constant; the percentage of this age group enrolled in high schools, however, has increased steadily (Figure 12-2). The high-school graduating class of 1899–1900 numbered 62,000. The graduating class of 1980–1981 numbered almost 3 million.

EDUCATIONAL ATTAINMENT IN THE 1980s

At the beginning of the decade of the 1980s, approximately 75 percent of 18-year-olds were high-school graduates (U.S. Bureau of the Census). The remaining 25 percent had dropped out of high school for one reason or another, although some of the dropout group can be expected to finish high school at a later date. About half of the high school graduates of the 1980s attend college in one of its many forms, from technical colleges to liberal-arts institutions. The remaining half of high-school graduates do something else—become full-time homemakers, enter the labor force, or go into military service.

FIGURE 12-2
A comparison of the percentages of persons aged 5–17 with the percentage of this age group enrolled in school, by academic year (1899–1900 to 1979–1980).

(From U.S. Bureau of the Census, *Historical Abstract of the United States, Colonial Times to 1970; Statistical Abstract of the United States, 1980.*)

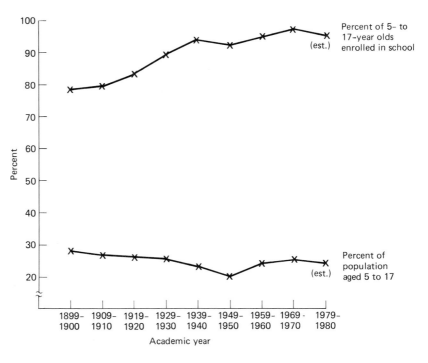

Half of the high-school graduates of the early 1980s attend college. Based on data from recent cohorts, we can estimate that about half of those who attend college will actually earn a Bachelor's degree (U.S. Bureau of the Census). Figure 12-3 shows the breakdown of expected educational attainment in the early 1980s in terms of 1,000 adolescents in the 18-year-old birth cohort. Of the 1,000 18-year-olds, about 800 will graduate from high school, 400 of those will go on to college, and 200 will actually attain the baccalaureate degree.

Sorting Mechanisms

In our examination of the educational system as it applies to American adolescents, we are interested in some of the factors that influence decisions about educational attainment. A variety of environmental forces—including peers, parents and other significant adults, and social class—impinge on adolescents' educational and vocational decision-making. These environmental forces serve as sorting mechanisms; they help to sort high-school students into educational and vocational channels. The impact of some of these sorting mechanisms is considered as we discuss different levels of educational attainment.

FIGURE 12-3
Slices of the educational-attainment pie for recent cohorts of 18-year-olds in the United States.

(From U.S. Bureau of the Census, *Statistical Abstract of the United States;* Trent & Medsker, 1969; Bachman, Green, & Wirtanen, 1971.)

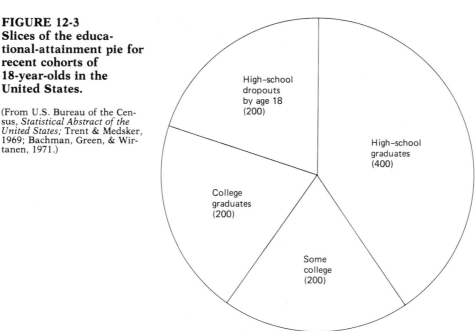

High-school dropouts by age 18 (200)

High-school graduates (400)

College graduates (200)

Some college (200)

High-School Dropouts   Most people believe that a high-school education is necessary for effective citizenship in a complex industrial society. In addition, there is a democratic ideal in American society that holds that schooling reduces social-class differences. As Douvan and Gold put it, "It is apparent to parents and youngsters alike that school provides the main path for social mobility in contemporary America" (Douvan & Gold, 1966, p. 500). Who, then, are the adolescents who drop out of high school, and why do they do it?

Two major longitudinal studies of high-school students provide information on dropouts. The first is the massive Project Talent study (Combs & Cooley, 1968) of nearly half a million high school students, begun in 1960. Ninth-grade students were selected in 1960, and followed up in 1964, when they would have been out of high school one year. From the sample of 440,000 9th-graders, 1,864 males and 1,817 females were selected who had dropped out of school before graduation. They were compared with random samples of 1,757 males and 2,056 females who completed high school but did not go on to college.

The second major longitudinal study is The Youth-in-Transition project (Bachman, Green, & Wirtanen, 1971), which we discussed in an earlier chapter (Chapter 10). A large group of 10th-grade boys was first interviewed as part of the Youth-in-Transition project in the fall of 1966, and again in each subsequent spring through 1970, 1 year after high school graduation would have taken place. One aspect of the study was dropping out of high school. Students who completed high school could be compared to dropouts on several measures prior to the actual event of dropping out. Unfortunately, no girls were included in this longitudinal study.

Three major classes of factors appear to be predictors of educational attainment. One class of variables concerns family background and includes such factors as socioeconomic status, discipline, and family stability. A second class of factors is labelled academic ability and includes grade failure, school attitudes, and intellectual ability. Academic ability may also be influenced by family background variables. A final class of factors, with unknown relationships to family background, falls under the heading "personality characteristics." The Youth-in-Transition project and the Project Talent study gathered information relevant to these factors with respect to the issue of dropping out of high school.

Family Background Characteristics Socioeconomic status exerted an effect on high-school boys' decisions to drop out of school. When socioeconomic status is defined as the combination of father's occupation, father's education, mother's education, and number of rooms per person in the house, there is a strong relationship to dropping out. Of those adolescents in the bottom sixth of the Youth-in-Transition sample in socioeconomic status, 23 percent dropped out of high school, compared to only 4 percent of the top sixth in socioeconomic status. In the Project Talent study, there was a significant relationship between dropping out of high school and lower socioeconomic status for girls, but not for boys (Combs & Cooley, 1968). Other studies have also confirmed the social-class effect (Havighurst, Bowman, Liddle, Matthews, & Pierce, 1962).

Race as a background factor has little power in predicting dropout rates by itself when socioeconomic status is controlled. Blacks from integrated schools have almost identical dropout rates to whites; blacks from segregated schools have higher dropout rates than whites (Bachman et al., 1971).

Other family background factors are also related to dropping out. For example, dropping out was about twice as likely for boys from broken homes as for those in intact families. The overall nature of family relationships is assumed to be a factor in educational attainment.

The better a boy reports getting along with his parents, the higher is his self-esteem, his self-concept of school ability, his attitude toward school, and his feelings of personal efficacy. The poorer the family relations he reports, the more likely the boy is to admit to delinquency, rebellious behavior in school, test anxiety, and negative school attitudes. (Bachman et al., 1971, p. 33)

One index of faulty family relationships is parental punitiveness, measured by a special scale of 10 items (Table 12-1). The dropout rate was lower in families where parental punitiveness was

TABLE 12-1
Items Comprising the Parental Punitiveness Index

1. How often do your parents completely ignore you after you've done something wrong?
2. How often do your parents act as if they don't care about you any more?
3. How often do your parents disagree with each other when it comes to raising you?
4. How often do your parents actually slap you?
5. How often do your parents take away your privileges (TV, movies, dates)?
6. How often do your parents blame you or criticize you when you don't deserve it?
7. How often do your parents threaten to slap you?
8. How often do your parents yell, shout, or scream at you?
9. How often do your parents disagree about punishing you?
10. How often do your parents nag at you?

Source: Bachman, Green, & Wirtanen 1971.

lower; at high levels of parental punitiveness, the dropout rate increased dramatically, as shown in Figure 12-4.

Academic Ability Factors   Measures of performance in school, as one might expect, are strongly related to dropping out of high school. More than half of the dropouts had failed at least one grade in school, compared to only 27 percent of the high-school graduates. Average grades in school, which are obviously related to grade failure, show the same overall relationship to dropping out. Measures of rebelliousness in school, including items about arguing with other students, goofing off in class, skipping school, and cheating, are also associated with dropping out. In interviews, students gave reasons for dropping out consistent with low academic ability. One said, "I was mostly just discouraged because I wasn't passing" (Bachman et al., 1971, p. 155).

Ability tests show a similar relationship to dropping out. Students who are lower in academic ability, as measured by standardized tests, are more likely to drop out. Among the 10th-graders in the Youth-in-Transition study who scored in the high-IQ range (125–150), only 7 percent dropped out of high school, in contrast to 33 percent of those who scored below 90 (Bachman et al., 1971). Among both male and female students in the Project Talent study,

FIGURE 12-4
Dropout rate as a function of parental punitiveness.

(From Bachman, Green, & Wirtanen, 1971.)

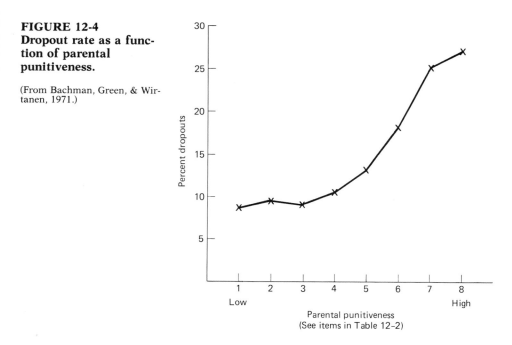

dropouts were of lower academic ability, as measured by a battery of ability tests. These differences are shown in Figure 12-5. Although there is a strong relationship between ability-test profiles and dropping out, some of the most able students were included in the dropout group in both major studies. Five percent of the male dropouts and 7 percent of the female dropouts were in the top quarter of ability (Combs & Cooley, 1968).

Personality Characteristics   Students in the Youth-in-Transition study were given Rotter's (1966) Internal–External Scale, a personality test measuring an individual's sense of the locus of control of reinforcement. Those who score high on the scale seem to believe that forces controlling their lives are external to themselves, in the hands of fate or chance. The students who were high "externals" on Rotter's test when they took it in 10th grade were more likely to drop out of high school than those who were low "externals" (Bachman et al., 1971).

The 10th-graders who subsequently dropped out of school were also lower in self-esteem than their counterparts who graduated. The low self-esteem preceded the actual event of dropping out. "Long before the events actually occurred, those destined to drop out indicated below average feelings of personal efficacy, while those bound for college were above average" (Bachman et al., 1971, p. 78).

FIGURE 12-5
Percentages of male and female dropouts in each quarter of ability. Students whose test profiles place them in the bottom quarter of ability are far more likely to drop out of school than those in higher quarters of ability.

(From Combs & Cooley, 1968.)

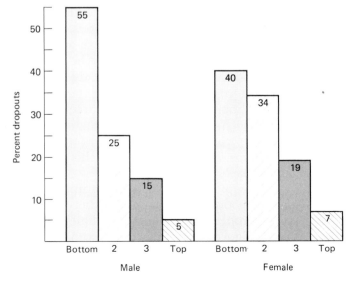

Students in the Project Talent study of dropouts were also given tests of self-perception. The graduates, in comparison to the dropouts, viewed themselves as more tidy, calm, vigorous, self-confident, and sociable. The dropout males (but not dropout females) scored higher on leadership and impulsiveness (Combs & Cooley, 1968). With the exception of the higher score of the male students on leadership, the personality and self-perception tests show a more negative profile for dropouts than for high-school graduates.

Finally, the future dropouts were more likely to report bodily ailments in 10th grade, such as headaches, nervousness, and insomnia, than their counterparts who stayed in school (Bachman et al., 1971).

Effects of Dropping Out of High School Given the high value our culture places on education, one would expect that the ramifications of dropping out of high school would be strongly negative. Although there are some differences between high-school dropouts and those who graduate from high school, they are not as striking as many had predicted.

We mentioned earlier that dropouts were somewhat lower in self-esteem than other groups of students, especially those who went on to college. While the self-esteem scores of dropouts are lower than their college-bound peers, they do not decrease after they have dropped out of school. In fact, the self-esteem level of all three groups—dropout, high-school graduate, college-bound—increases over time by about the same amount. Whatever the mechanisms for an association of self-esteem and dropping out may be, they *precede* the actual event (Bachman et al., 1971).

Other personality dimensions revealed that differences among the three groups of students were greater in 10th grade, before the students had dropped out, than they were 4 years after high-school graduation would have taken place. All groups of students became less "external" over time on Rotter's scale. Even academic values became more similar for the three groups during the intervening years (Bachman et al., 1971). One difference in social attitudes did emerge: Dropouts expressed more negative attitudes against minority groups than did the high-school graduates or the college students (Bachman et al., 1971).

Despite lower academic ability profiles, and despite the pattern of poorer self-perception, there are no striking differences between employed dropouts and high-school graduates in terms of income. Figure 12-6 shows the average annual income of the dropouts and graduates for the year 1964, one year out of high school (in 1964 dollars). Although the difference is not great, the male dropouts ac-

FIGURE 12-6
A comparison of the average annual salaries for male and female high-school dropouts versus high-school graduates. These data are based on a four-year follow-up of 9th-grade students who were studied in 1960. The average salaries are for the year 1964 and have not been adjusted to reflect current purchasing power.

(From Combs & Cooley, 1968.)

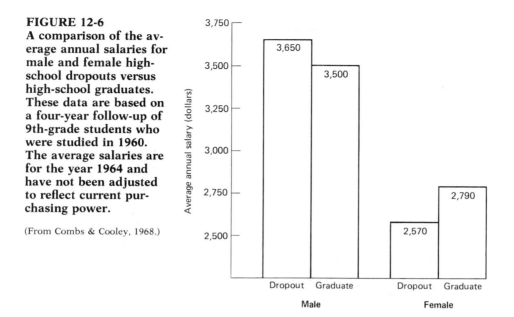

tually made more money than the high-school graduates for that year. Average annual salary for females was lower than for males overall, and lower for dropouts than for high-school graduates (Combs & Cooley, 1968).

The Youth-in-Transition students, who were all males, showed a similar income difference. The dropouts had a slightly *higher* average income than the high-school graduates. Furthermore, their satisfaction with their jobs was about the same as that of the high-school graduates (Bachman et al., 1971). Their higher incomes, in other words, are not the result of highly undesirable working conditions.

Comparison of dropouts and high-school graduates do show some important employment differences. One is the actual likelihood of getting a job in the first place, which of course is not a trivial difference. While 87 percent of the high-school graduates were fully employed four years after high school, only 71 percent of the dropouts were fully employed at that time.

The unemployment rate rose between 1980 and 1981 for those workers who had less than a high-school education. Unemployment was particularly high among young black high-school dropouts (U.S. Bureau of the Census, 1981).

Another major difference between high-school graduates and dropouts is the type of job a person can expect to obtain, irrespec-

A teenager selling news-papers on the streets of Chinatown in San Francisco. High-school drop-outs are far more likely to hold blue-collar or service jobs than high-school graduates. Furthermore, dropouts face a higher rate of unemployment and greater re-strictions on the types of jobs available to them.

(Photo copyright © by Freda Leinwand/Monkmeyer Press Photo Service)

tive of income. Table 12-2 shows the percentage of white and non-white graduates and dropouts in three major segments of the labor force: white collar, blue collar, and service/farm workers. Both white and nonwhite high-school graduates are more likely to hold white-collar jobs than their counterparts who dropped out of school. High-school dropouts are far more likely to hold blue-collar or service/farm jobs (Young, 1973).

Adolescents drop out of high school for a variety of reasons, as we have seen in this section. Many of the factors that impinge on adolescents and influence their decisions to drop out or stay in

TABLE 12-2
Percentage of White and Nonwhite High-School Graduates and High-School Dropouts in Three Major Segments of the Labor Force

	HIGH-SCHOOL GRADUATES		HIGH-SCHOOL DROPOUTS	
	WHITE	NONWHITE	WHITE	NONWHITE
White collar	51.7	41.0	13.1	11.1
Blue collar	35.4	40.5	65.8	58.9
Service/Farm	12.9	18.5	21.2	30.0

Source: Young, 1973.

school can be described as *sorting mechanisms*. Social class is a powerful sorting mechanism, as is ability measured by standardized tests. High-school dropouts appear to view themselves as "tracked" or "sorted" in a way that makes a high-school education irrelevant to their lives. As one dropout described school, "It didn't teach me true things. It didn't teach me how to cope with society once I got out of school doors" (Bachman et al., 1971, p. 155).

Cliques in High Schools As the functions of high school grew more diverse in the early 20th century (Kett, 1977), students divided themselves along social lines as well as academic tracks. Hollingshead was one of the first researchers to study clique formation in an American high-school. A high-school teacher in Hollingshead's Elmtown told him the following about cliques:

This school is full of cliques. You go into the hall, or the Commons Room between classes or at noon, and you will find the same kids together day after day. Walk up Freedom Street at noon, or in the evening, and you'll see them again. These kids run in bunches just like their parents. (Hollingshead, 1949, p. 204)

Hollingshead studied 259 cliques in Elmtown High School, and concluded that there were three major categories. The *elite* were the social leaders. They ran the extracurricular activities and were recognized as the social leaders by teachers as well as other students. The *good kids* were the majority of students at Elmtown, those who did not distinguish themselves in any particular way. The third group was the *grubby gang*, those who were bad for several reasons. Some were from lower socioeconomic strata and shunned for that reason; others were troublemakers in school itself.

More recent studies of high-school cliques have also found a small number of clique types in schools. Leona (1978), for example, examined cliques in a suburban Boston high school. In addition to the undistinguished majority of students, and the intellectual group of *smart kids*, there were *jocks*, mostly male students who were identified by their participation in athletics. There were *motorheads*, boys who were interested in working on cars more than any other pastime. And there were *druggies*, cliques of drug users including both male and female students.

Gifted High-School Students High schools have recently devoted more attention to gifted students, those who have superior academic ability (Hogan, 1980). Special programs have been created to help these students develop their potential as much as possible. In a typical enrichment program for gifted students (McGinn, Viernstein, & Hogan, 1980), 7th- and 8th-graders who scored very high on the SAT-Verbal test were placed in college-level courses in creative writing or in the social sciences. Despite their initial high SAT-Verbal scores, these students made impressive gains in verbal reasoning after their participation in the academic program (McGinn et al., 1980).

The educational track followed by gifted students is noticeably different from the tracks which other students pursue. A group of high-school students identified as National Merit Scholars were followed 8 years after high-school graduation. Among the males, only 6 percent had not achieved at least a Bachelor's degree, and 82 percent either had advanced degrees or were still in school. Comparable figures for females were 7 percent and 68 percent, respectively (Watley, 1969).

The Ecology of the High School

The educational system for adolescents in the United States has been described as a "main line with side tracks" (Kandel & Lesser, 1972). The main line of high-school education is a straight academic line leading to the high-school diploma. The diploma certifies to the community at large—and especially to prospective employers—that students have put in their required time. The experiences that students have in high school are very different, depending on the "side track" involved. Vocational and technical programs, as well as termination of study before graduation, are examples of side tracks.

For a significant number of students, high school is a place where they "go" during the day. Very little educational intervention takes place with these students. It is as if the educational system has written them off as hopeless. Schools, for them, are "temporary holding places on the way to adulthood," as Coleman (1975, p. 35) put it. Coleman, a major critic of the ecology of the American high school, has been concerned about the expansion of the role of "student" in American life. Other important figures in the field of adolescent psychology have shared Coleman's concern (e.g., Douvan & Gold, 1966).

Historical and technological changes in the way of life in our society created the need to remove adolescents from the labor force. In addition, the increasingly complex nature of society created a need for more education. The role of student was thus expanded, through compulsory education laws, to the point that young people now must spend a significant portion of their lives in the educational system. Coleman described the results of this expanded role for many of the students on side tracks in high schools.

The consequences of the expansion of the student role, and the action poverty it implies for the young, has been an increased restiveness among the young. They are shielded from responsibility, and they become irresponsible; they are held in a dependent status, and they come to act as dependents; they are kept away from productive work, and they become unproductive. (Coleman, 1975, p. 35)

Coleman also argued that schools gradually moved away from the teaching of basic skills—reading, writing, arithmetic—to specific occupational tutoring for some students and the teaching of topics irrelevant to occupational success to others. In the former category are high-school curricula in subjects from auto mechanics to cosmetology; in the latter are courses like music appreciation. High school as a main line with side tracks gradually evolved.

In the United States, high schools also differ a great deal in the ways they socialize adolescents depending on their overall educational philosophy. Alternative schools that reject the traditional "basics" of education are likely to emphasize relationship dimensions, such as involvement between students and teachers. Competition is emphasized in vocational high schools, and much less so in alternative schools (Trickett, 1978).

Schooling and Economic Production Bowles and Gintis (1976), in a critique of American education from an economic-system perspective, postulated a link between social class, economic production, and types of schooling. Structural features of schools, in their view, reinforce the production needs of the Capitalist economy. Students are tracked to provide training that will prepare them for specific jobs in the economy. Mickelson (1980) interviewed school personnel in two very different high schools in the Los Angeles area to test some of the notions presented by Bowles and Gintis (1976).

Morningside High School, in Inglewood, serves a predominantly working-class population. Yearly per pupil expenditure at Morningside was $1,300 in 1976. Beverly Hills High School is in an upper middle-class area, with a per pupil expenditure in 1976 of $2,129.

Morningside High has structural features that contrast sharply with those of Beverly Hills High. The former has a dress code, a closed campus surrounded by a fence, and assigned classes in which students have no choice of period or teacher. Beverly Hills High operates more like a college community. Students may schedule their own classes and move about freely on the open campus. There is no dress code; and classes meet on Monday, Wednesday, and Friday or on Tuesday and Thursday, rather than daily as at Morningside.

Mickelson felt that the structural differences of schools like Morningside and Beverly Hills High are part of larger social-class distinctions designed to track students and socialize them in ways appropriate to their tracks.

Thus vocational and general tracks, where most working-class adolescents are channeled, emphasize rule following and close supervision, whereas college-bound tracks, where more upper- and middle-class children [sic], are channeled, tend toward a more open atmosphere emphasizing internalization of norms and standards of control. (Mickelson, 1980, p. 84)

Decisions that high-school graduates make about college attendance are influenced by many factors, including financial considerations, scores on aptitude tests, family influences (such as belief in education), and motivation. Sorting mechanisms impinge on high-school graduates, however, channeling students in one direction or another. This channeling of students appears to be consistent with a view of education as guardian of an economic and philosophical system.

Beyond High School

High-school graduation marks an especially significant decision point in the lives of adolescents. It is a time when many young people decide to end their educations and attempt to find a place in the work force. As shown in Figure 12-3, this decision accounts for the largest number of young people at the present time; about 40 percent of the late adolescent population make this decision, according to recent trends provided by the Census Bureau. This effectively means that adolescence as a transitional stage between childhood and adulthood is coming to a close for the high-school graduates. They are ending their economic and, to some extent, their psychological dependence on their parents by accepting positions in the labor force. Two researchers in the field of adolescent education, James Trent and Leland Medsker, put it this way: "Graduation from high school marks a major point at which decisions must be made that may have a profound effect on a way of life and permanently shape a future career" (Trent & Medsker, 1969, p. 219).

High-school graduation is also a time when many adolescents decide to get married. For a substantial number of female adolescents, this means full-time work within the home, if not as members of the paid labor force. This decision also effectively closes the period of adolescence, although there may remain elements of psychological dependence on parents.

Half of the high-school graduates of the late 1980s will go on to further education at this important decision point. They will therefore remain semidependent on their parents, both financially and psychologically, for a few years more. Most college-bound students will continue to think of their parents' address as a home base to which they will periodically return over school holidays and summer vacations. Indeed, a large percentage of these students seeking postsecondary education will continue to live at home while they commute to classes.

Many of the same sorting mechanisms that influenced the decisions of younger adolescents to drop out of high school also impinge upon high-school graduates when they are deciding about college attendance. Among the most important of these sorting mechanisms are social class and ability level.

Social Class and Ability Level The social-class factor as a sorting mechanism for college attendance is even stronger than it is for dropping out of high school. In the top quarter of social class, far more students attend college than in the lowest quarter of social class. Among boys, 15 percent in the highest quarter attend college, compared to 2 percent in the lowest quarter. The figures for girls are comparable, 18 percent and 1 percent, respectively (Havighurst & Neugarten, 1962).

Flanagan and Cooley calculated probabilities of entering college by combining the effects of social class and of ability measured on standardized tests for the Project Talent students (Berg, 1970). Table 12-3 shows the strong effects produced by the two sets of measures. Low-ability, low social-class students are highly unlikely

TABLE 12-3 **Probability of Entering College, by Ability and Socioeconomic Status**		SOCIOECONOMIC QUARTER		
ABILITY QUARTER	LOW 1	2	3	HIGH 4
	MALES			
Low 1	0.06	0.12	0.13	0.26
2	0.13	0.15	0.29	0.36
3	0.25	0.34	0.45	0.65
High 4	0.48	0.70	0.73	0.87
	FEMALES			
Low 1	0.07	0.07	0.05	0.20
2	0.08	0.09	0.20	0.33
3	0.18	0.23	0.36	0.55
High 4	0.34	0.67	0.67	0.82

The samples from which these probabilities were calculated were high-school juniors in 1960.
Source: Berg, 1970.

to go to college (6 out of 100 males; 7 out of 100 females); high-ability, high social-class students are highly likely to go to college (87 out of 100 males; 82 out of 100 females).

Income, which is related to social class, is one factor in college attendance. For the high school class of 1972, median family income for those students who went on to college was $13,260; for high school graduates who did not attend college, median family income was $10,470 (Young, 1973). Differential income affects both physical access to college—in terms of having the opportunity to attend college in the absence of financial aid, and psychological access to college—in the sense of feeling that college is appropriate or inappropriate to one's station in life.

Social Class and Tracking   Critics of the American educational system argue that the power of social class and ability tests as sorting mechanisms is too strong, and that these factors have racist overtones. McClelland has argued that SAT tests, for example, "have served as a very efficient device for screening out black, Spanish-speaking, and other minority applicants to colleges" (McClelland, 1973, p. 1). Furthermore, he argues, even if minority students are good at taking tests, they may be screened out of college tracks because they are in the wrong social class. "Very few children, even with good test-taking ability, go to college if they are from poor families. One could argue that they are victims of oppression: they do not have the opportunity or the values that permit or encourage going to college" (McClelland, 1973, p. 6).

Consider the following example of the power of social class in tracking students into college. It is an example from Hollingshead's major anthropological study of American high-school students that we discussed earlier. A girl from a family of high social standing was given a college scholarship instead of a boy with equally good grades who was from a lower social class. One of the high-school girls described the incident to Hollingshead.

Joe Brummit was the brightest student in the class. He was a whiz at mathematics and science. He was awfully good in mechanics. Joe worked his last two years in high school in a gas station. He wanted to go to the university and study aeronautical engineering; now he is down at the Mill. His father's a carpenter, so he is not in a position to send him off. I suppose he should have been given the "Special College" Scholarship, but it was given to Willa Cross. I guess when you compare the two, Willa is more of an all-around person than Joe. (Hollingshead, 1949, p. 182)

A parent from a lower social class was more bitter in her description.

You see, that's the way things go around here. If you're inside the ring, you're all right, but if you're outside, they keep you out. (Hollingshead, 1949, p. 183)

College Attendance

Although about half of high school graduates are currently furthering their education beyond the high-school level, the attrition rate from college is fairly high. Approximately half of those who attend college ultimately graduate while the other half drop out along the way (U.S. Bureau of the Census; Trent & Medsker, 1969).

One might guess that financial need and academic difficulty would be strong predictors of college withdrawal; however, neither turns out to be a major factor (Trent & Medsker, 1969). Those students who score higher on aptitude tests are more likely to persist in college; however, when ability level is held constant, those who persist are just as likely to report academic difficulty as those who withdraw. Financial difficulty is reported by about the same proportion of persisters and withdrawers.

The major factors that appear to contribute to persistence in college can be subsumed under the heading "academic orientation" (Trent & Medsker, 1969). Those students who thought college was "extremely important," for example, were more likely actually to graduate from college than those who thought it less important. Among male students, 72 percent of those who ultimately graduated thought college was "extremely important" when they were still in high school, while only 44 percent of those who withdrew thought college "extremely important." Comparable figures for female students were 69 percent and 40 percent, respectively.

What students see as the main purpose of college is another aspect of academic orientation. Vocational training was seen as the main purpose by the largest number of students who subsequently withdrew from college. In contrast, gaining knowledge or an appreciation of ideas was viewed as the main purpose by the largest number of those who remained in college (Trent & Medsker, 1969).

There were also some differences between persisters and withdrawers in intellectual disposition, as measured by the Omnibus Personality Inventory. Persisters were more likely to prefer reflective, abstract thought, and to exhibit independent, unbiased, and flexible thought (Trent & Medsker, 1969).

Finally, a major indication of academic orientation is the amount of time students devoted to studying. Those students who persisted in college studied more than those who withdrew. Twice as many of the males who withdrew said they studied less than 10 hours a week; three times as many persisters as withdrawers reported studying 20 hours or more per week. Although differences in study time were not as striking among women, the trends were similar (Trent & Medsker, 1969).

Academic orientation is the by-product of early socialization and is itself influenced by the sorting mechanisms that we have already discussed in some detail. One of the most profound determinants of academic orientation is parental encouragement. Those students who persisted in college reported far more encouragement from their parents than those who subsequently withdrew. Furthermore, the lower socioeconomic level of the students' families, the less parental encouragement they reported, regardless of whether they withdrew or persisted. The academic orientation associated with completion of college is strongly associated with encouragement within the family (Trent & Medsker, 1969). Parental influences on adolescents' educational aspirations are far stronger than peer influences, and do not decline over the adolescent years (Davies & Kandel, 1981).

EFFECTS OF EDUCATION

One of the major figures in the study of the effects of education on students is Theodore Newcomb. A simple series of questions about students in educational institutions has guided his and others' research: "Have they changed between entry and exit? If so, how and why?" (Newcomb, 1978, p. 114). These are the issues with which we are concerned in the following section.

Measurement of the Effects of Education

Newcomb's questions are deceptively simple. As we have seen, adolescents attain different levels of education due to a variety of complex psychological and sociological factors. Background characteristics—what the student brings to the institution—interact with the characteristics of the institution itself to influence the type of changes students go through. In addition, there is a developmental component: Some of the changes that occur might well have occurred independent of the institution, simply through the processes of psychological maturation.

We are concerned with two broad classes of educational effects. First, we discuss *affective* changes that may result from education. Affective changes that have been studied include changes in self-concept, interests, values, attitudes, and beliefs (Astin, 1973). Second, we consider *cognitive* changes that may be a function of education. The most obvious cognitive changes concern growth of general knowledge or intelligence; in addition, we examine studies of changes in students' intellectual dispositions as a function of education.

Affective Changes

Changes in Values Much of the research on change in values during the college years has used paper-and-pencil scales to measure changes, scales such as the Allport-Vernon-Lindzey Scale of Values.

This scale breaks down values into six areas: theoretical, economic, aesthetic, social, political, and religious. Longitudinal studies of value changes in college typically administer the scale during the freshman year, and again during the senior year to assess changes over the 4 years of college. For example, Huntley (1965) gave the scale to freshmen at Union College and administered it again upon graduation. He provided data for over 1,000 college males, grouped according to their majors (Table 12-4).

Studies of value changes in college typically show an increase in aesthetic values, and a decrease in religious values, as Huntley found (see also Feldman & Newcomb, 1970). The increase in aesthetic values and the decrease in religious values appear to be independent of college major. Some of the other value changes are linked to the course of study one chooses, either because initial value differences impelled one to choose a field of concentration, or because special types of training were encountered in the major. Probably there is a little bit of both aspects operating. As Table 12-4 shows, theoretical values decreased for humanities majors and increased for science majors. Economic values decreased for all majors to some extent, but more so for humanities majors. Political values increased to some extent for all types of majors, but far more among humanities majors (Huntley, 1965).

The study of value changes described above included only college students. Therefore, it is impossible to assess value changes as a function of college attendance because nonstudents were not tested. Studies are available that indicate that some value changes are associated with college attendance. It is consistently reported, for example, that nonauthoritarianism increases with college attendance (Newcomb, 1978). (*Authoritarianism* includes feelings of dependence, punitiveness, compulsivity, dogmatism, and prejudice; *nonauthoritarianism* is its opposite.) Figure 12-7 shows changes in nonauthoritarianism for men and women who went to college in

TABLE 12-4
Changes in Values over the 4 Years of College

MAJOR	VALUE AREA					
	THEORETICAL	ECONOMIC	AESTHETIC	SOCIAL	POLITICAL	RELIGIOUS
Humanities	−2.95	−4.22	+12.18	−1.89	+2.53	−5.86
Social studies	−0.36	−0.20	+5.86	−0.20	+0.23	−5.63
Science	+2.23	−1.79	+5.30	−1.93	+0.36	−4.55

Source: Huntley, 1965.

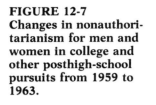

FIGURE 12-7
Changes in nonauthoritarianism for men and women in college and other posthigh-school pursuits from 1959 to 1963.

(From Trent & Medsker, 1969.)

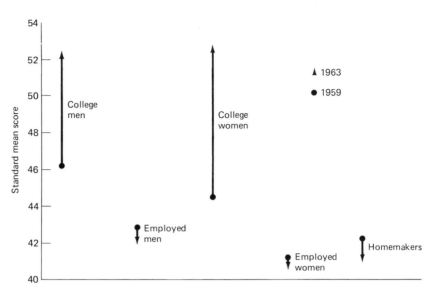

comparison to other posthigh-school pursuits. Although the high-school students who ultimately went to college scored somewhat higher on nonauthoritarianism to begin with, the differences were not striking. However, 4 years after high school, those students who went to college had increased in nonauthoritarianism, whereas all the other groups had decreased slightly (Trent & Medsker, 1969).

In general, noncollege youth of equivalent ages appear to be more traditional in their value orientation. They are more likely to express respect for authority, endorse law-and-order values, and support sexual conservatism (Thornburg, 1971). In comparison to high-school graduates who do not go on to college, college students become less judgmental and moralistic over time (Frantz, 1971). Although the evidence is less than perfect, studies suggest that college students, in comparison to youth of the same age who do not go to college, adopt values systems emphasizing existential moral relativism (Feldman & Newcomb, 1970).

The Youth-in-Transition study (Bachman et al., 1971) provides some empirical information on racial awareness by level of educational attainment in a longitudinal study. Questions were asked to assess the students' perceptions of racial discrimination in jobs, housing, and schooling. Students who pursued their educations in the years after high school perceived more racial discrimination; those who dropped out of high school or who ended their educations with high-school graduation perceived less racial discrimination over time (Bachman et al., 1971).

Political Knowledge and Awareness As we saw in Chapter 9 on political socialization, high school has a less powerful impact on students' political knowledge and beliefs than parents do. Some researchers (e.g., Jennings & Niemi, 1974) have concluded that the high-school civics curriculum has very little impact on students' political knowledge. Students and their parents do about equally poorly on a simple test of political knowledge (Jennings & Niemi, 1974).

Participants in the Youth-in-Transition study actually declined in their political knowledge during the late high-school and early posthigh-school years. Researchers asked these respondents periodically to name the President of the United States, the Secretary of Defense, the Secretary of State, and the two United States Senators from their own state. Although political knowledge measured this way decreased over time and finally leveled off, college students were more knowledgeable at each assessment than either high-school graduates or high-school dropouts (Bachman et al., 1971).

Political awareness, in contrast to political knowledge, appears to increase somewhat during the four years of college. Furthermore, political awareness is greater among college students than noncollege age-mates. Again, the changes are parallel for college and noncollege youth:

Although college appears to "press" students in the direction of greater political awareness, this change is actually no greater than that for noncollege persons. . . . Thus, the passage of time, in conjunction with other facets of life, is responsible for changes in political concern. (Rich, 1976, p. 75)

In interviews, high-school students were asked "What are your political beliefs?" Two typical answers were, "Most of the time I'm more liberal—as yet I haven't given politics much thought. . . . I don't care too much about that." "I can vote, but I don't want to." (Trent & Medsker, 1969, p. 1968). Political apathy was the usual stance of these high-school students.

In the arena of politics, it would appear that two parallel trends are operating. First, there are differences between students of different levels of educational attainment with regard to political knowledge. Longitudinal studies are consistent in their findings that college-bound students are more knowledgeable about political matters than either high-school graduates only or high-school dropouts. Nevertheless, neither of the three groups is as knowledgeable as one might hope; and for a few years in late adolescence, there even appears to be a decline in political knowledge.

The second trend in the political arena has to do with age-related changes. Political awareness increases at a parallel rate for all three educational-attainment groups. These changes appear to be age-related changes in political interest, rather than the effects of schooling per se.

Cognitive Changes

The most obvious place to look for changes in adolescents between entry into and exit from an educational institution is the store of knowledge the adolescents have. Interestingly enough, none of the major longitudinal studies of schooling has assessed factual knowledge obtained (Ellison & Simon, 1973). Many of the studies have tested students for overall intellectual ability; as we have seen, this factor serves as a powerful sorting mechanism for educational attainment. However, there are some intellectual-disposition factors that appear to differentiate between students who achieve different levels of education.

Intellectual Disposition Students who attend college and who remain until they achieve the baccalaureate degree have different scores on measures of intellectual disposition than their counterparts who drop out of college. College graduates prefer reflective thought and show more interest in ideas for their own sake. In contrast, college dropouts tend to evaluate ideas more for their practical significance (Trent & Medsker, 1969).

College dropouts also show less intellectual curiosity than their counterparts who finish college. The dropout students prefer structured, unambiguous situations, whereas the graduates seek out new ideas and situations (Trent & Medsker, 1969).

Perry's Scheme Research on changes in intellectual dispositions during the college years suggests that there is a developmental sequence in approaches to knowledge. William Perry interviewed students at Harvard College each year, beginning in their freshman year, to find out what was salient to the students themselves about their college experience. Although there is no single-track movement in intellectual disposition, there is a rough theme that can be isolated. Perry (1970) described his approach to studying the development of intellectual disposition this way:

Of course a person will use a variety of forms in construing different areas of his experience at any given time. However, we made the assumption in this study that within this variety it is possible to identify a dominant form (or central tendency among the forms) in which the person is currently interpreting his experience. (p. 3)

Perry argued that the forms of intellectual development used by undergraduates in his study are not limited to the college years. "We proffer our scheme of development for its more general implications. We presume its relevance to the understanding of the intellectual and ethical development of late adolescence in a pluralistic culture" (Perry, 1970, p. 3).

The main line of development in Perry's scheme has three main phases: dualism, relativism, and commitment. In the *dualistic phase*, students express frustration with college teachers who fail to provide the "correct" answers, as this freshmen did with the following:

A certain amount of theory is good but it should not be dominant in a course. I mean theory might be convenient for them, but it's nonetheless—the facts are what's there. And I think that should be, that should be the main thing. (Perry, 1970, p. 67)

Another freshmen provided this opinion of the courses he had encountered:

There seem to be so many conflicting doctrines and opinions that I guess that the tendency is just to keep quiet until you really know just what the answer is. (Perry, 1970, p. 87)

At least partly as a function of the educational experience, students begin to abandon the notion of dualism, in favor of a disposition to *relativistic* thinking. One sophomore described his relativism and its attendant questioning this way:

I think the main thing that was interesting this year was questioning basic assumptions. . . . It was interesting in anthropology, particularly, which I didn't go into very deeply, but what I saw is the very basic differences, things that never occurred to me to question before. I don't know whether I'm questioning them now, but at least I know that it's possible to question. That is a frightening thought to say it didn't occur to me to question. Sounds like 1984 or something. Well, it didn't feel out, or anything, before. So I'm sure there are things that I'm not questioning now that I should be. Whatever "should be" is. (Perry, 1970, p. 117)

This intellectual disposition is not limited to courses in anthropology. Rather, there is a wide range of application, even to the understanding of the world beyond the classroom.

Toward the end of college, for most students, there is a recognition that *commitments* have gradually been made. The awareness of commitments leads to a comforting sense of psychological identity and belongingness. One student, musing about his college experience, expressed it this way:

I've come to a fairly settled idea of what I want to do as far as my career is concerned, and also my general values have become oriented, kind of settled to some degree. Also one thing I've noticed, I've finally become at home. I feel at home in this atmosphere here, and coming from out where I do it took me quite a long time to do that. As far as my values are concerned, I guess in my junior year—hard to really pinpoint—I really severely questioned my basic beliefs about things. Intellectually there hasn't been any big jump. Ever since I came here, slowly I've learned new things. Slowly. (Perry, 1970, pp. 165–166)

Perry's scheme for intellectual development in late adolescence has many similarities to Erikson's model of identity development, which we discussed in Chapter 3. Both models view the adolescent as searching among alternatives and both recognize that commitment to one of those alternatives is a necessary intermediate step toward affirmation of identity, which becomes a life-long process rather than an unchanging status.

At present, very few empirical studies have been done to test Perry's ideas about intellectual dispositions in older adolescents. One such study, with only a small number of student participants, yielded information consistent with Perry's scheme (Kurfiss, 1977). Positions in Perry's scheme appeared to be sequential; however, they lacked the structural unity that one would expect for pure developmental stages. Recall that this was also an issue for Piaget's formal-operational stage, in terms of the lack of "structures of the whole," referred to in Chapter 5.

Despite the relative lack of empirical validation of the Perry scheme, it has been used in comparisons of distinct types of classroom styles. One such study (Clinchy, Lief, & Young, 1977) compared traditional and progressive high schools on the basis of Perry's positions. Sophomores did not differ with respect to their position in the scheme; seniors in the progressive school, however, were farther along in the scheme of intellectual disposition.

In a related study, classrooms within the same school system were manipulated with respect to Perry's ideas about intellectual change with education. Three groups of students were used. In an experimental group, students were taught by a teacher trained in Perry's different positions. This instructor challenged students by providing as much diversity in points of view as possible, combined with experiential learning. A traditional classroom employed traditional teaching methods under an instructor who had no knowledge of Perry's work. Students in a mixed classroom were taught by a teacher who knew Perry's work but who did not attempt to integrate it into the curriculum.

Figure 12-8 shows the average position movement in the three types of classroom. Far more movement occurred in the class-

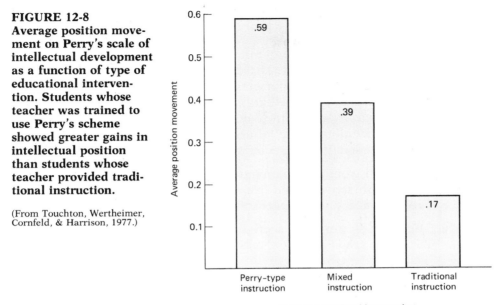

FIGURE 12-8
Average position movement on Perry's scale of intellectual development as a function of type of educational intervention. Students whose teacher was trained to use Perry's scheme showed greater gains in intellectual position than students whose teacher provided traditional instruction.

(From Touchton, Wertheimer, Cornfeld, & Harrison, 1977.)

rooms that employed information from Perry's scheme of cognitive development. In addition, instructors who were aware of Perry's work, even if they did not attempt to use it in the classroom, elicited more movement in intellectual disposition than instructors who were unaware of Perry's work (Touchton, Wertheimer, Cornfeld, & Harrison, 1977).

SUMMARY

1. Over the past 20 years, aptitude-test scores of American high-school students have declined. One explanation for this decline has been deterioration in the quality of secondary education.

2. During the 20th century, the emphasis of secondary education shifted away from "basics" toward occupational training and preparation for college. This emphasis is consistent with a view of education as serving a major socialization function, of preparing young people for future roles in society.

3. In the 1980s, approximately 20 percent of 18-year-olds are high-school dropouts. Another 40 percent terminate their education at high-school graduation, while 40 percent go on for further ed-

ucation. Of those who attend college, approximately half receive a baccalaureate degree.

4. Several factors operate to influence a given individual's level of educational attainment. These factors are referred to as *sorting mechanisms*. Three major classes of factors appear to serve as sorting mechanisms: (1) family background, including socioeconomic status, discipline, and family stability; (2) academic ability, including grade failure, school attitudes, and aptitude; and (3) personality characteristics.

5. In general, young people who are especially prone to dropping out of high school come from a lower socioeconomic status, a broken home, and a punitive household.

6. High-school dropouts score low on academic aptitude tests, have low grades, and express negative attitudes about school. These students are lower in self-esteem and other personality characteristics in comparison to high-school graduates.

7. Although high-school dropouts have a higher unemployment rate, those who do work make about the same money as high-school graduates. Dropouts are, however, more likely to work in blue collar and service occupations than high-school graduates.

8. High schools have been characterized as a "main line with side tracks." School tracks depend, at least in part, on sorting mechanisms leading to a particular position in the capitalist economic system.

9. Social cliques in high school also follow social class lines, as well as being grouped by interests such as sports or academic studies.

10. One high school track is for gifted students, a group receiving greater attention from educators. Gifted students—those who score high on aptitude tests—can profit from special educational intervention. Their educational career paths are distinctively different from those of other students.

11. High-school graduation is a very special decision point in young people's lives. Many adolescents get married or enter the full-time labor force following graduation. About 40 percent go on to college.

12. Sorting mechanisms, such as those we discussed in point 4, operate at the college-decision juncture just as they did earlier at the high-school level. There is an even stronger relation between

social class and college attendance than there is for dropping out of high school.

13. Once in college, persistence to the bachelor's-degree level is relatively independent of social class. *Academic orientation*, such as feelings about the importance of college, is more strongly predictive of persistence.

14. Students appear to change in complex ways, partly as a function of education itself. In the affective domain, college induces changes in values, such as an increase in aesthetic values and a decrease in religious values. College students are also less authoritarian and less conservative than noncollege peers.

15. In the cognitive domain, college appears to induce, to some extent, changes in intellectual disposition. College students prefer abstract, reflective thought in comparison to noncollege youth.

16. College students progress, during the course of the college years, from dualistic thinkers in right and wrong absolutes, to relativistic thinkers who recognize a legitimate diversity in points of view. A final element of cognitive style includes commitment to a position within this diversity.

A FINAL WORD: MOVEMENT INTO ADULTHOOD

Adolescence has been portrayed in this book as a time of transition between childhood and adulthood. A transition between two great developmental epochs implies psychological change. Indeed, there are important and dramatic changes in physical, cognitive, and social status in these transitional years. And yet, at the same time, human beings manage to hold onto a strong sense of individual continuity. We view ourselves as having continuous identities even when changes are relatively dramatic, as at puberty. In this epilogue, some themes of change and continuity in adolescence are reviewed.

THEMES OF CHANGE AND CONTINUITY

Physical Change and Continuity

The physical changes associated with puberty mark the beginning of the adolescent years. Within a relatively short span of time, adolescents undergo dramatic physical changes. They experience a growth spurt in height and weight; they develop secondary sex characteristics; they acquire reproductive capabilities. Puberty is perhaps the most abrupt physical discontinuity in the entire life span.

That most adolescents manage to endure these physical changes with relatively good grace is worthy of admiration and even a little awe. For those adolescents who are out of step with the modal developmental timetable that their peers are experiencing, the admiration is even more deserved. Research indicates that adolescents who are obviously out of step with the rest of their peers are unhappy and troubled. They feel different and isolated, and maybe a little weird. But there is resilience in human development. Negative effects of precocious or delayed puberty do not appear to be debilitating or even necessarily long-lasting.

Puberty also occurs within a cultural tradition. Societies offer their adolescents a set of norms for dealing with the discontinuity that puberty brings. Historically, nontechnological societies have provided rituals at the time of puberty to dramatize the status transition from childhood to adulthood. Whatever psychological hardship might be associated with physical discontinuity in these societies is relatively brief. In technological societies, such as the United States, norms specify a longer period of preparation for adult status; adolescents may experience several years of experimentation—especially in our age-graded educational system—before they make adult commitments.

Identity

The self-structure undergoes its greatest change in adolescence, when young people must integrate the physical changes of puberty with the social demands of upcoming adulthood. In particular, adolescents are concerned about occupational roles, and other expectations of adulthood. It is this state of affairs that led Erik Erikson to describe late adolescence as a period of identity crisis—a point in the life cycle when there is a heightened sense of vulnerability with respect to identity.

The identity crisis may be experienced as a turning point in the life cycle, a point at which commitments are made that determine many later events in a person's life. Even so, the outcome of the identity crisis is in part a product of all that has gone before. As Erikson pointed out, identity implies both a "sense of individual uniqueness" and a "striving for a continuity of experience." Adolescents view their lives as continuous and connected, despite the crisis of identity.

Sex-Role Consolidation

Adolescence is a very important phase of the life cycle for sex-role development, which is itself a major part of the identity equation. Sex-role identity includes many elements. Gender identity, the sense of being either male or female, is firmly established in childhood and undergoes no further elaboration across the life cycle. Cultural expectations for masculine and feminine behavior, however, are in part a function of life-cycle stage.

It is during adolescence that sex-role stereotyping is strongest. And it is during adolescence that many important elements of sex-role identity are consolidated within the personality. For example, the developmental history of spatial and verbal abilities reveals no great differences between boys and girls during childhood. However, shortly after puberty, male and female adolescents begin to show consistent average differences in these two cognitive abilities. Males are superior at spatial tasks, and females are superior in verbal performance.

Cognitive Development

The themes of change and continuity are well illustrated by changes in thinking across the life span. For a given individual, changes in thinking occur as a gradual process of cognitive elaboration. One's understanding of the world is not noticeably different from one day to the next. Nevertheless, it is useful to distinguish stages in cognitive orientation despite the fact that stages merge gradually.

Modes of thinking characteristic of childhood give way to more formal modes of thinking in adolescence. Thought becomes more systematic and logical; reasoning abilities extend from the concrete to the hypothetical and abstract; point-of-view becomes less egocentric, and at the same time more self-reflective. There is no strong line of demarcation between child and adolescent modes of thinking, and yet they are in many ways qualitatively different. Stages of thinking, as well as many other aspects of development in adolescence, are an exciting mixture of change and continuity.

Moral Development

The transition to new modes of thinking is not limited to traditional cognitive domains. In fact, the way people think about any issue, from political ideology to moral philosophy, can be examined. In recent years, many psychologists have focused attention on developmental approaches to moral reasoning—reasoning about dilemmas that have moral overtones. Again, the themes of change and continuity are strikingly apparent. People change, in regular and even predictable ways; their moral reasoning appears to follow a stage sequence from individualistic reasoning to rule-governed and conventional reasoning, to reasoning based on principles of a higher order than mere rules. And yet adolescents are unlikely to be aware of shifts in their thinking about moral issues, even though they are very likely to go through one or more of these shifts during adolescence. Changes in modes of thinking form a continuous bridge between the morality of childhood and the morality of adulthood by virtue of their orderly sequence.

Social Orientation

In the moral mode, shifts in thinking are directed at value issues. In the social mode, shifts occur in the ways adolescents construe interpersonal situations. Changing patterns of parent and peer interaction are consistent with shifts in thinking about the social world.

Adolescents become more oriented toward their peers than they were as children; at the same time, they become somewhat less oriented toward their parents. Despite this shift in interpersonal orientation, most adolescents maintain friendly relations with their parents. Although they are likely to spend their leisure time with peers, they continue to be heavily influenced by the opinions of their parents on important issues such as educational and occupational plans.

One expected change in social orientation occurs in the way adolescents construe male–female interaction. They become much more likely to interpret male–female interaction in romantic terms during the adolescent years. This shift coincides, quite naturally, with the increased likelihood of dating and other forms of heterosexual interaction.

Adolescent Sexuality

Freud's highly influential work on psychosexual development firmly established the notion that sexual aspects of personality do not originate in adolescence. Children also have sexual curiosity and sexual experiences, although of a qualitatively different sort from those of adolescents and adults. The qualitative shift in sexuality following puberty is one of the most forceful shifts in human development. The maturation of the reproductive system, in conjunction with the shifts in cognitive and social orientations, focuses adolescent attention on sexual issues much more intensely than in childhood. Thoughts about sexuality are more frequent in adolescence than at any other time in the life cycle.

A highly publicized "sexual revolution" occurred in the 1960s and 1970s. Sexual preoccupation, however, has probably not undergone much change from one cohort to another. Rather, the likelihood of a sexual "rite of passage," such as loss of virginity, is now more likely to play a part in the psychological transition from child to adult than in earlier generations.

Youth Culture

In our culture, and indeed in all cultures, status is defined in part on the basis of age. Adolescents often find themselves age-segregated. There is generational continuity in this phenomenon. Each successive generation of adolescents engages in a collective search for identity, for a way of making sense out of its own unique historical experience.

Many adolescents in the 1950s turned to rock-and-roll music as an expressive medium for their feelings. A substantial minority of 1950s youth, in a kind of cultural alienation, described themselves as the "beat generation." The 1960s and 1970s spawned other generational themes, such as drug experimentation and activist protest. The civil-rights movement and the antiwar movement provided rallying points for the collective identity search among substantial numbers of adolescents.

As we move into the 1980s, new generation units are emerging. Many young people are making the transition from childhood to adulthood in cult movements, while others quest for a place in an uncertain economic system. As the pace of technological development becomes more rapid, self-definition becomes more difficult. It is hard to decide what direction to take when the overall trend of technological development is unclear. Rejection of all conventional standards, exhibited by some adolescents in the punk-rock generation unit, may be one result of this uncertainty.

Problems in Adolescence

The rapid pace of modern technology may be responsible, at least in part, for some of the problems of adolescence in the 1980s. Depression and suicidal behavior have increased among adolescents in recent years. Juvenile delinquency is by no means a novel phenomenon, but it too is on the increase. The period between childhood and adulthood is to some extent an unstable situation in the best of times; when the social context is also uncertain, instability is enhanced.

As Carol Gilligan (1979) pointed out, "Conceptions of the life cycle represent attempts to order and make coherent the unfolding experiences and perceptions, the changing wishes and realities of everyday life. But the truth of such observations depends in part on the position of the observer" (p. 431). The position of the adolescent observer is by definition a position of transition, and that position appears to be in flux now more than ever before.

THEMES OF CHANGE IN CHILDREN'S LITERATURE

A great deal of children's literature is about character transformation. Pinnochio is transformed from a wooden puppet into a live little boy. Snow White matures into a beautiful young woman, which is the prelude to another transformation: After eating the jealous queen's poison apple, she falls into suspended animation, awaiting the arrival of a lover—in the form of a prince—to be brought back to consciousness. Alice in Wonderland likewise undergoes transformations, as she alternately grows larger and smaller through drinking potions. In the story of Cinderella, the theme of change in human development suggests the fantasies of everyday life, where we dream of impossible but highly desirable goals. In this story, the miserable servant girl becomes a beautiful dancer at the palace ball, unrecognized even by her own stepsisters. Her magical metamorphosis is eventually rewarded with marriage to the prince.

Much has been written about the psychological significance of this body of children's literature. Bruno Bettelheim (1976), in *The Uses of Enchantment*, suggested that fairy tales provide children with a mechanism to sort out good and evil when they are grappling with the anxiety engendered by their own preliminary moves toward independence. For example, Bettelheim argued that tales about a long period of sleep, such as "Snow White" and "The Sleeping Beauty," are tales which reassure children about characteristics of adolescence that they themselves may experience.

In major life changes such as adolescence, for successful growth opportunities both active and quiescent periods are needed. Those fairy tales which, like "The Sleeping Beauty," have the period of passivity for their central topic, permit the budding adolescent not to worry during his inactive period: he learns that things continue to evolve. (Bettelheim, 1979, p. 225)

Poet Anne Sexton also viewed fairy tales as carriers of significant, hidden messages. Sexton had observed her 17-year-old daughter's absorption with Grimm's fairy tales, and Sexton herself began a study that resulted in one of her most unusual collections of poems, *Transformations*. In Sexton's version of "The Frog Prince," the theme of sexual awakening and sexual anxiety in adolescence emerges as the tale's hidden meaning. The young princess has promised a frog three things in exchange for the return of her lost golden ball. She will allow him to eat from her plate, drink from her cup, and sleep in her bed.

Next came the bed.
The silky royal bed.
Ah! The penultimate hour!
There was the pillow
with the princess breathing
and there was the sinuous frog
riding up and down beside her.
I have been lost in a river
of shut doors, he said,
and I have made my way over
the wet stones to live with you.
She woke up aghast.
I suffer for birds and fireflies

but not frogs, she said,
and threw him across the room.
Kaboom!
Like a genie coming out of a samovar,
a handsome prince arose in the
corner of her royal bedroom.
He had kind eyes and hands
and was a friend of sorrow.
Thus they were married.
*After all he had compromised her.**

The transformation of frog into prince is a startling device, in Grimm's original tale and in Sexton's poem. But the princess's sexual transformation is the basis for a developmental interpretation of the poem.

Once the ball is out of the princess's hands, she becomes involved in a fatal negotiation. She makes promises to the frog with childish ease, that is, without intending to keep them; but when the king steps in to enforce her commitments, the princess discovers she is in a situation governed by adult rules. She has been handed over by her father, the guardian of her sexuality. (Middlebrook, 1978, p. 77)

Two developmental psychologists have recently written about the importance of these fairy tales.

Such tales about change in personality after childhood center on the two fundamental dramatic conflicts inherent in the process of change. The first is the conflict between the person's wish to change while maintaining a sense of identity. The second is the conflict between the person and society; the person may wish to change, yet society may demand constancy, or the person may wish to remain the same, yet society may demand that the person change. Our treasured stories about metamorphosis in children are especially poignant because they engage children's fascination with transformation of self and at the same time make them realize that there are some inescapable continuities with what they are now. (Brim & Kagan, 1980, pp. 17; 19)

For those of us who are not of royal or amphibian blood, the themes of change and continuity are probably more important during the developmental phase of adolescence than at any other time.

THE ADOLESCENT TRANSITION

For all of us in our adolescence, nonmembership in either the child or the adult world underscores the great themes of change and continuity. This book opened with passages from Carson McCullers'

---

*From Transformations *by Anne Sexton. Copyright © 1971 by Anne Sexton. Reprinted by permission of Houghton Mifflin Company.*

novel, *The Member of the Wedding.* McCullers elaborated on the themes of change and continuity in an article in the New York *Herald Tribune.*

To the spectator, the amateur philosopher, no motive among the complex ricochets of our desires and rejections seems stronger or more enduring than the will of the individual to claim his identity and belong. From infancy to death, the human being is obsessed by these dual motives. After the first establishment of identity there comes the imperative need to lose this new-found sense of separateness and to belong to something larger and more powerful than the weak, lonely self. (Carr, 1975, p. 14)

Her novel—and this book—is about that period of transition between childhood and adulthood. When *The Member of the Wedding* was performed as a play on the New York stage, McCullers described the larger context in which it should be understood. Her words provide a context for understanding the themes of this book as well: "The play is about adolescence, but that's not really what it's about. It's a play about identity and the will to belong. Everybody wants to be a member of something" (Carr, 1975, p. 34).

So we have come full circle. Everybody wants to be a member of something, and it is during adolescence—the transitional years between childhood and adulthood—that "membership" is sharpened and given psychological meaning in terms of what has happened before and in preparation for what may lie ahead.

REFERENCES

Abramson, P. R., & Mosher, D. L. Development of a measure of negative attitudes toward masturbation. *Journal of Consulting and Clinical Psychology*, 1975, *43*, 485–490.

Adelson, J., & Doehrman, M. J. The psychodynamic approach to adolescence. In J. Adelson (Ed.), *Handbook of adolescent psychology*. New York: Wiley, 1980.

Adelson, J., & O'Neil, R. P. Growth of political ideas in adolescence: The sense of community. *Journal of Personality and Social Psychology*, 1966, *4*, 295–306.

Adler, N. Ritual, release, and orientation: Maintenance of the self in the antinomian personality. In I. I. Zaretsky & M. P. Leone (Eds.), *Religious movements in contemporary America*. Princeton: Princeton University Press, 1974.

Ahlgren, A., & Johnson, D. W. Sex differences in cooperative and competitive attitudes from the 2nd through the 12th grades. *Developmental Psychology*, 1979, *15*, 45–49.

Allen, V. L., & Newtson, D. Development of conformity and independence. *Journal of Personality and Social Psychology*, 1972, *22*, 18–30.

Allen, W. R. Race, sex, grade level, and disadvantageness in feelings of alienation among adolescents in a southern school. (Doctoral dissertation, University of Georgia, 1974.) *Dissertation Abstracts International*, 1975, *35*, 5107A.

Allinsmith, W. The learning of moral standards. In D. R. Miller & G. E. Swanson (Eds.), *Inner conflict and defense*. New York: Henry Holt, 1960.

Alston, J. P., & Tucker, F. The myth of sexual permissiveness. *Journal of Sex Research*, 1973, *9*, 34–40.

Altbach, P. G., & Peterson, P. M. Before Berkeley: Historical perspectives on American student activism. In P. G. Altbach & R. S. Laufer (Eds.), *The new pilgrims: Youth protest in transition*. New York: David McKay, 1972.

Amundsen, W., & Diers, C. J. The age of menarche in classical Greece and Rome. *Human Biology*, 1969, *41*, 125–132.

Amundsen, W., & Diers, C. J. The age of menarche in medieval Europe. *Human Biology*, 1973, *45*, 363–369.

A nation of dunces? *Newsweek*, November 10, 1975, p. 84.

Annesley, P. T. Psychiatric illness in adolescence: Presentation and prognosis. *British Journal of Psychiatry*, 1961, *107*, 268–278.

Anthony, D., & Robbins, T. The Meher Baba movement: Its effect on postadolescent social alienation. In I. I. Zaretsky & M. P. Leone (Eds.), *Religious movements in contemporary America*. Princeton: Princeton University Press, 1974.

Arbuthnot, J. Modification of moral judgment through role playing. *Developmental Psychology*, 1975, *11*, 319–324.

Aries, P. [*Centuries of childhood: A social history of the family.*] (R. Baldick, trans.) New York: Random House, 1962. (Originally published, 1960.)

Armsby, R. E. A reexamination of the development of moral judgments in children. *Child Development*, 1971, *42*, 1241–1248.

Aronson, E., & Mills, J. The effects of severity of initiation on liking for a group. *Journal of Abnormal and Social Psychology*, 1959, *59*, 177–181.

Asch, S. E. Effects of group pressure upon the modification and distortion of judgment. In H. Guetzkow (Ed.), *Groups, leadership, and men*. Pittsburgh: Carnegie, 1951.

Asch, S. E. Studies of independence and conformity: I. A minority of one against a unanimous majority. *Psychological Monographs*, 1956, *70* (9, Whole No. 416).

Astin, A. W. Measurement and determinants of the outputs of higher education. In L. C. Solmon & P. J. Taubman (Eds.), *Does college matter? Some evidence on the impacts of higher education*. New York: Academic Press, 1973.

Avery, A. W., & Ridley, C. A. Interpersonal correlates of sexual intimacy. Paper presented at meetings of the American Psychological Association, New Orleans, 1974.

Bachman, J. G., Green, S., & Wirtanen, I. D. *Youth in transition, Volume III: Dropping out—problem or symptom?* Ann Arbor: Institute for Social Research, 1971.

Bachman, J. G., Johnston, L. D., & O'Malley, P. M. *Monitoring the future: Questionnaire responses from the nation's high school seniors: 1978*. Ann Arbor: Institute for Social Research, 1980.

Bachman, J. G., O'Malley, P. M., & Johnston, J. *Youth in transition, Volume 6: Adolescence to adulthood: Change and stability in the lives of young men*. Ann Arbor: Institute for Social Research, 1978.

Bailey, K. G., & Minor, S. W. Self-image and congruence in freshmen, seniors, and graduate students. *Journal of Genetic Psychology*, 1976, *129*, 301–309.

Bakan, D. Adolescence in America: From idea to social fact. In J. Kagan & R. Coles (Eds.), *12 to 16: Early adolescence*. New York: Norton, 1972.

Bakwin, H., & McLaughlin, S. M. Secular increase in height. Is the end in sight? *The Lancet*, 1964 (2), 1195–1196.

Balswick, J. O., & Macrides, C. Parental stimulus for adolescent rebellion. *Adolescence*, 1975, *10*, 253–266.

Bandura, A., & McDonald, F. J. Influence of social reinforcement and the behavior of models in shaping children's moral judgments. *Journal of Abnormal and Social Psychology*, 1963, *67*, 274–281.

Barenboim, C. Developmental changes in the interpersonal cognitive system from middle childhood to adolescence. *Child Development*, 1977, *48*, 1467–1474.

Barenboim, C. The development of person perception in childhood and adolescence: From behavioral comparisons to psychological constructs to psychological comparisons. *Child Development*, 1981, *52*, 129–144.

Barnes, G. M. The development of adolescent drinking behavior: An evaluative review of the impact of the socialization process within the family. *Adolescence*, 1977, *12*, 571–591.

Barratt, B. B. Training and transfer in combinatorial problem solving: The development of formal reasoning during early adolescence. *Developmental Psychology*, 1975, *11*, 700–704.

Barry, H., III, Bacon, M. K., & Child, I. L. A cross-cultural survey of some sex differences in socialization. *Journal of Abnormal and Social Psychology*, 1957, *55*, 327–332.

Barták, V., & Mellan, J. Changes in the sexual behavior of adolescents of Czechoslovakia and Germany. *Archives of Sexual Behavior*, 1971, *1*, 181–184.

Bauman, K. E. Volunteer bias in a study of sexual knowledge, attitudes, and behavior. *Journal of Marriage and the Family*, 1973, *35*, 27–31.

Bauman, K. E., & Wilson, R. R. Sexual behavior of unmarried university students in 1968 and 1972. *Journal of Sex Research*, 1974, *10*, 327–333.

Bayer, A. E. Early dating and early marriage. *Journal of Marriage and the Family*, 1968, *30*, 628–632.

Beall, C. M., Baker, P. T., Baker, T. S., & Haas, J. D. The effects of high altitude on adolescent growth in southern Peruvian Amerindians. *Human Biology*, 1977, *49*, 109–124.

Beck, P. A. The role of agents in political socialization. In S. A. Renshon (Ed.), *Handbook of political socialization: Theory and research*. New York: Free Press, 1977.

Beidelman, T. O. *The Kaguru: A matrilineal people of East Africa*. New York: Holt, Rinehart, Winston, 1971.

Bell, A. P., & Weinberg, M. S. *Homosexualities: A study of diversity among men and women*. New York: Simon and Shuster, 1978.

Bem, S. L. The measurement of psychological androgyny. *Journal of Clinical and Consulting Psychology*, 1974, *42*, 155–162.

Bem, S. L. Sex role adaptability: One consequence of psychological androgyny. *Journal of Personality and Social Psychology*, 1975, *31*, 634–643.

Bem, S. L., & Lenney, E. Sex typing and the avoidance of cross-sex behavior. *Journal of Personality and Social Psychology*, 1976, *33*, 48–54.

Bem, S. L., Martyna, W., & Watson, C. Sex typing and androgyny: Further explorations of the expressive domain. *Journal of Personality and Social Psychology*, 1976, *34*, 1016–1023.

Bemis, K. M. Current approaches to the etiology and treatment of anorexia nervosa. *Psychological Bulletin*, 1978, *85*, 593–617.

Benedict, R. *Patterns of culture*. Boston: Houghton Mifflin, 1934.

Bengston, V. L., Furlong, M. J., & Laufer, R. S. Time, aging, and the continuity of social structure: Themes and issues in generational analysis. *Journal of Social Issues*, 1974, *30*, 1–30.

Bengston, V. L., & Starr, J. M. Contrast and consensus: A generational analysis of youth in the 1970s. In R. J. Havighurst & P. H. Dreyer (Eds.),

Youth: The seventy-fourth yearbook for the National Society for the Study of Education. Chicago: University of Chicago Press, 1975.

Berg, I. *Education and jobs: The great training robbery.* New York: Praeger, 1970.

Berger, B. M. *Looking for America: Essays on youth, suburbia, and other American obsessions.* Englewood Cliffs, NJ: Prentice-Hall, 1971.

Berger, B. M., & Hackett, B. M. On the decline of age grading in rural hippie communes. *Journal of Social Issues,* 1974, *30,* 163–183.

Berger, D. G., & Wenger, M. G. The ideology of virginity. *Journal of Marriage and the Family,* 1973, *35,* 666–676.

Bernard, H. S. Identity formation during late adolescence: A review of some empirical findings. *Adolescence,* 1981, *16,* 349–358.

Berndt, T. J. Developmental changes in conformity to peers and parents. *Developmental Psychology,* 1979, *15,* 608–616.

Berry, J. W. Temne and Eskimo perceptual skills. *International Journal of Psychology,* 1966, *1,* 207–229.

Bettelheim, B. *The uses of enchantment: The meaning and importance of fairy tales.* New York: Knopf, 1976.

Bielicki, T., & Charzewski, J. Sex differences in the magnitude of statural gains of offspring over parents. *Human Biology,* 1977, *49,* 265–277.

Bieri, J., Bradburn, W. M., & Galinsky, M. D. Sex differences in perceptual behavior. *Journal of Personality,* 1958, *26,* 1–12.

Birnbaum, N., & Childers, M. The American student movement. In A. M. Orum (Ed.), *The seeds of politics: Youth and politics in America.* Englewood Cliffs, NJ: Prentice-Hall, 1972.

Bixenstine, V. E., DeCorte, M. S., & Bixenstine, B. A. Conformity to peer-sponsored misconduct at four grade levels. *Developmental Psychology,* 1976, *12,* 226–236.

Blatt, M., Colby, A., & Speicher, B. *Hypothetical dilemmas for use in moral discussions.* Cambridge: Moral Education and Research Foundation, 1974.

Block, J. H. Conceptions of sex roles: Some cross-cultural and longitudinal perspectives. *American Psychologist,* 1973, *28,* 512–526.

Block, J. H., Haan, N., & Smith, M. B. Socialization correlates of student activism. In A. M. Orum (Ed.), *The seeds of politics: Youth and politics in America.* Englewood Cliffs, NJ: Prentice-Hall, 1972.

Bloom, L. The formation of friendships among Zambian university students. *International Journal of Psychology,* 1971, *6,* 157–162.

Blos, P. *On adolescence: A psychoanalytic interpretation.* New York: Free Press, 1962.

Blumstein, P. W., & Schwartz, P. Bisexuality: Some social psychological issues. *Journal of Social Issues,* 1977, *33,* 30–45.

Bono, F. V. The effects of two teaching approaches on the moral judgment of sixth grade children. (Doctoral dissertation, Ohio University, 1975.) *Dissertation Abstracts International,* 1976, *36,* 6436.

Boodman, S. G. What makes Johnny steal in suburbia? *The Washington Post,* May 31, 1980, pp 1; 7.

Bowerman, C. E., & Kinch, J. W. Changes in family and peer orientation of children between the fourth and tenth grades. *Social Forces*, 1959, *37*, 206–211.

Bowles, S., & Gintis, H. *Schooling in capitalist America: Reform and the contradictions of economic life.* New York: Basic Books, 1976.

Brain, R. *Friends and lovers.* Frogmore, Herts: Paladin, 1976.

Braungart, R. G. Youth movements. In J. Adelson (Ed.), *Handbook of adolescent psychology.* New York: Wiley, 1980.

Braungart, R. G., & Braungart, M. M. Reference group, social judgment and student politics. *Adolescence*, 1979, *14*, 135–157.

Brill, N. Q., Crumpton, E., & Grayson, H. M. Personality factors in marijuana use: A preliminary report. *Archives of General Psychiatry*, 1971, *24*, 163–165.

Brim, O. G., Jr., & Kagan, J. Constancy and change: A view of the issues. In O. G. Brim, Jr., & J. Kagan (Eds.), *Constancy and change in human development.* Cambridge: Harvard University Press, 1980.

Brittain, C. V. Adolescent choices and parent-peer cross-pressures. *American Sociological Review*, 1963, *28*, 385–391.

Brittain, C. V. An exploration of the bases of peer-compliance and parent-compliance in adolescence. *Adolescence*, 1967, *2*, 445–458.

Broderick, C. B., & Weaver, J. The perceptual context of boy–girl communication. *Journal of Marriage and the Family*, 1968, *30*, 618–627.

Bromley, D. D., & Britten, F. H. *Youth and sex: A study of 1300 college students.* New York: Harper, 1938.

Bronfenbrenner, U. The origins of alienation. *Scientific American*, 1974, *231* (2), 53–61.

Brook, J. S., Lukoff, I. F., & Whiteman, M. Initiation into adolescent marijuana use. *Journal of Genetic Psychology*, 1980, *137*, 133–142.

Broude, G. Norms of premarital sexual behavior: A cross-cultural study. *Ethos*, 1975, 381–402.

Broughton, J. M. The divided self in adolescence. *Human Development*, 1981, *24*, 13–32.

Broverman, D. M., Broverman, I. K., Vogel, W., Palmer, R. D., & Klaiber, E. L. The automatization cognitive style and physical development. *Child Development*, 1964, *35*, 1343–1359.

Broverman, D. M., Klaiber, E. L., Kobayashi, Y., & Vogel, W. Roles of activation and inhibition in sex differences in cognitive abilities. *Psychological Review*, 1968, *75*, 23–50.

Brown, D., & Marks, P. A. Bakan's bi-polar constructs: Agency and communion. *Psychological Record*, 1969, *19*, 465–478.

Brown, J. K. A cross-cultural study of female initiation rites. *American Anthropologist*, 1963, *65*, 837–853.

Bruch, H. *The golden cage: The enigma of anorexia nervosa.* Cambridge: Harvard University Press, 1978.

Bruske, E., & Sager, M. Glorious Fourth: The best party in America is here. *The Washington Post*, July 5, 1980, pp. A1; A8.

Burke, R. J., & Weir, T. Sex differences in adolescent life stress, social support, and well-being. *Journal of Psychology*, 1978, *98*, 227–288.

Burrell, R. J. W., Healy, M. J. R., & Tanner, J. M. Age at menarche in South

African Bantu schoolgirls living in the Transkei Reserve. *Human Biology*, 1961, *33*, 250–261.

Byrne, D. Interpersonal attraction and attitude similarity. *Journal of Abnormal and Social Psychology*, 1961, *62*, 713–715.

Cairns, R. B. *Social development: The origins and plasticity of interchanges.* San Francisco: Freeman, 1979.

Cameron, P., & Biber, H. Sexual thought throughout the lifespan. *Gerontologist*, 1973, *13*, 144–147.

Carlsmith, L. Some personality characteristics of boys separated from their fathers during World War II. *Ethos*, 1973, *1*, 467–477.

Carlson, E. R., & Carlson, R. Male and female subjects in personality research. *Journal of Abnormal and Social Psychology*, 1960, *61*, 482–483.

Carlson, R. Sex differences in ego functioning: Exploratory studies of agency and communion. *Journal of Consulting and Clinical Psychology*, 1971, *37*, 267–277.

Carns, D. E. Talking about sex: Notes on first coitus and the double standard. *Journal of Marriage and the Family*, 1973, *35*, 677–687.

Carr, V. S. *The lonely hunter: A biography of Carson McCullers.* Garden City, New York: Doubleday, 1975.

Cauble, M. A. Formal operations, ego identity, and principled morality: Are they related? *Developmental Psychology*, 1976, *12*, 363–364.

Chaffee, S. H., with Jackson-Beeck, M., Durall, J., & Wilson, D. Mass communication in political socialization. In S. A. Renshon (Ed.), *Handbook of political socialization: Theory and research.* New York: Free Press, 1977.

Chagnon, N. A. *Yąnomamö: The fierce people.* New York: Holt, Rinehart, and Winston, 1968.

Chapman, M. Father absence, stepfathers, and the cognitive performance of college students. *Child Development*, 1977, *48*, 1155–1158.

Chess, S., Thomas, A., & Cameron, M. Sexual attitudes and behavior patterns in a middle class adolescent population. *American Journal of Orthopsychiatry*, 1976, *46*, 689–701.

Christensen, H. T., & Carpenter, G. R. Timing patterns in the development of sexual intimacy. *Marriage and Family Living*, 1962, *24*, 30–35.

Christensen, H. T., & Gregg, C. F. Changing sex norms in America and Scandinavia. *Journal of Marriage and the Family*, 1970, *32*, 616–627.

Ciseaux, A. (pseudonym). Anorexia nervosa: A view from the mirror. *American Journal of Nursing*, 1980, *80*, 1468–1470.

Clark, J. P., & Wenninger, E. P. Socio-economic class and area as correlates of illegal behavior among juveniles. *American Sociological Review*, 1962, *27*, 826–834.

Clinchy, B., Lief, J., & Young, P. Epistemological and moral development in girls from a traditional and a progressive high school. *Journal of Educational Psychology*, 1977, *69*, 337–343.

Cloward, R. A. Illegitimate means, anomie, and deviant behavior. *American Sociological Review*, 1959, *24*, 164–176.

Coleman, J. C. Friendship and the peer group in adolescence. In J. Adelson (Ed.), *Handbook of adolescent psychology.* New York: Wiley, 1980.

Coleman, J. S. *The adolescent society.* New York: Free Press, 1961.

Coleman, J. S. How do the young become adults? In R. E. Grinder (Ed.), *Studies in adolescence* (3rd ed.). New York: Macmillan, 1975.

Coleman, J., George, R., & Holt, G. Adolescents and their parents: A study of attitudes. *Journal of Genetic Psychology*, 1977, *130*, 239–245.

Collins, J. K. Adolescent dating and intimacy: Norms and peer expectations. *Journal of Youth and Adolescence*, 1974, *3*, 317–328.

Combs, J., & Cooley, W. W. Dropouts: In high school and after school. *American Educational Research Journal*, 1968, *5*, 343–363.

Cone, T. E., Jr. Secular acceleration of height and biologic maturation in children during the past century. *Journal of Pediatrics*, 1961, *59*, 736–740.

Constantinople, A. An Eriksonian measure of personality development in college students. *Developmental Psychology*, 1969, *1*, 357–372.

Constantinople, A. Masculinity-femininity: An exception to the famous dictum? *Psychological Bulletin*, 1973, *80*, 389–407.

Cooley, C. H. *Social organization: A study of the larger mind.* New York: Schocken Books, 1962. (Originally published, 1909.)

Corder, B. F., Page, P. V., & Corder, R. F. Parental history, family communication and interaction patterns in adolescent suicide. *Family Therapy*, 1974, *1*, 285–290.

Corder, B. F., Shorr, W., & Corder, R. F. A study of social and psychological characteristics of adolescent suicide attempters in an urban, disadvantaged area. *Adolescence*, 1974, *9*, 1–6.

Cowan, P., Langer, J., Heavenrich, J., & Nathanson, M. Social learning and Piaget's cognitive theory of moral development. *Journal of Personality and Social Psychology*, 1969, *11*, 261–274.

Crain, W. C., & Starace, J. Utopian visions of schizophrenic adolescents. *Journal of Youth and Adolescence*, 1976, *5*, 271–281.

Croake, J. W., & James, B. E. Attitudes toward premarital sexual behavior as a function of behavioral commitment. *College Student Journal*, 1972, *6*, 36–41.

Croake, J. W., & James, B. E. A four year comparison of premarital sexual attitudes. *Journal of Sex Research*, 1973, *9*, 91–96.

Crutchfield, R. A. Conformity and character. *American Psychologist*, 1955, *10*, 191–198.

Curran, J. P., Neff, S., & Lippold, S. Correlates of sexual experiences among university students. *Journal of Sex Research*, 1973, *9*, 124–131.

Curtis, R. L., Jr. Adolescent orientations toward parents and peers: Variations by sex, age, and socioeconomic status. *Adolescence*, 1975, *10*, 483–494.

Cutler, N. E. Political socialization research as generational analysis: The cohort approach versus the lineage approach. In S. A. Renshon (Ed.), *Handbook of political socialization: Theory and research.* New York: Free Press, 1977.

Damon, A., Damon, S. T., Reed, R. B., & Valadian, I. Age at menarche of mothers and daughters, with a note on accuracy of recall. *Human Biology*, 1969, *41*, 161–175.

Danner, F. W., & Day, M. C. Eliciting formal operations. *Child Development*, 1977, *48*, 1600–1606.

Darley, J. M., & Batson, C. D. "From Jerusalem to Jericho": A study of situational and dispositional variables in helping behavior. *Journal of Personality and Social Psychology*, 1973, *27*, 100–108.

Darley, J. M., Klosson, E. C., & Zanna, M. P. Intentions and their contexts in the moral judgments of children and adults. *Child Development*, 1978, *49*, 66–74.

Darling, L. The Rainbow People: Festival in the forest: The coal miners and the '60s counterculture. *The Washington Post*, July 7, 1980, pp. D1; D3.

D'Augelli, J. F., & Cross, H. J. Relationship of sex guilt and moral reasoning to premarital sex in college women and in couples. *Journal of Consulting and Clinical Psychology*, 1975, *43*, 40–47.

D'Augelli, J. F., & D'Augelli, A. R. Moral reasoning and premarital sexual behavior: Toward reasoning about relationships. *Journal of Social Issues*, 1977, *33*, 46–66.

Davidson, S. *Loose change: Three women of the sixties.* Garden City, NY: Doubleday, 1977.

Davies, B. L. Attitudes toward school among early and late maturing adolescent girls. *Journal of Genetic Psychology*, 1977, *131*, 261–266.

Davies, M., & Kandel, D. B. Parental and peer influences on adolescents' educational plans: Some further evidence. *American Journal of Sociology*, 1981, *87*, 363–387.

Davis, K. The sociology of parent-youth conflict. *American Sociological Review*, 1940, *5*, 523–535.

DeLamater, J., & MacCorquodale, P. *Premarital Sexuality: Attitudes, relationships, behavior.* Madison, Wisconsin: University of Wisconsin Press, 1979.

Demone, H. W., Jr., & Wechsler, H. Changing drinking patterns of adolescents since the 1960s. In M. Greenblatt & M. A. Schuckit (Eds.), *Alcoholism problems in women and children.* New York: Gruen and Stratton, 1976.

Deutscher, I. The quality of postparental life: Definitions of the situation. *Journal of Marriage and the Family*, 1964, *26*, 52–59.

DeVries, R. Relationships among Piagetian, IQ, and achievement assessments. *Child Development*, 1974, *45*, 746–756.

Dewey, J. *Democracy and education.* New York: Free Press, 1966.

Diamant, L. Premarital sexual behavior, attitudes, and emotional adjustment. *Journal of Social Psychology*, 1970, *82*, 75–80.

Doering, C. H. The endocrine system. In O. G. Brim, Jr., & J. Kagan (Eds.), *Constancy and change in human development.* Cambridge: Harvard University Press, 1980.

Donovan, J. M. Identity status and interpersonal style. *Journal of Youth and Adolescence*, 1975, *4*, 37–55.

Dornbusch, S. M., Carlsmith, J. M., Gross, R. T., Martin, J. A., Jennings, D., Rosenberg, A., & Duke, P. Sexual development, age, and dating: A comparison of biological and social influences upon one set of behaviors. *Child Development*, 1981, *52*, 179–185.

Dostoevski, F. [*Crime and punishment*]. (C. Garnett, trans.) New York: Random House, 1950. (Originally published, 1866.)

Douglas, J. W. B., & Ross, J. M. Age of puberty related to educational ability, attainment and school leaving age. *Journal of Child Psychology and Psychiatry*, 1964, *5*, 185–195.

Douvan, E., & Adelson, J. *The adolescent experience*. New York: Wiley, 1966.

Douvan, E., & Gold, M. Modal patterns in American adolescence. In L. W. Hoffman & M. L. Hoffman (Eds.), *Review of child development research* (Vol. 2). New York: Russell Sage, 1966.

Drake, C. T., & McDougall, D. Effects of the absence of a father and other male models on the development of boys' sex roles. *Developmental Psychology*, 1977, *13*, 537–538.

Draper, H. The student movement of the thirties: A political history. In A. M. Orum (Ed.), *The seeds of politics: Youth and politics in America*. Englewood Cliffs, NJ: Prentice-Hall, 1972.

DuBois, C. *The people of Alor*. Minneapolis: University of Minnesota Press, 1944.

Dulit, E. Adolescent thinking á la Piaget: The formal stage. In R. E. Grinder (Ed.,), *Studies in adolescence* (3rd ed.). New York: Macmillan, 1975.

Duncan, D. F. Attitudes toward parents and delinquency in suburban adolescent males. *Adolescence*, 1978, *13*, 365–369.

Dunphy, D. C. The social structure of urban adolescent peer groups. *Sociometry*, 1963, *26*, 230–246.

Dykeman, B. F. Teenage alcoholism—detecting those early warning signals. *Adolescence*, 1979, *14*, 251–254.

Eckhardt, K. W., & Schriner, E. C. Familial conflict, adolescent rebellion, and political expression. *Journal of Marriage and the Family*, 1969, *31*, 494–499.

Ehrmann, W. *Premarital dating behavior*. New York: Holt, 1959.

Eimas, P. D. A developmental study of hypothesis behavior and focusing. *Journal of Experimental Child Psychology*, 1969, *8*, 160–172.

Eisenberg, L. Student unrest: Sources and consequences. *Science*, 1970, *167*, 1688–1692.

Elder, G. H., Jr. Parental power legitimation and its effect on the adolescent. *Sociometry*, 1963, *26*, 50–65.

Elder, G. H., Jr. Adolescence in historical perspective. In J. Adelson (Ed.), *Handbook of adolescent psychology*. New York: Wiley, 1980.

Elias, J., & Gebhard, P. Sexuality and sexual learning in children. *Phi Delta Kappan*, 1969, *50*, 401–406.

Elkind, D. Cognitive structure and adolescence experience. *Adolescence*, 1962, *2*, 427 ff.

Elkind, D. Quantity conceptions in college students. *Journal of Social Psychology*, 1962, *57*, 549–465.

Elkind, D. Egocentrism in adolescence. *Child Development*, 1967, *38*, 1025–1034.

Elkind, D. Strategic interactions in early adolescence. In J. Adelson (Ed.), *Handbook of adolescent psychology*. New York: Wiley, 1980.

Ellison, A., & Simon, B. Does college make a person healthy and wise? In L. C. Solmon & P. J. Taubman (Eds.), *Does college matter? Some evidence on the impacts of higher education*. New York: Academic Press, 1973.

Elms, A., & Milgram, S. Personality characteristics associated with obedience and defiance toward authoritative command. *Journal of Experimental Research in Personality*, 1966, *1*, 282–289.

Emmerich, W., & Shepard, K. Development of sex-differentiated preferences during late childhood and adolescence. *Developmental Psychology*, 1982, *18*, 406–417.

Empey, L. T., & Erickson, M. L. Hidden delinquency and social status. *Social Forces*, 1966, *44*, 546–554.

Erickson, M. L., & Empey, L. T. Class position, peers and delinquency. *Sociological and Social Research*, 1965, *49*, 268–282.

Erikson, E. H. *Childhood and society* (2nd ed.). New York: Norton, 1963.

Erikson, E. H. *Insight and responsibility*. New York: Norton, 1964.

Erikson, E. H. *Identity: Youth and crisis*. New York: Norton, 1968.

Esterson, A. *The leaves of spring: Schizophrenia, family and sacrifice*. New York: Penguin, 1970.

Faust, M. S. Developmental maturity as a determinant in prestige of adolescent girls. *Child Development*, 1960, *31*, 173–184.

Faust, M. S. Somatic development of adolescent girls. *Monographs of the Society for Research in Child Development*, 1977, *42* (1, Serial No. 169).

Feighner, J. P., Robins, E., Guze, S. B., Woodruff, R. A., Winokur, G., & Munoz, R. Diagnostic criteria for use in psychiatric research. *Archives of General Psychiatry*, 1972, *26*, 57–63.

Feldman, K. A., & Newcomb, T. M. *The impact of college on students: Vol. I. An analysis of four decades of research*. San Francisco: Jossey-Bass, 1970.

Feldman, N. S., Klosson, E. C., Parsons, J. E., Rholes, W. S., & Ruble, D. N. Order of information presentation and children's moral judgments. *Child Development*, 1976, *47*, 556–559.

Feldman, S. E., & Feldman, M. T. Transition of sex differences in cheating. *Psychological Reports*, 1967, *20*, 957–958.

Fendrich, J. M. Activists ten years later: A test of generational unit continuity. *Journal of Social Issues*, 1974, *30*, 95–118.

Finger, F. W. Sex beliefs and practices among male college students. *Journal of Abnormal and Social Psychology*, 1947, *42*, 57–67.

Finn, P. Teenage drunkenness: Warning signal, transient boisterousness, or symptom of social change. *Adolescence*, 1979, *14*, 819–834.

Fischer, J. L., & Narus, L. R., Jr. Sex-role development in late adolescence and adulthood. *Sex Roles*, 1981, *7*, 97–106.

Fisher, W. A., & Byrne, D. Sex differences in response to erotica? Love versus lust. *Journal of Personality and Social Psychology*, 1978, *36*, 117–125.

Fishkin, J., Keniston, K., & MacKinnon, C. Moral reasoning and political ideology. *Journal of Personality and Social Psychology*, 1973, *27*, 109–119.

Fiske, E. B. College entry test scores drop sharply. *The New York Times*, September 7, 1975, p. 1.

Flavell, J. H. Historical and bibliographical note. In W. Kessen & C. Kuhlman (Eds.), *Thought in the young child*. Chicago: University of Chicago Press, 1962.

Flavell, J. H., & Wohlwill, J. F. Formal and functional aspects of cognitive development. In D. Elkind & J. H. Flavell (Eds.), *Studies in cognitive development: Essays in honor of Jean Piaget.* New York: Oxford University Press, 1969.

Floyd, H. H., Jr., & South, D. R. Dilemma of youth: The choice of parents or peers as a frame of reference for behavior. *Journal of Marriage and the Family,* 1972, *34,* 627–634.

Foll, C. V. The age at menarche in Assam and Burma. *Archives of Disease in Childhood,* 1961, *36,* 302–304.

Frank, A. *Anne Frank: The diary of a young girl.* Garden City, NY: Doubleday, 1952.

Frankel, J., & Dullaert, J. Is adolescent rebellion universal? *Adolescence,* 1977, *12,* 227–235.

Frantz, T. T. Student and non-student change. *Journal of College Student Personnel,* 1971, *12,* 49–53.

Freedman, M. B. The sexual behavior of American college women: An empirical study and an historical survey. *Merrill-Palmer Quarterly,* 1965, *11,* 33–48.

Freeman, H. R. The generation gap: Attitudes of students and of their parents. *Journal of Counseling Psychology,* 1972, *19,* 441–447.

Freeman, S. J. Individual differences in moral judgment by children and adolescents. (Doctoral dissertation, University of Wisconsin, 1974.) *Dissertation Abstracts International,* 1975, *35,* 4248.

Freemesser, G. F., & Kaplan, H. B. Self-attitudes and deviant behavior: The case of the charismatic religious movement. *Journal of Youth and Adolescence,* 1976, *5,* 1–9.

Freud, S. [*Three contributions to the theory of sex*] (A. A. Brill, trans.) New York: Dutton, 1962. (Originally published, 1905.)

Friedenberg, E. Z. *The vanishing adolescent.* New York: Dell, 1959.

Friedman, A. S. The family and the female delinquent: An overview. In O. Pollak & A. Friedman (Eds.), *Family dynamics and female sexual delinquency.* Palo Alto: Science and Behavior Books, 1969.

Frisch, R. E., & Revelle, R. The height and weight of adolescent boys and girls at the time of peak velocity of growth in height and weight: Longitudinal data. *Human Biology,* 1969, *41,* 536–559.

Frisch, R. E., & Revelle, R. Variation in body weights and the age of the adolescent growth spurt among Latin American and Asian populations, in relation to calorie supplies. *Human Biology,* 1969, *41,* 185–212.

Frisch, R. E., & Revelle, R. Height and weight at menarche and a hypothesis of menarche. *Archives of Disease in Childhood,* 1971, *46,* 695–701.

Frisch, R. E., & Revelle, R. The height and weight of girls and boys at the time of initiation of the adolescent growth spurt in height and weight and the relationship to menarche. *Human Biology,* 1971, *43,* 140–159.

Frisch, R. E., Revelle, R., & Cook, S. Height, weight and age at menarche and the "critical weight" hypothesis. *Science,* 1971, *174,* 1148–1149.

Froming, W. J., & McColgan, E. B. Comparing the Defining Issues Test and the Moral Dilemma Interview. *Developmental Psychology,* 1979, *15,* 658–659.

Furstenberg, F. F., Jr. *Unplanned parenthood: The social consequences of teenage childbearing.* New York: Free Press, 1976.

Furth, H. G. On language and knowing in Piaget's developmental theory. *Human Development,* 1970, *13,* 241–257.

Furth, H. G., & Youniss, J. Formal operations and language: A comparison of deaf and hearing adolescents. *International Journal of Psychology,* 1971, *6,* 49–64.

Gallatin, J. Political thinking in adolescence. In J. Adelson (Ed.), *Handbook of adolescent psychology.* New York: Wiley, 1980.

Gallo, P. G., & Savoia, G. The sexual maturation of the girls from the Valle Sabbia (BS) and their school progress. *Giornale Italiano di Psicologia,* 1978, *5,* 153–158. (Abstract.)

Ganzer, V. J., & Sarason, I. G. Variables associated with recidivism among juvenile delinquents. *Journal of Consulting and Clinical Psychology,* 1973, *40,* 1–5.

Garfagna, M., Figurelli, E., Matarese, G., & Matarese, S. Menarcheal age of schoolgirls in the District of Naples. *Human Biology,* 1972, *44,* 117–125.

Garmezy, N. Process and reactive schizophrenia: Some conceptions and issues. *Schizophrenia Bulletin,* 1970, *2,* 30–74.

Garn, S. M. Continuities and change in maturational timing. In O. G. Brim, Jr., & J. Kagan (Eds.), *Constancy and change in human development.* Cambridge: Harvard University Press, 1980.

Garwood, S. G., Levine, D. W., & Ewing, L. Effect of protagonist's sex on assessing gender differences in moral reasoning. *Developmental Psychology,* 1980, *16,* 677–678.

Gesell, A., & Ilg, F. L. *Infant and child in the culture of today.* New York: Harper, 1943.

Gilligan, C. In a different voice: Women's conceptions of self and morality. *Harvard Education Review,* 1977, *47,* 481–517.

Gilligan, C. Woman's place in man's cycle. *Harvard Education Review,* 1979, *49,* 431–446.

Gilligan, C., & Murphy, J. M. Development from adolescence to adulthood: The philosopher and the dilemma of the fact. In D. Kuhn (Ed.), *Intellectual development beyond childhood* (New Directions in Child Development Series No. 5). San Francisco: Jossey-Bass, 1979.

Givens, D. B. The nonverbal basis of attraction: Flirtation, courtship, and seduction. *Psychiatry,* 1978, *41,* 346–359.

Glick, J. Cognitive development in cross-cultural perspective. In F. D. Horowitz (Ed.), *Review of child development research* (Vol. 4). Chicago: University of Chicago Press, 1975.

Glueck, S., & Glueck, E. *Delinquents and nondelinquents in perspective.* Cambridge: Harvard University Press, 1968.

Goethals, G. W., & Klos, D. S. *Experiencing youth: First-person accounts* (2nd ed.). Boston: Little-Brown, 1976.

Gold, M., & Petronio, R. J. Delinquent behavior in adolescence. In J. Adelson (Ed.), *Handbook of adolescent development.* New York: Wiley, 1980.

Goldstein, J. On being adult and being an adult in secular law. *Daedalus,* 1976, *105* (4), 69–87.

Goodnow, J. J. A test of milieu effects with some of Piaget's tasks. *Psychological Monographs*, 1962, *76* (36, Whole No. 555).

Goodnow, J. J., & Bethon, G. Piaget's tasks: The effects of schooling and intelligence. *Child Development*, 1966, *37*, 573–582.

Gordon, R. A., Short, J. F., Jr., Cartwright, D. S., & Strodtbeck, F. L. Values and gang delinquency: A study of street-corner groups. *American Journal of Sociology*, 1963, *69*, 109–128.

Gossett, J. T., Lewis, J. M., & Phillips, V. A. Extent and prevalence of illicit drug use as reported by 56,745 students. *Journal of the American Medical Association*, 1971, *216*, 1464–1470.

Gottlieb, D. E., Taylor, S. E., & Ruderman, A. Cognitive bases of children's moral judgments. *Developmental Psychology*, 1977, *13*, 547–566.

Greeley, A. M. There's a new-time religion on campus. *New York Times Magazine*, June 1, 1969, p. 14 ff.

Greene, B. Beyond the sexual revolution. *Newsweek*, September 29, 1975, p. 13.

Grinder, R. Parental childrearing practices, conscience, and resistance to temptation of sixth-grade children. *Child Development*, 1962, *33*, 803–820.

Gruder, C. L., & Cook, T. D. Sex, dependency and helping. *Journal of Personality and Social Psychology*, 1971, *19*, 290–294.

Grueling, J. W., & DeBlassie, R. R. Adolescent suicide. *Adolescence*, 1980, *15*, 589–601.

Haan, N., Langer, J., & Kohlberg, L. Family patterns of moral reasoning. *Child Development*, 1976, *47*, 1204–1206.

Haan, N. Smith, M. B., & Block, J. Moral reasoning of young adults: Political-social behavior, family background, and personality correlates. *Journal of Personality and Social Psychology*, 1968, *10*, 183–201.

Haider, I. Suicide attempts in children and adolescents. *British Journal of Psychiatry*, 1968, *114*, 1133–1134.

Hamid, P. N., & Wyllie, A. J. What generation gap? *Adolescence*, 1980, *15*, 385–391.

Hansen, S. L. Dating choices of high school students. *The Family Coordinator*, April, 1977, 133–138.

Hansen, S. L., & Hicks, M. W. Sex role attitudes and perceived dating-mating choices of youth. *Adolescence*, 1980, *15*, 83–90.

Harrington, C. *Errors in sex-role behavior in teen-age boys*. New York: Teachers College Press, 1970.

Harris, G. W. Sex hormones, brain development and brain function. *Endocrinology*, 1964, *75*, 627–648.

Harrison, D. E., Bennett, W. H., & Globetti, G. Attitudes of rural youth toward premarital sexual permissiveness. *Journal of Marriage and the Family*, 1969, *31*, 783–787.

Hartshorne, H., May, M. A., & Shuttleworth, F. K. *Studies in the nature of character: Studies in the organization of character* (3). New York: Macmillan, 1930.

Haskell, M. R., & Yablonsky, L. *Juvenile Delinquency* (3rd ed.). Boston:

Houghton Mifflin, 1982.

Havighurst, R. J., Bowman, P. H., Liddle, G. P., Matthews, C. V., & Pierce, J. V. *Growing up in River City.* New York: Wiley, 1962.

Havighurst, R. J., & Neugarten, B. L. *Society and education* (2nd ed.). Boston: Allyn and Bacon, 1962.

Heilbrun, A. B., Jr. Conformity to masculinity-femininity stereotypes and ego identity in adolescents. *Psychological Reports,* 1964, *14,* 351–357.

Heilbrun, A. B., Jr. Measurement of masculine and feminine sex role identities as independent dimensions. *Journal of Consulting and Clinical Psychology,* 1976, *44,* 183–190.

Helmreich, R. L., Spence, J. T., & Holahan, C. K. Psychological androgyny and sex role flexibility: A test of two hypotheses. *Journal of Personality and Social Psychology,* 1979, *37,* 1631–1644.

Hendin, H. Growing up dead: Student suicide. In E. S. Shneidman (Ed.), *Suicidology: Contemporary developments.* New York: Grune and Stratton, 1976.

Henggeler, S. W., Borduin, C. M., Rodick, J. D., & Tavormina, J. B. Importance of task content for family interaction research. *Developmental Psychology,* 1979, *15,* 660–661.

Henley, J. R., & Adams, L. D. Marijuana use in post-collegiate cohorts: Correlates of use, prevalence patterns, and factors associated with cessation. *Social Problems,* 1973, *20,* 514–520.

Herold, E. S. A dating adjustment scale for college students. *Adolescence,* 1973, *8,* 51–60.

Herold, E. S. Stages of date selection: A reconciliation of divergent findings on campus values in dating. *Adolescence,* 1974, *9,* 113–120.

Herold, E. S. Variables influencing the dating adjustment of university students. *Journal of Youth and Adolescence,* 1979, *8,* 73–79.

Hessellund, H. On some sociosexual sex differences. *Journal of Sex Research,* 1971, *7,* 263–273.

Hetherington, E. M. Effects of paternal absence on sex-typed behaviors in Negro and White preadolescent males. *Journal of Personality and Social Psychology,* 1966, *4,* 87–91.

Hetherington, E. M. Effects of father absence on personality development in adolescent daughters. *Developmental Psychology,* 1972, *7,* 313–326.

Hill, M. N. Suicidal behavior in adolescents and its relationship to the lack of parental empathy. (Doctoral dissertation, Smith College, 1969.) *Dissertation Abstracts International,* 1970, *31,* 472A.

Himadi, W. G., Arkowitz, H., Hinton, R., & Perl, J. Minimal dating and its relationship to other social problems and general adjustment. *Behavior Therapy,* 1980, *11,* 345–352.

Hindelang, M. J. Age, sex, and the versatility of delinquent involvements. *Social Problems,* 1971, *18,* 522–535.

Hindelang, M. J. Variations in sex-race-age-specific incidence rates of offending. *American Sociological Review,* 1981, *46,* 461–474.

Hirschi, T., & Hindelang, M. J. Intelligence and delinquency: A revisionist review. *American Sociological Review,* 1977, *42,* 571–587.

Hodgson, J. W., & Fischer, J. L. Pathways of identity development in college women. *Sex Roles*, 1981, *7*, 681–690.

Hoffman, M. L. Father absence and conscience development. *Developmental Psychology*, 1971, *4*, 400–406.

Hoffman, M. L. Moral development in adolescence. In J. Adelson (Ed.), *Handbook of adolescent psychology*. New York: Wiley, 1980.

Hoffman, M. L., & Saltzstein, H. D. Parent discipline and the child's moral development. *Journal of Personality and Social Psychology*, 1967, *5*, 45–57.

Hogan, R. A dimension of moral judgment. *Journal of Consulting and Clinical Psychology*, 1970, *35*, 205–212.

Hogan, R. The gifted adolescent. In J. Adelson (Ed.), *Handbook of adolescent psychology*. New York: Wiley, 1980.

Hogan, R., Mankin, D., Conway, J., & Fox, S. Personality correlates of undergraduate marijuana use. *Journal of Consulting and Clinical Psychology*, 1970, *35*, 58–63.

Hollingshead, A. B. *Elmtown's youth*. New York: McGraw-Hill, 1949.

Holstein, C. B. Irreversible, stepwise sequence in the development of moral judgment: A longitudinal study of males and females. *Child Development*, 1976, *47*, 51–61.

Hopkins, J. R. Attention span and language-communication skills in three groups of children. Unpublished Honors Thesis, University of Virginia, 1968.

Hopkins, J. R. Sexual behavior in adolescence. *Journal of Social Issues*, 1977, *33*, 67–85.

Hopkins, L. B. Inner space and outer space identity in contemporary females. *Psychiatry*, 1980, *43*, 1–12.

Horrocks, J. E., & Benimoff, M. Isolation from the peer group during adolescence. *Adolescence*, 1967, *2*, 41–52.

Hunt, M. *Sexual behavior in the 1970s*. New York: Playboy Press, 1974.

Huntley, C. W. Changes in Study of Values scores during the four years of college. *Genetic Psychology Monographs*, 1965, *71*, 349–383.

Husbands, C. T. Some social and psychological consequences of the American dating system. *Adolescence*, 1970, *5*, 451–462.

Hyde, J. S., & Phillis, D. E. Androgyny across the life span. *Developmental Psychology*, 1979, *15*, 334–336.

Iacovetta, R. G. Adolescent-adult interaction and peer-group involvement. *Adolescence*, 1975, *10*, 327–336.

Inhelder, B., & Piaget, J. [*The growth of logical thinking from childhood to adolescence*.] (A. Parsons and S. Milgram, trans.) London: Routledge and Kegan Paul, 1958. (Originally published, 1955.)

Isen, A. M. Success, failure, attention, and reaction to others: The warm glow of success. *Journal of Personality and Social Psychology*, 1970, *15*, 294–301.

Jacobson, L. I., Berger, S. E., & Millham, J. Individual differences in cheating during a temptation period when confronting failure. *Journal of Personality and Social Psychology*, 1970, *15*, 48–56.

Jaffe, R. *Class reunion.* New York: Delacorte Press, 1979.

Jennings, M. K., Ehman, L. H., & Niemi, R. G. Social studies teachers and their pupils. In M. K. Jennings & R. G. Niemi (Eds.), *The political character of adolescence: The influence of families and schools.* Princeton: Princeton University Press, 1974.

Jennings, M. K., & Niemi, R. G. Continuity and change in political orientations: A longitudinal study of two generations. *American Political Science Review,* 1975, *69,* 1316–1335.

Jennings, M. K., & Niemi, R. G. *The political character of adolescence: The influence of families and schools.* Princeton: Princeton University Press, 1974.

Jessor, R., Costa, F., Jessor, L., & Donovan, J. E. The time of first intercourse: A prospective study. Unpublished manuscript, 1981. (*Journal of Personality and Social Psychology,* in press.)

Jessor, S., & Jessor, R. Transition from virginity to nonvirginity among youth: A social-psychological study over time. *Developmental Psychology,* 1975, *11,* 473–484.

Johnson, C. D., & Gormly, J. Academic cheating: The contribution of sex, personality, and situational variables. *Developmental Psychology,* 1972, *6,* 320–325.

Johnston, F. E. Control of age at menarche. *Human Biology,* 1974, *46,* 159–171.

Johnston, L. D. *Drugs and American youth.* Ann Arbor: Institute for Social Research, 1973.

Jones, M. C. The later careers of boys who were early- or late-maturing. *Child Development,* 1957, *28,* 113–128.

Jones, M. C., & Mussen, P. H. Self-conceptions, motivations, and interpersonal attitudes of early- and late-maturing girls. *Child Development,* 1958, *29,* 491–501.

Josselson, R. Ego development in adolescence. In J. Adelson (Ed.), *Handbook of adolescent psychology.* New York: Wiley, 1980.

Josselson, R., Greenberger, E., & McConochie, D. Phenomenological aspects of psychosocial maturity in adolescence. Part I: Boys. *Journal of Youth and Adolescence,* 1977, *6,* 25–56.

Judah, J. S. The Hare Krishna movement. In I. I. Zaretsky & M. P. Leone (Eds.), *Religious movements in contemporary America.* Princeton: Princeton University Press, 1974.

Jurich, A. P., & Jurich, J. A. The effect of cognitive moral development upon the selection of premarital sexual standards. *Journal of Marriage and the Family,* 1974, *36,* 736–741.

Kaats, G. R., & Davis, K. E. The dynamics of sexual behavior of college students. *Journal of Marriage and the Family,* 1970, *32,* 390–399.

Kacergius, M. A., & Adams, G. R. Erikson stage resolution: The relationship between identity and intimacy. *Journal of Youth and Adolescence,* 1980, *9,* 117–126.

Kagan, J. A conception of early adolescence. In J. Kagan & R. Coles (Eds.), *12 to 16: Early adolescence.* New York: Norton, 1972.

Kandel, D. B. Inter- and intragenerational influence on adolescent marijuana use. *Journal of Social Issues*, 1974, *30* (2), 107–135.

Kandel, D. B., & Lesser, G. S. Parental and peer influences on educational plans of adolescents. *American Sociological Review*, 1969, *34*, 213–223.

Kandel, D. B., & Lesser, G. S. *Youth in two worlds: United States and Denmark.* San Francisco: Jossey-Bass, 1972.

Kantner, J. F., & Zelnik, M. Sexual experience of young unmarried women in the United States. *Family Planning Perspectives*, 1972, *4*, 9–18.

Karpinos, B. D. Current height and weight of youths of military age. *Human Biology*, 1961, *33*, 335–354.

Katchadourian, H. *The biology of adolescence.* San Francisco: Freeman, 1977.

Keasey, C. B. Social participation as a factor in the moral development of preadolescents. *Developmental Psychology*, 1971, *5*, 216–220.

Keating, D. P. Precocious cognitive development at the level of formal operations. *Child Development*, 1975, *46*, 276–280.

Keating, D. P., & Clark, L. V. Development of physical and social reasoning in adolescence. *Developmental Psychology*, 1980, *16*, 23–30.

Keefe, D. R. A comparison of the effect of teacher and student led discussions of short stories and case accounts on the moral reasoning of adolescents using the Kohlberg model. (Doctoral dissertation, University of Illinois, Champaign-Urbana, 1975.) *Dissertation Abstracts International*, 1976, *36*, 2734.

Keniston, K. *The uncommitted: Alienated youth in American society.* New York: Dell, 1965.

Keniston, K. *Young radicals: Notes on committed youth.* New York: Harcourt, Brace, and World, 1968.

Kerckoff, A. C. Social class differences in sexual attitudes and behavior. *Medical Aspects of Human Sexuality*, 1974, *8*, 10.

Kerouac, J. *On the road.* New York: Signet, 1957.

Kett, J. F. *Rites of passage: Adolescence in America 1790 to the present.* New York: Basic Books, 1977.

Kiernan, K. E. Age at puberty in relation to age at marriage and parenthood: A national longitudinal study. *Annals of Human Biology*, 1977, *4*, 301–308.

Kimmel, D. C. *Adulthood and aging* (2nd ed.). New York, Wiley, 1980.

Kimura, D. Spatial localization in left and right visual fields. *Canadian Journal of Psychology*, 1969, *23*, 445–458.

Kimura, K. A consideration of the secular trend in Japanese for height and weight by a graphic method. *American Journal of Physical Anthropology*, 1967, *27*, 89–94.

King, K., Balswick, J. O., & Robinson, I. E. The continuing premarital sexual revolution among college females. *Journal of Marriage and the Family*, 1977, *39*, 455–459.

Kinsey, A. C., Pomeroy, W. B., & Martin, C. E. *Sexual behavior in the human male.* Philadelphia: W. B. Saunders, 1948.

Kinsey, A. C., Pomeroy, W. B., Martin, C. E., & Gebhard, P. H. *Sexual be-*

havior in the human female. Philadelphia: W. B. Saunders, 1953.

Klagsbrun, F. *Youth and suicide: Too young to die.* New York: Houghton Mifflin, 1976.

Klapp, O. E. *Collective search for identity.* New York: Holt, Rinehart, and Winston, 1969.

Klein, H. M., & Willerman, L. Psychological masculinity and femininity and typical and maximal dominance expression in women. *Journal of Personality and Social Psychology,* 1979, *37,* 2059–2070.

Kloos, P. *The Maroni River Caribs of Surinam.* Assen: Van Gorcu, 1971.

Knapp, C. W., & Harwood, B. T. Factors in the determination of intimate same-sex friendship. *Journal of Genetic Psychology,* 1977, *131,* 83–90.

Knox, D. H., Jr., & Sporakowski, M. J. Attitudes of college students toward love. *Journal of Marriage and the Family,* 1968, *30,* 638–642.

Kohlberg, L. A cognitive-developmental analysis of children's sex-role concepts and attitudes. In E. E. Maccoby (Ed.), *The development of sex differences.* Stanford: Stanford University Press, 1966.

Kohlberg, L. Stage and sequence: The cognitive-developmental approach to socialization. In D. A. Goslin (Ed.), *Handbook of socialization theory and research.* Chicago: Rand McNally, 1969.

Kohlberg, L. Continuities in childhood and adult moral development revisited. In P. B. Baltes & K. W. Schaie (Eds.), *Life-span developmental psychology: Personality and socialization.* New York: Academic Press, 1973.

Kohlberg, L. Moral stages and moralization: The cognitive-developmental approach. In T. Lickona (Ed.), *Moral development and behavior: Theory, research, and social issues.* New York: Holt, Rinehart, and Winston, 1976.

Kohlberg, L., & Kramer, R. Continuities and discontinuities in childhood and adult moral development. *Human Development,* 1969, *12,* 93–120.

Komarovsky, M. Cultural contradictions and sex roles. *American Journal of Sociology,* 1946, *52,* 184–189.

Komarovsky, M. Cultural contradictions and sex roles: The masculine case. *American Journal of Sociology,* 1973, *78,* 873–884.

Komarovsky, M. *Dilemmas of masculinity: A study of college youth.* New York: Norton, 1976.

Krakowski, A. J. Depressive reactions of childhood and adolescence. *Psychosomatics,* 1970, *11,* 429–433.

Kratcoski, P. C., & Kratcoski, J. E. Changing patterns in the delinquent activities of boys and girls: A self-reported delinquency analysis. *Adolescence,* 1975, *10,* 83–92.

Krauss, I. K. Some situational determinants of competitive performance on sex-stereotyped tasks. *Developmental Psychology,* 1977, *13,* 473–480.

Kraut, R. E., & Lewis, S. H. Alternate models of family influence on student political ideology. *Journal of Personality and Social Psychology,* 1975, *31,* 791–800.

Krebs, D., & Rosenwald, A. Moral reasoning and moral behavior in conventional adults. *Merrill-Palmer Quarterly,* 1977, *23,* 77–87.

Kuhn, D. Relation of two Piagetian stage transitions to IQ. *Developmental Psychology,* 1976, *12,* 157–161.

Kuhn, D. Short-term longitudinal evidence for the sequentiality of Kohlberg's early stages of moral judgment. *Developmental Psychology*, 1976, *12*, 162–166.

Kuhn, D., & Angelev, J. An experimental study of the development of formal operational thought. *Child Development*, 1976, *47*, 697–706.

Kuhn, D., & Brannock, J. Development of the isolation of variables scheme in an experimental and "natural experiment" context. *Developmental Psychology*, 1977, *13*, 9–14.

Kulik, J. A., Stein, K. B., & Sarbin, T. R. Disclosure of delinquent behavior under conditions of anonymity and nonanonymity. *Journal of Consulting and Clinical Psychology*, 1968, *32*, 506–509.

Kulin, H. E. The physiology of adolescence in man. *Human Biology*, 1974, *46*, 133–144.

Kurfiss, J. Sequentiality and structure in a cognitive model of college student development. *Developmental Psychology*, 1977, *13*, 565–571.

Kurtines, W., & Greif, E. B. The development of moral thought: Review and evaluation of Kohlberg's approach. *Psychological Bulletin*, 1974, *81*, 453–470.

LaVoie, J. C. Ego identity formation in middle adolescence. *Journal of Youth and Adolescence*, 1976, *5*, 371–385.

Lawrence, M. Anorexia nervosa—the control paradox. *Women's Studies International Quarterly*, 1979, *2*, 93–101.

Lawrence, T. S., & Velleman, J. D. Correlates of student drug use in a suburban high school. *Psychiatry*, 1974, *37*, 129–136.

Lee, M. M. C., Chang, K. S. F., & Chan, M. M. C. Sexual maturation of Chinese girls in Hong Kong. *Pediatrics*, 1963, *32*, 389–398.

Lehrke, R. A theory of x-linkage of major intellectual traits. *American Journal of Mental Deficiency*, 1972, *76*, 611–619.

Leona, M. H. An examination of adolescent clique language in a suburban secondary school. *Adolescence*, 1978, *13*, 495–502.

Lerner, R. M., & Knapp, J. R. Actual and perceived intrafamilial attitudes of late adolescents and their parents. *Journal of Youth and Adolescence*. 1975, *4*, 17–36.

Lester, G., & Lester, D. *Suicide: The gamble with death.* Englewood Cliffs, NJ: Prentice-Hall, 1971.

Levenson, M., & Neuringer, C. Problem-solving behavior in suicidal adolescents. *Journal of Consulting and Clinical Psychology*, 1971, *37*, 433–436.

LeVine, R. A., & LeVine, B. B. Nyansongo: A Gusii community in Kenya. In B. Whiting (Ed.), *Six cultures: Studies in child rearing.* New York: Wiley, 1963.

Levinson, D. J. *The seasons of a man's life.* New York: A. A. Knopf, 1978.

Lewis, R. A. Parents and peers: Socialization agents in the coital behavior of young adults. *Journal of Sex Research*, 1973, *9*, 156–170.

Lewis, R. A., & Burr, W. R. Premarital coitus and commitment among college students. *Archives of Sexual Behavior*, 1975, *4*, 73–79.

Libby, R. W., Gray, L., & White, M. A test and reformulation of reference group and role correlates of premarital sexual permissiveness theory. *Journal of Marriage and the Family*, 1978, *40*, 79–92.

Liben, L. S. Performance on Piagetian spatial tasks as a function of sex, field dependence, and training. *Merrill-Palmer Quarterly*, 1978, *24*, 97–110.

Lickona, T. (Ed.), *Moral development and behavior: Theory, research, and social issues.* New York: Holt, Rinehart, and Winston, 1976.

Lipton, D. N., & Nelson, R. O. The contribution of initiation behaviors to dating frequency. *Behavior Therapy*, 1980, *11*, 59–67.

Livson, N., & Peskin, H. Perspectives on adolescence from longitudinal research. In J. Adelson (Ed.), *Handbook of adolescent psychology.* New York: Wiley, 1980.

Loevinger, J. The meaning and measurement of ego development. *American Psychologist*, 1966, *21*, 195–206.

Looft, W. R. Egocentrism and social interaction across the life span. *Psychological Bulletin*, 1972, *78*, 73–92.

LoPiccolo, J. Mothers and daughters: Perceived and real differences in sexual values. *Journal of Sex Research*, 1973, *9*, 171–177.

Lorimer, R. M. The acquisition of moral judgments in adolescence: The effects of an exposition of basic concepts versus exposure to, and discussion of a filmed dramatic example. (Doctoral dissertation, University of Toronto, 1968.) *Dissertation Abstracts International*, 1970, *31*, 2187A.

Lovell, K. A follow-up study of Inhelder and Piaget's *The growth of logical thinking. British Journal of Psychology*, 1961, *52*, 143–153.

Lowrie, S. H. Dating theories and student responses. *American Sociological Review*, 1951, *16*, 334–340.

Luckey, E. B., & Nass, G. D. A comparison of sexual attitudes and behavior in an international sample. *Journal of Marriage and the Family*, 1969, *31*, 364–379.

Lunzer, E. Some points of Piagetian theory in the light of experimental criticism. *Journal of Child Psychology and Psychiatry*, 1960, *1*, 191–202.

MacArthur, R. Sex differences in field dependence for the Eskimo. *International Journal of Psychology*, 1967, *2*, 139–140.

Maccoby, E. E., & Jacklin, C. N. *The psychology of sex differences.* Stanford: Stanford University Press, 1974.

Maddock, J. W. Sex in adolescence: Its meaning and its future. *Adolescence*, 1973, *8*, 325–342.

Malina, R. M. Comparison of the increase in body size between 1899 and 1970 in a specially selected group with that in the general population. *American Journal of Physical Anthropology*, 1972, *37*, 135–142.

Malina, R. M. Secular changes in size and maturity: Causes and effects. In A. F. Roche (Ed.), Secular trends in human growth, maturation, and development. *Monographs of the Society for Research in Child Development*, 1979, *44* (Serial No. 179).

Malinowski, B. *The sexual life of savages in northwestern Melanesia.* London: Routledge and Kegan Paul, 1929.

Mannarino, A. P. Friendship patterns and altruistic behavior in preadolescent males. *Developmental Psychology*, 1976, *12*, 555–556.

Mannheim, K. The problem of generations. In P. B. Altbach & R. S. Laufer

(Eds.), *The new pilgrims: Youth protest in transition.* New York: McKay, 1972, (Originally published, 1952.)

Manosevitz, M. The development of male homosexuality. *Journal of Sex Research,* 1972, *8,* 31–40.

Marcia, J. E. Development and validation of ego-identity status. *Journal of Personality and Social Psychology,* 1966, *3,* 551–558.

Marcia, J. E. Identity six years after: A follow-up study. *Journal of Youth and Adolescence,* 1976, *5,* 145–160.

Marcia, J. E. Identity in adolescence. In J. Adelson (Ed.), *Handbook of adolescent psychology.* New York: Wiley, 1980.

Marcia, J. E., & Friedman, M. L. Ego identity status in college women. *Journal of Personality,* 1970, *38,* 249–263.

Marshall, D. S. Sexual behavior on Mangaia. In D. S. Marshall & R. C. Suggs (Eds.), *Human sexual behavior: Variations in the ethnographic spectrum.* New York: Basic Books, 1971.

Marshall, W. A., & Tanner, J. M. Variations in the pattern of pubertal changes in boys. *Archives of Disease in Childhood,* 1970, *45,* 13–23.

Martorano, S. C. A developmental analysis of performance on Piaget's formal operations tasks. *Developmental Psychology,* 1977, *13,* 666–672.

Masterson, J. F., Jr. Prognosis in adolescent disorders—schizophrenia. *Journal of Nervous and Mental Diseases,* 1956, *124,* 219–232.

Matza, D. *Delinquency and drift.* New York: Wiley, 1964.

McArarney, E. R. Adolescent and young adult suicide in the United States—a reflection of societal unrest? *Adolescence,* 1979, *14,* 765–774.

McAree, C. P., Steffenhagen, R. A., & Zheutlin, L. S. Personality factors and patterns of drug usage in college students. *American Journal of Psychiatry,* 1972, *128,* 890–891.

McClelland, D. C. Testing for competence rather than for "intelligence." *American Psychologist,* 1973, *28,* 1–14.

McCormick, N. B. Come-ons and put-offs: Unmarried students' strategies for having and avoiding sexual intercourse. *Psychology of Women Quarterly,* 1979, *4,* 194–211.

McCullers, C. *The member of the wedding.* New York: Penguin, 1946.

McGee, M. G. Human spatial abilities: Psychometric studies and environmental, genetic, hormonal, and neurological influences. *Psychological Bulletin,* 1979, *86,* 889–918.

McGinn, P. V., Viernstein, M. C., & Hogan, R. Fostering the intellectual development of verbally gifted adolescents. *Journal of Educational Psychology,* 1980, *72,* 494–498.

Mead, G. H. *Mind, self, and society.* Chicago: University of Chicago Press, 1934.

Mead, M. *Sex and temperament in three primitive societies.* New York: Dell, 1935.

Mead, M. *Male and female.* New York: Penguin, 1949.

Mead, M. Adolescence in primitive and in modern society. In E. E. Maccoby, T. M. Newcomb, & E. L. Hartley (Eds.), *Readings in social psychology* (3rd ed.). New York: Holt, Rinehart, and Winston, 1958.

Mead, M. Introduction. In W. Ehrman. *Premarital dating behavior*. New York: Henry Holt, 1959.

Meggitt, M. J. Male-female relationships in the highlands of Australian New Guinea. *American Antrhopologist*, 1964, *66*, 204–224.

Meilman, P. W. Cross-sectional age changes in ego identity status during adolescence. *Developmental Psychology*, 1979, *15*, 230–231.

Meredith, H. V. Findings from Asia, Australia, Europe, and North America on secular change in mean height of children, youths and young adults. *American Journal of Physical Anthropology*, 1976, *44*, 315–326.

Merelman, R. M. Moral development and potential radicalism in adolescence: A reconnaissance. *Youth and Society*, 1977, *9*, 29–54.

Merton, R. K. *Social theory and social structure*. Glencoe, Ill.: Free Press, 1957.

Mickelson, R. A. Social stratification processes in secondary schools: A comparison of Beverly Hills High School and Morningside High School. *Journal of Education*, 1980, *162*, 83–112.

Middlebrook, D. W. *Worlds into words: Understanding modern poems*. Stanford, Calif.: Stanford Alumni Association, 1978.

Milgram, R. M., Milgram, N. A., Rosenbloom, G., & Rabkin, L. Quantity and quality of creative thinking in children and adolescents. *Child Development*, 1978, *49*, 385–388.

Milgram, S. Some conditions of obedience and disobedience to authority. *Human Relations*, 1965, *18*, 57–76.

Milgram, S. *Obedience to authority*. New York: Harper and Row, 1974.

Miller, D. R. The study of social relationships: Situation, identity, and social interaction. In S. Koch (Ed.), *Psychology: A study of a science* (Vol. 5). New York: McGraw-Hill, 1963.

Miller, P. H., Kessel, F. S., & Flavell, J. H. Thinking about people thinking about people thinking about . . . A study of social cognitive development. *Child Development*, 1970, *41*, 613–624.

Miller, P. Y., & Simon, W. Adolescent sexual behavior: Context and change. *Social Problems*, 1974, *22*, 58–76.

Miller, P. Y., & Simon, W. The development of sexuality in adolescence. In J. Adelson (Ed.), *Handbook of adolescent psychology*. New York: Wiley, 1980.

Miller, W. B. Lower class culture as a generating milieu of gang delinquency. *Journal of Social Issues*, 1958, *14*, 5–19. (Reprinted in D. R. Cressey & D. A. Ward (Eds.), *Delinquency, crime and social process*. New York: Harper and Row, 1969).

Milne, L. *The home of an Eastern clan: A study of the Palungs of the Shan States*. Oxford: Clarendon, 1924.

Minturn, L., & Hitchcock, J. T. *The Rajputs of Khalapur, India*. In B. Whting (Ed.), *Six cultures: Studies in child rearing*. New York: Wiley, 1963.

Mirande, A. M. Reference group theory and adolescent sexual behavior. *Journal of Marriage and the Family*, 1968, *30*, 572–577.

Mischel, W., & Mischel, H. N. A cognitive social-learning approach to morality and self-regulation. In T. Lickona (Ed.), *Moral development and behavior*. New York: Holt, Rinehart, and Winston, 1976.

Money, J., & Clopper, R. R., Jr. Psychosocial and psychosexual aspects of errors of pubertal onset and development. *Human Biology*, 1974, *46*, 173–181.

Montemayor, R., & Eisen, M. The development of self-conceptions from childhood to adolescence. *Developmental Psychology*, 1977, *13*, 314–319.

Moos, R. H., Moos, B. S., & Kulik, J. A. College-student abstainers, moderate drinkers, and heavy drinkers: A comparative analysis. *Journal of Youth and Adolescence*, 1976, *5*, 349–360.

Morash, M. A. Working class membership and the adolescent identity crisis. *Adolescence*, 1980, *15*, 313–320.

Morgan, D. Seniors tell what high school didn't prepare them for. *The Washington Post*, June 25, 1980, p. A2.

Mosher, D. L., & Cross, H. J. Sex guilt and premarital sexual experiences of college students. *Journal of Consulting and Clinical Psychology*, 1971, *36*, 27–32.

Moshman, D. Consolidation and stage formation in the emergence of formal operations. *Developmental Psychology*, 1977, *13*, 95–100.

Munro, G., & Adams, G. R. Ego identity formation in college students and working youth. *Developmental Psychology*, 1977, *13*, 523–524.

Murray, F. B., & Armstrong, S. L. Adult nonconservation of numerical equivalence. *Merrill-Palmer Quarterly*, 1978, *24*, 255–263.

Mussen, P. H., & Jones, M.C. Self-conceptions, motivations, and interpersonal attitudes of late- and early-maturing boys. *Child Development*, 1957, *28*, 243–256.

Naftolin, F., Ryan, K. J., & Petro, Z. Aromatization of androstenedione by the diencephalon. *Journal of Clinical Endocrinology and Metabolism*, 1971, *33*, 368–370.

Nash, S. The relationship among sex-role stereotyping, sex-role preference, and the sex difference in spatial visualization. *Sex Roles*, 1975, *1*, 15–32.

Neuringer, C. Dichotomous evaluations in suicidal individuals. *Journal of Consulting Psychology*, 1961, *25*, 445–449.

Neuringer, C. Rigid thinking in suicidal individuals, *Journal of Consulting Psychology*, 1964, *28*, 54–58.

Newcomb, T. M. Youth in colleges and corrections; Institutional influences. *American Psychologist*, 1978, *33*, 114–124.

Nicolson, A. B., & Hanley, C. Indices of physiological maturity: Derivation and interrelationships. *Child Development*, 1953, *24*, 3–38.

Noe, F. P., & Elifson, K. W. The pleasures of youth: Parent and peer compliance toward discretionary time. *Journal of Youth and Adolescence*, 1976, *5*, 37–58.

Noller, P. Sex differences in the socialization of affectionate expression. *Developmental Psychology*, 1978, *14*, 317–319.

Norris, D. L., & Jones, E. Anorexia nervosa—a clinical study of ten patients and their family systems. *Journal of Adolescence*, 1979, *2*, 101–111.

O'Donnell, W. J. Adolescent self-esteem related to feelings toward parents and friends. *Journal of Youth and Adolescence*, 1976, *5*, 179–185.

Offer, D., & Offer, J. B. *From teenage to young manhood: A psychological study*. New York: Basic Books, 1975.

Orloff, H., & Weinstock, A. A comparison of parent and adolescent attitude factor structures. *Adolescence*, 1975, *10*, 201–205.

Oshman, H. P., & Manosevitz, M. Father absence: Effects of stepfathers upon psychosocial development in males. *Developmental Psychology*, 1976, *12*, 479–480.

Otto, U. Suicidal attempts in childhood and adolescence—today and after ten years. A follow-up study. In A. Annell (Ed.), *Depressive states in childhood and adolescence*. Stockholm: Almqvist and Wiksell, 1972.

Owen, D. *High school: Undercover with the class of '80.* New York: Viking Press, 1981.

Pable, M. W. Some parental determinants of ego identity in adolescent boys. *Dissertation Abstracts International*, 1965, *26*, 3480–3481.

Parish, T. S., & Copeland, T. F. The impact of father absence on moral development in females. *Sex Roles*, 1981, 7, 635–636.

Parsons, A., & Milgram, S. Translators' introduction: A guide for psychologists. In B. Inhelder & J. Piaget, [*The growth of logical thinking from childhood to adolescence*]. (A. Parsons and S. Milgram, trans.) New York: Basic Books, 1958.

Parsons, T., & Bales, R. F. *Family, socialization, and interaction process.* Glencoe, Ill.: Free Press, 1955.

Paton, S. M., & Kandel, D. B. Psychological factors and adolescent illicit drug use: Ethnicity and sex differences. *Adolescence*, 1978, *13*, 187–200.

Patrick, J. J. Political socialization and political education in schools. In S. A. Renshon (Ed.), *Handbook of political socialization: Theory and research.* New York: Free Press, 1977.

Peplau, L. A. Impact of fear of success and sex-role attitudes on women's competitive achievement. *Journal of Personality and Social Psychology*, 1976, *34*, 561–568.

Peplau, L. A., Rubin, Z., & Hill, C. T. Sexual intimacy in dating relationships. *Journal of Social Issues*, 1977, *33*, (2), 86–109.

Perry, W. B. *Forms of ethical and intellectual development in the college years: A scheme.* New York: Holt, Rinehart, and Winston, 1970.

Peskin, H. Influence of the developmental schedule of puberty on learning and ego functioning. *Journal of Youth and Adolescence*, 1973, *2*, 273–290.

Petersen, A. C. Physical functioning in adolescence. *Developmental Psychology*, 1976, *12*, 524–533.

Petersen, A. C., & Taylor, B. The biological approach to adolescence: Biological change and psychological adaptation. In J. Adelson (Ed.), *Handbook of adolescent psychology.* New York: Wiley, 1980.

Piaget, J. [*Thee moral judgment of the child*]. (M. Gabain, trans.) London: Routledge and Kegan Paul, 1932.

Piaget, J. [*The psychology of intelligence.*] (M. Piercy and D. E. Berlyne, trans.) London: Routledge and Kegan Paul, 1950. (Originally published, 1947).

Piaget, J. [*Genetic epistemology.*] (E. Duckworth, trans.) New York: Norton, 1970.

Piaget, J. Piaget's theory. In P. H. Mussen (Ed.), *Carmichael's manual of child psychology*, Vol. 1 (3rd ed.) New York: Wiley, 1970.

Piaget, J. The theory of stages in cognitive development. In D. R. Green, M. P. Ford, & G. B. Flamer (Eds.), *Measurement and Piaget*. New York: McGraw-Hill, 1971.

Piaget, J. [*The child and reality: Problems of genetic epistemology.*] (A. Rosen, trans.) New York: Viking Press, 1973. (Originally published, 1972.)

Piaget, J. Intellectual evolution from adolescence to adulthood. *Human Development*, 1972, *15*, 1–12.

Piaget, J., & Inhelder, B. [*The child's conception of space.*] (F. J. Langdon and J. L. Lunzer, trans.) New York: Norton, 1967. (Originally published, 1948.)

Piaget, J., & Inhelder, B. [*The psychology of the child.*] (H. Weaver, trans.) London: Routledge and Kegan Paul, 1969. (Originally published, 1966.)

Piliavin, I., & Briar, S. Police encounters with juveniles. *American Journal of Sociology*, 1964, *70*, 206–214.

Place, D. M. The dating experience for adolescent girls. *Adolescence*, 1975, *10*, 157–174.

Podd, M. H. Ego identity status and morality: The relationship between two developmental constructs. *Developmental Psychology*, 1972, *6*, 497–507.

Podd, M. H., Marcia, J. E., & Rubin, B. M. The effects of ego identity and partner perception on a prisoner's dilemma game. *Journal of Social Psychology*, 1970, *82*, 117–126.

Porges, S. W. Ontogenetic comparisons. *International Journal of Psychology*, 1976, *11*, 203–214.

Prince, R. H. Cocoon work: An interpretation of the concern of contemporary youth with the mystical. In I. I. Zaretsky & M. P. Leone (Eds.), *Religious movements in contemporary America*. Princeton: Princeton University Press, 1974.

Ralston, N. C., & Thomas, G. P. *The adolescent: Case studies for analysis*. New York: Chandler, 1974.

Raucher, H. *Summer of '42*. New York: Dell, 1971.

Ray, W. J., Georgiou, S., & Ravizza, R. Spatial abilities, sex differences, and lateral eye movements. *Developmental Psychology*, 1979, *15*, 455–457.

Reinhold, R. Census finds unmarried couples have doubled from 1970 to 1978. *The New York Times*, June 27, 1979, pp. 1; B5.

Reiss, I. L. The sexual renaissance: A summary and analysis. *Journal of Social Issues*, 1966, *22*, (2), 123–137.

Reiss, I. L. Social class and premarital sexual permissiveness: A re-examination. *American Sociological Review*, 1965, *30*, 747–756.

Reiss, I. *The social context of premarital sexual permissiveness*. New York: Holt, Rinehart, and Winston, 1967.

Rest, J. R. Longitudinal study of the Defining Issues Test of moral judgment: A strategy for analyzing moral change. *Developmental Psychology*, 1975, *11*, 738–748.

Rest, J. R., Cooper, D., Coder, R., Masanz, J., & Anderson, D. Judging the important issues in moral dilemmas. *Developmental Psychology*, 1974, *10*, 491–501.

Rest, J. R., Davison, M. L., & Robbins, S. Age trends in judging moral issues: A review of cross-sectional, longitudinal, and sequential studies of the Defining Issues Test. *Child Development*, 1978, *49*, 263–279.

Rich, H. E. The effect of college on political awareness and knowledge. *Youth and Society*, 1976, *8*, 67–80.

Richards, A. I. *Chisungu: A girl's initiation ceremony among the Bemba of northern Rhodesia*. London: Faber and Faber, 1956.

Richardson, T. F. Anorexia nervosa: An overview. *American Journal of Nursing*, 1980, *80*, 1470–1471.

Richey, M. H., & Richey, H. W. The significance of best-friend relationships in adolescence. *Psychology in the Schools*, 1980, *17*, 536–540.

Rierdan, J., & Koff, E. The psychological impact of menarche: Integrative versus disruptive changes. *Journal of Youth and Adolescence*, 1980, *9*, 49–58.

Robbins, T. *Even cowgirls get the blues*. New York: Bantam Books, 1976.

Roberge, J. J., & Flexner, B. K. Further examination of formal operational reasoning abilities. *Child Development*, 1979, *50*, 478–484.

Robey, A. The runaway girl. In O. Pollak & A. Friedman (Eds.), *Family dynamics and female sexual delinquency*. Palo Alto: Science and Behavior Books, 1969.

Robinson, I. E., King, K., & Balswick, J. O. The premarital sexual revolution among college females. *Family Coordinator*, 1972, *21*, 189–194.

Robinson, P. A. Parents of "beyond control" adolescents. *Adolescence*, 1978, *13*, 109–119.

Roche, A. F. Secular trends in stature, weight, and maturation. In A. F. Roche (Ed.), Secular trends in human growth, maturation, and development. *Monographs of the Society for Research in Child Development*, 1979, *44*, (Serial No. 179).

Root, A. W. Endocrinology of puberty, I. Normal sexual maturation. *Journal of Pediatrics*, 1973, *83*, 1–19.

Rosenberg, C. M. Young alcoholics. *British Journal of Psychiatry*, 1969, *115*, 181–188.

Rosenkrantz, P., Vogel, S., Bee, H., Broverman, I., & Broverman, D. M. Sex-role stereotypes and self-concepts in college students. *Journal of Consulting and Clinical Psychology*, 1968, *32*, 287–295.

Rothbaum, F. Developmental and gender differences in the sex stereotyping of nurturance and dominance. *Developmental Psychology*, 1977, *13*, 531–532.

Rothbaum, F. Comprehension of the objectivity-subjectivity distinction in childhood and early adolescence. *Child Development*, *1979, 50*, 1184–1191.

Rotter, J. B. Generalized expectancies for internal versus external control of reinforcement. *Psychological Monographs*, 1966, *80* (Whole No. 609).

Rubin, Z., Peplau, L. A., & Hill, C. T. Loving and leaving: Sex differences in romantic attachments. *Sex Roles*, 1981, *7*, 821–835.

Rudy, A. J. Sex-role perceptions in early adolescence. *Adolescence*, 1968, *3*, 453–470.

Saarni, C. I. Piagetian operations and field independence as factors in children's problem-solving performance. *Child Development*, 1973, *44*, 338–345.

St. Clair, R. E. A study of the changes in moral judgment patterns of college students. (Doctoral dissertation, University of Virginia, 1975.) *Dissertation Abstracts International*, 1976, *36*, 5656.

Salinger, J. D. *The catcher in the rye.* Boston: Little-Brown, 1951.

Schalmo, G. B., & Levin, B. H. Presence of the double standard in a college population. *Psychological Reports*, 1974, *34*, 227–230.

Schenkel, S., & Marcia, J. E. Attitudes toward premarital intercourse in determining ego identity status in college women. *Journal of Personality*, 1972, *40*, 472–482.

Schiff, E., & Koopman, E. J. The relationship of women's sex-role identity to self-esteem and ego development. *Journal of Psychology*, 1978, *98*, 299–305.

Schlossman, S., & Wallach, S. The crime of precocious sexuality: Female juvenile delinquency in the progressive era. *Harvard Education Review*, 1978, *48*, 65–94.

Schofield, M. *The sexual behavior of young people.* Middlesex, England: Penguin, 1965.

Schulz, B., Bohrnstedt, G. W., Borgatta, E. F., & Evans, R. R. Explaining premarital sexual intercourse among college students: A causal model. *Social Forces*, 1977, *56*, 148–165.

Schwartz, S. H., Feldman, K. A., Brown, M. E., & Heingartner, A. Some personality correlates of conduct in two situations of moral conflict. *Journal of Personality*, 1969, *37*, 41–57.

Schwartz, S. K. The validity of adolescents' political responses. *Youth and Society*, 1977, *8*, 212–243.

Scott, J. A. *Report on the heights and weights (and other measurements) of school pupils in the County of London in 1959.* London: County Council, 1961.

Sears, R. R., Maccoby, E. E., & Levin, H. *Patterns of child rearing.* Evanston, Ill.: Row, Peterson, 1957.

Sebald, H., & White, B. Teenagers' divided reference groups: Uneven alignment with parents and peers. *Adolescence*, 1980, *15*, 979–984.

Sebert, S. K., Jennings, M. K., & Niemi, R. G. The political texture of peer groups. In M. K. Jennings & R. G. Niemi (Eds.), *The political character of adolescence.* Princeton: Princeton University Press, 1974.

Seiden, R. H. *Suicide among youth.* United States Government Printing Office, Publication No. 1971, 1969.

Selman, R. Social-cognitive understanding. In T. Lickona (Ed.), *Moral development and behavior.* New York: Holt, Rinehart, and Winston, 1976.

Sexton, A. *Transformations.* Boston: Houghton Mifflin, 1971.

Shakir, A. The age at menarche in girls attending schools in Baghdad. *Human Biology*, 1971, *43*, 265–270.

Shanteau, J., & Nagy, G. F. Probability of acceptance in dating choice. *Journal of Personality and Social Psychology*, 1979, *37*, 522–533.

Shantz, C. U. A developmental study of Piaget's theory of logical multiplication. *Merrill-Palmer Quarterly*, 1967, *13*, 121–137.

Sherman, J. Mathematics, spatial visualization, and related factors: Changes in girls and boys, grades 8–11. *Journal of Educational Psychology*, 1980, *72*, 476–482.

Siegler, R. S. Development sequences within and between concepts. *Monographs of the Society for Research in Child Development*, 1981, *46*, (2, Serial No. 189).

Signorella, M. L., & Jamison, W. Sex differences in the correlations among field dependence, spatial ability, sex role orientation, and performance on Piaget's water-level task. *Developmental Psychology*, 1978, *14*, 689–690.

Silbiger, S. L. Peers and political socialization. In S. A. Renshon (Ed.), *Handbook of political socialization: Theory and research*. New York: Free Press, 1977.

Silverman, I. W. Incidence of guilt reactions in children. *Journal of Personality and Social Psychology*, 1967, 7, 338–340.

Simon, W. Sex. *Psychology Today*, July, 1969, pp. 23–27.

Simon, W., Berger, A. S., & Gagnon, J. H. Beyond anxiety and fantasy: The coital experiences of college youth. *Journal of Youth and Adolescence*, 1972, *1*, 203–222.

Simpson, E. L. Moral development research: A case study of scientific cultural bias. *Human Development*, 1974, *17*, 81–106.

Snyder, S, S., & Feldman, D. H. Internal and external influences on cognitive developmental change. *Child Development*, 1977, *48*, 937–943.

Sorensen, R. C. *Adolescent sexuality in contemporary America*. New York: World, 1972.

Spence, J. T., & Helmreich, R. L. *Masculinity and femininity: Their psychological dimensions, correlates, and antecedents*. Austin: University of Texas Press, 1978.

Spock, B. *Baby and child care*. New York: Pocket Books, 1976.

Starr, J. M. The peace and love generation: Changing attitudes toward sex and violence among college youth. *Journal of Social Issues*, 1974, *30*, 73–106.

Staub, E. A child in distress: The influence of nurturance and modeling on children's attempts to help. *Developmental Pscyhology*, 1971, *5*, 124–132.

Steinberg, L. D., Greenberger, E., Garduque, L., Ruggiero, M., & Vaux, A. Effects of working on adolescent development. *Developmental Psychology*, 1982, *18*, 385–395.

Steinberg, L. D., & Hill, J. P. Patterns of family interaction as a function of age, the onset of puberty, and formal thinking. *Developmental Psychology*, 1978, *14*, 683–684.

Stolz, H. R., & Stolz, L. M. *Somatic development of adolescent boys*. New York: Macmillan, 1951.

Stone, C. A., & Day, M. C. Levels of availability of a formal operational strategy. *Child Development*, 1978, *49*, 1054–1065.

Stone, L. H., Miranne, A. C., & Ellis, G. J. Parent-peer influence as a predictor of marijuana use. *Adolescence*, 1979, *14*, 115–122.

Sullivan, H. S. (H. S. Perry & M. L. Gawel, Eds.) *The interpersonal theory of psychiatry.* New York: Norton, 1953.

Sullivan, K., & Sullivan, A. Adolescent-parent separation. *Developmental Psychology*, 1980, *16*, 93–99.

Surber, C. F. Developmental precesses in social inference: Averaging of intentions and consequences in moral judgment. *Developmental Psychology*, 1977, *13*, 654–665.

Tanner, J. M. *Growth at adolescence* (2nd ed.) Oxford: Blackwell Scientific Publications, 1962.

Tanner, J. M. Sequence, tempo, and individual variation in growth and development of boys and girls aged twelve to sixteen. In J. Kagan & R. Coles (Eds.), *12 to 16: Early adolescence.* New York: Norton, 1972.

Tanner, J. M. *Fetus into man: Physical growth from conception to maturity.* Cambridge: Harvard University Press, 1978.

Tavris, C., & Offir, C. *The longest war: Sex differences in perspective.* New York: Harcourt, Brace, Jovanovich, 1977.

Tavris, C., & Sadd, S. *The Redbook report on female sexuality.* New York: Delacorte, 1977.

Thomas, H., & Jamison, W. On the acquisition of understanding that still water is horizontal. *Merrill-Palmer Quarterly*, 1975, *21*, 31–44.

Thomas, L. E. Family correlates of student political activism. *Developmental Psychology*, 1971, *5*, 206–214.

Thompson, E. A., Smith-DiJulio, K., & Matthews, T. Social control theory: Evaluating a model for the study of adolescent alcohol and drug use. *Youth and Society*, 1982, *13*, 303–326.

Thompson, N. L., Schwartz, D. M., McCandless, B. R., & Edwards, D. A. Parent-child relationships and sexual identity in male and female homosexuals and heterosexuals. *Journal of Consulting and Clinical Psychology*, 1973, *41*, 120–127.

Thornburg, H. D. Peers: Three distinct groups. *Adolescence*, 1971, *6*, 59–76.

Toby, J. Affluence and adolescent crime. In D. R. Cressey & D. A. Ward (Eds.), *Delinquency, crime, and social process.* New York: Harper and Row, 1969.

Toder, N. L., & Marcia, J. E. Ego identity status and response to conformity pressure in college women. *Journal of Personality and Social Psychology*, 1973, *26*, 287–294.

Tomlinson-Keasey, C., & Keasey, C. B. Long-term cultural change in cognitive development. *Perceptual and Motor Skills*, 1972, *35*, 135–139.

Tomlinson-Keasey, C., & Keasey, C. B. The mediating role of cognitive development in moral judgment. *Child Development*, 1974, *45*, 291–298.

Toolan, J. M. Suicide in childhood and adolescence. *American Journal of Psychotherapy*, 1975, *29*, 339–344.

Touchton, J. G., Wertheimer, L. C., Cornfeld, J. L., & Harrison, K. H. Career planning and decision-making: A developmental approach to the classroom. *Counseling Psychologist*, 1977, *6*, (4), 42–47.

Touhey, J. C. Birth order and virginity. *Psychological Reports*, 1971, *28*, 894.

Trent, J. W., & Medsker, L. L. *Beyond high school.* San Francisco: Jossey-Bass, 1969.

Trickett, E. J. Toward a social-ecological conception of adolescent socialization: Normative data on contrasting types of public school classrooms. *Child Development*, 1978, *49*, 408–414.

Tucker, G. H., & Suib, M. R. Conjugate lateral eye movement (CLEM) direction and its relationship to performance on verbal and visuospatial tasks. *Neuropsychologia*, 1978, *16*, 251–254.

Turiel, E. Developmental processes in the child's moral thinking. In P. Mussen, J. Langer, & M. Covington (Eds.), *Trends and issues in developmental psychology.* New York: Holt, Rinehart, and Winston, 1969.

Turiel, E. Conflict and transition in adolescent moral development. *Child Development*, 1974, *45*, 14–29.

Turnbull, C. *The forest people.* London: Pan Books, 1961.

Turnbull, C. *The mountain people.* London: Pan Books, 1973.

United States Bureau of the Census. *Historical Statistics of the United States, Colonial Times to 1970*, Bicentennial edition, Part 2. Washington, D. C., 1975.

United States Bureau of the Census. *Statistical Abstract of the United States: 1980.* Washington, D. C., 1981.

United States Federal Bureau of Investigation. *Uniform Crime Reports.* Washington, D. C., 1979.

Urberg, K. A. Sex role conceptualizations in adolescents and adults. *Developmental Psychology*, 1979, *15*, 90–92.

Urberg, K. A., & Labouvie-Vief, G. Conceptualizations of sex roles: A life span developmental study. *Developmental psychology*, 1976, *12*, 15–23.

Vaillant, G. E. *Adaptation to life.* Boston: Little-Brown, 1977.

van Gennep, A. [*The rites of passage*]. (M. B. Vizedom and G. L. Caffee, trans.) London: Routledge and Kegan Paul, 1960. (Originally published, 1908.)

Vedder, C. B., & Somerville, D. B. *The delinquent girl* (2nd ed.). Springfield, Illinois: Charles C. Thomas, 1975.

Vener, A. M., & Stewart, C. S. Adolescent sexual behavior in middle America revisited: 1971–1973. *Journal of Marriage and the Family*, 1974, *36*, 728–735.

Vlastovsky, V. G. The secular trend in the growth and development of children and young persons in the Soviet Union. *Human Biology*, 1966, *38*, 219–230.

Waber, D. P. Sex differences in mental abilities, hemispheric lateralization, and rate of physical growth at adolescence. *Developmental Psychology*, 1977, *13*, 29–38.

Walker, L. J. Cognitive and perspective-taking prerequisites for moral development. *Child Development*, 1980, *51*, 131–139.

Walker, L. J., & Richards, B. S. Stimulating transitions in moral reasoning as a function of stage of cognitive development. *Developmental Psychology*, 1979, *15*, 95–103.

Waller, W. The rating and dating complex. *American Sociological Review*, 1937, *2*, 727–734.

Wason, P. C. Reasoning about a rule. *Quarterly Journal of Experimental Psychology*, 1968, *20*, 273–281.

Waterman, A. S. Identity development from adolescence to adulthood: An extension of theory and a review of research. *Developmental Psychology*, 1982, *18*, 341–358.

Waterman, A. S., Geary, P. S., & Waterman, C. K. Longitudinal study of changes in ego identity status from the freshman to the senior year at college. *Developmental Psychology*, 1974, *10*, 387–392.

Waterman, A. S., & Goldman, J. A. A longitudinal study of ego identity development at a liberal arts college. *Journal of Youth and Adolescence*, 1976, *5*, 361–369.

Waterman, A. S., & Waterman, C. K. Relationship between freshman ego identity status and subsequent academic behavior: A test of the predictive validity of Marcia's categorization system for identity status. *Developmental Psychology*, 1972, *6*, 179.

Waterman, C. K., & Nevid, J. S. Sex differences in the resolution of the identity crisis. *Journal of Youth and Adolescence*, 1977, *6*, 337–342.

Watley, D. J. Career progress: A longitudinal study of gifted students. *Journal of Counseling Psychology*, 1969, *16*, 100–108.

Watt, N. F., & Lubensky, A. W. Childhood roots of schizophrenia. *Journal of Consulting and Clinical Psychology*, 1976, *44*, 363–375.

Weatherley, D. Self-perceived rate of physical maturation and personality in late adolescence. *Child Development*, 1964, *35*, 1197–1210. (Reprinted in R. E. Grinder (Ed.), *Studies in adolescence* (3rd ed.). New York: Macmillan, 1975.)

Webb, A. P. Sex-role preferences and adjustment in early adolescents. *Child Development*, 1963, *34*, 609–618.

Webb, R. A. Concrete and formal operations in very bright 6- to 11-year-olds. *Human Development*, 1974, *17*, 292–300.

Weiner, I. B. *Psychological disturbance in adolescence.* New York: Wiley, 1970.

Weiner I. B. The generation gap—fact and fancy. *Adolescence*, 1971, *6*, 155–166.

Weiner, I. B. Psychopathology in adolescence. In J. Adelson (Ed.), *Handbook of adolescent psychology.* New York: Wiley, 1980.

Weissman, M. M. The epidemiology of suicide attempts, 1960–1971. *Archives of General Psychiatry*, 1974, *30*, 737–746.

Wenz, F. V. Sociological correlates of alienation among adolescent suicide attempts. *Adolescence*, 1979, *14*, 19–30.

Westby, D. L., & Braungart, R. G. Class and politics in the family backgrounds of student political activists. In A. M. Orum (Ed.), *The seeds of politics: Youth and politics in America.* Englewood Cliffs, NJ: Prentice-Hall, 1972.

Whatley, A. E., & Appel, V. H. Convergence of attitudes among college students. *Journal of College Student Personnel*, 1973, *14*, 511–516.

Wheeler, L., & Nezlik, J. Sex differences in social participation. *Journal of Personality and Social Psychology*, 1977, *35*, 742–754.

Whitbourne, S. K., Jilsma, B. M., & Waterman, A. S. An Eriksonian measure of personality development in college students: A reexamination of Constantinople's data and a partial replication. *Developmental Psychology*, 1982, *18*, 369–371.

Whiting, B. B. Sex identity conflict and physical violence: A comparative study. *American Anthropologist*, 1965, *67*, 123–140.

Whiting, B. B., & Pope, C. A cross-cultural analysis of sex differences in the behavior of children aged three to eleven. *Journal of Social Psychology*, 1974.

Whiting, J. W. M. *Becoming a Kwoma: Teaching and learning in a New Guinea tribe*. New Haven: Yale University Press, 1941.

Whiting, J. W. M., Kluckhohn, R., & Anthony, A. The function of male initiation ceremonies at puberty. In E. E. Maccoby, T. M. Newcomb, & E. L. Hartley (Eds.) *Readings in social psychology* (3rd ed.). New York: Henry Holt, 1958.

Wieder, D. L., & Zimmerman, D. H. Generational experience and the development of freak culture. *Journal of Social Issues*, 1974, *30*, 137–161.

Williams, J. R., & Gold, M. From delinquent behavior to official delinquency. *Social Problems*, 1972, *20*, 209–229.

Wilson, D. C., & Sutherland, I. Age at the menarche. *British Medical Journal*, 1950, *1*, 1267.

Witkin, H. A., Goodenough, D. R., & Karp, S. A. Stability of cognitive style from childhood to young adulthood. *Journal of Personality and Social Psychology*, 1967, *7*, 291–300.

Woelfel, J. C. Political attitudes: Interpersonal sources for white, American youth. *Youth and Society*, 1978, *9*, 433–452.

Wohlwill, J. F. From perception to inference: A dimension of cognitive development. In W. Kessen & C. Kuhlman (Eds.), *Thought in the young child*. Chicago: University of Chicago Press, 1962.

Wolf, F. M., & Larson, G. L. On why adolescent formal operators may not be creative thinkers. *Adolescence*, 1981, *16*, 345–348.

Work force in the '70s better educated. *The Washington Post*, October 18, 1981.

Young, A. M. The high school class of 1972: More at work, fewer in college. *Monthly Labor Review*, 1973, *96*, 26–32.

Young, F. W. *Initiation ceremonies: A cross-cultural study of status dramatization*. Indianapolis: Bobbs-Merrill, 1965.

Yussen, S. R. Characteristics of moral dilemmas written by adolescents. *Developmental Psychology*, 1977, *13*, 162–163.

NAME INDEX

SUBJECT INDEX

A 2
B 3
C 4
D 5
E 6
F 7
G 8
H 9